Student Services
and the Law

Margaret J. Barr
and Associates

Student Services and the Law

A Handbook for Practitioners

 Jossey-Bass Publishers

San Francisco • London • 1988

STUDENT SERVICES AND THE LAW
A Handbook for Practitioners
by Margaret J. Barr and Associates

Copyright © 1988 by: Jossey-Bass Inc., Publishers
350 Sansome Street
San Francisco, California 94104

&

Jossey-Bass Limited
28 Banner Street
London EC1Y 8QE

Library of Congress Cataloging-in-Publication Data

Student services and the law: a handbook for practitioners / Margaret
    J. Barr . . . [et al.]. — 1st ed.
      p.   cm. — (The Jossey-Bass higher education series)
    Bibliographies: pp.
    Includes indexes.
    ISBN 1-55542-079-6 (alk. paper)
    1. College students—Legal status, laws, etc.—United States.
2. College student personnel administrators—Legal status, laws,
etc.—United States.   3. Student activities—Law and legislation—
United States.   4. Universities and colleges—Law and legislation—
United States.   I. Barr, Margaret J.   II. Series.
KF4243.S87   1988
344.73′0794—dc19
[347.304794]   87-46330
                                                                    CIP

Manufactured in the United States of America

The paper in this book meets the guidelines for
permanence and durability of the Committee on
Production Guidelines for Book Longevity of the
Council on Library Resources.

JACKET DESIGN BY WILLI BAUM

FIRST EDITION

Code 8803

The Jossey-Bass Higher Education Series

Consulting Editor
Counseling Psychology

Ursula Delworth
University of Iowa

Contents

Policy Development and Implementation • Summary
• References

Preface

We would all agree that the work of a student affairs administrator today is very different from that of a dean of women or dean of men thirty years ago. Behavioral mores have changed, student populations have altered, and society's expectations for higher education have expanded. Responsibilities for student affairs administrators have also changed. In addition to the more traditional areas of student life programs, services, and activities, many student affairs administrators also supervise complex budgets and physical facilities. Within the last three decades, there has also been a major increase in the influence of the law on the campus. No longer are institutions of higher education isolated from the larger society and the law. Therefore, responsible administration requires that professionals understand the legal implications of both their actions and their inactions.

I have long believed that student affairs administrators must increase their knowledge and understanding of the law. For many of these administrators, training, background, and experience have not provided a solid understanding of the law and its influence on professional practice. This volume will, I hope, help them gain that understanding. Its authors are professionals who have many years of practical experience in the administration of student services and who understand the legal implications of their work. It should not, however, be relied on as a definitive source of the law. The one verity we can count on is that the law is ever changing. New statutes, court decisions, and interpretations can create new issues for each of us to face in our daily practice. In fact, the law exhibits great variation from state to state, and decisions will depend on the facts of the situation. Administrators should be aware of differences between and among state laws and should always seek competent legal advice when making decisions that have legal implications and when developing policy.

Overview of the Contents

This book provides a broad overview of the most pressing issues influencing student affairs practice. It is designed to help practitioners understand these issues and apply legal principles in their daily work.

Part One explores the legal foundation for higher education and student affairs administration. Sources of the law are explained, the legal organization of higher education is discussed, and the essential legal similarities and differences between public and private institutions are explored. This section provides the reader with a basic understanding of the legal framework of higher education and therefore supplies a background for the specific areas of law discussed in later sections. Part Two is written by practitioners with legal training and explores the key areas of legal responsibility and liability for student services. Specific chapters focus on constitutional law, contract law, civil rights, administrative law, discipline and campus control, and liability. Part Three, written by student affairs professionals, applies these broad legal principles to the management of functional areas in student affairs (areas such as admissions, residence life programs, facility management, counseling and health centers, student organizations, the student press, records management, and staff supervision). Specific guidelines and implications for practice are provided by each of the authors.

Although I strongly believe that student affairs plays an important educational role, that role is not emphasized in this book. My associates and I have concentrated on defining the legal framework governing our work, with the hope that a more complete understanding of the law will let each of us concentrate more on our educational role and reduce our concern for the legal implications of our practice.

Acknowledgments

Obviously, such a volume would not be possible without the work, contributions, and support of many friends and colleagues. The contributing authors offer unique perspectives and a careful review of the legal standards in their chapters. Ursula Delworth, my consulting editor, provided a great deal of excellent advice. The staff at Jossey-Bass, who encouraged me to produce this volume, have my gratitude for their support and for their careful and professional work. William Mahoney, currently a law student at the University of Kansas, deserves thanks for his hours of legal research. Donna Jackson and Carolyn Shapard spent long hours carefully typing and proofing the complicated text, and my thanks go to both of them. The staff of the Division of Student Affairs at Texas Christian University deserve praise for their understanding and support during the completion of this project.

My interest in the law was heightened during my doctoral work at the University of Texas, Austin, where I had the privilege of studying with Lanier Cox, who directed my dissertation. His patience, interest, and direction started me on this path, and I will be forever grateful to him. Finally, the support of my family and friends must be acknowledged, for without them I would never have completed the book.

It is my hope that this volume will be useful and helpful and will serve as a tool for all of us who attempt to be fair, honest, and judicious in our approach to our work.

Fort Worth, Texas MARGARET J. BARR
February 1988

The Authors

Margaret J. Barr is vice-chancellor for student affairs at Texas Christian University in Fort Worth, Texas. She previously served as vice-president and assistant vice-president for student affairs at Northern Illinois University and as associate and assistant dean of students at the University of Texas, Austin. She received her B.S. degree (1961) from the State University College, Buffalo, in elementary education; her M.S. degree (1964) from Southern Illinois University, Carbondale, in college student personnel; and her Ph.D. degree (1980) from the University of Texas, Austin, in educational administration. Her dissertation focused on the legal aspects of facility use at public colleges and universities.

She is the author of over twenty articles, monographs, and chapters regarding student affairs and is the current editor of the New Directions for Student Services monograph series. Her works include *Effective Student Services: A Guide for Practitioners* (1985, coeditor with L. A. Keating) and *Student Affairs and the Law* (1983), a monograph in the New Directions for Student Services series. She received the 1986 Professional Service Award from the American College Personnel Association (ACPA) and in the same year received the award for Outstanding Contribution to Literature and Research from the National Association of Student Personnel Administrators (NASPA). She is a former president of ACPA and presently serves as a senior scholar for that association.

Edward G. Boehm, Jr. is associate vice-chancellor for academic affairs and dean of admissions at Texas Christian University in Fort Worth. He serves as vice-chairman of the Southwest Regional Assembly of the College Board.

William R. Bracewell is director of the Office of Judicial Programs at the University of Georgia in Athens. He has been active in ACPA, serving on Commission XV: Judicial Programs.

E. T. "Joe" Buchanan III is an attorney and dean of campus and community services at Tidewater Community College in Virginia Beach, Virginia. He is a former president of NASPA.

Donald R. Buckner is director of student housing services at Northern Illinois University in DeKalb. He has been active in the Association of College and University Housing Officers.

Richard J. Correnti is vice-president for student affairs at Florida International University in Miami. He is a former president of NASPA.

Jon C. Dalton is vice-president for student affairs at Northern Illinois University in DeKalb. He has long been active at both the national and regional levels in NASPA.

Larry H. Ebbers is professor and chairman of the Department of Professional Studies in Education at Iowa State University in Ames. He is the current president of NASPA.

David A. Emmerling is executive director of the National Wellness Institute at the University of Wisconsin–Stevens Point. He is the former director of the Counseling and Student Development Center at Northern Illinois University.

Stephen S. Janes is an attorney and serves as assistant vice-president for student affairs at the University of Texas, Austin.

Glenn W. Maloney is the assistant dean of students at the University of Texas, Austin, and is completing his doctoral work there.

Melissa Gasser Math serves as a law clerk for the Third District of the Illinois Appellate Court and teaches part time at Illinois Central College in East Peoria.

Shari R. Rhode is the chief trial attorney at Southern Illinois University, Carbondale.

John H. Schuh is associate vice-president for student affairs at Wichita State University.

Gwen Seaquist is an attorney and assistant professor of law at Ithaca College.

George M. Shur is the university attorney for Northern Illinois University in DeKalb. He is the vice-president of the National Association of College and University Attorneys.

Part One

Legal Foundations of Student Affairs Practice

Through court cases, statutes, administrative rulings, constitutional provisions at both the state and federal level, and the use of enforcement mechanisms by agencies and by contracts, the influence of law is being vigorously felt on the college campus. Thus, unilateral power and authority of college administrators have greatly diminished over the last three decades. Higher education also has not been isolated from the changed legal climate in the United States, where the courts are increasingly used to settle differences. In fact, student affairs administrators must confront legal questions on a daily basis.

This section focuses on the legal foundation for the practice of administration in colleges and universities. In Chapter One, the many sources of the law are discussed, and assistance is given in determining the influence of particular sources of the law on a specific campus. Although other chapters in this volume discuss the sources of the law in great detail, this introductory chapter provides basic information for interpreting more detailed discussions. In Chapter Two, issues of power and authority are discussed from a legal perspective, and essential questions of authority to act are reviewed and analyzed. In Chapter Three, the similarities and

1

differences between public and private institutions are presented. Each institutional type has specific legal constraints, which influence decisions, policies, and practices. Neither public nor private institutions are immune from the influence of the law, and astute professionals understand and appreciate the legal constraints on their work.

This section is designed to aid the practitioner in understanding the multiple sources of the law, as well as the constraints and opportunities provided by the law. It provides a foundation for the rest of the volume and a framework for understanding the influence of legal rights and responsibilities on our professional practice.

1   *Margaret J. Barr*

🌿   🌿   🌿

Sources of Laws Influencing Administrative Decisions in Student Affairs

A federal district court in another state rules that door-to-door solicitation for magazines can take place in a university residence hall at a public university. Your institutional policy does not permit such solicitation. Should you change your rules?

A father calls with a demand to see his son's transcript and current grade report. Should he be allowed to do so?

Last week you received notification that a former employee had filed a grievance with the state equal employment commission charging discrimination. What should you do?

A local business owner claims that the sale of some new items in the campus bookstore threatens his business. He charges that a tax-supported institution should not be in direct competition with private business and threatens litigation. Should you remove the contested items from the shelves?

A woman attending a conference on campus slips and falls in the Student Center. She sustains severe injuries and claims that the institution is responsible. Is her assertion correct?

The Ku Klux Klan wishes to rent the ballroom in the Student Center for a rally. You disapprove of everything that the Klan stands for, and you believe that such an organization has no place on a university campus. You want to refuse the request. Can you legally do so?

A residence hall director suspects that one of the residents is selling cocaine from his room. She wants to search his room for evidence. Should you permit the search?

These questions and others like them are part of the day-to-day administrative decisions on any university or college campus. Answers are not simple and depend on the facts in a particular situation and the applicability of the law or jurisdiction of the court. Other chapters in this volume will focus on some of these specific issues. In this chapter, the sources of the law influencing administrative decisions will be reviewed and implications for practice will be discussed.

There is no single, unchanging source of law to guide practice for the student affairs administrator. The law evolves, changes, and responds to changing societal demands and expectations. Thus, the influence of the law on administrative practice will differ from year to year and from institution to institution. Since the sources of the law influencing professional practice in student affairs are many and diverse, student affairs professionals—if they are to make sound decisions based on available facts—must understand the scope and influence that any one source of the law may have on decisions. In addition, they must recognize the legal differences between public and private institutions (see Chapter Three in this volume). Finally, they must know when to seek competent legal advice. Legal counsel often can aid in avoiding problems and in clarifying issues. In order to make best use of such legal advice, student affairs administrators should, however, understand what sources of law can influence higher education in general and in their own institutions.

In this chapter, eight specific sources of the law will be discussed: the federal Constitution; the applicable state constitution; statutes at the federal, state, and local ordinance levels; judicial decisions; rules and regulations of administrative agencies;

contracts; institutional rules and regulations; and academic tradition.

Federal Constitution

In *Tinker* v. *Des Moines Independent School District* (1969), the United States Supreme Court declared: "It can hardly be argued that either students or teachers shed their constitutional rights to freedom of speech at the schoolhouse gate" (at 736). Since then, the federal Constitution—the highest source for law in the country— has been a real and potent force in American higher education. "Constitutions are the fundamental source for determining the nature and extent of governmental powers. Constitutions are also the fundamental source of the individual rights guarantees that limit the power of the government and protect citizens generally, including members of the academic community" (Kaplin, 1985, p. 10).

Although the federal Constitution has no specific provision related to education (Kaplin, 1985, p. 10), it does have a number of provisions that directly affect student affairs practice in higher education. Three amendments of the Constitution are of particular concern to student affairs administrators: the First, Fourth, and Fourteenth Amendments. (For a complete discussion of these issues, see Chapter Four in this volume.)

The First Amendment states that "Congress shall make no law respecting an establishment of religion, or prohibiting the free exercise thereof; or abridging the freedom of speech, or of the press, or the right of the people peaceably to assemble and to petition the Government for a redress of grievances." Issues involving First Amendment rights of individuals and groups are the cause of much of the litigation involving student affairs practitioners today (see Chapter Four). The question of separation of church and state in the use of institutional facilities is not as clear as it was a decade ago (see Chapter Twelve); neither is the relationship with both the student press and off-campus publications (see Chapter Sixteen). First Amendment issues will continue to be litigated in the decade ahead, and astute practitioners should be aware of court cases (particularly at the Supreme Court level) that could influence their programs, policies, or procedures.

The Fourth Amendment provides protection against "unreasonable searches and seizures." It has had a profound effect on the management of university-owned residence halls and other facilities (see Chapters Eleven and Twelve). For institutions whose security or police function is legally recognized in the state, it will also influence policies and procedures of that department as well as judicial proceedings (see Chapters Eight and Fourteen).

The Fourteenth Amendment provides for equal protection under the law and requires due process of law for the denial of "life, liberty, or property." Student judicial codes, employment practices, evaluation practices, and supervision of all types of employees have been greatly influenced by the applicability of the Fourteenth Amendment to college and university campuses.

There are significant differences in the effect of these federal constitutional guarantees on the practice of student affairs work in public and private institutions (see Chapters Three and Four). As Kaplin (1985, pp. 16–18) notes, public institutions and their officers are fully subject to the constraints of the federal Constitution, whereas private institutions and their officers are not. Under the law, public institutions operate as an arm of the state (or government); and as an arm of the government, they are fully subject to the federal Constitution. Actions taken by public institutions and their officers are defined as state action and are thus subject to the provisions of the federal Constitution. Under certain conditions, the actions of private institutions and their officers may be defined as state action, and the federal Constitution will apply. (For a discussion of these circumstances, see Chapter Three.)

State Constitutions

The applicable state constitution can also have a very real and direct influence on the conduct of business at both public and private institutions. Through the residual powers of the federal Constitution, which delegates certain powers to the federal government and cedes all others to the state and the people, higher education institutions come primarily under state control (Alexander and Solomon, 1972, p. 42). There are differences, however, in how that control influences policy making and decisions in private and public institutions.

Constitutionally Autonomous Institutions. In Arizona, California, Colorado, Georgia, Idaho, Michigan, Minnesota, Nevada, and Oklahoma, the state constitution provides autonomy for the state university (Hofstadter and Smith, 1961). When a constitutionally autonomous institution is established, the control exercised by the state legislature and other state government entities is diminished. However, the constitutionally autonomous institution is not free from all control. Limitations may be imposed through the appropriation of funds, the general police powers of the state, and other provisions of some state constitutions relating to the legislative, executive, and judicial branches of state government (Glenny and Daglish, 1973). Usually, only one institution is granted constitutionally autonomous status within the state. Although the constitutions of twenty-seven states make explicit reference to higher education, autonomy is not guaranteed in all cases (Hofstadter and Smith, 1961).

Other Public Institutions. Whether or not the state constitution makes explicit reference to the state university, other constitutional provisions can greatly influence public higher education. State constitutions may establish "a state department of education or other governing authority with some responsibility for postsecondary education" (Kaplin, 1985, p. 10). In addition, some state constitutions have established provisions with "more expansive individual rights than those guaranteed by parallel provisions of the federal Constitution" (Kaplin, 1985, p. 10).

Private Institutions. Private institutions are also subject to some provisions of the applicable state constitution. In addition to the general police power of the state, individual rights may be protected on the campuses of private institutions by the applicable portion of the state constitution. For example, in *State* v. *Schmid* (1980), a nonstudent was charged with criminal trespass for distributing political material on the Princeton campus. The New Jersey Supreme Court held that the provisions of New Jersey's constitution did not permit the private institution to deny Schmid's expressional rights. Muhlenberg College, in Pennsylvania, was involved in similar litigation, because of the applicable portions of the state constitution of Pennsylvania (*Commonwealth of Pennsylvania* v. *Tate*, 1981). Although these cases are applicable only in the states mentioned, they do illustrate the power of the state constitution over private institutions under certain circumstances.

Statutes

Laws at the federal, state, and local ordinance level must be accounted for in the development of institutional policy and practice. The applicability of these laws will depend on the legal status of the institution and its public or private character (see Chapters Two and Three).

Federal Statutes. The laws of the federal government govern all the citizens of all the states and must be consistent with the powers reserved for the federal government under the United States Constitution. "All federal statutes (laws passed by the Congress) are codified in the *United States Code* (U.S.C.)" (Gehring, 1983, p. 540). Federal legislation influencing higher education is far reaching in its range and scope. Since passage of the Morrill Act in 1862, the federal government has become increasingly involved in higher education. The *United States Code* contains many volumes, and each volume has laws related to a specific topic (Gehring, 1983). Each general topic is referred to as an Arabic numeral title—for instance, Title 20, which contains the laws related to education. These Arabic numerals should not be confused with Roman numeral titles, such as Title VI and Title VII of the Civil Rights Act. Once the Civil Rights Act of 1964 became law, it was codified into a section of Title 42, containing all federal civil rights laws.

Some federal statutes of concern to student affairs administrators include the statutory authority for student financial aid, individual privacy, military training, loan support for facility construction, and discrimination. In addition, at the federal level as well as the state and local ordinance levels, other laws applying to other entities may also apply to higher education. Examples of this type of statute at the federal level include tax laws, retirement laws, Social Security legislation, and antitrust statutes.

State Statutes. By far the greatest number of laws controlling higher education are at the state level. Both public and private institutions are directly influenced by state law (Moos and Rourke, 1959). Both types of institutions must conform to the general laws of the state. Private institutions come under additional state control through statutes providing for incorporation, trusts, chartering, licensure, or coordination bodies. All states incorporate or charter private institutions. About two-thirds of the states also require licensing (Education Commission of the States, 1973). State-mandated coordination of degree programs, financial aid programs, and off-campus degree requirements can create another form of state statutory authority over private institutions.

Both private and public institutions are also subject to the regulation of state agencies whose primary function is not education. Such agencies may include, for example, unemployment compensation boards, hospital licensing agencies, and human relations commissions. Both public and private institutions also must comply with regulations derived from the general police power of the state.

Although constitutionally autonomous institutions do exist, most public institutions are created by state statute. A statutory institution is created by the legislature, and it is subject to control by the legislative body. Statutory institutions can be defined as either primary or secondary state agencies (Alexander and Solomon, 1972, p. 46) (see Chapter Two in this volume). However, primarily through the weight of academic tradition, some observers feel that statutory institutions enjoy greater autonomy than do other state agencies (Glenny and Daglish, 1973).

Public institutions are also controlled by lay boards. The composition of the board, the powers of the board, and procedures for appointment of board members are all governed by state statutes. The amount of explicit, implied, or inherent power given to a governing board by statutes or judicial decisions can directly affect the day-to-day operation of the institution. Although private institutions may also be controlled by lay boards, the effect of state statutes on their power and authority is different. The laws related to incorporation and chartering of the institution provide the parameters for the exercise of authority by the board.

Local Ordinances. The effect of local ordinances on an institution of higher education is determined in part by the charter or license of the private institution and by the statutory entitlement of the public institution. It is also determined by the statutory entitlement of the specific municipality or county where the institution is located and by the facts involved. In general, both public and private institutions are subject to local ordinances regarding general health and safety: fire codes, zoning laws, and the like. A public institution, as an arm of the state, generally has plenary powers over local government unless restrictions are placed by state or federal constitutional provisions (Thompson, 1976).

Further, as Meyers (1970, p. 3) notes, "The growing trend for institutions of higher education to become 'involved' with the communities they serve gives rise to even more relationships which have legal implications." For both public and private institutions, the local government's legal authority over institutional facilities, property, and actions can be determined only by careful comparison between the parameters of the legal authority of the local government body and that of the institution.

Judicial Sources

"A knowledge of case law to date gives one knowledge of established legal precedent applicable to one jurisdiction, or guidance where litigation may have occurred elsewhere but remains untested in one's own judicial area" (Owens, 1984, pp. 3–4). However, to understand case law and the influence it may have on institutional practice, one first must understand the court system.

All courts, including the Supreme Court of the United States, have three functions: settling controversies by applying appropriate laws or principles to a specific set of facts, interpreting enactments of the legislature, and determining the constitutionality of statutes (Alexander and Solomon, 1972, p. 8). The force of any judicial decision depends on the jurisdiction of the deciding court.

Federal Court System. The federal court system consists of a Supreme Court, courts of appeal, and district courts. Decisions of the United States Supreme Court are "binding precedents throughout the country" (Kaplin, 1985, p. 13) in matters related to federal constitutional issues and federal statutes. There is no right of appeal to the United States Supreme Court. Those who want their appeal considered must file a writ of certiorari with the Supreme Court. Hundreds of such writs are filed each year, and the Supreme Court agrees to hear only a relatively small number of cases. Denial of the writ of certiorari leaves the law as decided by the lower court for that jurisdiction. It does not change the law in other circuits or districts not affected by the original decision.

United States Supreme Court decisions and opinions are reported officially in the *United States Supreme Court Reports* (U.S.) and in two unofficial reporters, the *Supreme Court Reporter* (S. Ct.) and the *United States Supreme Court Reports—Lawyers' Edition* (L. Ed. or L. Ed. 2d). Opinions of the Supreme Court are also available more quickly through *United States Law Week* (U.S.L.W.).

Eleven federal circuits comprise the federal courts of appeals. The decisions of the federal courts of appeals (or circuits) are reported in the *Federal Reporter* (F. or F.2d). Each circuit serves as an intermediate appellate court, and cases can be appealed as a matter of right to the appropriate circuit. The decisions of one circuit are not binding on other circuits or on district courts in other circuits. Decisions of a federal appeals court are binding within all courts and jurisdictions of the circuit, unless they are successfully appealed to the United States Supreme Court.

Each federal district court is a one-judge trial court. Decisions of federal district courts are reported in the *Federal Supplement* (F. Supp.). Any decision of the district court is binding only in the district where judgment is rendered. However, decisions of other circuits and other districts also should be monitored, since they can (although not legally binding) serve as precedents for courts with jurisdiction over an institution. District court decisions may be appealed to the appropriate federal court of appeals and, in some cases, directly to the United States Supreme Court.

State Court System. Each state court system is unique; in general, however, state court systems are structured like federal courts. District courts are usually courts of general jurisdiction that have judicial responsibility for a specific geographical area. Decisions of state district courts are binding on the district in which

they are rendered, unless they are reversed on appeal. Most states
have separate district courts for civil and criminal matters and
continue this separation at the appellate level. State court systems
can also include courts with special or limited jurisdiction. For
example, Illinois has established a Court of Claims, with original
jurisdiction in monetary issues involving the state. Careful review
of the constitutional authority and statutory support for the state
court system is needed in order to determine the jurisdiction of the
individual decisions that emanate from each court.

The National Reporter System publishes important state
court options in seven regional reports, such as the *Northwestern
Reporter* (N.W. or N.W.2d). California and New York have special
reports for state court decisions in those states. As in the federal
judicial system, decisions of state courts in other jurisdictions and
other states can become the basis for decisions by a court that does
have jurisdiction over an institution.

Administrative Rules and Regulations

Administrative regulations and rules issued by state and
federal agencies can also carry the force of law. Kaplin (1985, p. 11)
indicates that the most rapidly expanding sources of postsecondary
education law are the directives of state and federal administrative
agencies. Proposed implementing regulations for federal statutes
are published in the *Federal Register* (Fed. Reg.), together with
invitations to comment. After the public comment period, final regulations—which have the status of laws—are issued. These regulations are published in final form in the *Code of Federal Regulations*
(C.F.R.). At the state level, administrative rules and regulations are
usually not found in a single source, although some states do have
a publication comparable to the C.F.R.

Kaplin (1985) cautions that legal advice should be sought to
determine the authority of a specific regulation. Like statutes,
administrative rules and regulations at either the state or federal
level must be consistent with applicable state and federal statutes
and constitutional provisions. Some agencies, such as labor and
human rights agencies, also have the legal right to settle disputes
on specific issues. If such power has been granted to an agency, legal

advice prior to contract with the agency is critical. Whether dealing with a compliance review, a request for information, or a complaint, the astute administrator seeks legal advice prior to responding.

Contracts

A contract creates a binding legal arrangement between the contracting parties, enforceable by either party if one party fails to comply with the terms of the contract. "An understanding of the elements of a contract, the authority to contract, and the implications for improper contracting are crucial in student affairs areas" (Owens, 1984, p. 4). As a matter of routine, student affairs administrators sign contracts for employment, goods, and services; thus, a clear understanding of the obligations of the contract is essential for administrative success. When disputes arise, the first source of law to be checked is the contract agreed upon between the parties. Each administrator must understand the rules governing contracts in the institution, any limitations on authority to contract, and the far-reaching implications of any contract.

In addition, an emerging body of case law is redefining the relationship between the student and the institution as contractual (see Chapter Five in this volume). Written materials published by the institution, as well as verbal presentations of institutional officials, have been viewed as an implied contract with the student. Careful attention to this emerging body of law is essential for sound administrative practice.

Institutional Rules and Regulations

Although institutional rules and regulations are subject to the sources of law previously mentioned, they can also be a source of law. These institutional rules and regulations must be consistent with other sources of the law; they must be as specific as is practical in an institution; they must be published; and they must be consistently enforced. Many institutions establish judicial bodies to enforce their rules and regulations (see Chapter Fourteen in this volume). The consistency of these bodies in enforcing regulations and in following published procedures has been a critical factor in a number of court cases. Careful review of the institutional rules and regulations is needed, at least annually, to ensure compliance with applicable law. Failure to do so could result in litigation.

Academic Tradition

Academic tradition—that is, traditional methods and practices not reflected in an institution's formal rules—is easily the most diffuse source of law influencing higher education. It can be discerned, for instance, in correspondence, speeches, statements to the news media, and other interpretations of the way that the institution does business. Sometimes called "campus common law," academic tradition is used to define the expectations of members of the academic community for the behavior of the institution and individuals who are part of the college or university. In a legal sense, academic tradition supplements more formal institutional rules and regulations by providing the explanatory backdrop of the institutional ethos. The use of academic tradition has been recognized by the courts in specific cases under specific circumstances (*Perry* v. *Sindermann,* 1972; *Krotkoff* v. *Goucher College,* 1978). In *Sindermann,* for example, academic tradition was relevant to determining whether a professor was entitled to a hearing prior to nonrenewal of his contract.

Summary

This chapter introduces specific sources of the law and describes their influence on administrative practice. Eight sources— each of them critical to the sound administration of student affairs units—are discussed. To establish a fair and just approach to their work, administrators must know what laws are applicable to the decisions they must make. The seven questions posed at the beginning of the chapter all require careful administrative decisions and all have legal implications. The answers to some of them can be found in this chapter; the answers to others will be found in later chapters in this volume.

References

Alexander, K., and Solomon, E. *College and University Law.* Charlottesville, Va.: Michie, 1972.

Education Commission of the States. *Model State Legislation: Report of the Task Force on Model State Legislation for Approval of Postsecondary Institutions and Authorizations to Grant Degrees.* Report no. 39. Washington, D.C.: Education Commission of the States, 1973.

Gehring, D. D. "An Introduction to Legal Research." In R. Winston, Jr., T. K. Miller, and W. R. Mendenhall (eds.), *Administration and Leadership in Student Affairs: Actualizing Student Development in Higher Education.* Muncie, Ind.: Accelerated Development, 1983.

Glenny, L. A., and Daglish, T. K. *Public Universities, State Agencies and the Law: Constitutional Autonomy in Decline.* Berkeley, Calif.: Center for Research and Development in Higher Education, 1973.

Hofstadter, R., and Smith, W. (eds.). *American Higher Education: A Documentary History.* Vol. 1 Chicago: University of Chicago Press, 1961.

Kaplin, W. A. *The Law of Higher Education: A Comprehensive Guide to Legal Implications of Administrative Decision Making.* (2nd ed.) San Francisco: Jossey-Bass, 1985.

Meyers, J. "The Conduct of Enterprises." In A. Knowles (ed.), *Handbook of College and University Administration.* New York: McGraw-Hill, 1970.

Moos, M., and Rourke, F. *The Campus and the State.* Baltimore: Johns Hopkins University Press, 1959.

Owens, H. F. "Risk Management and Professional Responsibility." In H. F. Owens (ed.), *Risk Management and the Student Affairs Professional.* Columbus, Ohio: National Association of Student Personnel Administrators, 1984.

Thompson, J. *Policymaking in American Public Education.* Englewood Cliffs, N.J.: Prentice-Hall, 1976.

2

Margaret J. Barr

Legal Organization and Control of Higher Education

Each day, a student affairs administrator must make numerous decisions that have legal implications. These decisions range, for example, from student discipline to contracting for goods and services. Such decisions can only be made legally, however, if the administrator has the power and authority to make them. To act without legal power and authority places both the administrator and the institution at risk.

Power and authority must also be exercised within the legal context of higher education. In Chapter One, specific sources of the law influencing American higher education were discussed. Each of these sources can place constraints on the actions of both individuals and institutions. However, the fundamental source of authority for institutional governance rests with the governing board of the institution. The power of the governing board is usually delegated for day-to-day operations to administrative officers and governance structures within the institution.

Governing Boards

Authority for action in public institutions is derived from the statutory or constitutional entitlement of the institution. Authority to act in private institutions is derived from the articles of incorporation, charter, or license of the institution. In both public and private institutions, laws or the articles of incorporation confer power on the governing board as an entity separate from the individual members of the board. To be legally valid, actions taken by individual members of the board, in the name of the board, must have explicit authority through bylaws, resolutions, or other board action. Board members also may have legal obligations, particularly in public institutions, mandated by laws dealing with conflict of interest, ethics, or fiduciary responsibilities.

A state may establish public institutions of higher education either as constitutionally autonomous entities or as statutory institutions. In states where a constitutionally autonomous state university has been established, the institution has increased protection from interference by other state agencies. The independence of the constitutionally autonomous state university has been challenged in the courts many times. In Michigan, the autonomy of the university was upheld against interference by other state agencies (*Board of Regents of the University of Michigan* v. *Auditor General*, 1911). In California, the courts refused to interfere in a matter involving the internal governance of the constitutionally autonomous university (*Wall* v. *Board of Regents of the University of California*, 1940). In *State ex rel. Peterson* v. *Quinlivan* (1936), a Minnesota case, the method of selection of the university's governing board was upheld. Although these challenges occurred in three different states and the constitutional provisions establishing the autonomy vary, the cases illustrate that courts tend to defer to the authority of governing boards of constitutionally autonomous public universities. However, the constitutionally autonomous state university is the exception rather than the rule. "The greater part of law defining the status of public institutions of higher education is legislative rather than constitutional" (Moos and Rourke, 1959, p. 17).

Statutory institutions are created by the legislature and are subject to the control of the legislative body. Alexander and Solomon (1972) define two types of statutory structures for public institutions of higher education. In the first type, the institution is organized as a primary agency and responds directly to the state legislature. In the second type, the institution is organized as a secondary agency and responds to the legislature only through another intermediate agency. In many states, a mixed reporting relationship is in effect; that is, the institution reports directly to the legislature on some matters and to the mid-level agency on others.

In private institutions, the power of the governing board may also be limited by other state statutes involving foundations, financial accounting, or other matters. For example, in the "Sibley Hospital" case (*Stern* v. *Lucy Webb Hayes National Training School for Deaconesses and Missionaries,* 1974), the court defined the fiduciary responsibilities of trustees for endowment management and financial dealings and indicated that the trustees must observe current statutes and regulations regarding the management of trusts. In *In re Antioch University* (1980), the power of a private board to control constituent units was defined through litigation regarding the institution's articles of incorporation. A careful understanding of the governing board's actual power and authority, and the limitations on such authority, must be reached on both public and private campuses. To do less invites problems, since the authority of the governing board is usually delegated to institutional officials and governance groups for the day-to-day management of the institution.

Concepts of Authority

Four legal concepts of authority can influence the work of student affairs administrators: explicit authority, implied authority, inherent authority, and apparent authority. Each type of authority flows from the authority vested in the governing board and has been defined through litigation.

Explicit Authority. Explicit or express authority "is that which is found within the plain meaning of a written grant of authority" (Kaplin, 1985, p. 41). Thus, explicit authority is clear and unambiguous. The statutes, the state constitution, or the institution's articles of incorporation clearly delineate the authority of the governing board.

The explicit authority of governing boards has been upheld by the courts many times. In Missouri, the courts held that the curators of the University of Missouri had explicit power through the state constitution and statutes to issue revenue bonds and to construct parking facilities (*State ex rel. Curators of the University of Missouri* v. *Neill,* 1966). The authority of the board of regents of the University of Texas to erect buildings and decide on their use was also confirmed in *Splawn* v. *Woodard* (1926).

Explicit authority to act must not be assumed by any officer or agent of the institution. Authority derived from the powers of the governing board must be confirmed through institutional rules, regulations, and policies. In order to claim explicit or express authority, the governing board must have "delegated authority to the alleged agent by words which expressly authorize the agent to do the delegated act" (*Brown* v. *Wichita State University*, 1975, at 74). Colleges and universities are complex organizations, and it is difficult to provide explicit authority for day-to-day institutional operations. The concept of implied authority has, therefore, also been confirmed by the courts.

Implied Authority. Implied authority provides much of the legal foundation for decisions in postsecondary institutions. Under the concept of implied authority, institutional officers and agents are permitted to assume prerogatives not specifically outlined in the powers of the board or by institutional rules. In Arizona, the court held that the governing board has not only such powers as those explicitly delegated to it but also such powers as may be reasonably implied for meeting its purposes (*Arizona Board of Regents* v. *Harper*, 1972). The court confirmed in Illinois that the board of trustees of the University of Illinois has, "by the statutes creating the University, the power and authority to do everything necessary for the management, operating and administration of the University including powers in the furtherance of the corporate purposes" (*Turkovich* v. *Board of Trustees of the University of Illinois*, 1957, at 229). In Texas, the Court of Civil Appeals ruled that the board of regents of the University of Houston has implied powers, holding in part that "the authority to make rules implies a power to modify or change the rules" (*Fazekas* v. *University of Houston*, 1972, at 299).

Inherent Authority. Inherent authority is derived from the legal status or position of the individual committing the act. There has not been a clear pattern, in case law, either sustaining or rejecting the concept of inherent authority. The concept of inherent authority was upheld in Texas when the court ruled that the statutes establishing the university "imply the power and if they do

not so imply then the power is inherent in University officials"
(*Morris* v. *Nowotny,* 1959, at 303). In New York, the court held that
the administrators of a college possess an inherent authority to
maintain order on campus for invited guests, students, and
members of the school staff (*Schuyler* v. *State University of New
York at Albany,* 1968).

Other courts have disagreed with these judicial interpretations, and several successful court challenges have been based on the
premise that the concept of inherent powers provides too much
discretionary authority for action by school officials (*Lieberman* v.
Marshall, 1970; *Esteban* v. *Central Missouri State College,* 1969;
Smith v. *Ellington,* 1971). Inherent authority is an "elusive concept
of uncertain stature and questionable value" (Kaplin, 1985, p. 41).
Both the concept of inherent authority and that of apparent
authority have received strict judicial scrutiny.

Apparent Authority. The idea of apparent authority pertains
when an individual causes others to believe that he or she has the
authority to act when, in fact, that authority does not exist.
Numerous examples of the exercise of apparent powers occurred in
higher education prior to the constitutionally based challenges in
the courts on student rights. For example, challenges to apparent
powers on the basis of the First Amendment were upheld in
Hammond v. *South Carolina State College* (1967) and in *Dickey* v.
Alabama State Board of Education (1967). It appears likely in an
increasingly litigious society that the exercise of apparent powers
will not continue without challenge in the courts. Actions taken
without authority can be ratified after the fact by an individual or
governing body with legal authority, although such an action
certainly does not constitute sound administration. Very often, the
concept of apparent authority is activated when an employee
without authority to do so makes promises in the name of the
institution (see Chapter Five in this volume). Thus, an understanding of the delegation of authority is essential to sound, legal
administrative practice.

Delegation of Authority

Authority to govern the institution flows from the governing
board. In general, in both public and private institutions, statutes

or articles of incorporation confer power on the board as an entity apart from individual members. As mentioned, actions taken by individual members of the board, in the name of the board, need explicit authority through bylaws, resolutions, or other board action in order to be legally valid.

Although, as Mortimer and McConnell (1978) indicate, the legal authority for decisions or actions rests with the board, delegation is necessary in order to manage daily operations. Such authority may be delegated to the institution's officers, faculty, administrators, internal governance groups, and—in rare cases— student organizations. In order to be legally valid, delegation of such authority by the governing board cannot be vague and ambiguous. Mager (1970) indicates that such delegation should include "touchstones of standards for rational policy development and decision making" (p. 37) and that such standards should be specific enough "for determination of the issues in a specific instance" (p. 46).

The question of delegation of authority by a governing board has also been litigated many times. In *People* v. *Ware* (1975), for example, a New York court upheld the power and authority of a system-wide governing board to delegate to campus administrators the responsibility for hiring peace officers. However, in *University of Colorado* v. *Silverman* (1976), the Supreme Court of Colorado held that hiring authority cannot be delegated unless the statutes specifically authorize such delegation. As these cases suggest, the authority to act for a campus administrator or group must be specifically defined. A board's ability to delegate such authority is also subject to constitutional, charter, or statutory provisions. For most institutions, delegation is accomplished through policies, rules, and regulations that create legal rights and responsibilities for the institution (Hollander, 1978).

Institutional Policy Development

Institutional policies provide the framework for the day-to-day management decisions within the institution. Since "wise decisions rest upon adequate awareness of the facts from which the decisions emerge" (Fellman, 1968, p. 121), effective policy development requires knowledge of legal constraints. In Chapter One, the complexity of the law as a source of "fact" for policy development was discussed. Policy formation is, indeed, a complex task; and a number of procedural, as well as legal, issues must be addressed. Awareness of the procedural issues listed below can assist administrators in developing policies that not only are consistent with identified legal constraints but also reflect the unique needs of the institution.

Institutional Mission. The philosophical base of the institution is perhaps the most important factor in policy formation. The institution's philosophy and mission define the parameters within which the legal constraints on policies must be met. For example, a community college may decide to adopt less stringent rules for the use of its facilities than a private residential institution would.

Governing Board's Authority. Any constraints on the authority of the governing board to act or to delegate authority should be clearly understood. Failure to do so can result in unnecessary litigation or problems.

Legal Advice. While appropriate legal advice during the process of policy development does not guarantee that the resulting policy will withstand judicial scrutiny if it is challenged, it can ensure that all identified legal standards have been included in the policy. Early legal review has great potential for increasing the possibility that the final policy will be fundamentally fair and reasonable. Understanding the implications of such legal advice also ensures that the policy will not only be sound but also educationally defensible.

Awareness of the Law. Every person who has policy formation responsibility needs to acquire at least a minimal understanding of the law. Acquisition of such understanding is a continuing process, because the law is always evolving.

Consolidation of Policies. At most institutions, policies can be found in handbooks, procedure manuals, and internal memoranda. A consolidated approach to policies is the

best defense against internal inconsistency. If it is not
feasible to develop a consolidated approach, then, at the
very minimum, a cross-reference index to all policies
should be available.

Broadening Policy Base. Besides being legally correct,
policies must also be reasonable and useful to those
charged with implementation. Since policies provide
guidance for daily decisions, inclusion of those who have
responsibility for policy implementation has many
advantages. Ambiguities can be resolved, potential
problems can be identified, and a broad-based development process can increase the basic knowledge of all
participants.

Development of policies is complicated by the intervention
of the courts in many issues (Kirp and Yudof, 1974). Sound policy
development will, however, lead to better management. The rules
and regulations derived from a governing board's policies should be
reasonably specific and influence only those activities intended by
the original policies. Such rules and regulations should also clearly
reflect the scope of authority for institutional agents in enforcement
of the policies.

Summary

The legal organization and control of higher education are
complicated by the many and varied sources of the law and the
concept of authority to act. A clear understanding of the range and
scope of authority given to a governing board is critical. Even more
important are the ways and means through which authority is
delegated to institutional agents. Specific authority to act must be
granted. Administrators should not rely on apparent authority, for
to do so invites litigation and unwarranted difficulty for both the
individual and the institution.

References

Alexander, K., and Solomon, E. *College and University Law.*
    Charlottesville, Va.: Michie, 1972.

Fellman, D. "The Academic Community: Who Decides What?" In
  C. Dobbins and C. Lee (eds.), *Whose Goals for American Higher
  Education?* Washington, D.C.: American Council on Education,
  1968.

Hollander, P. A. *A Legal Handbook for Educators.* Boulder, Colo.:
  Westview Press, 1978.

Kaplin, W. A. *The Law of Higher Education: A Comprehensive
  Guide to Legal Implications of Administrative Decision Making.*
  (2nd ed.) San Francisco: Jossey-Bass, 1985.

Kirp, D. L., and Yudof, M. G. *Educational Policy and the Law.*
  Berkeley, Calif.: McCutchan, 1974.

Mager, R. T. "Changes in Institutional Governance: Legal
  Restraints Involving Delegation of Authority by Governing
  Boards." *College Counsel,* 1970, *1,* 37–49.

Moos, M., and Rourke, F. *The Campus and the State.* Baltimore:
  Johns Hopkins University Press, 1959.

Mortimer, K. P., and McConnell, T. R. *Sharing Authority Effectively: Participation, Interaction, and Discretion.* San Francisco:
  Jossey-Bass, 1978.

3

Richard J. Correnti

How Public and Private Institutions Differ Under the Law

There is a perception that private institutions enjoy a level of legal autonomy free of constitutional constraint and external regulation and intervention not enjoyed by their public counterparts. Although, in many ways, private institutions have more control over their legal destinies than public institutions do, unbridled license certainly does not exist. The differences are not as extreme as many believe, and, in fact, the distinction between public and private institutions from a legal perspective has narrowed in the past few years.

The legal differences between public and private institutions stem from differences in organization and control. Because of differences in governance structure, each institutional type is affected differently by state statutes, the federal Constitution, and theories of trust, tort, and fiduciary responsibilities. Taken at face value, these distinctions suggest significant differences in the legal constraints placed on public, as opposed to private, institutions. Only a few decades ago, these differences did exist; and, to be sure, distinctions between the two types of institutions continue to exist. However, imposed regulation—in the form of legislation, receipt of government dollars, and court interpretations over the past few years—has blurred many of these distinctions.

In addition, a self-monitoring influence has evolved within private institutions. They are now taking more care to define their relationships with students and to deal with them in fair and equitable ways. Administrators in both public and private institutions have become much more knowledgeable and sophisticated about students' rights, the law, and cases affecting public as well as private institutions. Administrators in private institutions have used this knowledge and understanding—as well as the understanding that the courts are more prone to inserting themselves into matters involving private institutions—both to clarify and articulate policies and procedures and to apply policies in ways that recognize and respect students' rights.

There are also as many differences among private, independent institutions as there are between private and public colleges and universities. Both institutions with a single, well-defined mission and philosophy and multipurpose universities can be found in the private sector. The mission and educational philosophy of the private institution will have as much to do with administrative decisions as the legal constraints on the institution.

In this chapter, the similarities and differences between private and public institutions will be discussed from a legal perspective. The actual application of that perspective will depend, in large part, on the unique mission and character of the private institution.

Governing Boards

The structure and source of authority of public and private governing boards are very different, leading to differences in application of the law to their respective institutions. Public institutions are established through state constitutions or legislative acts. (See Chapter Two in this volume for further discussion of patterns of organization and control.) No matter what the organizational pattern, the authority of the trustees in public institutions is defined by constitutional provision or state statute, and ultimate control rests with the state government. Private institutions are established through state incorporation or trust laws. The authority of the trustees of private institutions is determined by the corporate charter of the institution, the restrictions placed on it by the incorporation laws of the state in which it is chartered, and other applicable state laws. Corporate charters are considered to provide either a license to do business, a franchise with a property interest, or a permanent contract between the state and the donors of the institution. In no way is the authority of the governing board controlled by the state unless another state statute impinges (Alexander and Solomon, 1972). Given these differences in structure and sources of authority, it is easy to see why private institutions are perceived to have considerably more legal autonomy than public institutions, even those constitutionally established.

The Federal Constitution: Application to Higher Education Law

The First, Fourth, Fifth, and Fourteenth Amendments to the federal Constitution provide the basis for the application of constitutional law to higher education. Although a number of specific legislative regulations have been applied to institutions of higher education over the years, these constitutional amendments have had the most significant influence on case law regarding the relationship between students and institutions and the differences between public and private institutions. The rights provided by these amendments include free speech, free press, freedom to assemble, due process, and freedom from unreasonable search and seizure. As Kaplin (1985, pp. 17-18) explains, the application of these amendments to public institutions differs from their application to private institutions: "Public institutions and their officers are fully subject to the constraints of the federal Constitution, whereas private institutions and their officers are not. Because the Constitution was designed to limit only the exercise of government power, it does not prohibit private individuals or corporations from impinging on such freedoms as free speech, equal protection, and due process." Since private institutions are technically free of constitutional constraints, must students who attend private colleges forfeit their rights? Certainly not! Many individual rights are protected by statutes, such as Title VII of the Civil Rights Act of 1964, Title IX of the Education Amendments of 1972, or the Family Educational Rights and Privacy Act of 1974. These are only examples; there are many more. In addition, other rights are protected by precedent established in recent case law. Still others are protected by the emerging definition of a contractual relationship between students and institutions.

First Amendment. A number of cases have been litigated regarding the protection of First Amendment rights of students in public institutions. (See Chapter Four in this volume for a full discussion of these issues.) In most of these cases (for example, *Healy* v. *James,* 1972; *Aryan* v. *Mackey,* 1978; *Gay Students Organization of the University of New Hampshire* v. *Bonner,* 1974), the courts have ruled on behalf of the students, indicating that their First Amendment rights had been violated. On the other hand, there have been circumstances where public institutions may exercise control that does not infringe on First Amendment rights. In *Brush* v. *Pennsylvania State University* (1977, 1980), the court ruled that the university regulation prohibiting door-to-door canvassing did not violate students' First Amendment rights. In a similar case, *American Future Systems, Inc.* v. *Pennsylvania State University* (1984), the court held that prohibition of group sales demonstrations in students' residence hall rooms was not unconstitutional. On appeal, the Supreme Court refused to review the case, thereby upholding the decision of the U.S. Court of Appeals for the Third Circuit.

In the private sector, several cases have been litigated under the freedom of religion clause of the First Amendment. Court decisions have generally not restricted state support where it would not be used specifically for sectarian purposes. In *Lendall* v. *Cook* (1977), a federal district court ruled that an Arkansas scholarship program which provided scholarships to approved public and private institutions within the state did not violate the First Amendment establishment of religion clause of the Constitution. In *Smith* v. *Board of Governors of the University of North Carolina* (1977), a similar ruling occurred. However, in *d'Errico* v. *Lesmeister* (1983), another federal district court ruled that the state of North Dakota could not provide funds to Bible colleges whose primary purpose was to prepare men and women for the ministry.

The right of private institutions to regulate who may use their property and under what circumstances has also been tested in court. In *State* v. *Schmid* (1980), Princeton University attempted to prohibit a nonstudent from distributing and selling political materials on the campus. The institution had a regulation requiring off-campus groups or nonstudents to obtain permission to distribute materials. In this instance, the defendant had also been warned that his presence would result in arrest. The court ruled that the university was not engaged in "state action" but did not rule on whether the university restriction interfered with the defendant's First Amendment rights. However, it did find the university's actions in violation of the New Jersey constitution, which protects the free speech and assembly rights of individuals against both government bodies and private persons. Under appeal, the United States Supreme Court dismissed the case because the university had changed its regulations controlling such activity.

In general, the courts have ruled that private institutions are not constrained by the First Amendment of the Constitution in their dealings with students, as long as they follow the policies and procedures outlined in official institutional publications. On the other hand, public institutions are constrained because the federal Constitution is designed to limit governmental power, including that of educational institutions. This area of the law must continue to be monitored by both public and private institutions.

Search and Seizure. The Fourth Amendment provides protection against unreasonable search and seizure. Again, the courts have made distinctions between public institutions and private institutions; even within public institutions, rulings have differed. In fact, in two similar public institution cases in the state of Alabama, the final disposition of the cases varied. In the first case, *Moore* v. *Student Affairs Committee of Troy State University* (1968), the court upheld the regulation that the college could enter student rooms for inspection purposes, holding that such inspections were "reasonable and necessary to the institution's performance of its duty to operate as an educational institution" (Alexander and Solomon, 1972, p. 429). In the second case, *Piazzola* v. *Watkins* (1971), two students were arrested, tried, convicted, and sentenced to prison when marijuana was found in their rooms. The rooms were searched at the initiation of the police with the cooperation of the dean of men, since the university had a policy allowing it to enter rooms for inspection purposes. On appeal, the court reversed the original convictions, ruling that the warrantless searches were unconstitutional.

Two interesting private institution cases also resulted in different outcomes on search and seizure. Although private institutions are not generally constrained by the Constitution, in *People* v. *Cohen* (1968), a search of a student's room was found to be in violation of the Fourth Amendment. In this case, "police, accompanied by two Hofstra University officials, entered a student's dormitory room without announcing their purpose and without a search warrant. Consent was not given by the student; in fact, no one was in the room at the time so there was no immediate danger that the evidence would be removed" (at 730). As in *Piazzola*, the court did not feel that the institutional search policy took precedence over the student's rights. In both cases, the court seemed to be swayed by the fact that the searches were initiated by the police instead of college officials and that warrants were not obtained to conduct them.

In the second case, *People* v. *Boettner* (1974, 1975), the New York Supreme Court, Appellate Division, upheld a ruling that the search of a room by officials at the Rochester Institute of Technology was not "state action" and therefore was not subject to the Fourth Amendment. The court arrived at this finding as a result of establishing that police were not involved in the search, did not initiate it, and in fact were not even aware that it occurred. A similar finding occurred in the case of *People* v. *Kelly* (1961), where police and college officials searched the room of a student without a warrant and found stolen property. The court upheld the search.

Four principles arise out of these cases. First, a student does not forfeit constitutional rights by occupying a residence hall room, even in a private institution. Second, if consent to a search is stated or implied in a contract or college publication as a result of a student's residing in a residence hall room, it is implied to the institution, not to the police. Third, a search warrant should be obtained prior to any search, except in emergencies. It should be noted, however, that institutions are not limited to involving police and obtaining a search warrant from a civil court. An institution may have a policy and procedure for issuing search warrants to be used within the institution's judicial system. Fourth, a private college has the right to establish reasonable rules and regulations necessary to carry out its function as an educational institution.

Due Process. The Fifth and Fourteenth Amendments address the issue of providing due process of law. As with other constitutional provisions, public institutions are required to meet specific due process standards. Although private institutions are less constrained by constitutional mandate, court decisions over the past few years clearly indicate that the courts expect private institutions to meet due process guidelines similar to those in the public sector.

The landmark case regarding due process is *Dixon* v. *Alabama State Board of Education* (1961). In addition to eliminating the concept of *in loco parentis,* this case clearly outlined the requirement of procedural due process for students. The U.S. Court of Appeals for the Fifth Circuit ruled that students have the right to a hearing when the possible sanction is suspension or expulsion and that written notice of the hearing, including specific charges, must be provided. Procedural due process requirements were sharpened considerably by *Esteban* v. *Central Missouri State College* (1969). This case was far more specific than *Dixon* in defining due process requirements. The court specified that the institution must provide written notice of specific charges, as well as the hearing, and written indication of the evidence on which the case was based; that the student must be allowed to present evidence and witnesses at the hearing; and that sanctions could not be imposed unless a preponderance of the evidence indicated student guilt.

Other public institution rulings substantiate these due process requirements. In *Woody* v. *Burns* (1966), expulsion of a student from a public institution was overturned because a faculty committee had usurped the authority of a disciplinary committee, which should have heard the case. Similar circumstances occurred in *Escobar* v. *State University of New York, College at Old Westbury* (1977), where the president imposed a sanction of suspension based on state-mandated Rules for the Maintenance of Public Order after a hearing board had heard the case and given a lesser sanction. In *DePrima* v. *Columbia-Greene Community College* (1977), the same Rules for the Maintenance of Public Order were employed. Although the hearing body was convened appropriately, the student was not allowed to bring witnesses or to cross-examine college witnesses. The court remanded the case back to the panel to meet these requirements, even though the original sanction was only disciplinary probation.

To analyze the development of the principle of due process in private institutions, it is necessary to present a historical perspective. In the early years of the century, students could be, and were, dismissed for nearly any reason. In *Anthony v. Syracuse University* (1928), for example, the court upheld a student's dismissal even though the university had given no reason for its action. The court simply assumed that the institution had a reason and that the expulsion fell within the purview of its authority. In *Carr v. St. John's University, New York* (1962), the courts ruled that a student could not be arbitrarily dismissed from a private institution. Although this ruling represented a small step forward for due process in private institutions, the issue in this instance was the dismissal of four students for participating in a non-Catholic wedding ceremony. The dismissals were upheld under a principle published in the college catalogue, which stated, "In conformity with the ideals of Christian education and conduct, the university reserves the right to dismiss a student at any time on whatever grounds the university judges advisable" (Kaplin, 1985, p. 294).

Due process for students in private institutions was strengthened in *Kwiatkowski v. Ithaca College* (1975), where the court ruled that a student who had not been permitted to have a representative at his hearing, as allowed by the institution's judicial code, should be granted a new hearing with the institution's appeal board. In *Slaughter v. Brigham Young University* (1975), the court upheld the dismissal of a graduate student for academic dishonesty, although it did so only after determining that the action was not arbitrary and that the proceedings met the same procedural due process requirements applied to public institutions.

Clearly, the courts no longer give private institutions great latitude—indeed, license—in the area of procedural due process; private institutions now must meet conditions similar to those required of public institutions. Given recent case law and public sentiment, the judicious private institution administrator will provide due process protections for students in institutional judicial processes. Some caution is in order, however. Institutions are not expected to duplicate the procedural or evidence requirements of the civil courts with prosecutors, student advocates or public defenders, or professional attorneys; they are simply expected to follow basic due process guidelines and to adopt a general tone of reasonableness and fairness. Whatever guidelines an institution follows, they should be clearly set out in the rules, regulations, and procedures included in institutional publications. (See Chapter Fourteen in this volume for further discussion of these issues.)

State Action. Given the differences in authority and autonomy of public and private governing boards and the constitutional restraints on public institutions, the doctrine of "state action" has been employed in an attempt to provide a level of protection for student rights in private institutions equal to that of students enrolled in public colleges and universities. If a private institution can be shown to be acting on behalf of, or in place of, the state, the same constitutional restraints under which public institutions operate may be applied to private colleges and universities. (See Chapter Six in this volume for a full discussion of the state action doctrine.)

There are two major types of cases where the doctrine of state action has been tested. The first is where state funding, or some other kind of state support for private institutions, has been challenged. The second is where the actions of private institutions have been challenged because these institutions receive some form of state support. In most instances, the courts have ruled in favor of private institutions on state action issues. In *Smith* v. *Board of Governors of the University of North Carolina* (1977) and in *Lendall* v. *Cook* (1977), the courts ruled that state funds could be used for scholarships and grants at private institutions. In *Alabama Education Association* v. *James* (1979) and in *Americans United for Separation of Church and State* v. *Blanton* (1977), similar rulings resulted. In *Roemer* v. *Board of Public Works of Maryland* (1976), the state of Maryland had enacted a statute that provided grants for private institutions, including those with religious affiliation. The U.S. Supreme Court ruled that the grants, administered by the Council for Higher Education, could continue as long as the institution was not established to award theological degrees solely and as long as the funds were not used for sectarian purposes. In *d'Errico* v. *Lesmeister* (1983), funds were not allowed to be provided to certain sectarian private institutions in North Dakota. It is clear from these examples that the courts have been supportive of public dollars to private institutions as long as their expenditure was not restricted to sectarian purposes.

In state action cases that have challenged the actions of private institutions, the most interesting and unique is *Powe* v. *Miles* (1968). This case is to the doctrine of state action as *Dixon* (discussed above) is to due process. In *Powe*, seven students were suspended from Alfred University because they had participated in a campus demonstration that interfered with an ROTC ceremony. Four of the students were enrolled in the private liberal arts school of the university. The remaining three students were enrolled in the State College of Ceramics, a statutory division of the university. The court found in favor of the appeal of the State College students, ruling that the action against them constituted "state action." However, the suspension of the students enrolled in the university proper was upheld.

In three similar cases, the courts ruled in favor of the institutions, holding that state action did not exist. In *Naranjo* v. *Alverno College* (1980), a private women's college received financial assistance from the state. The court ruled that receipt of such assistance did not constitute state action and that therefore the college was not required under Title IX to admit a male to its nursing program. In *Grossner* v. *Trustees of Columbia University* (1968), students who had occupied buildings at Columbia University were dismissed. They contended that the university's action constituted state action because the university received government funds. The court did not accept their argument. The same ruling occurred in *Browns* v. *Mitchell* (1969), in which students suspended by the University of Denver contended that the institution's tax-exempt status required it to conform to the federal Constitution's requirements. The court found in favor of the institution.

Except under unusual circumstances, the courts have generally not found "state action" against private institutions. There have been such unusual cases, and although they have not occurred in student affairs, they are relevant to this discussion. In

Braden v. *University of Pittsburgh* (1977), a professor was dismissed from the University of Pittsburgh. Because the Commonwealth Act for the University of Pittsburgh created more than simply a financial connection between the university and the state, the court ruled that the university's action constituted "state action" and that due process for the dismissed professor was required. The decision in this case was based, at least partially, on the case of *Burton* v. *Wilmington Parking Authority* (1961). In this case, the owner of a private restaurant refused service to a customer because of the customer's race. Because the restaurant was operated in a building owned by a state-created parking authority, the U.S. Supreme Court ruled that the restaurant did not fall outside the scope of the Fourteenth Amendment and was therefore operating under the principle of state action. In *Isaacs* v. *Board of Trustees of Temple University* (1974), a case of sexual discrimination, the court found in favor of the plaintiff because the Temple University Commonwealth Act links the university to the state—just as the University of Pittsburgh was linked in the *Braden* case. These two cases are unusual because they both occurred in Pennsylvania under circumstances where private institutions, because of financial difficulties, became linked to the state through statutory actions.

Contract Theory

In response to the limitations of the federal Constitution and the state action doctrine, contract theory has been used to protect students' rights and to define the relationship between a private institution and its students. The contract theory "assumes that the student and the university are parties to a contract, each giving certain benefits and detriments in order to fulfill the agreement. The school in advertising and seeking students, in effect, makes an offer to the student and the student by registering accepts. The student agrees to pay tuition and fees and the school agrees to provide instruction and subsequently a degree, if the student remains in good standing academically and abides by the school's rules and regulations" (Alexander and Solomon, 1972, pp. 412–413). It is clear from this statement that the student must meet both the academic and the conduct requirements of the institution. Given these conditions, academic and conduct standards must be carefully developed and clearly articulated in campus publications as conditions of the contract.

There are differences of opinion regarding whether contract theory may be applied to public institutions in the same way that it is applied to private institutions. Those who question its applicability point out that public institutions cannot freely choose the parties with whom they will share the contract, since many public institutions cannot deny admission to resident students. Despite this question, it is a fact that both public and private institutions maintain contractual relationships with students in the areas of housing, food service, and student loan agreements.

Differences of opinion also exist about whether a contractual relationship between institutions and students is the most appropriate legal link between them. Some believe that only through a strict contractual approach can the rights of students in private institutions be protected. On the other hand, detractors argue that the contractual relationship swings the balance of power so far in the direction of the institution that the student is left with few, if any, rights. Those who take this position believe that university documents are generally vague and that, in any event, the student has little recourse because the courts have recognized "implied" or "inherent" institutional powers (as indicated in Chapter Two of this volume) beyond what is presented in writing.

There is little question that the contractual approach creates problems. White (1979–80) indicates that students do not generally regard college publications as contracts. Thus, although the contractual relationship is clear to the institution, it may not be to the student. Second, the fact that the student may be a minor is also a problem. Although institutions may treat students as adults at age eighteen, many students enter college before that age. The third problem is that public institutions are not necessarily free to decide whether or not to enter into the contract.

A number of cases illustrate the application of contract law to higher education. Most of them have occurred in private institutions, but there are some examples of contract theory applied to public institutions.

In *Zumbrun* v. *University of Southern California* (1972), it was established that "the basic legal relationship between a student and a private university or college is contractual in nature" (Edwards and Nordin, 1979, p. 420).

In *Steinberg* v. *Chicago Medical School* (1976), the plaintiff alleged that criteria other than those published in the institution's brochure were used in assessing his application for admission. The school contended that no contract existed because it was simply a brochure in which information was printed. However, the court ruled that the brochure constituted an invitation to make an offer and that the student, by applying and paying the application fee, made that offer. Therefore, the school's voluntary acceptance of the fee created the contract.

In *King* v. *American Academy of Dramatic Arts* (1980), a student was expelled for being too much of an "exhibitionist." The student had paid $410 in tuition and fees, and institutional publications indicated that the student was responsible for these costs if he left the institution for any reason before the end of the year. The court found in favor of the student because it interpreted "leaving" the institution to be a voluntary act. Since the student was dismissed, it was not voluntary. Unfortunately, institutional publications did not mention that tuition fees would be retained if a student was dismissed.

In *Clayton* v. *Trustees of Princeton University* (1985), a student was granted relief because the institution did not follow its published procedures. In *Slaughter* v. *Brigham Young University* (1975), the court upheld the dismissal of a student for violating the Student Code of Conduct, which the court viewed as part of the contract.

In a case involving student fees, *Basch* v. *George Washington University* (1977), an institutional publication specified a medical school tuition fee of $3,200 for the 1974–75 academic year. It further indicated that increases for the next few years would occur in increments of $200 and that every effort would be made to keep increases within that limit. However, the following year, tuition was increased by $1,800. Students filed a class action suit to hold the university to its published increases. The court ruled in favor of the institution, indicating that it could not be expected to project economic factors and concomitant costs precisely.

Although there have been fewer contract cases in public institutions than in private ones, there are cases where contract theory has been applied to public institutions. In *Mahavongsanan* v. *Hall* (1976), a district court had forced the defendants, a dean and Georgia State University's board of regents, to award a degree to the plaintiff. As directed, the defendants awarded the degree even though they determined that she had not met the university's requirements for the degree. On appeal, the U.S. Court of Appeals for the Fifth Circuit ruled in favor of the institution, indicating that it had not breached the contract because academic institutions have wide latitude and discretion in determining degree requirements and that the courts should not interfere in such matters.

In a second, more complex, case, involving an implied contract, an appeals court ruled against the university. In *Behrand* v. *State* (1977), the appellants were former architectural students at Ohio University. They had claimed damages against the university because the School of Architecture lost its accreditation after they were enrolled. Subsequently, the administration of the institution, and the board of trustees, made a decision to eliminate the School of Architecture from the university due to financial exigency. Although the original ruling by the Court of Claims did not grant the students relief, the Ohio Court of Appeals reversed this decision, ruling that the university had an implied contract with the former students. Further, it required that they be reimbursed for the loss of credit and time which resulted from their transfer to other schools or from their delay in taking state professional exams.

In *Eden* v. *Board of Trustees of the State University of New York* (1975), the court considered an appeal by students who had been admitted to a new School of Podiatry at the Stony Brook campus. Before the school opened, the state withdrew its fiscal support. The court ruled that a contract existed because the institution had accepted the students' applications, and it required the institution to open the school and to enroll the students for the following year.

Although there remains some question whether public institutions can truly enter into contracts with students, the courts have certainly acted in a manner indicating that they can. It is true that more contract cases have occurred in private institutions than in public ones, but the courts have not felt limited in this regard.

The specific role of institutional publications as contract documents still needs to be clarified by the courts. For example, to what extent do publications constitute part of the contract? What terms and conditions need to be spelled out in these publications? In addition, to what extent do institutions retain implied or inherent authority when policies, rules, and regulations are not expressly stated in writing? It is likely that many of these questions will be addressed in the courts over the next few years. (See Chapter Five in this volume for a further discussion of these issues.)

Tort Theory

As stated above, there are those who believe that contract theory applied to the student-institution relationship is so heavily weighted in favor of the institution that other definitions should be applied. Because tort liability is applied to relationships between individuals and/or groups when a wrong or injury has occurred, tort theory may be the most applicable principle. Tort concepts are inserted into contractual situations, and private institutions have been sued for both negligence and defamation. Although in some states public institutions are protected from tort liability by government immunity, numerous suits against public institutions have been settled in favor of the plaintiffs. In *Lamphear* v. *State* (1982) and in *Lavoie* v. *State* (1982), for instance, students who were injured as a result of unsafe conditions at the schools were awarded significant settlements. In private institutions, the most prominent recent cases are *Bradshaw* v. *Rawlings* (1980), *Mullins* v. *Pine Manor College* (1983), and *Whitlock* v. *University of Denver* (1987).

In *Bradshaw,* the college was found not liable for serious injuries received by a student in an automobile accident that occurred after a school picnic where alcohol was served. The driver of the car was also a student and was intoxicated at the time. In *Pine Manor,* a female student was raped by a male intruder who had gained entrance to her residence hall room. The institution and the vice-president of operations were found to be negligent. In *Whitlock,* a student was seriously injured in a trampoline accident at a fraternity house located on the university campus. Drinking occurred prior to the accident. The university was found negligent by the state district court and the Colorado Court of Appeals. The student was awarded a $5 million settlement. In November 1987, the Colorado Supreme Court reversed the judgment and found that the university did not owe a duty of care to Whitlock.

Defamation suits often involve personnel actions. In *Greenya* v. *George Washington University* (1975), however, when a part-time instructor brought suit claiming defamation because of a statement in his personnel file, the district court upheld the university. The court stated in part that "officers and faculty members of educational organizations enjoy a qualified privilege to discuss the qualifications and character of fellow officers and faculty members if the matter communicated is pertinent to the functioning of the educational institution" (at 563). In *Shearer* v. *Lambert* (1976), the court also upheld this qualified privilege in a public university when the alleged defamatory statement was published in the performance of official duties. (For a complete discussion of tort liability, see Chapter Nine in this volume.)

There is little question that tort cases have increased in number and have become more common over the past few years, presumably as a result of an increasingly litigious society. Tort theory certainly provides another means of protection for students who have been wronged in both public and private institutions. However, there are serious questions whether it is· an across-the-board solution to all differences between institutions and students, or even a majority of them. Most can and should be solved through other means. Cash settlements are not the answer to most problems in higher education.

Other Theories

Trust and fiduciary theories also have been considered applicable to the student-institution relationship in certain circumstances. In the former, "the school is considered the trustee administrating a charitable or educational trust, with the student as the beneficiary" (Alexander and Solomon, 1972, p. 413). In the latter, the institution is seen as existing for the benefit of the student; therefore, institutional representatives "act in a fiduciary capacity to the students" (Seavey, 1957, p. 1407). It is incomprehensible how either of these principles could be applied to the student-institution relationship as it presently exists, except in the most unusual of circumstances. In dispute situations, students and parents certainly do not regard the institution as beneficent or as existing for their benefit.

Government Regulation

Over the past twenty years, the government has inserted itself into the operation of institutions of higher education in a number of ways. Intervention and regulation have occurred through passage of a number of statutes. The most prominent are the Vietnam Era Veterans' Readjustment Assistance Act, Titles VI and VII of the Civil Rights Act, Title IX of the Education Amendments of 1972, Section 504 of the Rehabilitation Act, the Fair Labor Standards Act, and the Family Educational Rights and Privacy Act. (See Chapters Six and Seven in this volume for a complete discussion of these issues.) Implementation of most of these regulations is consistent for both public and private institutions. However, there are exceptions.

The Fair Labor Standards Act did not apply to public institutions in the same way that it applied to private institutions until a Supreme Court decision in *Garcia* v. *San Antonio Metropolitan Transit Authority* (1985). In an important student affairs case prior to that, *Marshall* v. *Regis Educational Corp.* (1981), suit was brought against Regis College by the Department of Labor for not keeping appropriate hourly records and for not paying the minimum wage to student residence hall assistants (RAs). The department challenged the reduced room rate, free phone, and tuition stipend that RAs received, arguing that it did not equal minimum wage requirements. Both the district court and the appeals court acknowledged the educational value of the RA position and likened resident assistants to student athletes and student government leaders, whose experiences are important components of their overall education. As a result, both courts upheld the institution's position.

Under the Family Educational Rights and Privacy Act (FERPA), students are classified as dependent if they are claimed as dependents on their parents' tax forms. Although most students, particularly those between the ages of eighteen and twenty-two, are claimed on tax forms by parents, many public institutions have chosen to consider students "independent." On the other hand, most private institutions classify them as "dependent." When the student is considered independent for the purposes of FERPA, only the student has a right to information in his or her educational records maintained by the institution. Information may not be released to parents without the student's consent. When the student is considered dependent by the institution, information in that student's educational records may be routinely released to parents. (See Chapter Seven in this volume for a complete discussion of these issues.)

Implications for Student Affairs Administrators

A comprehensive look at the similarities and differences between public and private institutions in regard to the law reveals that a fine line does not exist between the two types of institutions. The commonly held perception that private institutions have license to promulgate and implement policies, rules, and regulations at will is largely a myth. Legislation and the results of court cases have shown that, in regard to the law, public and private institutions are more alike than they are different. Nonetheless, administrators should seek legal counsel in developing policies and should not assume that each source of the law (see Chapter One in this volume) applies equally to both public and private institutions.

The legal framework within which public and private institutions of higher education operate has been extensively expanded over the past twenty-five years. It will continue to be honed over the immediate future as more and more disputes between students and institutions are litigated and settled. Given the blurring of the differences between public and private institutions over the past few years, it is safe to predict that these differences will continue to diminish, particularly in areas for which students affairs administrators are responsible.

References

Alexander, K., and Solomon, E. *College and University Law.* Charlottesville, Va.: Michie, 1972.

Edwards, H., and Nordin, V. *Higher Education and the Law.* Cambridge, Mass.: Institute for Educational Management, Harvard University, 1979.

Kaplin, W. A. *The Law of Higher Education: A Comprehensive Guide to Legal Implications of Administrative Decision Making.* (2nd ed.) San Francisco: Jossey-Bass, 1985.

Seavey, W. "Dismissal of Students: Due Process." *Harvard Law Review,* 1957, *70,* 1406–1407.

White, R. "Wanted: A Strict Contractual Approach to the Private University/Student Relationship." *Kentucky Law Journal,* 1979–80, *68,* 439–456.

Part Two

Key Areas of Legal Responsibility and Liability

As Part One of this volume has indicated, the law is multifaceted, ever changing, and derived from many sources. In Part Two, areas of the law that are especially relevant to student services are covered in detail. Each author provides an overview of the important legal concerns and addresses the specific implications that those concerns have for practice in both public and private institutions. The authors are lawyers or have substantial training in the law. Their insight from both a legal and an administrative perspective should provide valuable guidance to the practitioner.

The greatest change that has occurred in higher education involves the enforcement of federal constitutional rights in colleges and universities. Although this phenomenon is felt most deeply on public campuses, private institutions may also be subject to the Constitution's provisions. Similarly, state constitutional provisions can influence both private and public institutions. In Chapter Four, E. T. "Joe" Buchanan III outlines the constitutional questions that must be accounted for in the administration of student services.

Contract law is currently emerging as a way to define the relationship between the student and the institution. This area of law is particularly important to practitioners in private institutions, although there are implications for public institutions as well. George Shur reviews contractual issues in detail in Chapter Five.

Nondiscrimination laws also have far-reaching implications for student affairs. In Chapter Six, Gwen Seaquist provides an analysis of the relevant federal statutes on discrimination. Enforcement mechanisms are discussed in detail, and methods to ensure compliance are also analyzed in this chapter.

Student affairs practice is also influenced by laws ranging from those influencing record keeping to copyright. In Chapter Seven, Stephen Janes describes the federal statutes that are relevant to administrative practice. He points out parallel laws at the state level and provides sound advice for the practitioner.

In Chapter Eight, Shari Rhode and Melissa Math provide a full discussion of the statutory and constitutional issues involved in campus discipline and control—issues such as due process requirements, control of outsiders, and possible responses to violations of state law.

The last chapter in this section focuses on liability questions. Liability, in this litigious society, is of increased concern to college administrators. Chapter Nine contains an analysis of pertinent areas of concern regarding liability and provides suggestions for managing this complex area of the law on campus.

4   E. T. "Joe" Buchanan III

Constitutional Issues: Protecting the Rights and Interests of Campuses and Students

The United States Constitution, now two hundred years old, is alive and well on the college campuses of this country. Such was not always the case. From the adoption of the Constitution in 1787, through the adoption of the amendments of the Civil War era, until the civil rights movement of the late 1950s, the Constitution had only a limited role on college campuses.

The legal basis for United States constitutional principles to be applied to the campuses came in four movements. First, the Bill of Rights, the first ten amendments to the federal Constitution, guaranteed such rights as due process and equal protection, free speech, free press, the right to assembly, the right of association, and restriction on unreasonable search and seizure. Second, the Civil War amendments to the Constitution—the Thirteenth, Fourteenth, and Fifteenth Amendments, dealing with voting rights, race equity, due process, and equal protection—provided the basis for the application of federal constitutional provisions to the actions of state officials. Third, *Brown* v. *Board of Education* (1954), although an elementary and secondary education case, began a number of legal challenges to segregation at the higher education level. Fourth, the civil rights actions of the late 1950s—including the

47

lunch counter sit-ins and freedom rides, and efforts by public college administrators in all-black colleges to discipline black students for civil disobedience—led judges to reexamine the relationship of public college students to their institution and its officials. In *Dickey* v. *Alabama State Board of Education* (1967), for example, the court concluded that civil rights protests by students were often protecting free speech, that the dean who acted in *Dickey* was a state official, that the "state action" doctrine prohibits arbitrary and capricious actions by a state official, and that actions by a public school official must meet the twin tests of due process and equal protection. *Dickey* was the first of a long line of cases discussed in this chapter that support these conclusions.

These four movements (the Bill of Rights, the Civil War amendments, desegregation of the schools, and civil rights) led, perhaps inexorably, to the "free-speech" movement at the University of California, Berkeley. Many of the leaders of this movement had spent a summer in Mississippi, participating in civil rights activities. On returning to campus in the fall, they found that the House Un-American Activities Committee (HUAC) had scheduled hearings in the Bay area. A student demonstration outside the committee's hearing room and the attendant police action provided the intellectual spark for the "free-speech" movement at Berkeley. That movement initiated the protests and demonstrations that continued during the Vietnam War and reappeared in the 1980s as students reacted against apartheid.

Because constitutional principles are now applied at our colleges and universities, many believe that college campuses are much more sane, reasonable, and humane places than they were even a few years ago. Students, faculty, and staff enjoy a level of due process in decisions about their academic futures or job security that promotes reasoned, factually based, decision making. Public institutions in particular, which fall clearly under the "state action" doctrine, must grant students the rights specified in the federal Constitution. Private colleges also have adopted principles of fair play in college catalogues and other documents that constitute the "contract of enrollment."

This chapter will discuss the implications of these federal constitutional rights for both public and private institutions. The private-public dichotomy will be explored, and the implications for administrative decisions that arise from state constitutional provisions will be discussed. Two major themes will emerge in this chapter. First, there is a fundamental, though eroding, distinction between public and private institutions. Second, the power of state officials can and should properly be restrained by the federal Constitution.

State Action: The Public-Private Dichotomy

The Fourteenth Amendment to the United States Constitution provides that no state "shall deprive any person of life, liberty, or property, without due process of law; nor deny to any person within its jurisdiction the equal protection of the laws." The Fourteenth Amendment was clearly intended to apply only to the actions of *public* officials and was *not* intended to reach the actions of private businesses or of nonprofit corporate directors, officers, and employees.

The issue of whether a college is public or private continues to be litigated. The plaintiff is usually a person who has been aggrieved by some administrative action and who seeks to have that administrative action declared "state action," so as to invoke federal constitutional protections. For many of the clearly public colleges in the country, this is not a debatable issue. For private institutions, however, it may be debatable, since many of these institutions receive some state financing and some federal funds, including funds for student aid. Cornell University, while private in control, has academic programs that are public in support. Should a student who is enrolled in the publicly supported home economics program at Cornell be entitled to federal constitutional protections of free speech and assembly, whereas a Cornell student who is enrolled in the privately funded English department is not so entitled?

As a practical matter, private institutions are continuing to adopt federal constitutional principles in defining the student-institution relationship. These private colleges are not generally responding to court action but are seeking to adopt—as part of the contract of enrollment evidenced in a catalogue, student handbook, or other publication—policies and procedures that fairly and reasonably reflect the spirit of what some call the American tradition of fair play. Once adopted, a private college's policies and procedures are generally enforceable, though the term *contract of enrollment* has almost as many meanings as there are judges who have ruled on the issue. Readers are urged to review Davenport's definitive article on the contract of enrollment (1985) and Chapter Five in this volume for further clarification.

An illustrative case in this area is *Clayton* v. *Trustees of Princeton University* (1985). Clayton was found, under Princeton's procedure, to have cheated in a laboratory practical exam. When disciplined, he sued on grounds that he was not afforded due process. At issue in *Clayton* was the level of due process required in a *private* college. The court held that the discipline procedures used by Princeton were fundamentally fair and adequate to safeguard a student from being unfairly found guilty of cheating. (It should be noted that Princeton students have resorted to the federal courts frequently in recent years, asserting a variety of claims, including sex discrimination, discipline, and outsiders' access to the campus, so that New Jersey's federal judges enjoy a relatively high level of sophistication in these matters.)

Much of the recent litigation on the public-private question has focused on the "symbiotic relationship" test of "state action." That is, if a court finds that a private institution is engaged in a "joint venture" with government (as the Supreme Court found in *Burton* v. *Wilmington Parking Authority*, 1961), the actions of that institution then will constitute state action; as a result, a suit alleging violation of constitutional rights can be brought.

Also relevant to this question is Section 1983 of the Civil Rights Act of 1871, which imposes liability on individuals who, "under color of" state law, deprive others of their constitutional rights. In *Wood* v. *Strickland* (1975), the United States Supreme Court established *personal* liability for officials who knowingly and willfully violate the well-known constitutional rights of a plaintiff. More recently, the Supreme Court decided, in *Daniels* v. *Williams* (1986) and *Davidson* v. *Cannon* (1986), that no cause of action arises under Section 1983 for mere negligent deprivation of well-known rights. These two cases overrule in part *Parrett* v. *Taylor* (1981), which authorized Section 1983 suits where mere negligence, as opposed to willful activity, violated fundamental rights. Under *Daniels* and *Davidson,* "egregious or oppressive" conduct should give rise to Section 1983 liability (Horen and Frels, 1985; see also Chapter Six in this volume).

In *Krynicky* v. *University of Pittsburgh* (1984), the Third Circuit held that, because the University of Pittsburgh received state appropriations and approximately one-third of the trustees of the university were state appointed, the symbiotic relationship test was met and the state action doctrine applied to the University of Pittsburgh. The United States Supreme Court refused to review the case. Another Pennsylvania case also illustrates the test for a symbiotic relationship (*Cohen* v. *Temple University of Commonwealth System of Higher Education,* 1984). Temple also received state appropriations and had state-appointed governing board members. Although *Cohen* involved a number of other issues regarding the relationship of the university to the city and its Civil Rights Commission, the significant finding was that the action by the university was state action.

Further insight into the state action doctrine is provided by *Grove City College* v. *Bell* (1984). In this case, Grove City College asserted that its receipt of federal student aid funds did not subject it to federal jurisdiction under Title IX of the Education Amendments of 1972, barring sex discrimination. The United States Supreme Court held that Title IX applied *only* to the college's financial aid program and to other specific federal programs (there are at least thirty research grants) and not to the institution in general. By extrapolation, Grove City College is likely not a "public" institution under the "symbiotic relationship" test, so that liability under the Fourteenth Amendment or Section 1983 probably could not be found.

Athletics, the source of an increasing volume of litigation, is not immune from the state action question. A typical case might involve a suit against a quasi-regulatory agency, such as the National Collegiate Athletic Association (NCAA), and an attempt to establish a federal constitutional level of due process in that agency's conduct of an investigation of an athletic program. Nolte's (1986) article "The Judicial Struggle with What Is State Action in Athletics" provides an excellent summary of these issues.

As several of the cases discussed illustrate, the federal courts have taken a strong position that officials must not arbitrarily, willfully, and capriciously deprive students or others of their "basic, unquestioned constitutional rights" (*Wood,* 1975, at 322) and that *personal* monetary damages will be assessed in an appropriate case. Clearly, attention to due process and to substantive rights is an important professional obligation, if only to protect the pocketbook of both the institution and the administrator. A federal statute (42 U.S.C. sec. 1988 *et seq.*) authorizes the award of attorneys' fees to the plaintiffs in such cases. This reimbursement is intended to encourage litigation protecting fundamental constitutional values. (See Chapter Nine in this volume for additional discussion of these issues.)

We now turn to an examination of specific provisions of the United States Constitution. The two lodestones of this examination are the "due process" and "equal protection" clauses of the Fifth and Fourteenth Amendments, which require a fundamentally fair process for resolving questions and equality of treatment under the law. Thus, both the substance of the law and its application must meet substantive and procedural constitutional tests.

Article I, Section 10: Contracts

The rationale of the Constitution and its progenitor, the Magna Carta, is largely one of both empowering and restricting government. Therefore, it is not surprising that one of the first principles of the Constitution is the "sanctity of contract" principle. Section 10 of Article I reads, in pertinent part, "No State shall . . . pass any . . . Law impairing the Obligation of Contracts."

One of the earliest higher education cases in this country, *Trustees of Dartmouth College* v. *Woodward* (1819), established the principle that a state legislative or regulatory action cannot impair a legally authorized contract between a college and another entity. (This is the famous case in which Daniel Webster, appearing on behalf of his alma mater, Dartmouth College, is reported to have argued that "It [Dartmouth] is but a small college, but there are those who love it!")

For a contract to be valid, a duly authorized institutional officer or employee must sign it on behalf of the institution. This point is occasionally missed by student affairs staff or students who seek to sign contracts for a variety of services, including food/beverage service, housing, transportation, and printing. Frequently, only the chief executive officer or that officer's duly designated appointee (one authorized by law or board action to act in the president's place) may bind the institution. Clearly, when a contract is signed by an unauthorized institutional representative who has no authority to sign, and when the institution has taken steps to restrict any "holding out" of this person as an authorized signatory, there is no binding contract, and the "sanctity of contract" doctrine will not validate the contract. (See Chapters Five and Nine in this volume for further information.)

Amendment I: Religion

The First Amendment reads, in pertinent part, "Congress shall make no law respecting an establishment of religion, or prohibiting the free exercise thereof." Pursuant both to state constitutional provisions and to the state action doctrine, public institutions must neither "establish" religion nor prohibit "free exercise," whereas private institutions, which frequently have a religious origin or a religious mission, are free to "establish" a religion and to prohibit "free exercise" of any but the established religion.

Over the years, a number of "free exercise/establishment" accommodations have been reached on college campuses. By the 1960s, religious denominations serving public colleges met the religious needs of the institutional community by a facility usually located off campus but adjacent to it. Facilities and staff were generally nonpublicly funded, while student union space, or other space constructed and maintained with nonappropriated fees and funds, might be made available to religious groups. Less occasionally, a "chaplain to the university," paid by appropriated funds, might be found, even in a public institution.

The school prayer decisions of the 1960s raised questions about quasi-religious practices in some public colleges. The issue was sharpened in the 1970s, with decisions authorizing socialists (*Healy* v. *James*, 1972) and homosexuals (*Gay Students Organization of the University of New Hampshire* v. *Bonner*, 1974) to utilize public institutional facilities for meetings and other purposes. Students seeking religious "free exercise" asked why an avowed political group could meet on campus to plan the overthrow of the United States, whereas students with a religious orientation could not meet on campus to pray. After several lower-court cases sought to resolve the issue of the access of religious groups to public institutional facilities, the United States Supreme Court, in *Widmar* v. *Vincent* (1981), held that a neutral accommodation of a number of active student religious groups would not constitute an establishment of religion, even though some groups might use institutional facilites paid for with appropriated (not fee-generated) dollars for religious worship or religious teaching. It is interesting to note that Missouri, the state in which *Widmar* arose, has a very strong public policy maintaining a strict separation of church and state, similar to Virginia's *Statute of Religious Freedom*, which was drafted by Thomas Jefferson and which disestablished the Episcopal Church as Virginia's state church. Prior to disestablishment, non-Episcopal clergy in Virginia were jailed, beaten, and otherwise harassed on occasion.

The following principles, discussed by Jones (1981), appear to reflect the current state of the law regarding freedom of religion on campus.

1. Students in public colleges have a constitutional right to organize sectarian religious groups, to have those groups recognized by the institution, and to receive all rights generally accruing to that status.
2. These sectarian religious groups may limit membership to those sharing a particular sectarian belief.
3. The question of student activity fee support for sectarian groups does not appear to be settled; the issue of the use of campus facilities is clearly in favor of the student sectarian religious group.

The emergence of religious cults, nondenominational groups, and evangelical groups on campuses has continued both debate and litigation over this issue. Nonetheless, a national consensus appears to have been reached on the general issue with the adoption of the Equal Access Act (Public Law 98-377, sec. 801 *et seq.*). This 1984 federal statute authorizes voluntary student-initiated religious activities in *public* school buildings on the same basis as other student extracurricular activities. Thus, both voluntary student-initiated prayer and scriptural teaching are now authorized by federal statute in the K–12 public schools. None of the case law arising from the Equal Access Act has settled the issue of the constitutionally of this statute. Administrators seeking guidance on this issue might examine "Standards and Guidelines for Religious Programs," which appears in the *CAS Standards and Guidelines for Student Services/Development Programs* (Council for the Advancement of Standards, 1986). This helpful document includes a summary of applicable case law and discusses the balance between the "establishment" clause of the First Amendment and "free exercise" interests. Further, it clearly distinguishes the legal issues for both public and private institutions.

Amendment I: Speech

The First Amendment also reads, in pertinent part, "Congress shall make no law . . . abridging the freedom of speech."

Employee Free Speech. Freedom of speech is one of the most cherished traditions of the academic community, and for good cause; a community of scholars cannot pursue the truth without the ability to discourse and publish information critical of the established order. Particularly for *public* employees, the last fifteen years have seen a growth of recognized free-speech rights. In a series of cases involving K–12 teachers, the rights of teachers to criticize a school board, testify before the legislature, relate the substance of a school memo over a radio station, and speak about alleged racially discriminatory policies have been affirmed (*Pickering* v. *Board of Education*, 1968, and its progeny). Despite these rulings, it should be noted that an employee in a *private* college or university, by definition, has no First Amendment rights.

Similarly, a public employee can be discharged for the irresponsible exercise of free-speech rights. In *Landrum* v. *Eastern*

Kentucky University (1984), a professor who verbally assaulted the administration over individual grievances was discharged, and a federal district court sustained his dismissal. Of considerable assistance on this point is the case of *Professional Association of College Educators* v. *El Paso County Community College* (1984), where the court held that the lawful exercise of free speech will be upheld in a job termination, even under conditions where all due process requirements were met. The emerging rule appears to be that only speech related to racial discrimination and political activity is so fundamental to our basic constitutional values as to always enjoy First Amendment protection. Less likely to enjoy First Amendment protection is speech on such topics as an individual's salary, job tenure, or work assignment, and where no racial or political issue is present (Lavin, 1983–84).

The other side of the free-speech coin is the employee who is libeled by the free speech of another. In *Fleming* v. *Moore* (1985), a developer ran an advertisement in a student paper, stating that a professor opposed a proposed development adjacent to the college on racial grounds. The professor sued and recovered $250,000 in the trial court. The award was reduced considerably on appeal, but the verdict stood.

What rights do public employees have when a union contract is in place and they are not union members? Can they be denied participation in academic governance, or may they claim First Amendment protection? In *Minnesota State Board for Community Colleges* v. *Knight* (1984), the U.S. Supreme Court held that a union contract making the union the sole contact with the administration excluded nonunion members from participation in academic governance committees. *Knight* includes an excellent discussion of public employees' First Amendment rights.

Finally, does a public employee have a First Amendment right to engage in a religious exercise in an effort to enhance communication with a student? A complaint filed with the Equal Employment Opportunity Commission (EEOC) in 1984 by a discharged employee is illustrative of this quest. In 1984, an assistant dean of students was fired from a California public college for using an Indian ritual involving the burning of herbs during a disciplinary hearing. She claimed that she was attempting to improve the atmosphere of the hearing. The outcome of the EEOC complaint is unknown but should be an interesting outcome to watch.

   Student Speech. The right of free speech has been very carefully protected by the courts. In order for speech to be curtailed, it must present a clear and present danger to the community (*Bridges* v. *California,* 1941). In *Bridges,* the Supreme Court held that the "substantive evil must be extremely serious, and the degree of imminence extremely high, before utterances can be punished" (at 252). Cases involving the free speech of students have supported this position. However, as Wright (1969) suggests, case law indicates that First Amendment activity can be regulated as to time, place, and manner. Wright suggests three principles that have been borne out by the judicial decisions:

1.   Expression cannot be prohibited because of a disagreement with or a dislike for its contents.
2.   Expression is subject to reasonable regulation as to time, place, and manner.
3.   Expression can be prohibited if it becomes action that materially and substantially interferes with the normal activities of the institution or invades the right of others.

   Wright's article was followed by *Tinker* v. *Des Moines Independent School District* (1969). *Tinker* established the First Amendment free-speech rights of K–12 students in a case involving the wearing of black armbands as a silent protest against the Vietnam War. In *Harrell* v. *Southern Illinois University* (1983), the court held that a university can lawfully regulate the time, place, and manner of political candidates conducting campaign activity in residence halls at public colleges. However, an absolute ban on political campaigning in such residence halls may violate First Amendment rights. A number of cases have been filed but have yet to be litigated. Among the issues at stake are the rights of an artist to show sexually explicit and racially offensive artwork at a public college and a student group's right to show X-rated films in the classrooms of public colleges. A recent case regarding the right of students to operate cars on campus has been decided. This is not a protected First Amendment right (*Miami University Associated Student Government* v. *Shriver*, 1984). The Supreme Court, in its 1986 term, decided *Bethel School District #403* v. *Fraser* (1986). Fraser gave a speech in a high school assembly, endorsing a candidate for school office. Because the speech contained a number of sexually allusive comments, he was disciplined by the school and subsequently brought suit, alleging that his First Amendment rights had been abridged. The trial court found in his favor and awarded him $12,750 for his attorney's fees and costs and $278 in damages. The Supreme Court reversed the decision and the award. *Fraser* is one of the most significant K-12 student speech cases since *Tinker*. The Court held that *Tinker* controlled but that K-12 students using lewd, vulgar, or indecent language at official functions may be disciplined.

Outside Speakers' Speech. Private institutions may limit the appearance of outside speakers as they wish. Public institutions may totally ban all outside speakers, but when they do allow an outside speaker to appear, they must observe constitutional requirements, such as "equal protection." Under the "equal protection" clause, a college cannot ban some speakers and authorize others to speak. Under the "clear and present danger of substantive harm to the institution" test, more than mere dislike is necessary to ban a speaker. The fact that a speaker's mere *presence* causes riotous conduct is not a sufficient reason for banning that speaker. The speaker must reasonably appear to advocate, in the course of the speech, violent overthrow of the government, willful destruction or seizure of property, forceful disruption of the institution's daily work, physical harm or invasion of rights, or other violent campus disorder (*Stacy* v. *Williams*, 1969).

An institution can, however, regulate outside speakers as to time, place, and manner. It cannot regulate the content of a speech, but it can—at least in the state of Florida—refuse to pay speakers who violate the "clear and present danger" test. (Needless to say, it may not be easy to decide when a speaker has crossed the line, as this author learned in trying to administer the Florida statute!)

Commercial Speech. The leading case on on-campus commercial solicitation by off-campus sales staff is *American Future Systems, Inc.* v. *Pennsylvania State University* (1980, 1982, 1983,

1984). American Future Systems (AFS) sought to sell cookware, crystal, china, and silverware on campus by first contacting students by phone and arranging sales demonstrations in dormitory rooms. The university prevailed at the trial court, which held that a "commercial vendor has no First Amendment right to disseminate information in any manner he chooses," (1980, at 253). The court pointed out that other means of communication—such as radio, newspaper, bulletin board, mail service, or telephone—were available to AFS. As long as a college's regulation does not impede alternative forms of communication and does not aim at commercial content, such a regulation will likely pass constitutional muster. (See Chapter Eleven for a complete discussion of this case.)

Amendment I: Assembly

The First Amendment reads, in pertinent part, "Congress shall make no law . . . abridging . . . the right of the people peaceably to assemble."

Student Organizations. Private institutions can, of course, prevent, limit, or refuse to authorize the peaceful assembly of student organizations of any type. Public institutions may not. In *Healy* v. *James* (1972), the United States Supreme Court determined that a public college must recognize a student organization—in this case, a local chapter of Students for a Democratic Society (SDS), which, the college alleged, espoused a philosophy of overthrow of the government—unless the college can show that the organization engaged in "advocacy directed to inciting imminent lawless action and . . . likely to produce such action" and had a "knowing affiliation with a group possessing unlawful goals, and a specific intent to further these goals" (at 2339).

More recent cases involve the gay rights movement and efforts to obtain institutional recognition and attendant benefits by gay groups. For public institutions, the law is now relatively clear that a duly organized gay student group must be recognized (*Student Coalition for Gay Alliance of Students* v. *Matthews,* 1976); efforts to deny recognition on grounds of illegality of homosexual acts, public policy concerns, or homosexuality as a mental illness have failed; and a state legislature may not withhold appropriations to a public college simply on the basis of that college's recognition of a gay student group (*Department of Education* v. *Lewis*, 1982). (See Chapter Fifteen in this volume for a full discussion of this issue.)

Single-Sex Organizations. Assuming that a student group may organize and be recognized, may it establish sex-based eligibility for membership? At a private institution, the answer is now a qualified "yes." In 1985, Harvard University separated nine all-male student groups from the university because these groups refused to admit women. As a result of the university's action, the nine groups lost university support, including the use of telephones and alumni lists. Princeton University has taken similar administrative action. As of this writing, no lawsuits have been filed on this issue. Although *Grove City College* v. *Bell* (1984) establishes the limits of Title IX in higher education, the issue of Title IX is not settled. Lawsuits involving the admission of women to single-sex men's volunteer groups have been filed in several jurisdictions. (See Chapter Six in this volume.)

For public institutions generally, student organizations must be open to all, regardless of sex. However, fraternities and sororities have a specific federal statutory exemption from Title IX, and student religious groups ought to be able to select only those who hold beliefs consistent with the group's mission.

Sexual Harassment and Hazing. Among the activities of student groups *not* subject to constitutional protection are sexual harassment and hazing. *This is true whether the institution is private or public.*

The U.S. Supreme Court in *Vincent* v. *Taylor* (1986) has recently upheld a civil claim arising out of sexual harassment in the workplace; it thereby provided judicial imprimature for EEOC regulations that define sexual harassment in the workplace. In addition to the EEOC regulation, there may be applicable state law, city ordinances, institutional policy, or applicable case law. A comprehensive review of sexual harassment cases is provided in "Sexual Advances by Employee's Supervisor as Sex Discrimination with Title VII" (44 A.L.R. Fed. 224). Title IX would presumably prohibit sexual harassment as a matter of student right, while a student in an employee situation should enjoy the protection of Title VII (29 C.F.R. sec. 1604.11a.10).

Hazing activity also enjoys no constitutional protection. At least twenty states have, by statute, made hazing a criminal violation, and it is frequently a civil tort. Fraternity policy prohibits hazing for all known national organizations. Interestingly, sexual harassment appears to be prosecutable under many of the antihazing statutes.

Amendment I: Press

The First Amendment reads, in pertinent part, "Congress shall make no law . . . abridging the freedom of . . . the press." The student press in a private college has, by definition, no constitutional protection, and an editor or a reporter may be dismissed at will, as long as institutional policies and procedures are followed. At public colleges, the student press was one of the first beneficiaries of the Constitution's coming to campus. In a series of cases arising during the civil rights demonstrations of the 1960s, the constitutional protection of the student press, when the press criticized public officials, was carved out. See *Dickey* v. *Alabama State Board of Education* (1967) for one example.

Regrettably, the constitutional protection afforded the editor under the *Dickey* line of cases created a legal monster. Under traditional law, the publisher of a paper is absolutely liable for the defamatory acts of the paper's editorial and writing staff, and the publisher of virtually every college paper in the country was the institutional president. After *Dickey*, public college presidents had *very* limited authority to remove editors, but presidents, at least theoretically, continued to be held strictly liable for the defamatory publications of an editor whom they had not hired and could not, under the case law, fire.

In this context, two interesting cases were decided. The first, *Carey* v. *Piphus* (1978), involved a Section 1983 claim by students suspended from school without due process. The U.S. Supreme Court held that, in the absence of actual injury, only nominal damages (in this case $1) were recoverable in Section 1983 cases. This case provided some comfort to those college presidents faced with removing an editor who might respond by filing a Section 1983 action. The second case, *Minnesota Daily* v. *University of Minnesota* (1983), suggested that the president was not legally the publisher of the paper and, therefore, had no liability for the paper's errors and omissions.

Minnesota Daily also brought some bad news. College presidents could no longer rid themselves of an objectionable paper by eliminating or restricting activity fee support. In June 1979, the *Daily* had published a humor issue, which included racial and religious commentary. In response, the governing board changed fee support from mandatory to optional, and the editor filed suit on a *Joyner* v. *Whiting* (1973) theory that First Amendment rights of freedom of speech are more fundamental and therefore entitled to greater protection than the race-conscious rights guaranteed by the Thirteenth, Fourteenth, and Fifteenth Amendments. The trial court held for the university, but the Eighth Circuit reversed, finding a First Amendment violation in the trustees' change in support. In the final settlement of this case, the university was required to restore the mandatory fee support; pay an attorney's fee of $182,000 to the editor's lawyer; and set up a $20,000 fund to support a speakers' series on First Amendment issues.

Minnesota Daily is helpful in defining the balance between the Bill of Rights amendments (such as freedom of the press) and the Civil War amendments, which are race-conscious. This case also points toward another developing trend, the use of federal civil procedure rules governing lawsuits brought in "bad faith" to authorize substantial awards of attorneys' fees against the losing party bringing a "frivolous" case. In a recent University of Washington case, a "bad-faith" award of attorneys' fees in the $40,000 range was made against the faculty member plaintiff. Needless to say, utilization of this rule by federal judges will have a chilling effect on weakly capitalized plaintiffs.

This discussion must be placed in the context of judicial definitions of obscenity and the "clear and present danger" test. In *Papish* v. *Board of Curators of the University of Missouri* (1973), Papish, a University of Missouri journalism student, was expelled for distributing a newspaper that included a cartoon of police raping the Statue of Liberty and a headline containing the

"M...F..." word. The U.S. Supreme Court found that neither the cartoon nor the headline was "constitutionally obscene or otherwise unprotected" (at 1198). Papish was ordered reinstated as a graduate student in the journalism school, and the university was required to restore the credits that he should have earned.

Interestingly, despite the clarity of the case law, newspaper editors and administrators continue to clash. Recent unreported cases have included litigation over rules banning abortion agency ads, unsigned editorial endorsements, and editorial claims that the Holocaust was a myth.

It is comforting, in this context, to read *Mazart* v. *State* (1981), which reaffirmed that a public university may not exercise prior restraint but may discipline for violation of constitutionally valid rules. The institution was held not to be liable for the libelous articles of the student press. Further, no agency relationship was held to exist between the newspaper staff and the president.

In the K-12 setting, the rights of administrators to control the press are considerably greater than in the postsecondary setting. Bartlett and Engel (1984) concluded that the courts have more frequently ruled in favor of the elementary and secondary school administration and against the student plaintiffs. (See Chapter Sixteen in this volume for a more detailed discussion of these issues.)

Amendments IV, V, and XIV

The Fifth and Fourteenth Amendments include due process/ equal protection language, while the Fourth Amendment includes language limiting unreasonable searches and seizures and establishing a "probable cause" requirement as a condition precedent to the issuance and execution of a search warrant.

Search and Seizure. No criminal law issue has been the subject of more litigation in the last two decades than search and seizure. For the college search and seizure cases, there are two divergent lines of case law. One line, which authorizes warrantless searches, is represented by *Moore* v. *Student Affairs Committee of Troy State University* (1968). The other line, represented by *Smyth* v. *Lubbers* (1975), holds that such searches are unlawful. In *Moore*, the dean of men and two agents of the Alabama State Health Department conducted a successful warrantless search for drugs in a residence hall. The court sustained the search against a Fourteenth Amendment challenge, finding that "a special relationship" exists between a college and its students and that "reasonable cause," a standard lower than "probable cause," was sufficient to authorize a warrantless dorm search.

Smyth involved a warrantless search of a dormitory room by campus police. The court in *Smyth* rejected the "special relationship" rationale, denied a claim of a right to search under the dormitory contract, asserted that a dorm room is a home entitled to full constitutional protection, and repudiated the "reasonable cause" test, insisting that a search warrant based on "probable cause" be obtained to search a dormitory room. The *Smyth* rationale was adopted in several other jurisdictions (see *Piazzola* v. *Watkins*, 1971; *State* v. *Mora*, 1976; *White* v. *Davis*, 1975; *People* v. *Cohen*, 1968).

Fortunately, the residence hall search and seizure issue found its way to the U.S. Supreme Court in 1982. Unfortunately, the case presented involved a police officer operating under the "plain view" exception to the requirement for a warrant, rather than the typical "resident assistant (RA) who suspects dope" case. In *Washington* v. *Chrisman* (1982), a campus police officer arrested a student outside his dorm because the student had illegal alcohol in his possession. The arresting officer accompanied the student to his room to get the student's ID card. The officer did not enter the room but, while standing in an open doorway, observed a pipe and seeds on a table eight to ten feet away. The officer then entered the room and seized the marijuana seeds and the pipe. The students already in the room were arrested and charged with possession. When prosecuted, they filed a Fourth Amendment challenge to the seizure. The U.S. Supreme Court upheld the search as being within the "plain view" exception to warrantless searches.

Of more value in discerning the current direction of the Supreme Court is *New Jersey* v. *T.L.O.* (1985). In *T.L.O.*, a high school vice-principal conducted a warrantless search of a student's purse, seeking contraband. The Court held that officials may conduct warrantless searches of their pupils' purses on the basis of "reasonable suspicion," a standard less rigorous than the "probable cause" standard. According to Keller (1986), the *T.L.O.* case suggests that the Court is moving away from the view expressed in *Smyth* and toward the adoption of the *Moore* rationale in such cases.

In *T.L.O.*, the Court invoked a balancing test, weighing the privacy interests of the student against the state's interest in violating the student's privacy. The school official's authority to search was found to be based on a duty to carry out clearly mandated legislative social policy—curbing drug abuse. By not upholding a "probable cause" requirement, the Court held that a warrantless search is justified when there are "reasonable grounds for suspecting that the search will turn up evidence that the student violated either the law or school rules" (at 744). Despite the assistance that this case provides, it is important to note that *T.L.O.* is *not* a higher education case. The state of Fourth Amendment search and seizure law on college campuses has *not* been definitely resolved, and existing case law at times is conflicting.

How would *T.L.O.* affect the typical "RA suspects drugs, presents self in room, is admitted, finds drugs, student is suspended or prosecuted" case? On these facts, there is no probable cause for a search warrant, since the RA has only a "mere suspicion." Under the *Smyth* line of cases, failure to obtain a warrant would be fatal to the seizure of the drugs. Under the *Moore/T.L.O.* line of cases, the RA's seizure of the drugs would be lawful, and use of the seized evidence, either in a campus disciplinary case or a criminal proceeding, would also likely be lawful.

This issue may receive considerably more public scrutiny over the next years. The 1986 Higher Education Amendments include language mandating an institution-wide drug abuse program. The issue of drug possession/use in residence halls, and of a campus's disciplinary efforts, including its search and seizure policy, is certain to be the focus of newspaper stories, legislative inquiry, parental inquiry, and other audits of a potentially embarrassing nature. There may be suggestions that college administrators should be subject to criminal prosecution for their failure to rid their campus of drug users, distributors, or manufacturers. Ellman (1985) has suggested that civil liability might attach to K–12 administrators who choose to look the other way. This might well be an accurate assessment in states such as California, where a "safe, habitable school environment" is required by statute. In any event, a half-dozen lower-court decisions have sought to apply *T.L.O.* These judges have been generally willing to grant to K–12 school officials considerable discretion in assessing "reasonable suspicion." Under *T.L.O.*, only the most flagrant abuse of administrative discretion will likely lead courts to declare a search invalid (Nuger and Strope, 1986).

Student Discipline. The discipline of students is perhaps the most litigated issue in higher education. Nearly two hundred cases, in virtually every federal jurisdiction across the country, have been reported. The U.S. Supreme Court has spoken to the issue of student discipline at least twice in the postsecondary context (in *Regents of the University of Michigan* v. *Ewing,* 1985; and in *Board of Curators of the University of Missouri* v. *Horowitz,* 1978). Student discipline in the K–12 context has been the subject of several U.S. Supreme Court decisions, including *Wood* v. *Strickland* (1975), which established personal liability for a public official's violation of federal civil rights.

Much of the student discipline litigation involves public institutions and their duties under the Constitution. Nonetheless, private institutions have a duty to follow their published rules (*Harvey* v. *Palmer School of Chiropractic,* 1984; *Cloud* v. *Trustees of Boston University,* 1983) in resolving disciplinary disputes, and have a general obligation to treat a student fairly (*Clayton* v. *Trustees of Princeton University,* 1985).

The requirements of due process and equal protection in public colleges and universities are discussed in detail in other chapters in this volume. Conduct regulation violations, as contrasted with academic regulation cases, have been thoroughly litigated. In addition, a full discussion of these issues can be found in Buchanan (1978).

Gehring, Nuss, and Pavela's (1986) recent monograph on *Issues and Perspectives on Academic Integrity* provides excellent advice in assessing current institutional practice in handling general student misconduct and academic misconduct. The authors emphasize that both conduct and academic violations should be treated under a single disciplinary system and that legal concerns are created when faculty members act unilaterally. For example, a faculty member who ignores established policy and procedure for handling academic misconduct, and instead assigns a grade of *F* to a student alleged to have committed an act of academic dishonesty, could be in violation of the student's contractual or constitutional rights, as well as the faculty member's own contractual obligation to the institution. The authors found no reported decision in which administrators, faculty, or students have been assessed damages for reporting acts of apparent academic dishonesty.

The U.S. Supreme Court's most recent ruling on this issue, *Regents of University of Michigan* v. *Ewing* (1985), reemphasized the authority of faculty in reaching academic judgments. Judges "may not override . . . the substance of a genuinely academic decision . . . unless it is such a substantial departure from accepted academic norms as to indicate that the faculty member or the committee did not actually exercise professional judgment" (at 507). Absent arbitrary or capricious evaluation, a federal court should not, under *Ewing,* find grounds to overturn a faculty decision to fail a student, drop a student from a program, deny a test retake, or deny readmission to a program. Nonetheless, reaching any of these decisions without some fundamentally fair process being made available to a student, in the form of a grade appeals procedure, might create a constitutional claim.

The current trend toward restoring some measure of *in loco parentis* (for example, the movement to restore the legal drinking age to twenty-one) has renewed interest in the issue of the college's jurisdiction over its students' off-campus behavior. During the last two decades, many colleges had abandoned responsibility for assisting in collecting debts owed to local merchants, or enforcing disciplinary rules in off-campus settings, and had otherwise generally restricted jurisdiction to the boundaries of the campus, or perhaps to include adjacent fraternity/sorority structures.

The social shift toward more conservative values (compare *T.L.O.* and *Smyth*), the fraternity hazing deaths and injuries, sexual harassment rules and regulations, and concerns about widespread academic and athletic misconduct have caused many a college to reexamine its "hands-off, let the police handle it" view of off-campus incidents. Many colleges now are finding it difficult to uphold the values explicit in antihazing or sexual harassment policy if they do not assert jurisdiction over off-campus actions (Nolte, 1985b).

A college has always had the inherent authority to discipline its students if their conduct is inconsistent with behavior reasonably expected by the academic community and if the college has a written rule prohibiting the conduct. A college may assert jurisdiction regardless of where a prohibited act occurs. An incident on campus, in town, in the next county, or in the next state (or even a foreign country!) is within the college's jurisdiction. Many of an institution's current legal obligations and duties—for instance, to discourage drug abuse, to limit hazing, and to deter harassment based on sex—likely will encourage institutions to assert jurisdiction over some off-campus incidents occurring on privately owned premises.

Student Athletes: "Jar Wars." An interesting application of several constitutionally protected values—including search and seizure, due process, and equal protection—is present in the relationship of scholarship athletes and their collegiate institution. Some cases suggest a contractual or a federally protected property interest in an athletic scholarship, while the institution of mandatory random drug testing in 130 colleges had led to the filing of at least one search and seizure case challenging this practice under the Fourth Amendment.

Water v. *University of South Carolina* (1984) suggests that a public institution has at least a contractual obligation, if not a federally protected property interest, to consider when dealing with a scholarship athlete who is injured and who seeks the balance due and owing under the scholarship. Interestingly, in two unreported private college cases involving Mercer University and Wake Forest, no liability on behalf of the institution was found, but the student-institution relationship was characterized as contractual in nature.

As mentioned, the issue of mandatory random drug testing, now practiced by an estimated 130 colleges with major athletic programs, is beginning to be litigated. The first reported suit was filed against a public college in the West in the fall of 1986. (Mandatory random drug testing is now routinely practiced in the military, the federal civil service, and many of the Fortune 500 companies, and a number of cases have been filed in these contexts.) The American Council on Education (1986) has prepared a helpful "self-regulation" initiative on this topic. This ACE document emphasizes that tests should be used only to identify performance-enhancing drugs, so that the integrity of athletic competition is sustained; they should not be smoke screens for a fishing expedition seeking evidence of more general drug use. The document emphasizes the importance of involvement of counsel, due process, and confidentiality; it does not encourage institutions to engage in drug testing, and it states several well-advised cautions.

Some lawyers have expressed serious doubts about the constitutionality of mandatory random drug testing—especially testing that is predicated on the *T.L.O.* test of "reasonable ground for suspecting that the search will turn up evidence that the student violated either the law or school rules." Remember that *T.L.O.* involved a public high school, an environment remarkably distinct from a college campus and even more remarkably distinct from the tightly regimented environment of a Division I college scholarship athletic program. Some of these lawyers argue that most current drug-testing programs violate the spirit and the letter of the ACE document and have as their primary purpose avoiding institutional embarrassment and ensuring a full stadium. Others argue that a legitimate social purpose—namely, protection of the public—is served by mandatory random drug testing of some students: ROTC students who handle firearms with live ammunition; medical students, nurses, and students in health-related programs with direct responsibility for patient care; and students who routinely handle hazardous substances, including radioactive materials. However, these observers argue, the public has no need to be protected from the drug-related acts of student athletes; therefore, society has no compelling state interest to ensure by such testing.

Interestingly, mandatory random testing of police, firemen, and even prison guards has been judicially declared a constitutional violation. It seems somehow inconsistent that a campus police officer who is armed may not be subjected to mandatory random drug testing but that a scholarship athlete should be subjected to such an intrusive search. Furthermore, a number of institutions, under the *Smyth* v. *Lubbers* (1975) rationale, now require a search warrant to search an athlete's room; at the same time, under NCAA policy, a search of an athlete's body—perhaps the most intrusive search of all—is required and authorized. It seems curious that a search warrant, issued under the "probable cause" standard, is required to search an athlete's room where drugs are alleged to be made and distributed, whereas no search warrant is required to search and seize evidence that is the product of that same athlete's body. (So much for what Washington observers have taken to calling "Jar Wars!")

State Constitutions

In addition to the federal Constitution, state constitutions may be an important source of authority. The federal Constitution reserves to the states all powers not specifically granted to the United States (see Article X). Thus authorized, a state may elect to have constitutional provisions reaching issues not treated by the federal Constitution. These provisions may have considerable significance for college administrators. One such topic is discrimination. Despite efforts over the years, the required number of states did not ratify the equal rights amendment to the U.S. Constitution. Some states have, as a consequence, adopted a state constitutional provision banning discrimination on the basis of sex and have implemented this provision by creating a "human rights commission" empowered to review allegations of discrimination that are sex based or otherwise countenanced under traditional discrimination laws. Similarly, some state constitutions prohibit discrimination against the disabled, thereby providing them with an alternative remedy to a federal claim under Section 504 of the federal Rehabilitation Act. (See Chapter Six in this volume.)

One of the most difficult state constitutional issues has been the provision of state support, frequently in the form of student financial aid, to students in private, sectarian colleges. Virtually every state constitution prohibits appropriating funds for sectarian purposes, while at least five states—Louisiana, Massachusetts, Nebraska, South Carolina, and Virginia—have amended their state constitutions to authorize various forms of aid to students in private or sectarian institutions. Virginia's constitutional provision (Art. VIII, Education sec. 11) authorizes aid to students in private or sectarian colleges who are not engaged in religious study. (For a definitive study of this subject, including an analysis of the laws of all fifty states, see Olliver, 1975.)

A state constitutional provision may be applicable to *both* public and private colleges in the absence of a state "state action" doctrine. Also, many state constitutions contain a "little" Bill of Rights, which may track the federal Bill of Rights. A state Bill of Rights may impose duties and create rights as a matter of state law, which may fill gaps in the body of federal law in areas where the federal law has not preempted state authority. See, for example, the California constitution's guarantee of free exercise of religion (Art. 1, sec. 4).

State constitutional provisions are of considerable moment, especially for the human rights commissions created in more than forty states to resolve discrimination claims, since they may authorize redress for claims not cognizable under the federal Constitution (for example, claims alleging discrimination on the basis of sex). However, the considerable body of reported case law involving the federal Constitution is of perhaps greatest concern to the college administrator, if only because the volume of that litigation is so great.

Summary

This chapter has attempted to cover those major constitutional issues affecting the management and operation of student affairs offices in both public and private colleges. In general, private colleges are not bound by the federal Constitution, except as to search and seizure, while public colleges fall under the obligations of the federal Constitution. The public-private distinction, as a matter of technical legal theory, is critical. As a practical matter, many private colleges meet or exceed federal constitutional standards and have elected to incorporate such standards in their contract of enrollment.

State constitutional provisions may be applicable to both public and private institutions. Such provisions, which may provide authority not found in the federal Constitution (for example, a constitutional basis for banning discrimination based on sex) may also include a state Bill of Rights.

Federal constitutional claims, involving intentional and willful disregard of well-known federal rights, may lead to the imposition of personal damage if actual injury occurs.

References

American Council on Education. *Statement on Drug Testing of Student Athletes.* Washington, D.C.: American Council on Education, 1986.

Bartlett, L., and Engel, R. "A Second Look at the Student Press and Discipline." *West's Education Law Reporter,* 1984, *16,* 705–709.

Buchanan, E. T., Jr. "Student Disciplinary Systems in Collegiate Institutions: Substantive and Procedural Due Process Requirements." In E. Hammond and R. Shaffer (eds.), *The Legal Foundations of Student Personnel Services in Higher Education.* Washington, D.C.: American College Personnel Association, 1978.

Council for the Advancement of Standards. "Standards and Guidelines for Religious Programs." In *CAS Standards and Guidelines for Student Services/Development Programs.* Washington, D.C.: Council for the Advancement of Standards, 1986.

Davenport, D. "The Catalog in the Courtroom: From Shield to Sword." *Journal of College and University Law,* 1985, *12* (3), 201–226.

Ellman, J. "After *T.L.O.:* Civil Liability for Failure to Control Substance Abuse." *West's Education Law Reporter,* 1985, *24,* 1099–1105.

Gehring, D., Nuss, E., and Pavela, G. *Issues and Perspectives on Academic Integrity.* Columbus, Ohio: National Association of Student Personnel Administrators, 1986.

Horen, J., and Frels, K. "The Death Knell to the Negligence Cause of Action Under 42 U.S.C. 1983." *West's Education Law Reporter,* 1985, *31,* 1–6.

Jennings, E., and Strope, J. "Procedural Due Process in Academia:

Board of Curators v. *Horowitz* Seven Years Later." *West's Education Law Reporter*, 1985, *28*, 973–983.

Jones, G. "Students and the Practice of Religion on Campus." *NASPA Journal*, 1981, *18* (3), 2–8.

Keller, M. "Shall the Truce Be Broken?" *New Jersey* v. *T.L.O.* and Higher Education." *Journal of College and University Law*, 1986, *12* (3), 415–427.

Lavin, T. "Grounds for Dismissing Tenured Post Secondary Faculty for Cause." *Journal of College and University Law*, 1983–84, *33* (10), 419–427.

Nolte, C. "The Judicial Struggle with What Is State Action in Athletics." *West's Education Law Reporter*, 1986a, *31*, 363–371.

Nolte, C. "Rape on Campus: When Is the Landlord Liable." *West's Education Law Reporter*, 1986b, *31*, 697–701.

Nuger, K., and Strope, J. *"New Jersey* v. *T.L.O.:* The Lower Court Response." *West's Education Law Reporter*, 1986, *32*, 415–427.

Olliver, J. *Non-Public Colleges and Universities in the United States.* Tallahassee: Department of Higher Education, Florida State University, 1975.

Wright, C. A. "The Constitution on the Campus." *Vanderbilt Law Review*, 1969, *22*, 1027–1088.

5

George M. Shur

❧❧❧   ❧❧❧   ❧❧❧

Contractual Agreements: Defining Relationships Between Students and Institutions

The courts have recognized that the relationship between a student and a college or university is contractual in nature. In one of the first cases where this argument was recognized, the court held that the admissions brochures of a medical college set forth the terms of a contract between the student and the institution (*People ex rel. Cecil* v. *Bellevue Hospital Medical College,* 1891; see also *Niedermeyer* v. *Curators of the University of Missouri,* 1895). In the last decade, the number of court cases involving institutions of higher education and alleged contractual obligations to students has dramatically increased. Since the courts are increasingly using contract law as a basis for the settlement of claims, prudent administrators must increase their knowledge in this area.

This chapter will present an overview of the current status of contract and consumer actions brought by students (prospective, current, or former) against educational institutions. A specific review of litigation involving contractual obligations in admissions, academic dismissals, degree denial, degree revocation, requirement alternatives, termination of academic programs, program quality, tuition alterations, discipline, and housing arrangements will be offered. The chapter concludes with a review of required information in publications and suggested guidelines for administrative practice.

Background

Virtually every oral and written contract between the student and the institution becomes part of the mutually binding contractual obligation. The findings in a number of court cases have supported the concept that students no longer need to be passive consumers who pay their tuition and fees, yet have no legal standing in the courts to ensure that the university will meet legitimate contractual obligations. It must be emphasized that the obligation runs both ways; in fact, two of the earliest cases involved private institutions arguing the contract theory in order to collect unpaid tuition and to enforce social rules. In *William* v. *Stein* (1917), a student left the institution before the end of the year, and the institution sued the parents for unpaid tuition for the entire year. The New York court held that the institution's contract with the student and/or the parents made it clear that full tuition must be paid even if the student left school. In another New York decision, *Anthony* v. *Syracuse University* (1928), the student was dismissed because she was not a "typical Syracuse girl." In successfully defending the suit, the university argued that the student had signed a statement that attendance was a privilege rather than a right, and the university could require dismissal to maintain a "proper, moral atmosphere."

Although the existence of the contractual relationship is now freely acknowledged, the *nature* of that relationship may be difficult to define. A contract, in its most basic form, is set forth in all the written and oral representations made between the parties during the application for admission and thereafter. These items clearly include the admissions application form, admissions brochures, the institution's catalogue, course descriptions, and promises or representations made by highly placed (or even not so highly placed) college or university officials.

Another early case concerning a student's rights was *Trustees of Columbia University* v. *Jacobsen* (1959), cited here, if for no other reason, to show how inventive a plaintiff can be. In a counterclaim to a collection suit brought by the university, the former student listed some fifty claims and asked for $7,000 in damages. His lawsuit was based on a variety of charges, including fraud and misrepresentation, but the crux of his claim was that the university had made certain written and oral promises that it had failed to keep. He claimed that the university had represented that it would teach him "wisdom, truth, character, enlightenment, understanding, justice, liberty, honesty, courage, beauty, and similar virtues and qualities; that it would develop the whole man, maturity, well-roundedness, objective thinking, and the like" (*Trustees*, 1959, at 65). Because it had failed to do so, Jacobsen argued, he suffered pecuniary loss. During the course of the litigation, Jacobsen cited the university's motto, "In your light, we shall see the light"; the inscription over the chapel, "Wisdom dwelleth in the heart of him who hath understanding"; and speeches at alumni dinners. It became clear that his real charge was that Columbia had somehow, fraudulently, deceitfully, and in breach of its representations and promises, failed to teach him wisdom. The court found that wisdom is not a subject that can be taught and that no rational person would accept such a claim from any man or institution.

Although Jacobsen lost the case, it was a beginning. Since the early 1970s, the number of more responsible student challenges in the area of tuition changes, student discipline, admissions, academic dismissal, change in academic programs, and, most recently, degree revocation has multiplied. In addition to the contract argument, most of the cases have relied on other theories of recovery, such as the tort of misrepresentations, the tort of fraud, and constitutional deprivation. In virtually every case cited in this chapter, the written or oral representations of the institution have provided the basis for the claims. Students have prevailed more often on cases involving representations in handbooks or rules and regulations regarding conduct. Generally speaking, institutions have prevailed in cases relating to course catalogues, syllabi, and claims involving the academic program.

Students rely, as they should, on the college catalogue, which, in these days of declining admissions pools, can contain some incautious prose on the school's programs or advantages. Most institutions have included disclaimers in their catalogues, but these disclaimers are usually set in very small type and are not prominently displayed. The presence of these disclaimers may be crucial, as will be discussed later in this chapter. Furthermore, according to Bender (1976), it may just be a matter of time before the Federal Trade Commission seeks to impose the same consumer-based regulations on nonprofit institutions that it places on proprietary schools.

Admissions

Two cases point out the necessity for an institution to carefully consider the criteria used in admitting students. In *Steinberg* v. *Chicago Medical School* (1976), a description in a medical school brochure outlined the terms under which an application would be evaluated. Steinberg claimed that the admissions committee had failed to evaluate his application pursuant to those criteria and alleged a "hidden agenda" on the part of the committee. The medical school, in its motion to dismiss the case, relied on the traditional discretion accorded to professional schools in making decisions about admissions. But the Illinois Supreme Court refused to grant the dismissal and gave Steinberg the right to present evidence on his claim.

A somewhat more traditional view was taken by the Massachusetts Court in *Donnelly* v. *Suffolk University* (1976), where the court held that giving weight to letters of recommendation from alumni or benefactors was neither a breach of the published admissions criteria nor a violation of state unfair practice in consumer protection status and regulations. The court relied on catalogue language giving Suffolk the broadest possible discretion in setting admissions criteria and in making decisions based on those criteria. Someone had taken the time to carefully draft language in the catalogue and the admissions material, thus allowing a court to defer to the good-faith discretion of academic administrators.

One cannot overemphasize the importance of reservations of rights on the part of the institution. In *Tinkoff et al.* v. *Northwestern University et al.* (1947), the Illinois court held that the institution was protected when its admissions materials reserved the right to reject an applicant for *any* reason. Admissions officers should be wary, however, of arbitrary or capricious treatment of applicants; not even carefully created disclaimers may be helpful where there has been reckless behavior. The Ohio federal district court decision in *Nuttleman* v. *Case Western Reserve University* (1981) illustrates that the judicial system will not interfere with the *academic* decision not to admit a student to a Ph.D. program, absent a showing that the denial was arbitrary and capricious. If, however, the decision not to admit was based on allegations of misconduct, a federal district court in Minnesota has ruled that the unsuccessful applicant may have some affirmative right to confront these accusations (*Hall* v. *University of Minnesota et al.*, 1982).

In the even more recent decision of *Martin* v. *Helstad* (1983), a federal court in Wisconsin wrestled with a *revocation* of an admission to the state university's law school. The successful applicant had failed to disclose a criminal background; when this apparent misrepresentation was discovered, the law school decided to revoke his admission. The court held that the initial acceptance into the academic program created a "property right," which could not be revoked or taken away without some procedure. The procedure involved did not necessarily have to include the full panoply of due process protections; presumably, sufficient procedural due process in a revocation situation would include notifying the student and giving him the opportunity to explain an apparent misrepresentation on the admissions application.

Academic Dismissals

In the absence of any "contract" provisions in the catalogue (that is, student conduct codes or academic dismissal procedures), the courts require different procedures for dealing with conduct-related and academic dismissals. These standards can vary even more between public and private institutions. Where a public institution alleges a disciplinary infraction, the student is entitled to at least a modicum of "due process," according to the U.S. Supreme Court in *Goss* v. *Lopez* (1975). However, no such procedures are required where academic failure is the cause for dismissal from the university. Notwithstanding these distinctions, most institutions (both public and private) have opted to promulgate detailed disciplinary or conduct codes as well as procedures by and through which a student can question, at least to the level of department head or dean, an adverse academic judgment (see Chapter Eight in this volume). These policies become part of the contract between the student and the institution, and any deviation from the written procedures can be dealt with as a breach of that contract. However, if proper procedures are followed, the courts will rarely interfere with the academic judgment of the faculty, absent a showing of arbitrary and capricious behavior.

Challenges to an institution's right to make academic decisions usually include constitutional claims, contractual claims, or both. Courts recognize that similar standards of judicial review attend, regardless of the formal nature of the claim. A federal district court in Texas stated: "A student with a grievance may not . . . transform a . . . court into a sort of educational ombudsman whose function is to review the everyday actions of local school officials. It is difficult to imagine an area of academia more suitable for judicial abstention" (*Keys* v. *Sawyer*, 1973, at 937).

When dealing with professors or with areas of study that are highly technical or that require great expertise, the courts have recognized that even more weight should be given to the judgment of trained professionals. To illustrate, a student of history who is found by faculty to be incapable of developing empathic relations with fellow students or faculty might arguably be allowed to graduate with a degree in history, it being presumed that character or personality problems would not in any way affect the person's competency as a historian, nor would a young historian be in a position where, by sole reason of her training and academic degree, she could adversely affect others. In contrast, a similar type of student in medicine or a medically related field, such as mental health counseling, by reason of training and a degree from an institution of higher education, can wreak havoc with the mental or physical well-being of others. In a North Carolina case, *Lai* v. *Board of Trustees of East Carolina University* (1971), a student was barred from enrolling in a practice teaching program because he admitted that he smoked marijuana cigarettes. In upholding the decision of East Carolina University, the court found as fact that

"As a result of the conference with [the student] in the department, [the faculty] felt they had some serious questions about his character in terms of suitability for teaching" (at 906). The court further stated that colleges and universities "are entitled to wide discretion in the regulation of the training of their students."

One of the first cases to recognize the necessity of strict standards was *Connelly* v. *University of Vermont and State Agricultural College* (1965). In this case, the court asked two questions. The first question involved the student's qualifications and his ability to meet academic standards. The court concluded that this was not a matter for judicial review. The second question centered on the motivation of the school authorities for the student's dismissal. Had they acted in an arbitrary or capricious manner? The court held that "a student dismissal motivated by bad faith, arbitrariness, or capriciousness may be actionable" (at 159-160).

A decision by the Washington Supreme Court amply defined "arbitrary and capricious action" in a case involving the University of Washington's medical school: "Arbitrary and capricious action of administrative bodies means willful and unreasoning action without consideration and in disregard of facts or circumstances. Where there is room for two opinions, action is not arbitrary or capricious when exercising honesty and upon due consideration, even though it may be believed that an erroneous conclusion has been reached" (*McDonald* v. *Hogness,* 1979, at 717). As a trial judge in Maine stated, "No one has a right to expect decisions to be always correct, only that they be fairly, thoughtfully, and legally arrived at" (*Robertson* v. *Haaland,* 1977, at 3). In *Gaspar* v. *Bruton* (1975, at 851), the U.S. Court of Appeals for the Tenth Circuit recognized: "The court may grant relief as a practical matter only in those cases where the student presents positive evidence of ill will or bad motive." A federal district court judge in Iowa succinctly underscored this concept when he declared: "The absence of such evidence coupled with the authorities' discretion to determine scholastic grades requires the decision in favor of defendants" (*Greenhill* v. *Bailey,* 1975, at 635).

In a landmark 1978 decision, *Board of Curators of the University of Missouri* v. *Horowitz,* the U.S. Supreme Court commented in great detail on the different standards to be used in

disciplinary and academic cases. Charlotte Horowitz had challenged her dismissal from medical school on every imaginable
ground, including her human and constitutional rights (both
procedural and substantive) and breach of what she claimed were
certain standards that the school used in making academic and
disciplinary decisions. The Court did not uphold her claim.

In *Giles* v. *Howard University* (1977), in which a student
argued that the university should be held to the medical school
retention policies in effect at the time of his matriculation, the
federal district court found no violation of the student's rights. It
was shown that the university had made reasonable changes in
standards and had gone out of its way to help the plaintiff remain
in medical school without compromising its academic standards (at
606). The court made it clear that, since institutions reserve to
themselves the right to dismiss a student who fails a course, they
"also reserved the right to require such a student to comply with any
reasonable condition to retain his student status" (at 606). Accordingly, the student's contract claim was denied.

Within the area of academic dismissals, courts have uniformly held that commercial contract doctrines should not be
applied rigidly. Students must be prepared to read and understand
the regulations affecting their continued academic good standing.
In *Lyons* v. *Salve Regina College* (1977), the court cautioned the
student that merely because a faculty panel made a "recommendation" in her favor, the use of that word did not preclude higher
college authorities from making an adverse decision. Obviously, the
First Circuit relied on the universally recognized chain of command
at institutions of higher education.

One can hope that the U.S. Supreme Court put this entire
area to rest in its 1985 decision in *Regents of the University of
Michigan* v. *Ewing*. Ewing, a medical student, was dismissed from
the academic program because he failed a portion of the National
Board of Medical Examiners examination. It appears from the
record in the case that this was not the plaintiff's only area of
academic failure; indeed, his failure in the national examination
was only the latest in a long line of well-documented academic
difficulties and deficiencies. The district court found for the
university, but the Sixth Circuit reversed and cited a university

promotional pamphlet stating that a qualified student would be
given a second chance to take the national examination. The
university publication was deemed important *regardless of whether
the student saw it.* The appellate court rejected the university's
argument that it could use broad discretion in cases of academic
competence. The Supreme Court, in unanimously reversing the
court of appeals, has made it clear that the university acted properly
in academically dismissing the plaintiff after having afforded him
an opportunity (within the written academic procedures of the
institution) to argue against the dismissal. As an interesting
sidelight, even though the majority assumed that the plaintiff had
a "property right" in continued enrollment, the concurring
opinion of Justice Powell strongly hints that the Court may be
inclined to take another look at the property rights implications of
academic dismissals should the right case reach it.

From the court decisions just cited, it appears that, in the
area of academic standards, use of a reservation of rights or a
disclaimer can be helpful if the institution's decision is challenged.
Courts seem to give even more leeway to faculty academic decisions
than they do to disciplinary determinations, but the importance of
a reservation or disclaimer cannot be overemphasized.

Denial of a Degree

Courts have also been reluctant to interfere with institutional
decisions to deny the award of the final degree, even where a student
may have successfully completed basic course requirements. Again,
appropriate disclaimers, the less ambiguous the better, in the
catalogue can make all the difference. If published standards have
not been met, a student cannot rely on the lack of warning from his
adviser concerning his academic deficiences (*Wilson* v. *Illinois
Benedictine College,* 1983). Similarly, a federal court in Georgia
found that the mere fact that a student was allowed to remain in a
dental program, albeit on academic probation, did not stop the
institution from conducting a final evaluation of competency and
determining that the degree would not be awarded (*Jansen* v. *Emory
University,* 1977).

Reservations of rights can be important, especially in programs that certify competence in highly technical (or medical) specialties. In *Balogun* v. *Cornell University* (1971), the New York court based its decision on a bulletin statement that the final determination of satisfactory work was to be based not on a set of course grades but on the student's entire record and potential. Therefore, the affected student was denied his degree in veterinary medicine. In sum, the courts will generally uphold the *inherent* right of trained faculty and administrators to determine fitness to obtain a degree (or enter a learned or skilled profession), but it is even more helpful for the catalogue or bulletin to state that the institution can conduct a final review which examines more than course grades.

Degrees can be denied for failure to demonstrate required competence (see, for instance, the discussion on the *Horowitz* and *Ewing* cases previously cited). The determination of competence is admittedly highly subjective, but is a judgment that can best be made by trained academics. If that judgment is based on academic performance and competency, minimal due process is required; however, if it is based on violations of rules of personal conduct, the student may have more "due process" available before the decision becomes final. Administrators should be sensitive to the fact that what might initially appear to be an academic problem is, in reality, a conduct-related problem, or vice versa. In order for a conduct-related failing to affect an academic decision, there ought to be some nexus between the two. For instance, in the *Horowitz* case, the conduct and personal habits of the medical student became inextricably linked with her clinical shortcomings. Administrators must be sensitive to the distinction between personal and academic conduct, and to the gray areas in between.

Of course, there are some cases where even the written requirements in the bulletin or catalogue may not protect the institution. Where a college official, with the apparent authority to do so, waives requirements, a student may be entitled to rely on this waiver. Two New York cases have held that the actions of an agent can indeed bind the institution (*Blank* v. *Board of Higher Education of the City of New York*, 1966; *Healy* v. *Larsson*, 1971, 1973).

Revocation of an Academic Degree

Even though a particular administrator may have little to do with the determination of whether a previously awarded degree ought or ought not to be revoked, he or she should—as a member of the administration of the institution—be sensitive to the contract implications in this area. Until recently, the authority of an institution to revoke a degree has not been well established. The Michigan federal district court, in *Crook* v. *Baker* (1984), stated: "The court will assume, without deciding, that the University is possessed of the legal authority which it claims to rescind a previously conferred academic degree." The question is one of both inherent power and authority, whether by statute or corporate charter, and whether the institution ever reserved the right to revoke the degree in the contract between individual and the student.

In 1986, the Ohio Supreme Court ruled that universities must be permitted to revoke degrees, even where they have no specific power to do so. Otherwise, a university would, in effect, be required to "continue making false certification to the public at large of the accomplishment of persons who in fact lack the very qualifications that are certified" (*Waliga* v. *Board of Trustees of Kent State University*, 1986, at 852). The court concluded that the revocation could be effected only after the former student had an opportunity to review the documentation and to present evidence at a hearing on campus. There is no requirement that legal counsel be involved. In the *Crook* decision, the federal trial court explored the type of due process protection available to a former student whose degree was in jeopardy. The court imposed such "minimal procedural protections" as (1) adequate notice of charges and evidence given sufficiently in advance to allow for adequate preparation of defense; (2) effective opportunity to be heard and present evidence; (3) representation by counsel; (4) opportunity to confront and cross-examine witnesses; (5) opportunity to present any and all evidence; (6) decisions based solely on the evidence at the hearing; and (7) an impartial decision maker. It appears that the trial court imposed criminal due process standards on what is clearly a civil process. Indeed, the finding in *Crook* requires a process far more detailed than that mandated in disciplinary cases. Accordingly, the University of Michigan has appealed the lower court's decision, and, as of this writing, the appellate decision has not yet been received.

Changes or Amendments in Requirements

Recently, the question of a university's right to alter or redefine course or graduation requirements has been litigated. The old argument (in *Niedermeyer* v. *Curators of the University of Missouri*, 1895)—that the parties entered into a continuing and basically unalterable contract upon the student's original matriculation—has been all but obliterated by a series of cases beginning with *Mahavongsanan* v. *Hall* (1976). Georgia State University added to and changed graduation requirements after the student matriculated. The federal appeals court held that the change in graduation requirements was "a reasonable academic regulation within the expertise of the University's faculty" (at 450). The court found that the student had received reasonable notification of the new graduation requirements and that the university had made efforts to devise a special program to resolve her dilemma. Finally, the court rejected the breach of contract argument out of hand, stating: "Implicit in the student's contract with the University upon matriculation is the student's agreement to comply with the University's rules and regulations, which the University clearly is entitled to modify so as to properly exercise its educational responsibility" (at 450).

Many jurisdictions have followed this rationale. Other important cases include *Hines* v. *Rinker* (1981), *Craft* v. *Board of Trustees of the University of Illinois* (1981), *Anderson* v. *Banks* (1981), and *Lavash* v. *Kountze* (1979). A 1983 First Circuit Court of Appeals case, *Cuesongle* v. *Ramos*, again underlines the importance of catalogue statements, including the right to change or amend programs, courses, requirements, and tuition. The courts continue to defer to the necessary evolution of academic process and programs and to the expectations of both parties to the contract. Indeed, it can be argued that the average college student is not a total innocent. After twelve or more years of public or private education, the student should be sophisticated enough to realize that discretion is built into the educator's or administrator's role.

Where it can be shown that the institution has exercised its judgment without malice or discriminatory intent or result, the student who challenges an academic failure or dismissal or a change in academic criteria will have no case.

Termination of Academic Programs

As new academic programs are born and institutions shift priorities, other programs must die. Courts have recognized the right of institutions to change the direction of academic programs and emphasis, but they have also taken steps to protect students whose academic careers would be unduly interrupted or affected by such changes. Program discontinuation has been upheld where there has been a legitimate lack of resources to maintain high quality in a program or where the accreditation has been lost (*Moore* v. *Board of Regents,* 1978). However, great care must be taken that the rights of students are not adversely affected, because a number of courts have held that the cancellation of a program constitutes a breach of contract (see *Behrand* v. *State,* 1977; *Eden* v. *Board of Trustees of the State University of New York,* 1975; and the federal decision, *Peretti* v. *State of Montana,* 1979, 1981).

Where such a breach has occurred, and absent a reasonable notice during which existing students could either complete degree requirements or arrange a transfer to another institution, a student may be entitled to monetary damages. In *Lowenthal* v. *Vanderbilt University* (1977), the Tennessee court concluded that damages should be awarded to students who had enrolled in a graduate management program which, shortly thereafter, failed to meet the academic standards of the university. A tuition refund was allowed by the court, but requests for loss of future earnings were rejected.

Students adversely affected by program termination can also request injunctive relief. In the *Eden* case, the State University of New York (SUNY) system claimed that it could not open the School of Podiatric Medicine to already enrolled students because of a state fiscal crisis. The court found that this action constituted a breach of preexisting contract with those students who had been notified of their acceptance. It may be significant that the court conditioned its ruling on a finding that the postponement of the opening of the new school was arbitrary and capricious, because SUNY was unable to prove that any money would be saved. In another New York case, *Wagner* v. *Cooper Union* (1976), the court refused to issue an injunction against discontinuation of certain programs, since the school bulletins had stated: "The Cooper Union reserves the right to change or amend its regulations, curricula, fees and admissions procedures without prior notice." Further, Cooper Union had announced the termination early enough to allow the transfer of students to other institutions and was able to bring in evidence that schools were prepared to accept transferees at the same tuition rate.

Any member of the management team of a college and university will undoubtedly have concern about the impact on students of decisions to eliminate programs. In determining whether students have been treated fairly (and whether an institution may bear some court-imposed liability), university officials should make sure (1) that the reasons for the decision are legitimate (that there is a *real* financial exigency); (2) that the loss of accreditation has not been occasioned by acts or negligence of the institution itself; (3) that students have received sufficient notice; and (4) that comparable programs are available elsewhere, and at comparable tuitions. Institutional planning should include not only a reservation of rights in a catalogue but also a good deal of thought and planning on campus to ensure that the decision to terminate is well grounded both academically and legally and that the students have been and will be treated fairly. Where there is even a remote possibility that programs will be eliminated, an institution ought to consider a detailed statement in the catalogue, setting forth the rights of the various parties in the event of such a termination. Such a statement would then become part of the contract between the student and the institution.

Quality of Academic Programs

Contract claims in the area of quality or adequacy of academic programs have also increased over the last two decades. One of the first cases was *Ianiello* v. *University of Bridgeport* (1977), in which the student claimed that the institution was in breach of contract because the course content and what the student gained from the course were not consistent with the contractual promises contained in the course catalogue. The Connecticut trial court refused to allow the issue to go to a jury because the plaintiff had failed to sustain her burden of proof. However, it was clear that, if the plaintiff has produced appropriate expert testimony to counter the educational experts presented by the institution, her case would have gone to the jury. An Idaho court has recently allowed plaintiffs to amend a complaint so as to allege breach of contract when students discovered that they could not be employed as certified mechanics after successful completion of the course of study; the catalogue had promised that graduates would be qualified for employment as entry-level journeymen (*Wickstrom et al.* v. *North Idaho College,* 1986). The case has been returned to the trial court.

As stated in the section on Termination of Academic Programs, courts have imposed very strict standards on schools when the quality or availability of a certain program has been altered. In *Behrand* v. *State* (1977), the student catalogue had indicated that the school of architecture at Ohio University was fully accredited. During the plaintiff's attendance, the academic program deteriorated, and the school lost its accreditation; for this reason, Behrand held the university accountable in breach of contract. The plaintiff had relied on catalogue descriptions and matriculated with the intention of graduating from an accredited program. This reliance, and especially the payment of significant tuition monies, created the contract, and the court so held.

In *Peretti* v. *State of Montana* (1979, 1981), students whose course of study was interrupted by a cut in legislative appropriations argued successfully that they had the contractual right to complete the training period of six academic quarters and to receive a diploma evidencing such completion. The state was held liable to each of the numerous student plaintiffs. The federal appellate court limited its reversal of the case to Eleventh Amendment grounds of governmental immunity and declared that no money could be awarded out of state coffers. *Peretti* continues to be widely and favorably cited for its contract arguments.

In *Lowenthal* v. *Vanderbilt University* (1977), the court ordered damages to students in the doctoral program at the graduate school of management as a result of significant changes in the course of study. The court adopted an ends-oriented test. It acknowledged that a rule change alone is not enough to constitute a breach of contract, but it also found that the changes in the program were so severe that the doctoral program had, in essence, ceased to exist as a matter of fact. The court recognized that, at least in this case, the contract between the parties was one of "adhesion." Courts often refuse to enforce contracts that are excessively one-sided and in which the relative bargaining positions of the parties are not fairly balanced. In *Lowenthal,* the court found that Vanderbilt received substantial tuition and gave little or nothing in return.

Tuition: Refunds and Changes

Most catalogues describe a tuition refund policy—usually a proration of billed or paid fees, depending on the date of withdrawal. Institutions argue that, by accepting a student, they are committed to certain fixed expenses, especially for faculty salaries, which are based on enrollment, and that these fixed expenses continue whether a particular student is present or not. It is always a question of fact—hence, it is always an issue to be determined at trial—whether a particular tuition refund plan is fair and equitable (*Cazenovia College* v. *Patterson,* 1974). An institution could choose to rely on the strict rules and regulations outlined in the catalogue, but a court, exercising its inherent, equitable power, could determine that an institution was unjustly enriching itself by strict enforcement of its refund policy. Again, the facts of the case would control.

To illustrate: At a school with a residence hall waiting list, a student's withdrawal from the residence hall would impose little if any financial hardship on the institution. To impose a significant penalty on the withdrawing student when the residence hall room would be immediately occupied at full rental by a new student could be seen as manifestly unfair. The school might be able to justify a small penalty to discourage disruption in the living arrangements at the residence hall and to cover administrative costs. In contrast, if the school had a number of empty beds, loss of one residence hall occupant could impose a significant financial hardship on the institution, absent a rigid refund policy. In determining whether the refund policy—that is, the contract—should be strictly enforced against a student, most courts will seek to determine which party was responsible for breach of contract. The student bears the burden of proving that the withdrawal was prompted by a material breach of the school's obligations. The concept of material breach of contract was recognized by a New York court in *Paynter* v. *New York University* (1971), where a student sought to hold the university liable for refund of tuition as a result of breach of contract when classes were canceled after the Kent State incident. The court found that the closing was within the discretion of the institution; in light of such a minor breach, the court would not interfere with this discretion. In another case occasioned by the Kent State incident, a student failed to prove his claim that he was a third-party beneficiary in the contract between the instructor and the school. If his claim had been upheld, he would have been awarded damages based on the failure of his professor to teach in accordance with his employment contract (*Zumbrun* v. *University of Southern California*, 1972). Students who make contractual claims not only must surmount both the broad discretion traditionally given to school administrators and the judiciary's unwillingness to interfere but also must prove that contract documents, such as the catalogue, do not specifically provide for such discretion.

The importance of an appropriate disclaimer is underscored by some recent cases involving changes in tuition during the student's academic career. The equitable principles of contract law recognize that it may be impossible for one party to perform a contract. While a court will not protect a party who has simply made a bad deal, the contract may be altered if the circumstances are beyond the party's control, especially if a disclaimer is part of the contract. Accordingly, even a school that optimistically projects moderate tuition increases but that later is forced to impose radical increases is protected. Among the leading cases in this area is *Basch* v. *George Washington University* (1977), where the court found that a general catalogue statement projecting future tuition was far too indefinite to create an enforceable promise, even though over a two-year period tuition rose from $3,200 to $12,500. The rationale of the

Basch case was followed by an Illinois court in a case involving medical students at Northwestern University (*Eisele* v. *Ayers,* 1978). The Appellate Division of the New York Supreme Court was recently faced with a claim that a State University of New York (SUNY) campus had no right to increase tuition after accepting students, but before they actually enrolled. The court held that "since specific disclaimers were included in the bulletins provided to claimants to the effect that the tuition charges were subject to change, [SUNY] was not contractually obligated to adhere to the initial $6000 charge," even where the letter of acceptance had included that fee (*Prusack* v. *State,* 1986, at 456–457). However, a Kansas trial court refused to give *absolute* discretion to the institution in tuition increases (*Hermann* v. *Hiersteiner,* 1978).

In short, courts increasingly are rejecting the theory of the *Niedermeyer* case that the initial contract of enrollment continues throughout the entire course of study. Instead, the courts have adopted what appears to be a more reasonable rule: that the school has the right to make changes, with appropriate notice, from time to time in such areas as tuition. Courts will not force an institution to operate at a financial loss, which would adversely affect the quality of the education that the school could provide.

Student Discipline

Dixon v. *Alabama State Board of Education* (1961) made it clear that the general concept of procedural due process is appropriate and necessary in student discipline cases, at least in public institutions. Accordingly, most institutions, both public and private, have adopted disciplinary or conduct codes that set forth procedures to be used in the event of a problem requiring investigation, disciplinary action, or both. Most codes contain either a general or a specific list of offenses and possible sanctions, as well as detailed procedures for handling them. The wise institution recognizes that the student disciplinary process, since it clearly is not criminal, does not require the specificity found in a criminal indictment or proceeding; therefore, the institution keeps the list of offenses fairly general, so that it retains appropriate latitude.

The courts have been most understanding if an institution

strays innocently from due process procedures, especially where there has been no real prejudice. As a general constitutional principle, the administrative process, administered by lay administrators acting in good faith, will be upheld even if there is some departure from due process (*Bishop* v. *Wood,* 1976). However, once the procedures are codified as part of catalogues or student handbooks, they become part of the contract between the institution and the student. In such cases, an institution can satisfy the somewhat amorphous requirements of constitutional due process but still be exposed to liability for breach of contractual due process.

Clearly, private institutions have a great deal more latitude than publicly supported schools in defining standards of student behavior, possible sanctions, and procedures. However, private institutions can also be charged with breach of contract if they do not follow their own published procedures. Since the concept of state or federal constitutional due process applies to state-supported institutions, students at private schools can rarely if ever prevail on these grounds. They must rely solely on contract arguments to secure what can be called appropriate process rather than due process. In *Tedeschi* v. *Wagner College* (1980), the court expressed reservations regarding the strict applicability of the contract relationship; nevertheless, the court held that the school had to follow its own procedures. Federal courts also have expressed reservations about the application of strict commercial contract principles to the relationship between a student and an institution (*Slaughter* v. *Brigham Young University,* 1975). In any case, institutions are bound to follow their own published procedures.

Housing Contracts

At the time of this writing, no decisions involving the housing or residence hall agreement or the meals contract between students and institutions have been reported. There is no doubt that a court would apply contract principles to the interpretation of such an agreement. For that reason, institutions should review this document carefully, to make sure that its language is appropriate; such documents should also include disclaimers and reservations of rights by the institution.

For instance, the institution may want to consider whether the dormitory contract should contain some language on conduct and on the handling of unacceptable or disruptive dormitory conduct. Should such misconduct be placed under the general student conduct or disciplinary code, or should there be special provisions and procedures pursuant to the dormitory contract itself? Should there be clauses allowing the institution to transfer the student for general reasons, such as the best interests of the institution? Should language providing for immediate eviction in the event of a breach of dormitory rules and regulations be included in the contract itself?

Where dormitory occupancy is required, the dormitory contract may be interpreted as one of *adhesion,* and the court might review the respective bargaining positions of the parties when deciding whether a contract should be enforced. A student who must live in a campus residence hall has no bargaining position and must sign the contract regardless of the fairness of its provisions. Further, some schools are so located that adequate or comparable housing is not available within a reasonable distance. There, too, a student must sign a contract simply because other suitable accommodations are not available. For these reasons, the institution would do well to review its housing or meal contracts with an eye on the realities of the local real estate and restaurant markets. If the school's facilities are the only suitable accommodations readily available or if the use of them is required by school policy, a student may be able to argue successfully that onerous contractual provisions should not be enforced.

The question can also arise as to what type of contract is involved. Both leases and licenses are contracts, but each involves potentially different rights and obligations. All states have procedures for terminating a lease and evicting a tenant. These procedures are usually cumbersome, expensive, and time consuming. Accordingly, many institutions, such as the University of Maine and Northern Illinois University, include in their residence hall agreement a statement that the contract constitutes a license to occupy space, not a lease. That statement has not been directly tested in a court of law, but its inclusion will allow the institution to argue that a contract can be terminated via simple legal procedures.

There is one decision that, by analogy, may prove helpful. Illinois law requires specific accounting for damage deposits required by rental or lease agreements. A court has held that the contractual relationship between a privately owned dormitory and a student is that of a license and not a lease, at least for the purpose of accounting for damage deposits. Since "a license is 'an agreement which merely entitles one party to use property subject to the management and control of the other party,' " and the management had reserved a right to move licensees from room to room, no leasehold interest exists (*Cook* v. *University Plaza*, 1981, at 407).

The prudent institution will explore the laws and procedures of its particular jurisdiction to determine whether a dormitory contract is likely to be construed as a lease or as a simple license, and it will analyze the consequences that follow from each construction.

Other Cases

Some theories of recovery seem to defy categorization. For instance, a parent chooses a school because, among other things, it features strict dormitory parietal rules. Sometime during the enrollment period, the rules are liberalized, and the enraged parent sues the college. Faced with the fact pattern, a New York court gave great deference to the professional judgments of administrators and held that the rule change did not constitute a breach in the contract of admissions or enrollment (*Jones* v. *Vassar College*, 1969).

In a case that seems to have some interesting implications for schools with both an active intercollegiate athletic program and a substantial grants-in-aid program (*Taylor* v. *Wake Forest University*, 1972), a student athlete sued the university for continuation of his scholarship after he opted not to continue his athletic career. While his grades were more than adequate and he had not suffered any debilitating injury, the court held that his relationship with Wake Forest was contractual and that he had agreed to participate in intercollegiate athletics, in return for which he would be given a scholarship. The court ruled that he had breached his contract and declined to enforce his scholarship. Recently, the national news wires publicized the decision of a workers' compensation commission in a midwestern state that awarded benefits to an injured college football player. The student successfully argued that his relationship with the institution was one of employer-employee, at least when it came to football. Only time will tell whether this case is an isolated incident or the beginning of similar claims throughout the country.

Required Information

Although discussion continues in Washington, the federal government has not generally entered into the arena of controlling university or college catalogues. One of the few exceptions is the requirement that institutions make certain consumer information available, especially for recipients of financial aid. These regulations, contained in 45 C.F.R. Part 178, have been in effect since November 18, 1977. It is significant that the regulations require only that consumer-oriented data (such as scholarship or grant criteria, total cost of attending the institution, refund policies, and student retention) must be available on request, not that they must be contained in a formal catalogue or made generally available to students. At least one state, New York, now requires such data to be included in the catalogue or otherwise made available to all students. Student affairs administrators need to monitor moves to establish such legislation in other states. Disclosure of information or the creation of certain procedures can also be required by federal programs controlling veterans' benefits, Title IX, Section 504 of the Rehabilitation Act of 1973, the Family Educational Rights and Privacy Act of 1974, and the like. *Keeping Your School or College Catalog in Compliance with Federal Laws and Regulations* (Federal Interagency Committee on Education, 1979) provides helpful guidance.

Role of the Administrator

Part of the administrator's responsibility is to limit, or at least control, potential institutional contractual liability. Here are

some guidelines for administrative action that can serve as a useful
starting point:

- Consider a periodic and careful review of all printed material,
  including admissions brochures, catalogues, student handbooks, syllabi, and the like. Times do change, and claims made
  yesterday are not always valid today.
- Include appropriate disclaimers in this material. Make sure that
  requirements or policies are not so specific as to preclude the
  reasonable exercise of good-faith discretion. This holds true for
  academic as well as for athletic and disciplinary matters.
- In both internal policies and published materials, clarify the
  academic or administrative level at which final discretion will
  be exercised. Try to limit the institution's being bound by the
  well-intentioned but uninformed representations of someone
  acting outside the scope of his or her authority.
- Make sure that all professional employees understand that
  anything they say or write could be considered a contractual
  representation of the institution and that it is therefore
  potentially binding.
- In administering the affairs of the institution, act in good faith.
  Courts are loath to interfere with the good-faith decision-
  making process in higher education.
- Do not be afraid to request assistance of legal counsel, even in
  the earliest stages of a challenge based on a so-called contract.
- Never apologize for making a difficult decision or ruling. An
  apology can be taken as a sign of weakness and actually
  encourage litigation.
- Be sensitive to the fact that a potential litigant will often go
  from office to office seeking a sympathetic ear, support, or a slip
  of the tongue. Insist that the student follow the proper
  administrative chain of command on any specific policy that
  has been promulgated to deal with the particular situation.

These guidelines can help institutions avoid contractual
litigation. Legal challenges to institutions of higher education are
growing in the area of contract law. The prudent administrator

should be aware of contractual representations and attempt to avoid unrealistic or unenforceable legal contracts.

References

Bender, L. W. "Will Your Catalog Stand FTC Scrutiny?" *American Governing Board Reports,* March/April 1976, pp. 1–3.

Federal Interagency Committee on Education. *Keeping Your School or College Catalog in Compliance with Federal Laws and Regulations.* Washington, D.C.: U.S. Government Printing Office, 1979.

6

Gwen Seaquist

Civil Rights and Equal Access: When Laws Apply— and When They Do Not

Few terms in the law have acquired as many meanings as *civil rights* has. Added to the multiple connotations given the phrase by nonlawyers, the courts themselves do not consistently define the phrase, making a simple starting place difficult. Therefore, this chapter limits the discussion of civil rights to "the enjoyment of such guarantees as are contained in constitutional or statutory law . . . designed to prevent discrimination in the treatment of persons by reason of their race, color, age, sex, religion, previous condition of servitude, or national origin" ("Civil Rights," 1976, p. 141).

At this starting point, it is important to remember that no one has "civil rights" unless a specific statute or constitutional provision grants that right. It is a commonly held belief that "all people" in the United States are somehow protected in "all activities," a misperception corrected by an understanding of civil rights laws.

The various civil rights laws, individually and as a whole, affect virtually every aspect of administering a student affairs office; indeed, defining areas *not* covered is the difficult task. The application of the laws is as varied as the institutions and the laws themselves. In this chapter, each civil rights law will be reviewed separately, so that readers can acquire a superior understanding of how the laws of civil rights affect different types of institutions. To assist in this understanding, a summary follows each major piece of civil rights legislation discussed in this chapter and serves as a quick referral guide to major provisions of each Act.

State Action and the Fourteenth Amendment

No understanding of civil rights concepts is possible without a basic familiarity with the Bill of Rights and the Fourteenth Amendment. The Bill of Rights consists of ten amendments to the United States Constitution. These amendments were added to the original document as it became clear that the original drafters had omitted important rights—for example, the First Amendment guarantee of "free speech." The U.S. Supreme Court, in its earlier decisions, held that these amendments did not apply to states. Thus, if the federal Congress passed a law that contravened the Bill of Rights, and if the law was challenged in court, it would be held unconstitutional; the same law, however, if passed by a *state* legislature, could not be declared unconstitutional, since these amendments did not apply to states. In order to rectify this situation, Congress enacted the Fourteenth Amendment shortly after the Civil War. The amendment provides: "No State shall make or enforce any law which shall abridge the privileges or immunities of citizens of the United States; nor shall any State deprive any person of life, liberty, or property without due process of law; nor deny to any person within its jurisdiction the equal protection of the laws."

The Fourteenth Amendment was used as a bridge between the Bill of Rights and actions by states; or, as legal writers term its application, the Fourteenth Amendment was used to *incorporate* the first ten amendments to the states. Therefore, if federal action or state action takes place in the form of laws, actions by federal or state employees, or any type of formal connection between the federal or state government and a private individual, *state action* will have taken place.

What is the significance of a finding that *state action* took place? If state action takes place and serves to deprive a citizen of *due process* or *equal protection,* the action violates the Fourteenth

Amendment. A violation, thus, is enforceable because the "state action" makes not only the Fourteenth Amendment but the entire Bill of Rights applicable to the situation. Suppose, for example, that a state university refuses to admit blacks. State action is present because a state university is a state governmental entity; therefore, blacks are entitled to Fourteenth Amendment *due process* and *equal protection*. Furthermore, the Fourteenth Amendment bridges over to the entire Bill of Rights, drawing in other amendments, such as the Fifth Amendment, which also guarantees due process. On the other hand, suppose that a private individual refuses to admit a black person to his home. No state action exists, since the individual homeowner has no connection to state or federal governments. Therefore, the black person cannot use the Fourteenth Amendment for protection; and without the Fourteenth Amendment, the Bill of Rights does not apply either. In short, the black person in this example would have no "constitutional rights" and would lose a lawsuit in which he invoked those rights.

Since the Fourteenth Amendment does not protect wholly private acts, some institutions of higher education have successfully used this argument to avoid liability in discrimination lawsuits. In the presence of *state action,* however, the Fourteenth Amendment and possibly the Fifth Amendment protect citizens from violation of due process and equal protection; for purposes of this chapter, such violation equates with discrimination against certain protected classes, such as those protected on the basis of race.

State action is a recurring theme throughout any discussion of civil rights legislation; therefore, an understanding of the term is essential in any discussion of the implications of civil rights legislation. Other constitutional issues are covered in Chapter Four in this volume. An additional excellent resource is *Constitutional Law* (Nowak, Rotunda, and Young, 1977).

Section 1981

Section 1981 of the Civil Rights Act of 1866 (42 U.S.C. sec. 1981) is considered one of the broadest remedies available to a plaintiff in a discrimination lawsuit. Because of the language used by Congress when writing the law, Section 1981 applies to many types of plaintiffs. The text of the statute states as follows:

> All persons within the jurisdiction of the United States have the same right . . . to make and enforce contracts, to sue, be parties, give evidence, and to the full and equal benefit of all laws and proceedings for the security of persons and property as is enjoyed by white citizens, and shall be subject to like punishment, pains, penalties, taxes, licences, and exactions of every kind, and to no other.

Application. This statute is used primarily as a remedy against racial discrimination; it does not protect claimants from discrimination based on sex, religion, or national origin. Enacted by Congress immediately after the Civil War, this provision grants blacks those rights specifically enumerated in the statute: contract, civil procedure, and property rights.

Section 1981 has broad application in the sense that it applies to any situation where white citizens enjoy privileges over nonwhite citizens. Thus, a lawsuit brought pursuant to Section 1981 must have as its *basis* the granting of rights to whites and the denying of rights to blacks or other minorities because of a disparity in contract, civil procedure, or property rights. Section 1981 also has broad application because a showing of state action is *not* required for the law to apply in a given situation. Thus, private as well as public discrimination is subject to federal regulation. A "state action" showing is not required (1) because Section 1981 is based on the Thirteenth Amendment, prohibiting slavery, and that amendment itself reaches into both public and private acts; and (2) because the prohibition against discrimination in a contractual context is by definition private behavior. For example, in *McCrary* v. *Runyon* (1976), the court held that private schools could not deny admission to students because of their race, notwithstanding a lack of state action. The decision was based on a statutory right to contract under Section 1981. "The section [1981] is violated by the school as long as the basis of exclusion is racial, for it is then clear

that the black applicant is denied a contractual right which would
have been granted to him if he had been white" (*McCrary*, at 1097).

Despite the fact that Section 1981 grants broad coverage in its
prohibition against racial discrimination, that no state action is
necessary, and that the statute applies to both public and private
actions, relatively few cases in the higher education context use
Section 1981 as their basis—mainly because Section 1981 has some
major disadvantages. The greatest disadvantage to a plaintiff
bringing a lawsuit under this statute is that he or she has the burden
of establishing a prima facie case of discriminatory intent. It is not
enough for a plaintiff to prove that he or she was actually
discriminated against, or a simple discriminatory event. Instead, the
plaintiff must prove *purposeful* discrimination by the defendant. In
Williams v. *DeKalb County* (1978), for example, the court held that
"the named plaintiff and the class must make a showing of
purposeful discrimination before casting the burden on the
defendant to rebut the charge; . . . a claim under Section 1981 is, for
this purpose, to be equated with a claim under the Fourteenth
Amendment . . . rather than under Title VII" (at 2-3).

Some courts allow proof of purposeful discrimination to be
based on a showing by the plaintiff of disparate treatment or
disparate impact (*Ingram* v. *Madison Square Garden Center, Inc.*,
1983). In North Carolina (*Tate* v. *Dravo Corp.*, 1985), the plaintiff
failed to sustain the burden of proving discrimination. The court
held in part that, to establish a prima facie case of discrimination,
"the plaintiff must prove actions taken by the employer from which
one can infer, if such actions remain unexplained, that it is more
likely than not that such actions were based on discriminatory
criterion under the Act" (at 1102). Even in those jurisdictions
allowing such an inference, this requirement places an enormous
evidentiary burden on the plaintiff.

Implications for Student Affairs. Section 1981, thus, prohibits racial discrimination based on contracts, civil procedures, and
property rights; it applies to both public and private institutions;
and the courts have held that the plaintiff has the burden of
establishing discriminatory intent. With these fundamental aspects
of Section 1981 in mind, what application does this provision have
to the student affairs administrator in both the private and public

sector? Quite simply, no programs may be offered that give privileges to white students without giving the same to nonwhites.

To protect a nonwhite student under this particular statute, the plaintiff must find a connection to Section 1981 provisions. Such a connection is not difficult to find, since the basis of most relationships between student affairs administrators and students is contractual, and a contract is a relationship that Section 1981 specifically protects. Considering that the college typically makes promises in catalogues and admissions brochures, and that students frequently enter into housing, parking, and food services contracts, the potential for discriminatory practices flows into virtually every aspect of administering student programs.

As is clear from litigation in nonacademic sectors, any plans, statistics, and programs that use discriminatory criteria may be the subject of successful litigation under this statute. Therefore, programs coming under the student affairs area warrant analysis to determine whether white students are receiving different benefits from nonwhite students, so that immediate correction can be made to prevent discrimination.

Section 1983

Unlike Section 1981, Section 1983 of the Civil Rights Act of 1871 (42 U.S.C. sec. 1983) is commonly found in litigation involving institutions of higher education. Since the mid-1960s, Section 1983 seems to have been rediscovered as the basis for a panoply of lawsuits. This Act states:

> Every person who, under color of any statute, ordi-
> nance, regulation, custom, or usage, of any state or
> territory or the District of Columbia, subjects, or
> causes to be subjected, any citizen of the United States
> or other person within the jurisdiction thereof to the
> deprivation of any rights, privileges, or immunities
> secured by the Constitution and laws, shall be liable
> to the party injured in an action at law, suit in equity,
> or other proper proceeding for redress.

While the language of the statute may appear complicated, a plaintiff bringing a lawsuit under Section 1983 must prove only two elements for recovery: First, a plaintiff must show that he or she has been deprived of a right protected by either the Constitution or the laws of the United States. Second, a plaintiff must show that the defendant was acting "under color of" state law (Simon, 1985). In other words, two elements exist under Section 1983: constitutional or federal statutory rights and interpretation of the term "under color of state law."

Constitutional or Federal Statutory Rights. What is a right protected by the Constitution or laws of the United States? Basically, the plaintiff's lawsuit must stem from a denial of a specific constitutional provision, such as the denial of Fourteenth Amendment due process rights, or must stem from a federal statute. For example, in *Bellnier* v. *Lund* (1977), a public elementary school conducted searches of students, which is an action protected by the Fourth Amendment. The court found that the defendants *may* be held liable under Section 1983 if the search is found to have violated students' constitutional (Fourth Amendment) rights. Likewise, in *University of Missouri at Columbia–National Education Association* v. *Dalton* (1978), Section 1983 applied to the university's refusal to permit students to use campus mail and campus meeting rooms in furtherance of collective bargaining, an action protected by federal statutes.

Many actions taken by colleges and universities, however, do not fall under Section 1983. Therefore, in lawsuits filed under this statute, the institution would not be found liable for such actions. For example, in *Staheli* v. *University of Mississippi* (1985), a nontenured professor who was not rehired by the university did not have any protected constitutional or property rights to use as a "springboard" into a Section 1983 lawsuit; there is no constitutional or statutory right to employment. Failing the first part of the Section 1983 two-part test, he could not proceed further with a lawsuit under this statute.

Actions Carried Out "Under Color of State Law." It is not enought for a plaintiff to establish that the defendant's actions violated a constitutional or statutory standard. The plaintiff also must show that the defendant's act was carried out under color of state law. This is a particularly tricky element in that the parameters for what constitutes "under color of state law" are not well defined.

"Under color of state law" basically means that the federal or state government cannot impose federal or state standards on private persons unless there is some connection or nexus between that individual and the government. For example, if the government supports a college financially, there is a nexus; therefore, the state or federal government now has the legal foundation on which to force to college to comply with particular laws, such as Section 1983.

One of the clearest tests of whether a sufficient nexus exists to find state action (or to find that the action of the college or university is under color of state law) is *Weise* v. *Syracuse University* (1975). In this case, two female professors sued the university, alleging sex discrimination in hiring and promotion. The court used a five-part test to determine whether or not state action existed. The five-part test (see *Weise,* at 406) included the following elements (here paraphrased as questions):

1. To what degree does the private organization depend on government aid?
2. How extensive and intrusive is the governmental regulatory scheme?
3. Does the governmental regulatory scheme connote governmental approval of the activity?
4. To what extent does the organization serve a public function?
5. Does the organization have legitimate claims to recognition as a "private" organization in associational or other constitutional terms?

To further complicate a state action analysis, the courts have also recognized the existence of a "double standard," which is particularly important to the student affairs administrator. If the claim is based on racial discrimination, the courts will use a "less onerous test" to find state action; that is, the likelihood of finding state action will greatly increase. If, on the other hand, it is another type of claim, then the court will set forth a more "vigorous" standard before state action will be found.

Other cases litigated on this same topic are helpful in determining specific instances where "state action" applies. In *Rackin* v. *University of Pennsylvania* (1974), a female faculty member charged the university with sex discrimination when her application for tenure was denied. In finding that the private University of Pennsylvania was engaged in activities under color of state law, the court deemed the following activities significant: scholarship and loan aid from the state; over $16 million in construction grants from the federal government; state financing of construction; an alumni committee to influence state legislators; and the university's submission, on a quarterly basis, of financial statements to the state.

Other courts, however, have not found state action under certain circumstances involving private institutions. In *Greenya* v. *George Washington University* (1975), no state action was found even though the state granted a corporate charter and tax-exempt status and even though the university received government loans. The court also found no state action in *Spark* v. *Catholic University of America* (1975, at 1282): "The fact that the federal government contributes funds to the University by itself is insufficient to show the exercise of influence on University decision-making or the encouragement of specific policies."

Further cases illustrating Section 1983 "under color of state law" boundaries include *Stewart* v. *New York University* (1976), where the court held that "tax exempt status alone will not suffice" (at 1309–1310); *Gilinsky* v. *Columbia University* (1980), where the court held that "financial assistance to a private university does not constitute state action" (at 1312); and *Jackson* v. *Metropolitan Edison Co.* (1974), where the court held that "government regulation alone will not mandate state action" (at 350–351).

Implications for Student Affairs. In two cases dealing specifically with actions brought by students, state action was not found in either case. In *Robinson* v. *Davis* (1972), the action of a college in detaining and questioning students was not state action despite the fact that the "college and town were administratively intertwined." Similarly, in *Grafton* v. *Brooklyn Law School* (1973), a suit by two students expelled from school for scholastic deficiencies, the court acknowledged that the "state's peripheral involvement" was not sufficient to constitute state action. Both cases illustrate that a high standard (onerous test) is applied by the courts in nonracial Section 1983 cases and that a strong showing of involvement is necessary to prove state action. Again, if a plaintiff fails to prove that an institution was "acting under color of state law," a court will find that Section 1983 is inapplicable.

To further complicate a lawsuit brought pursuant to Section 1983, many courts recognize that the special nature of colleges and universities warrants a policy of noninterference. In student affairs, this concept becomes particularly important. For example, if a decision against a student is based on a purely academic matter in which the institution's expertise would be in question, the courts have been loath to interfere (*Board of Curators of the University of Missouri* v. *Horowitz*, 1978). On the other hand, in situations where an institution sets up particular procedures, requirements, or expectations, and then violates its own internal policies, Section 1983 lawsuits are more successful. In student affairs, it is common to have a wide variety of such policies; dormitory regulations, conduct review boards, and admissions catalogues are all examples. "Written standards and procedures are precisely the types of guarantees that create interests protectable under Section 1983" (*Board of Curators*, note 12). (For further discussion of liability under Section 1983, see Chapter Nine in this volume.)

Section 1983 applies to any situation where the plaintiff can find a deprivation of civil rights based on the Constitution or on a federal law. The plaintiff must prove that the deprivation exists and that the defendant is operating under color of state law. Thus, Section 1983 can apply to both public and private institutions. Student affairs administrators should make sure that printed and oral representations of institutional services are accurate. Obviously, the institution should avoid treating a protected class differently from others. Furthermore, in its treatment of students, it should make sure that their fundamental constitutional rights are protected.

Title VI

In 1954, in the now historic case of *Brown* v. *Board of Education*, the United States Supreme Court outlawed racial discrimination in the schools. Despite *Brown*'s far-reaching ramifications in all sectors of education throughout the United States, the case failed to reach a segment of society in which racial discrimination could flourish without recourse: the private sector. Obviously, without a federal nexus, enforcement of federal law remained unconstitutional. As a result of this "loophole," Congress passed Title VI of the Civil Rights Act of 1964 (42 U.S.C. sec. 2000d) to prohibit discrimination on the basis of race, color, or national origin in those programs receiving federal financial assistance. The limitation to "race, color, or national origin" limits Title VI "to proscribe only those racial classifications that would violate the Equal Protection Clause of the Fifth Amendment" (*Regents of the University of California* v. *Bakke*, 1978, at 284). Title VI provides:

> No person in the United States shall, on the ground of race, color, or national origin, be excluded from participation in, be denied the benefits of, or be subjected to discrimination under any program or activity receiving Federal financial assistance.

The Supreme Court commented that "Title VI is majestic in its sweep" (*Bakke*, at 284). In fact, Title VI is so broad that the actual statute (stated above) gives college administrators, as well as everyone else, little guidance about how to apply the law. For this reason, Title VI is "accompanied by" lengthy enabling legislation (found at 34 C.F.R. secs. 10.1–10.13) that explains the law in more detail. Unfortunately, the explanation is so detailed that the entire text cannot be set out in full here, but the more important provisions are outlined below.

Federal Financial Assistance. Title VI applies only to those institutions receiving money from the federal government; but how much assistance must be received, and what form it must take before Title VI applies to a given institution, is not clearly defined. The enabling legislation does list the specific types of assistance that make Title VI applicable. Some of the types of assistance include construction of facilities for higher education, construction of educational broadcast facilities, allowances to institutions training graduate fellows under the National Defense Education Act (NDEA), Educational Opportunity Grants and assistance for states and private programs in the form of low-interest insured loans, Basic Educational Opportunity Grants, and Guaranteed Student Loans. The full list is extensive and should be consulted before a determination of applicability is made.

An additional important question remains, however: If an institution receives assistance as defined in the enabling legislation, does Title VI apply to the institution as a whole or only to the program receiving assistance? In anticipation of this problem, Congress limited the sanctions of Title VI to what is known as the "pinpoint provisions." This means that noncompliance with Title VI may result in "the termination of such program or activity in which discrimination is found," but that "such termination shall be limited to the particular political entity . . . in which noncompliance has been found" (42 U.S.C. sec. 2000d-1). In short, once an institution is subject to Title VI, a finding of discrimination cuts off funds to the program receiving such funds and acting discriminatorily, but it does not cut off funds to other programs (*Stewart v. New York University*, 1976, at 1314).

Assurances. Institutions receiving Title VI money must file written assurances with the Department of Education that the program will be conducted in compliance with all requirements imposed by this part. Of specific importance to student affairs administrators, Title VI requires that this assurance "shall extend to admission practices and to all other practices relating to the treatment of students" (34 C.F.R. sec. 10.5(d)(2)).

Specific Discriminatory Provisions. The enabling legislation (at 34 C.F.R. sec. 100.3(b)) sets forth clear examples of discrimination prohibited by the Act. According to the regulations, a recipient of Title VI funds cannot:

(i) Deny an individual any service, financial aid, or other benefit provided under the program;

(ii) Provide any service, financial aid, or other benefit to an individual which is different, or is provided in a different manner, from that provided to others under the program;

(iii) Subject an individual to segregation or separate treatment in any matter related to his receipt of any service, financial aid, or other benefit under the program;

(iv) Restrict an individual in any way in the enjoyment of any advantage or privilege enjoyed by others receiving any service, financial aid, or other benefit under the program;

(v) Treat an individual differently from others in determining whether he satisfies any admission, enrollment, quota, eligibility, membership, or other requirement or condition which individuals must meet in order to be provided any service, financial aid, or other benefit provided under the program;

(vi) Deny an individual an opportunity to participate in the program through the provision of services or otherwise or afford him an opportunity to do so which is different from that afforded others under the program (including the opportunity to participate in the program as an employee but only to the extent set forth in paragraph (c) of this section);

(vii) Deny a person the opportunity to participate as a member of a planning or advisory body which is an integral part of the program.

Disparate Impact and Disparate Effect. Title VI clearly prohibits discrimination based on race, color, or national origin in programs receiving federal financial assistance. The enabling legislation further provides that "a recipient . . . may not, directly or through contractual or other arrangements, utilize criteria or methods of administration which have the effect of subjecting individuals to discrimination because of their race . . . or have the effect of defeating . . . the objectives of the program" (34 C.F.R. sec. 100.3(b)(2)).

For example, in *Lau* v. *Nichols* (1974), non-English-speaking Chinese students brought suit under Title VI because of their language disadvantage in the public schools: the system failed to provide English instruction or to teach courses in Chinese. While the school system had no proven *intent* to so discriminate, failure to provide instruction was unlawful because it had the *effect* of discriminating (*Lau,* at 568). In *Guardians Association* v. *Civil Service Commission of the City of New York* (1983), black and Hispanic police officers challenged examinations used to make appointments to entry-level positions. While the tests themselves were not discriminatory on their face, the challenged examinations had a discriminatory impact on the scores of blacks and Hispanics, who were then ranked lower for entering positions. It appears well settled that, if programs or tests have the effect of discriminating, they violate Title VI, even in the absence of discriminating intent (*Guardians,* at 586) and will be held unlawful.

Reverse Discrimination. Title VI outlaws discrimination, but what then are the consequences of intentional discrimination to "remedy past discrimination"? Fortunately for college administrators, the now famous *Bakke* decision answered some of the more important questions concerning "reverse discrimination." In the case, the University of California, a public institution, had set up a special admissions program under which minorities were considered for sixteen out of one hundred places in a medical school class. While no single opinion emanated from the Supreme Court, Abernathy (1978) drew the following conclusions about what *Bakke* actually did decide:

1. Colleges and universities are given the leeway to take race into account as one factor in diversifying their student bodies.
2. Colleges and universities may use affirmative action and "probably even numerical quotas to cure specific cases of prior racial discrimination" (p. 1234).
3. Colleges and universities are forbidden to make race the dispositive factor in the admissions process.

Perhaps one of the keys to *Bakke* is the admonition that race not be the only factor but one of many factors, as employed by Harvard College in its admissions policies.

Enforcement by the Federal Government. As previously indicated, an institution must file assurances of compliance with the federal government. As a result of receiving federal financial assistance and giving assurances, the institution of higher education is subject to "investigations" in which various records and files may be requested to determine compliance with Title VI. Court decisions on this topic indicate that, in spite of the inconvenience that results from a request to copy hundreds of files, the courts mandate cooperation. In *United States* v. *El Camino Community College District* (1979), the Office of Civil Rights (OCR) requested information about the college's work force, student body, recruiting and hiring, student hiring, and financial and academic assistance programs for students. The college objected on the grounds that the request exceeded those programs receiving federal assistance. The court said: "We cannot excuse the College for its failure to comply with the regulations that it accepted in obtaining federal funding . . . extending the investigation to those areas enumerated in [34 C.F.R. sec. 100.6(c)] including 'books, records, accounts, and any other sources of information'" (at 1259). (See also *United States* v. *Phoenix Union High School District,* 1982.)

The phrase "exhausting administrative remedies" means that a plaintiff must seek administrative review before that same plaintiff may utilize the courts. Under Title VI, is a plaintiff compelled to "exhaust" before suing? The courts "hold that there exists a private cause of action under Title VI which may be asserted without preliminary recourse to agency remedial procedures" (*NAACP* v. *Medical Center, Inc.,* 1979, at 1248). Furthermore, the Supreme Court now treats Title VI analogously with Title IX in holding that "administrative exhaustion is not required under Title IX" or under Title VI (*Cannon* v. *University of Chicago,* 1979, at 677).

If an institution fails to comply with the requirements of Title VI, the Department of Education may seek informal attempts at compliance, followed by the termination of funds. The department also has authority to recommend the case to the Justice Department for proceedings. However, termination of funds will not take place without notice to the recipient, a hearing, and a review by appropriate federal committees.

Enforcement by Individuals. Despite the fact that a complainant has the right under Title VI to file a complaint with the Department of Education, and, as discussed above, the department may attempt informal as well as formal dispute resolution, the question remains: May the complainant seek redress as a private individual, or must an individual rely on action by the federal agency? Recent cases indicate that the balance of jurisdictions are recognizing a private cause of action. In *Bakke,* the Court simply assumed, without deciding, that a private cause of action existed because the lower courts in that case had done so (*Bakke,* at 281). Since the enactment of Title VI, the courts have allowed a private right of action without exhausting all administrative remedies (*Lau* v. *Nichols,* 1974). However, in *Cannon,* the court refused to follow *Lau* in a Title IX case, saying that it applied only to suits involving large numbers of similarly situated individuals. In *Guardians Association* v. *Civil Service Commission of the City of New York* (1983), the United States Supreme Court distinguished between intentional and unintentional discrimination: "Compensatory relief or other relief based on past violations of the conditions attached to the use of federal funds is not available as a private remedy for Title VI violations not involving intentional discrimination" (at 602–603). Therefore, unless a plaintiff can show intentional discrimination, compensatory damages will not be awarded.

Implications for Student Affairs. Title VI prohibits discrimination on the basis of race, color, or national origin in programs at either public or private institutions receiving federal financial assistance. If there is disparate impact on members of a protected class in the program, then discrimination exists. The enabling legislation sets out numerous requirements that colleges and universities must give *all* students assurance of nondiscriminatory programs, including participation, admission, eligibility, membership, and opportunity. However, admissions may take race into consideration if it is one of many factors. Colleges and universities attempting to correct prior discriminatory behavior probably may engage in affirmative action admissions programs. Finally, the institution must file assurances with the federal government, turn over records, and comply with OCR on-site units.

Title VII

Unlike actions brought pursuant to civil rights acts such as Section 1981, Section 1983, and Title VI, the provisions of Title VII of the Civil Rights Act of 1964 (42 U.S.C. sec. 2000e *et seq.*) apply only to issues regarding employment. Title VII also "expands" the protected class of persons to prohibit discrimination on the basis of race, color, national origin, sex, or religion in businesses engaging fifteen or more employees.

Two initial comments concerning the Act are warranted. First, Title VII is so complex and has been the subject of so much litigation that this treatment can provide only a brief summary of Title VII, with some cautionary provisos. For those seeking a more detailed discussion, a number of excellent texts exist, including Schlie and Grossman's (1984) volume on *Employment Discrimination Law*. Second, since Title VII deals only with employment problems and not to "civil rights" issues of students, it is important to focus this particular provision on the student affairs staff: hiring procedures, training programs, and termination of employees. Such procedures, however, concern not only the student affairs administrator but also the institution's personnel office; therefore, they must be coordinated on a campus-wide basis.

Section 2000e-2(a) of Title VII provides:

> It shall be an unlawful practice for an employer (1) to fail or refuse to hire or discharge any individual, or otherwise to discriminate against any individual with respect to his compensation, terms, conditions, or privileges of employment, because of such individual's race, color, religion, sex, or national origin; or (2) to limit, segregate, or classify his employees or applicants for employment in any way which would deprive [them] of employment opportunities . . . because of . . . race, color, religion, sex, or national origin.

Academic Employment. At the onset, one should be aware that much litigation under Title VII involving higher education involves academic tenure matters and not student affairs. This distinction is important. In academic matters (for example, a charge that an institution discriminated on the basis of sex in its refusal to grant tenure), the courts resist looking into the subjective criteria of a tenure grant. Therefore, statistics that might imply discrimination are discounted. "Disparate impact is not used in university faculty hiring because it is viewed as *each* job having its own criteria" (Kramer, 1982, p. 1206). On the other hand, courts are likely to view the student affairs side of the house in a more conventional manner. Therefore, an alleged Title VII violation will be subjected to a more traditional two-method test.

Under the first "test," a court will find discrimination based on *disparate impact*. That is, the "discriminatory impact of the employment practice does not have to be intentional for the court to find a Title VII violation" (Kramer, p. 1209); even when an act is neutral on its face, it will be regarded as discriminatory if the overall impact discriminates against one of the five classes protected by Title VII. The college or university can protect against a Title VII disparate-impact claim by demonstrating that the challenged practice is "a necessary part of the business or related to job performance" or "necessary to the safety and efficiency of the business" (*Griggs* v. *Duke Power Co.*, 1971, at 434). Consider, for example, a student affairs operation that each year hires a staff of resident assistants. Recruitment of staff is done by "word of mouth" until, year after year, all the staff are white males. Although those in charge of hiring do not intentionally plan to exclude others, this method of "recruitment" has a disparate impact on the protected classes and would be considered violative of Title VII.

Likewise, the second "test," *disparate treatment,* usually examines the legality of a particular employment decision. In *McDonnell Douglas Corp.* v. *Green* (1973), the United States Supreme Court set fourth a four-step analysis to determine whether this type of discrimination has taken place. A plaintiff must show that he or she (1) belongs to a racial minority; (2) applied and was qualified for the job; (3) despite these qualifications, was rejected; and (4) after the rejection occurred, the position remained open and the employer continued to seek applications from persons with the same qualifications (*McDonnell Douglas*, at 802).

"Of particular importance to public colleges and universities, the U.S. Supreme Court upheld amendments in 1972 to Title VII extending coverage . . . to state employees and, consequently, to academicians employed in public institutions of higher education" (Edwards and Nordin, 1979, p. 590).

The Hiring Process. For the student affairs administrator preparing to hire new staff members, careful training of current staff members may prevent discriminatory activities. One area of particular concern is that of preemployment inquiries. Because certain questions may unfairly affect certain classifications (race, for example), certain preemployment activities may be violative. Specifically, the following activities should be avoided: requesting photographs of applicants; advertising in sex-segregated publications; announcing jobs through word of mouth; posting jobs at educational levels not truly necessary to perform the work; using tests as a screening device when the tests do not judge skills necessary for the job; inquiring about arrests (with or without convictions); inquiring about children, child rearing, pregnancy, or abortion; inquiring about marital status or spouse's occupation, education, or background; inquiring about race, religion, or national origin.

Employment Activities. The enabling legislation of Title VII (29 C.F.R. Parts 1600–1610) should be consulted for a complete discussion of "on-the-job" activities that might be considered discriminatory. In general, any "terms, conditions, and privileges" of employment that favor one class over another are suspect. Section 703 of Title VII also specifically prohibits a number of actions, including the following:

- Forbidding the use by employees of any languages other than English
- Addressing an employee in certain (discriminatory) ways
- Using derogatory epithets based on race, color, religion, sex, or national origin
- Maintaining separate assignments, grade levels, classifications,

and lines of progression on the basis of race, color, religion, sex, or national origin

Terminating an employee is the one action most likely to bring on a Title VII lawsuit. A fired employee may understandably assume that termination arose from membership in a minority group. For the student affairs administrator in a position of terminating an employee, it is especially important that personnel policies of the institution are closely followed and that clear documentation is kept on the matter, ensuring that the cause was failure to perform properly and not one of discrimination.

Pregnancy. In 1978, Congress amended Title VII to include the Pregnancy Discrimination Act, "which prohibits . . . discrimination in employment on the basis of sex: pregnancy, childbirth, or related medical conditions." The Act specifically protects a woman from being fired or denied a promotion because of pregnancy or an abortion. In addition, if other employees who take disability leave are entitled to use disability or sick leave benefits for other types of medical reasons, such benefits must be provided for the pregnant woman. Finally, the Act guarantees a job when the individual is returning from a pregnancy leave if other employees who take disability leave are entitled to get their jobs back when they are able to again work.

Religious Discrimination. Student affairs administrators have an obligation under this section of Title VII "to provide reasonable accommodation for the religious practices of their employees . . . unless to do so would create an undue hardship." Employees have a duty to notify the employer of the need for religious accommodation, "and the employer has an obligation to reasonably accommodate the individual's religious practices" (29 C.F.R. Part 1605).

National Origin. Student affairs administrators have an obligation under this section of Title VII not to discriminate on the basis of national origin. Under the Act, employment activities cannot be denied because of an individual's foreign accent or inability to communicate well in English. Employees also must be allowed to speak their primary language at times, and total prohibition on the job of languages other than English is prohibited. Finally, the employer is responsible for acts of harassment of employees in the workplace on the basis of national origin *if* the employer "knew or should have known" of the conduct and failed to take action (29 C.F.R. Part 1606).

Sexual Harassment. Harassment on the basis of sex is a violation of Section 703 of Title VII. According to the enabling legislation, "Unwelcome sexual advances, requests for sexual favors, and other verbal or physical conduct of a sexual nature constitute sexual harassment when (1) submission to such conduct is made either explicity or implicitly a term or a condition of an individual's employment; (2) submission to or rejection of such conduct . . . is used as the basis for employment decisions affecting such individual; (3) such conduct has the purpose or effect of unreasonably interfering with an individual's work performance" (29 C.F.R. sec. 1604.11). This provision applies not only to the individual student affairs administrator but also to the staff that the administrator may supervise. The employer is liable for the acts of employees even when the employer did not authorize (or even forbade) the specific acts and did not know of their occurrence.

Implications for Student Affairs. Title VII directly influences hiring and supervision practices in student affairs. Preemployment activities must be carefully monitored to avoid questions regarding race and sex. Supervision requires institution-wide guidelines for assignments, grade levels, and classifications that are not discriminatory. Pregnant staff members have specific rights pertaining to their job, disability benefits, and leave. Religious practices must be accommodated within reason. Non-English speakers have certain rights to speak their native language. Finally, the administrator may be liable for on-the-job sexual harassment of employees by staff members who are supervised by the administrator. These provisions thus mandate staff and supervisory training as well as careful monitoring of the employment process. (See Chapter Eighteen in this volume for a full discussion of these issues.)

Title IX

Title IX of the Education Amendments of 1972 (20 U.S.C. secs. 1681–1686) prohibits discrimination on the basis of sex in any

educational program that receives federal financial assistance. Title
IX differs from Title VI, since Title VI does not prohibit sex
discrimination; and from Title VII, since Title VII applies only to
discrimination *in employment* on the basis of race, color, religion,
sex, or national origin. Note also that Title IX applies specifically
to education and educational programs.

Title IX is a comprehensive Act that includes many provisions directly applicable to the student affairs administrator. As a
result of the many provisions that apply to student affairs, it is
extremely important that administrators obtain and review the
enabling legislation found at 34 C.F.R. Part 106. Title IX provides:

> No person in the United States shall, on the basis of
> sex, be excluded from participation in, be denied the
> benefits of, or be subjected to discrimination under
> any education program or activity receiving Federal
> financial assistance."

Limitations of Application. Only certain types of educational institutions are subject to the provisions of Title IX.
Specifically, Title IX does *not* apply to educational institutions
controlled by religious organizations or to military and merchant
marine institutions. Furthermore, nondiscrimination on the basis
of sex in *admissions* practices is prohibited only in vocational,
professional, graduate higher education, and public institutions of
undergraduate higher education. The admissions practices of
private undergraduate institutions are exempt from the Act.

Private Cause of Action and Exhaustion of Remedies. Title
IX does not expressly grant a plaintiff the right to bring an action,
but it now appears well settled that an *implied* remedy is present.
In *Cannon* v. *University of Chicago* (1979), a woman brought suit
under Title IX when she was rejected as a candidate for medical
school. The Supreme Court stated: "Title IX presents the atypical
situation in which all of these circumstances that the Court has
previously identified as supportive of an implied remedy are
present" (at 717). In short, aggrieved parties may use Title IX as
individual plaintiffs. Furthermore, exhaustion of administrative
remedies is not mandated.

Program Specificity. If one part of the institution receives federal funding, does Title IX apply only to that program or to the institution as a whole? The Supreme Court held in *Grove City College* v. *Bell* (1984, at 564) that "receipt of BEOGs [Basic Educational Opportunity Grants] by some of Grove City's students does not trigger institution-wide coverage under Title IX." This means that enforcement power under Title IX is limited to the specific program receiving funds and does not extend to the entire institution.

It does not matter whether monies to the institution are direct or indirect. For example, if BEOG funding goes directly to students, it is still money to the institution. Therefore, Title IX is applicable. "Nothing in Section 901(a) [of Title IX] suggests that Congress elevated form over substance by making the application of the nondiscrimination principle dependent on the manner in which a program or activity receives federal assistance" (*Grove City,* 1984, at 717). (See Chapter Seven in this volume for a full discussion of these issues.)

Implications for Student Affairs. The enabling legislation accompanying Title IX is replete with provisions applicable to student affairs.

• *Admissions.* Discrimination on the basis of sex is prohibited. Gender cannot be used as a basis for preference; ranking; numerical limitations; separate types of tests; or questions pertaining to parental, family, or marital status or to pregnancy, childbirth, or termination of pregnancy. Inquiries regarding sex of a candidate are permissible if the same question is asked of all candidates and is not used in a discriminatory manner.

• *Housing.* It is permissible to provide separate housing, but such housing must be proportionate; it must be comparable in quality and cost; and the same policies or practices must be used for both sexes.

• *Facilities.* Locker rooms, toilets, and shower facilities must be comparable.

• *Course Offerings.* Separate contact sport programs are permissible, but other course offerings on the basis of sex are not.

• *Counseling.* Internal procedures must be developed to

ensure that materials used in counseling do not discriminate on the basis of sex.

- *Financial Assistance.* It is impermissible, on the basis of sex, to provide different amounts or types, to limit eligibility, or to apply different criteria in making determinations for financial assistance. Financial aid offices must develop internal procedures to ensure nondiscrimination. If financial aid from an outside source, such as a trust or organization, is designated for one sex in a legal instrument, that is permissible as long as the overall effect is nondiscriminatory. Athletic scholarships must afford a reasonable opportunity for members of each sex.

- *Employment Assistance.* A policy of nondiscrimination applies "in-house" as well as to those outside the educational institution who make employment available to any of its students.

- *Health Care.* Health care coverage may not discriminate on the basis of sex. If full-coverage health care is provided, then gynecological care must be provided.

- *Medical or Parental Status.* An institution may not discriminate or exclude a student from classes or extracurricular activities on the basis of pregnancy, childbirth, false pregnancy, or termination of pregnancy. Such conditions must be treated as a disability, allowing students a leave of absence.

- *Athletics.* Institutions may have separate teams on the basis of sex. However, if the institution has a team for members of one sex only and athletic opportunities for the opposite sex have traditionally been limited, then all students must be given the opportunity to try out unless the sport is a contact sport. Otherwise, students are entitled to equal access to supplies, travel and per diem allowances, coaches and tutors, and medical and training facilities.

As has been shown, Title IX has implications for almost every area in student affairs. It generally applies to educational institutions, but, with regard to admissions, it does not apply to private undergraduate institutions. Title IX prohibits discrimination in programs receiving federal money but does not necessarily apply to the entire institution. Because of the intertwining of many student affairs functions (most notably, financial aid and housing), special attention must be paid to Title IX in policies, procedures, and practices.

Section 504

Section 504 of the Rehabilitation Act of 1973 (29 U.S.C. secs. 791-794) refers to federal law mandating nondiscrimination on the basis of handicap. It is interesting to note that, "although disabled persons constitute over 10% of the population of the United States, they make up less than 1% of the students at colleges and universities and an even smaller proportion of students in graduate and professional schools" (Cook and Luski, 1980, p. 418). The purpose of this Act is to make higher education available to all qualified applicants, regardless of physical disability, thereby increasing the representation of the disabled student on campuses nationwide.

For purposes of this chapter, discussion pertaining to Section 504 is limited to the Act as it addresses academic institutions, but it is not the intent of this discussion to include employment aspects of the Act. Rather, the focus is on the duty of the college or university to accommodate disabled students.

The applicable section of the law provides:

> No otherwise qualified handicapped individual in the United States . . . shall, solely by reason of his handicap, be excluded from the participation in, be denied the benefits of, or be subjected to discrimination under any program or activity receiving federal financial assistance or under any program or activity conducted by any Executive agency or by the United States Postal Service.

A handicapped individual means any individual who (1) has a physical or mental impairment that substantially limits one or more of such person's major life activities; (2) has a record of such impairment; or (3) is regarded as having such an impairment (34 C.F.R. sec. 104.3(j)).

Further definitions and more specific examples of what constitutes an impairment are found in the regulations that explain the meaning of the Rehabilitation Act in detail. The following list of disabilities is provided: "The term includes . . . such diseases and conditions as orthopedic, visual, speech, and hearing impairments, cerebral palsy, epilepsy, muscular dystrophy, multiple sclerosis, cancer, heart disease, diabetes, mental retardation, and emotional illness. . . . Environmental, cultural, and economic disadvantages are not in themselves covered; nor are prison records, age, or homosexuality" (34 C.F.R. Part 104, Appendix A(3)). The Act is applicable in a number of ways to institutions of higher education.

Direct and Indirect Financial Assistance. Discrimination against students on the basis of handicap is prohibited "under any program or activity receiving federal financial assistance." The question then arises: What constitutes the receipt of federal financial assistance? It is clear that a college or university receiving "direct" federal funding—for example, monies for construction—is subject to the Act. The courts have struggled, however, with situations where monies to the college or university are indirect— for example, colleges whose only source of federal funding is through federal financial aid to students. In *Haffer* v. *Temple University* (1982), the award of federal Basic Educational Opportunity Grants to students constituted federal financial assistance, thereby making Title IX sex discrimination provisions applicable. More important, in *Grove City College* (discussed above), the Supreme Court met the same issue squarely in a case involving a private college's refusal to comply with Title IX despite the fact that a large number of students received BEOGs. The Court said: "The economic effect of direct and indirect assistance often is indistinguishable . . . and the BEOG program was structured to ensure that it effectively supplements the College's own financial aid program. The drafters of Title IX envisioned that the receipt of student aid funds would trigger coverage, and since they approved identical language, we discern no reason to believe that the Congressmen who voted for Title IX intended a different result" (*Grove City*, at 565). *By analogy*, it appears that the receipt of either indirect or direct federal financial assistance to colleges and universities also makes the prohibition against discrimination on the basis of handicap applicable.

Pinpointing. Also by analogy to *Grove City*, the receipt of federal financial assistance by a college or university does not necessarily make the entire institution subject to the provisions of the Act. Rather, as with Title IX, the courts tend to "pinpoint," meaning that the government can only enforce the prohibition against discrimination in the specific program receiving federal financial assistance (*Doyle* v. *University of Alabama in Birmingham*, 1982).

Private Causes of Action and Exhaustion of Remedies. Two unsettled areas under this Act concern whether a plaintiff has a right to bring a private lawsuit and whether exhaustion of administrative remedies is first required. It appears that most courts are allowing private lawsuits, despite the fact that Section 504 does not specifically address this issue. Again, by analogy with Title IX and Title VI provisions, courts are finding "surer footing" for making the argument that such a right exists. For an excellent discussion on the evolution of the law in this area, see Wegner (1984).

With regard to the second question, must a plaintiff exhaust federal agency complaint procedures before litigation must proceed, courts have concluded that this sort of exhaustion is not required, at least since the Supreme Court held that "exhaustion of administrative remedies is not required under Title IX" (*Cannon* v. *University of Chicago*, 1979, at 706 *n.*41).

Implications for Student Affairs. The Rehabilitation Act of 1973 has numerous provisions of particular importance to the student affairs administrator. A review of the implementing guidelines found at 34 C.F.R. Part 104 (which effectuate Section 504) is highly recommended, especially "Subpart E," which applies to postsecondary institutions that receive or benefit from federal financial assistance. Some of the more important provisions appear below.

• *Admissions and Recruitment.* This section mandates that discrimination not take place on the basis of handicap but on "individual capabilities rather than stereotyped conceptions of the abilities of disabled persons" (34 C.F.R. sec. 104.42 (b)(2)). Schools may not apply limitations on the number or proportion of handicapped persons admitted. Nor may they use tests that have an adverse effect on handicapped persons unless the test is validated as a predictor of success and no alternate testing is available. In *Southeastern Community College* v. *Davis* (1979), an applicant to the college's nursing program was rejected from the program because she suffered from a congenital hearing impairment in both ears. In its decision upholding the college's right to exclude Davis, the U.S. Supreme Court noted that a college may take into consideration limitations resulting from handicaps because "no otherwise qualified handicapped individual" means one "who is able to meet all of a program's requirements in spite of handicap(s)" (at 405-406). The requirement imposed by the college that "students have the ability to understand speech without reliance on lipreading" was a reasonable and necessary physical qualification for the clinical phase of Southeastern Community College's nursing degree (at 407). In short, it appears that applicants must meet all of a college's entrance requirements in spite of handicap.

• *Testing.* If applicants must take entrance examinations, the regulations require that such testing take place "in a manner that insures accurate results for those with impaired sensory, manual or speaking skills" (34 C.F.R. sec. 104.42).

• *Academic Services.* Exclusion of handicapped individuals from any course or courses of study is prohibited. Note, however, that, under the *Davis* ruling, exclusion is not necessarily discriminatory if a student is not able to meet the standards of a course safely and effectively. The college is required to take "affirmative steps to assure that services are as effective as those provided to others" (34 C.F.R. sec. 104.42). For example, an institution may be required to provide and to pay for auxiliary aids if vocational rehabilitation agencies do not pay.

• *Nonacademic Services.* For the student affairs administrator, the nonacademic services provisions are particularly applicable. The regulations require that the following services be provided to disabled students in a nondiscriminatory manner:

1. Housing—must be "comparable" to that provided nonhandicapped and must be "accessible." Note that all housing does not need to be made accessible so long as the effect is not to segregate disabled students within a single setting.
2. Counseling—must be "comparable." Furthermore, disabled students must not be "counseled" toward "more restrictive career objectives."
3. Financial assistance—must be provided without regard to

disability. Financial aid may not be limited because a student is disabled; this stricture applies whether aid is directly from the school or is distributed by another entity through the school.

4. Accessibility—must be ensured for all programs at the college and university. For example, "Colleges must operate their programs and activities so that, when reviewed in their entirety, they are readily accessible to handicapped persons." Specifically, classrooms may need to be moved to a location that is accessible to handicapped students; laboratory equipment may need to be redesigned; and existing facilities may need to be changed or modified.

Age Discrimination Act

The Age Discrimination Act of 1975 (42 U.S.C. sec. 6101 *et seq.*) prohibits age discrimination in federally funded programs and activities. Such discrimination thus is prohibited in many programs and activities in the domain of student affairs, including admissions, employment, financial aid, and housing. Both public and private institutions receiving federal funds are controlled by the Act. Section 90.14 of the implementing regulations (45 C.F.R. Part 90) permits age distinctions necessary to the "normal operation" or the achievement of a "statutory objective" of a federally funded program or activity (Kaplin, 1985, p. 251).

In *Purdie* v. *University of Utah* (1978), the court considered a case where a woman claimed that she had been denied admission because she was too old. The trial court dismissed her claim; however, on appeal, the Utah Supreme Court reversed, holding that rejection of a qualified fifty-one-year-old would violate equal protection unless the university could show that there was a relationship between the use of age as an admissions criterion and the legitimate purposes of the state.

The regulations do permit use of physical fitness tests as a factor in selecting participants to train or continue in positions. However, the physical activity tested must relate directly and substantially to the position and not be merely a ploy to discriminate on the basis of age.

Summary

Civil rights legislation is both complex and far reaching. Private and public institutions may be differentially influenced by statutes in this area. If, however, a private institution is engaging in state action, these federal statutes apply. Attention must be given to all policies, practices, and procedures in the institution, to ensure that they do not have differential impact on protected classes of persons and thus are discriminatory. For students, statutory implications begin prior to admissions (see Chapter Ten in this volume) and continue throughout matriculation. Similarly, statutory protections begin during the screening phase and continue throughout the employment period. Understanding of applicable civil rights laws increases the ability of both the institution and the individual administrator to avoid litigation and risk loss of a lawsuit. More important, adherence to civil rights laws ensures equity and access for all persons.

References

Abernathy, C. "Affirmative Action and the Rule of *Bakke.*" *American Bar Association Journal,* Aug. 1978, *64,* 1233–1237.

"Civil Rights." In *American Jurisprudence.* (2nd ed.) Vol. 15, sec. 1. Rochester, N.Y.: Lawyers Cooperative Publishing, 1976.

Cook, T., and Luski, F. "Beyond *Davis:* Equality of Opportunity for Education of Disabled Students Under the Rehabilitation Act of 1973." *Harvard Civil Rights–Civil Liberties Law Review,* 1980, *15,* 415–473.

Edwards, H., and Nordin, V. *Higher Education and the Law.* Cambridge, Mass.: Institute for Educational Management, Harvard University, 1979.

Kaplin, W. A. *The Law of Higher Education: A Comprehensive Guide to Legal Implications of Decision Making.* (2nd ed.) San Francisco: Jossey-Bass, 1985.

Kramer, G. R. "Title VII on Campus: Judicial Review of University Employment Decisions." *Columbia Law Review,* Oct. 1982, pp. 1206–1235.

Nowak, J., Rotunda, R., and Young, J. *Constitutional Law.* St. Paul, Minn.: West, 1977.

Schlie, B., and Grossman, P. *Employment Discrimination Law.* Washington, D.C.: Bureau of National Affairs, 1984.

Simon, T. F. "Of Colleges and Kings: Academic Defendants Under 42 U.S.C. Section 1983." *St. Johns Law Review,* 1985, *59,* 228–290.

Wegner, J. "The Antidiscrimination Model Reconsidered: Ensuring Equal Opportunity Without Respect to Handicap Under Section 504 of the Rehabilitation Act of 1973." *Cornell Law Journal,* 1984, *69,* 401–516.

7

Stephen S. Janes

🌿 🌿 🌿

Administrative Practice: A Day-To-Day Guide to Legal Requirements

A discussion of legislation with implications for student affairs practitioners is not complete without consideration of a number of federal statutes besides those discussed in the preceding chapters. The applicability of these statutes in a particular institutional setting depends, of course, on the nature of its control and the specific responsibilities of the division of student affairs. This chapter will examine federal legislation that applies to all institutions as well as certain statutes that apply only to private institutions. The statutes selected for discussion are federal laws that apply to higher education and have particular relevance to student affairs professionals. The relationship of federal legislation to church-related institutions is a frequent source of litigation; administrators at these institutions should consult counsel for guidance when doubt exists.

A number of cases are mentioned in this chapter. They have been selected for inclusion as much for the value of their discussion and review of relevant points of law as for their holdings. Since both case law and statutes are in relatively constant flux, student affairs practitioners should ascertain the current status of both when investigating a particular legal question. It is also important to keep in mind that the laws discussed in this chapter apply to specific activities or administrative functions regardless of the locus of responsibility for their conduct within the institution. For example, the federal law regarding privacy of educational records must be followed whether the record-keeping functions are handled in student affairs or elsewhere. Similarly, the regulations implementing the federal student assistance programs delineate a number of activities that may cross institutional lines of authority.

While the discussion in this chapter is devoted to federal legislation, administrators should be mindful that states often enact statutes dealing with the same subject matter. As a general rule, valid federal laws preempt conflicting state laws, thus minimizing the problems associated with jurisdictional disputes and legal interpretation. Federal statutes with general application only to privately controlled institutions typically have state counterparts dictating similar provisions for public institutions. It is not uncommon for states to pass "reception statutes," which adopt the provisions of certain federal statutes as state law or stipulate that the state defers to federal law under specified conditions. Prudent student affairs administrators will verify the existence and terms of state laws on any important legal matters, even when it seems clear that federal law is supervening, since it may be necessary to reconcile overlapping provisions of federal and state laws.

Family Educational Rights and Privacy Act

The Family Educational Rights and Privacy Act of 1974 (as amended) has significant implications for nearly all postsecondary institutions. This statute, popularly known as "FERPA" or the "Buckley Amendment," was signed into law in 1974. The implementing regulations (now at 34 C.F.R. Part 99) were issued by the then Department of Health, Education and Welfare in June 1976. The early history of this law is a testimonial to the difficulties often associated with implementing federal legislation that bears on the activities of several thousand postsecondary institutions, each with somewhat unique internal procedures and practices. The problem is exacerbated, of course, if those institutions are subject to conflicting provisions of state laws.

The purpose of FERPA is to regulate educational record-keeping practices in postsecondary institutions. The intent of the legislation is to protect the rights of students and parents and to ensure the privacy and accuracy of educational records. Through it, the Congress has codified certain rights of individual students and of the parents of students who are dependents under federal income tax regulations. FERPA does not apply to the records of applicants for admission or of admitted students until they have actually attended the institution maintaining the educational records. An exception to the enrollment requirement provides for coverage of educational records, such as grade reports and transcripts, in cooperative and correspondence study programs. Attention should be given to the definition of educational records in the regulations for this legislation, since what constitutes educational records within an institution may depend on the uses the institution makes of the data it maintains. For example, commingling of information from the campus law enforcement unit with other educational record information or sharing educational record information with the law enforcement unit may bring the records of the law enforcement unit under the provisions of FERPA.

FERPA provisions must be heeded by all institutions receiving Department of Education (ED) funds directly or through students in attendance who are receiving funds from programs administered by ED. Direct receipt of funds includes federal grants or contracts, whether the institution is the prime recipient or assumes a subgrant or subcontracting role. Indirect receipt of funds occurs when students pay all or part of any funds they receive from the federal government to the institution to meet educational expenses. The most common forms of indirect payments are funds paid through the federal student assistance programs (*Grove City College* v. *Bell*, 1984).

The records covered by FERPA are defined to include nearly anything containing the names or identifiers of students who have attended the institution. The litany of exceptions mentioned in the regulations is extensive. The more significant exclusions from the Act are the personal records of an institution's personnel; certain campus law enforcement, administrative, medical, and counseling records; data on alumni; and certain records relating to religious matters. The Act applies regardless of the methods used to maintain the records subject to its provisions. There are few restrictions on destruction of educational records except those relating to pending requests for review by eligible students and "explanations" placed in the records as the result of record-related hearing.

The thrust of FERPA is to enumerate the protections afforded educational records, as a means of ensuring that institutions follow what has come to be widely recognized as sound practice in record maintenance. Primary emphasis is given to the right of students to inspect their own educational records. Students are entitled to challenge the contents of their records and to request formal hearings to resolve disputes. The Act prevents disclosure of information from educational records without approval of the student, and it enumerates circumstances under which disclosure may be made without consent. Institutions may extend protections to educational records that are more stringent than those stipulated in this legislation.

FERPA regulations require institutions to develop written procedures for its implementation. Students (and their parents in specific instances) must be informed annually of their rights under the Act by such means as are reasonably likely to inform them. Students may waive their rights of access to certain materials, such as letters of reference or materials found in credential files. Such waivers must be in writing and cannot be a condition for receiving any service, such as placement, from the institution and cannot be used as a requirement for letters of recommendation in an admissions process. Letters of recommendation and similar materials that were provided with the understanding that they remain confidential may be withheld from a student if the student has executed a waiver. In the latter instance, a number of associated requirements are nicely met by forms described by the American Association of Collegiate Registrars and Admissions Officers (1976) in *A Guide to Postsecondary Institutions for Implementation of the Family Educational Rights and Privacy Act of 1974, as Amended.*

FERPA places important restrictions on the redisclosure of information from educational records, particularly among third parties such as institutions or individuals who have been authorized by the student to receive educational record information. The day-to-day administrative requirements for intrainstitutional exchange of information are facilitated by a provision allowing other educational officials within the institution access to appropriate record information without prior approval from the student.

Two provisions of the regulations warrant special attention because the conditions they govern frequently generate questions. First, FERPA allows disclosure of "directory information" without prior student approval if certain conditions are met. Directory information is defined in the regulations as "the student's name, address, telephone number, date and place of birth, major field of study, participation in officially recognized activities and sports, weight and height of members of athletic teams, dates of attendance, degrees and awards received, the most recent previous educational agency or institution attended by the student and other similar information" (34 C.F.R. sec. 99.3).

The institution must make public its designation of the data it considers directory information, and it must give each student an opportunity to refuse to permit the release of some or all of these data. Prudent interpretation of the Act dictates against an excessively broad definition of directory information. The mechanics through which the designation is made public and the means by which students' restrictions are implemented differ widely among institutions and may be a source of difficulty in larger institutions with unsophisticated technical resources.

Student-requested restrictions on designation of portions of the educational record as directory information may present special difficulties if the institution does not coordinate the timing of these restrictions with the annual notification of rights under the Act. Therefore, most institutions require at least an annual filing of requests to withhold the release of directory information, usually at the beginning of the fall term.

Another source of particular concern involves the request for information from educational records by law enforcement agencies or as part of a civil suit. The FERPA regulations describe a number of conditions under which prior permission for release of educational record information is not required. One such condition is "To comply with a judicial order or lawfully issued subpoena; Provided, that the educational agency or institution makes a reasonable effort to notify the parent of the student or the eligible student of the order or subpoena in advance of compliance therewith" (34 C.F.R. sec. 99.31(a)(9)).

Law enforcement officials may prefer to avoid using the subpoena process any more frequently than is absolutely necessary, in part because of the time and effort involved. However, the institution should avoid succumbing to pressure to release educational record information without following the requirements of FERPA. Special attention should be paid to the requirement that the subpoena be lawfully issued. Since there are several kinds of subpoenas with varying legal status, many institutions follow the wise practice of seeking review of all such documents by legal counsel before responding. Yet another difficulty relates to determining the best means of proceeding when a subpoena mandates that the institution may not attempt to contact the student whose records are being sought, usually for a specified period or until a pending investigation has been completed. Since the regulations require an attempt to notify the student, generally satisfied by sending a letter to the last-known address and waiting for a reasonable period of time before releasing information, there is often a conflict between FERPA and state or local legal procedures. FERPA is administered by the FERPA Office, Department of Education, 400 Maryland Avenue, S.W., Washington, D.C. 20202. That office should be contacted at any time guidance about the Act is required.

Provisions of FERPA are also to some extent in conflict with regulations implementing laws administered by the Immigration and Naturalization Service (INS), which mandate the release of certain educational record information without either subpoena or prior consent of the students under INS jurisdiction (8 C.F.R. sec. 214.4(a)(i)). Resolution of these conflicts may also require the advice of counsel.

Enforcement of FERPA requirements may involve the filing of a complaint by an aggrieved student and an investigation by the Department of Education. Penalties for noncompliance involve the withdrawal of federal funds. The Act does not confer standing to sue on individuals, as indicated in *Girardier* v. *Webster College* (1977).

Another federal statute related to record keeping, the Privacy Act of 1974, applies primarily to federal agencies. It reaches public postsecondary institutions to the extent that it prohibits governmental bodies from requiring the disclosure of the Social Security number, except as permitted by other federal legislation or if the institution was required to collect it by statute or regulation and was doing so before January 1, 1975. This legislation also applies to any postsecondary institution that maintains a system of records for the federal government under contract.

Higher Education Act

The Higher Education Act of 1965 (as amended) contains a number of titles providing support services for higher education. The principal areas of focus in this statute for student affairs administrators are the sections dealing with the federal student financial aid programs. This legislation is "reauthorized" on a periodic basis, during which time the Congress undertakes a fairly exhaustive review of experience with the various programs and entertains suggestions for modifications. The most recent extension of the Act was published as the Higher Education Amendments of 1986 in the *Congressional Record* on September 22, 1986. Current regulations for federal student assistance programs may be found in the following parts of the *Code of Federal Regulations:*

Auxiliary Loans to Assist Students (34 C.F.R. Part 638)
College Work-Study program (authority: 42 U.S.C. sec. 2751 *et seq.*) (34 C.F.R. Part 675)
Guaranteed Student Loan program (34 C.F.R. Part 682)
Health Professions Student Loan program (42 C.F.R. Part 57, subpart C)
National Direct Student Loan program (34 C.F.R. Part 674)
Pell Grant program (34 C.F.R. Part 690)
State Student Incentive Grant program (34 C.F.R. Part 692)
Supplemental Educational Opportunity Grant program (34 C.F.R. Part 676)

Title IV. Student Assistance (Title IV) contains enabling legislation for a wide range of grant programs, loans, and the College Work-Study program; it also contains a number of requirements relating to the calculation of financial need and administrative procedures of the Department of Education. The specific provisions of Title IV vary with each reauthorization, both in the number and types of programs covered and in the administrative requirements pertaining to those programs. Student affairs administrators with responsibilities involving student financial aid must heed a wide range of federal accounting, auditing, and administrative requirements. Particular attention must be paid to the eligibility of applicants for each of the federal student assistance programs. The eligibility requirements include maintenance of satisfactory academic progress (as defined by the institution, subject to statutory and regulatory constraints) and a complex formula for determining financial need. Recent changes in this statute have curtailed the eligibility of students for federally guaranteed student loans and substantially limit the freedom of student applicants to present themselves as financially independent of their parents.

Regulations for the Title IV programs have added progressively complex validation requirements at the institutional level. These requirements provide that the institution must perform a secondary audit of certain data elements on the financial aid application, must entirely audit certain application files by obtaining additional documentation (such as the federal form 1040), and must ensure that appropriate changes are made to the applications before awarding funds. The 1986 reauthorization places limits on the scope of the Department of Education's validation efforts.

Another series of regulatory requirements relates to the failure of some students to make payments on federal loans. An excessive default rate among federally subsidized loans made through a specific institution may result in administrative sanctions. (See the section on loan defaults, below.)

Recent federal initiatives, published December 1, 1986, in the *Federal Register,* suggest the implementation of new quality control procedures for Title IV programs at the institutional level. These procedures may supplant the Title IV validation requirements, but they will also contribute significantly to the institutional work load. The Act requires that participating institutions follow very specific information dissemination requirements to meet the needs of prospective and enrolled students. These requirements include descriptions of financial aid programs available through the institution, delineation of application procedures, and statements about the cost of attendance, student rights and responsibilities, the institutional refund policy, academic programs, standards regarding satisfactory progress, institutional contact persons, special facilities and services available to handicapped students, and institutional accreditation. An additional requirement is imposed on those institutions that advertise job placement rates as an enrollment incentive, stipulating that they must provide data to substantiate the truthfulness of their advertisements.

Enforcement. There are several enforcement mechanisms specified in Title IV, depending on the nature of the violation involved. In some instances, the Secretary of Education may rescind the institution's eligibility to participate in federal student assistance programs. This penalty generally is imposed if an institution fails to represent itself properly in communications to students or regarding compliance with this or related federal statutes. A useful discussion of these issues is contained in the *Grove City* case.

A second type of penalty, civil assessments ranging to $25,000 per violation, is associated with either misrepresentation by the institution or its failure to comply with provisions of the Act and implementing regulations. The civil penalty may be deducted from sums payable to the institution from any source of federal funding, including payments due the institution as part of the administrative cost allowances provided for in the Higher Education Amendments of 1986 (42 U.S.C. sec. 489(a)). Institutions are routinely required to replace funds when an audit has determined that federal funds have not been properly administered. The Department of Education has shown that it will go to court to enforce its Title IV regulations, as demonstrated by its successful efforts in *United States* v. *Institute of Computer Technology* (1975).

Criminal penalties are also associated with this statute. They range up to $10,000 and five years' imprisonment for violations by any individual for offenses involving fraud, forgery, false statements, concealment of relevant information in the assignment of loans, fraudulent inducements, or obstruction of justice.

Loan Defaults. An area of growing concern related to Title

IV programs is that of defaults in the repayment of student loans. Recognizing a growing tendency among borrowers to ignore their obligations, the federal government has resorted to a number of collection techniques that require institutional cooperation. Among these are the provision of information to credit bureaus at certain stages of the collection process, due diligence in the collection of loans that have come due, and a variety of reporting and auditing requirements.

The discharge of student loans through bankruptcy has been limited substantially by provisions of the Bankruptcy Reform Act of 1978 (as amended). In general, student loans made, funded, or guaranteed by governmental bodies at any level, as well as those made through nonprofit postsecondary institutions, may not be discharged in bankruptcy until payments have been due for at least five years. This provision excludes periods during which repayment is suspended and allows consideration of undue hardship as an extenuating circumstance.

There are important distinctions between discharge through Chapter 7 and repayment plans developed under Chapter 13 of the federal bankruptcy laws. For the most part, courts have not applied the five-year requirement to petitions for relief under Chapter 13, as exemplified by the discussion and holding of *In re Eichelberger* (1980). The five-year period begins after the first installment payment becomes due rather than after the debtor's last actual repayment (*In re Nunn*, 1986). The 1978 revisions of this Act effectively nullified part of the decision in *Girardier* v. *Webster College* (1977), which allowed institutions to withhold transcripts of students with delinquent accounts during bankruptcy proceedings or after they had been declared bankrupt. However, the courts have upheld an institution's right to withhold transcripts for delinquent accounts that have not been discharged after bankruptcy proceedings have concluded (*Johnson* v. *Edinboro State College*, 1984).

Related Requirements. A source of contention for postsecondary institutions has been the tendency of Congress to tie corollary requirements to the administration of Title IV programs at the institutional level. A recent instance of this problem was a requirement mandating selective service registration by certain students as a condition for receipt of assistance under Title IV programs (34 C.F.R. Part 668). Institutions were told that they must present statements certifying draft registration before federal student aid could be disbursed, a much lamented burden on student financial aid officers. The requirement was upheld in *Selective Service System* v. *Minnesota Public Interest Research Group* (1984).

Another example of "tangential" administrative requirements is reflected in the Higher Education Amendments of 1986, stipulating that a participating institution must certify that it has in operation a drug abuse prevention program accessible to any officer, employee, or student at the institution (42 U.S.C. sec. 487(a)).

Beyond the administrative burdens created by these legislative conditions are the difficulties posed when students or other citizens find themselves in disagreement with a given requirement. On balance, resort to the judicial process will ultimately decide the validity of such matters. Nonetheless, student affairs administrators may occasionally be faced with constituents who do not wish to acquiesce in a specific federal mandate and who do not care that the requirement is not one of the institution's own making. When such occasions arise, the advice of legal counsel should be sought. Often, counsel can help administrators demonstrate to the appropriate agency that the institution has acted in good faith to meet the requirements. Additionally, legal counsel can provide advice on what other administrative options are open to the institution. Ignoring the issue is not wise administrative practice, and some resolution must be sought in the conflict.

Relevant provisions of the Veterans' Educational Assistance Act, as Amended (38 U.S.C. sec. 1651) should be read to gain a complete understanding of the overall requirements placed on an institution by the federal government's student financial assistance programs. The status of veterans receiving assistance under this Act must be certified by the institution on a periodic basis, and the "financial aid package" of veterans who are Title IV aid recipients must reflect the total payments they receive from all funding sources. Enforcement of these requirements has been tested in court and upheld (*United States* v. *Garrahan,* 1985).

Immigration Issues

The Immigration Reform and Control Act of 1986 affects all institutions that enroll students from foreign countries. The provisions of this legislation govern the status of these students, and the implementing regulations impose requirements that must be carefully followed. There are few areas so clearly the domain of the federal government, as evidenced by recent Supreme Court decisions (*Toll* v. *Moreno*, 1982; *Plyler* v. *Doe*, 1982) overriding actions at the state and local level. The Court has affirmed that residency status and citizenship are the domain of the federal government, and state and local actions may not contravene such statutory authority. This Act comprises a complete revision of the United States immigration laws. The revisions may result in some modifications to the regulations governing foreign students at United States institutions.

Federal law provides for entry into the United States of persons from other countries who wish to engage in a program of study here. The legislation has been interpreted in regulations promulgated by the Immigration and Naturalization Service (INS), placing individuals in a series of classifications. Most international students are now classified as "J-1—exchange students," "M-1—vocational or technical students," or "F-1—academic or language program students." Professionals charged with administering the immigration laws on United States campuses frequently contend that INS regulations place restrictions on foreign students beyond those intended by Congress. This contention is an important consideration for student affairs administrators, since loose interpretations of INS regulations by administrators or "tests" by the students themselves tend to be a major source of legal problems for institutions.

This legislation requires campus personnel to process documents associated with applications for admission and to certify that foreign applicants meet academic requirements, are able to speak English well enough for study here, and have the financial means to cover expenses for study. INS allows participating schools to issue a form (now, an I-20) for use by the foreign applicants as they apply for entry into this country. Other administrative requirements that must be followed are that foreign students—and there are exceptions to these requirements, depending on the visa type and the program of study—are engaged in full-time study and that they are not working off campus. Exceptions to the restriction to on-campus employment may be made for students who have been here sufficiently long (usually twelve months) to demonstrate the capacity for serious study but who suffer serious financial reverses.

INS requires participating institutions to maintain specific records and to report information on a periodic basis, usually through completion of lists provided for that purpose. The objective of these lists is to ascertain the status of foreign students studying at each institution. INS requires institutions to release certain types of information, and current regulations stipulate that an institution must agree to provide that information without a subpoena, as mentioned earlier in this chapter. The nature and quantity of information requested can depend on which INS office is making the request. The legal fallback for this approach is based on a statement or "waiver" that foreign students sign as they complete the United States entry procedures. It is advisable to consult with counsel before releasing any educational record information, to ensure compliance with the provisions of FERPA, since this apparent conflict between regulations implementing federal statutes has not reached clear resolution.

A specific example of this problem involves the validation by INS of credentials presented by foreign students, such as standardized test scores on the Test of English as a Foreign Language (TOEFL) or the Scholastic Aptitude Test (SAT) or the American College Testing Program (ACT). Institutions enrolling substantial numbers of foreign students may receive frequent requests for information contained in the educational records of foreign students who are the subject of INS or other law enforcement agency investigations. Recent court decisions have extended to noncitizens in this country rights under the Fifth and Sixth Amendments (*Wong Wing* v. *United States*, 1896) and the Fourth Amendment (*United States* v. *Barbera*, 1975). Given that trend and the invalidation of a state law restricting the rights of undocumented alien children to attend public schools (*Plyler* v. *Doe*, 1982), there is every reason to believe that the direction of our laws is to accord noncitizens, no matter what their status or classification, protections similar to those afforded citizens, as long as they remain within our borders. Accordingly, the "releases" on INS documents that must be signed by foreign students when they complete their applications may ultimately be subjected to the same legal scrutiny by the courts as would be any release or waiver executed by a United States citizen.

There are important distinctions between the status of nonimmigrant aliens and the status of immigrant aliens, and these distinctions may require different treatment of students in those classifications. In addition to their constitutional protections, resident or immigrant aliens are entitled to preferential treatment paralleling that of United States citizens in other specific instances. These include consideration for residency at state-supported institutions and eligibility for most forms of student financial aid.

Some uncertainty exists regarding the conditions under which institutions may be required to report students who are no longer maintaining the INS status they were granted on enrollment. Current regulations set no requirement that students who are working without authorization be reported, just as there is no requirement that information not "officially" a part of a particular student's record must be disclosed. Administrators can avoid a number of legal problems if they will reexamine the institution's overall record-keeping policy (including information accumulated by the international office, law enforcement units, counseling centers, and health centers) and try to avoid the commingling and intrainstitutional sharing of information that might not be considered part of an educational record.

The primary mechanism through which INS enforces its regulations is the withdrawal of an institution's approval to enroll nonimmigrant foreign students. The process generally begins with a letter or complaint from a regional officer and requires the same procedural due process accorded any other major administrative action by a federal agency (*Blackwell College of Business* v. *Attorney General*, 1971).

Fair Labor Standards Act

The Fair Labor Standards Act of 1938 (as amended) (FLSA) (29 U.S.C. sec. 201 *et seq.*) sets minimum wage and hour requirements for employees who are not exempt from its provisions. The exempt classification includes executives, senior administrators, and others in a "professional capacity" and is a fruitful source of legal inquiry, since the range of positions that may be included or excluded is the subject of incessant litigation.

This statute has a checkered history with respect to its applicability to higher education. There has never been a question about its applicability to private institutions, but the courts have vacillated in applying it to public institutions. The most recent case interpreting this statute, *Garcia v. San Antonio Metropolitan Transit Authority* (1985), reasserted the application of the Act to state and local government employers, a holding that can readily be interpreted to include most public postsecondary institutions.

The *Garcia* holding requires state and local employers to provide overtime pay instead of granting compensatory time off for nonexempt employees. Private employers (including private colleges and universities) have been subject to that requirement since 1974. Subsequent pressure from public employers resulted in the passage by Congress of the Fair Labor Standards Amendments of 1985, exempting state and local government employers from a strict requirement to pay overtime wages for nonexempt employees, effective April 15, 1986. All postsecondary institutions must still comply with the minimum wage requirements of the FLSA, although there are exceptions allowing subminimum wages for certain classes of employees, including full-time students. Independent institutions may also implement a "time-off" plan to avoid paying overtime wages. The regulations implementing this legislation contain very specific criteria governing the interpretation of which positions qualify individuals as exempt employees (29 C.F.R. Part 541). There is also a considerable history regarding what constitutes an "employee" (*Marshall v. Regis Educational Corp.* 1981). Both issues will almost certainly continue to be actively litigated.

Enforcement of the provisions of this legislation generally emanates from the complaint of an individual concerning the behavior of an employer, usually concerning pay or hours worked. If the parties cannot be satisfied by the hearing and appeal procedures provided for administratively under the regulations, there are provisions for resort to the courts. The Supreme Court has agreed that the contract rights of an individual are independent of rights under other legislation, such as Title VII of the Civil Rights Act of 1964 (*Barrentine* v. *Arkansas-Best Freight System, Inc.*, 1981), and that suits may be brought in both instances. Penalties for violation of this statute may include fines, imprisonment, damages, back payments for lost wages, and civil assessments for child labor violations.

While student affairs administrators must heed the provisions of this legislation for those employees who are covered by it, the primary responsibility for its implementation rests with the personnel or business officers at most institutions.

Other Labor Laws

There are a number of federal statutes that affect the functions of the student affairs administrator to a lesser extent than those discussed to this point, since they are most frequently within the line responsibility of the personnel or business officers. Nonetheless, student affairs professionals should be aware of their existence and general requirements.

The Occupational Safety and Health Act (or OSHA, as the Act and its federal administrative agency have come to be known) requires institutions and agencies covered by its provisions to meet specific health and safety standards. Although the federal statute applies only to private higher education, public institutions are usually covered by similar statutes enacted at the state level. Partial state control or support is not sufficient to remove a private institution from OSHA jurisdiction (*University of Pittsburgh*, 1980).

The Secretary of Labor is responsible for developing and promulgating occupational safety and health standards. These standards may cover almost any conceivable topic related to health or safety in the workplace. Cases have included such subjects as smoking in the workplace, the potential health risks to pregnant women who must sit before a cathode-ray tube for prolonged periods, and the more obvious problems of radioactivity, highly toxic chemicals, and falling objects.

OSHA inspections, generally conducted by a compliance officer without advance notice, are the heart of the enforcement mechanism for this legislation. The history of these inspections is complex, particularly as regards the requirement for a warrant, which has been the subject of considerable litigation. The Occupational Safety and Health Review Commission, with quasi-judicial powers and a substantial amount of independence, conducts hearings on alleged violations and imposes penalties. The commission has great latitude in setting penalties. Fines may include $1,000-per-day assessments for certain kinds of activity. The legislation also provides for criminal penalties. Although this statute does not confer a private right of action by an employee against an employer, there is no preemption of the right of individuals to enforce their remedies under state law or common law protections. Violations of OSHA standards have been allowed as evidence in a wide range of litigation. The legislation specifies a broad range of record-keeping and reporting requirements, particularly when an injury has occurred. Employees may also request inspections and may not be discriminated against by an employer when they seek redress under OSHA regulations.

Another labor law, the Labor-Management Relations Act, applies only to private institutions with a significant impact on interstate commerce. Again, public institutions may be subject to similar provisions under applicable state laws. This statute derives from the process of amending the Taft-Hartley Act of 1947, although the two names are often used interchangeably. Its basic provisions prohibit unfair labor practices, establish federal preemption in labor disputes, provide mediation alternatives to collective bargaining in specific instances, and ensure the rights of association and organization for covered employees. The primary enforcement mechanisms are injunctive relief and suits for damages, which may be brought by either employers or employees.

Most higher education cases under this legislation have dealt with the right of faculty members to organize and the jurisdiction of the National Labor Relations Board over such matters, as in *National Labor Relations Board* v. *Wentworth Institute* (1975). The NLRB has asserted jurisdiction over educational institutions on the basis of the nature of their charters and the sources of their funding.

A good discussion of these issues can be found in *University of Vermont and State Agricultural College* (1976).

Labor law, whether codified at the federal or the state level, is an area requiring resort to legal expertise in what may seem to be the simplest of problem situations. Further, the National Labor Relations Board is the federal agency responsible for administering the Labor-Management Relations Act, and it tends toward a "case method" approach to defining coverage of the Act rather than the straightforward regulatory approach followed by most other federal agencies. Given these complications, and the possibility of uncertainty regarding state court jurisdiction in particular cases, reference to counsel by administrators concerned about problems in this area is an absolute necessity.

Copyright

Congress enacted a total revision of United States copyright law in 1976. The General Revision of the Copyright Law (as amended) (17 U.S.C. sec. 101 *et seq.*) has implications for all student affairs administrators. The statute describes what may be copied and under what conditions. The revised law provides "grandfather" protections for materials that were actually published or registered before 1978. The new law applies common rules to unpublished or unregistered works regardless of the date of origination.

The basic protection afforded owners of copyrightable materials is what amounts to absolute domain over most works for a period of the life of the author plus fifty years. Works made for hire, which are generally defined as those produced by an employee, have similar protections but for seventy-five years from date of publication or one hundred years from the date of origination, whichever is the shorter term.

Common law copyright protection is automatic for any original work, but notice must be affixed before publication to avoid loss of ownership rights and the protection of the copyright law. Notice is defined as affixing the word *copyright*, the copyright marking ©, the year of first publication, and the name of the copyright owner in specific locations on the materials. International protection requires additional markings, such as "All rights reserved," depending on the countries involved.

In addition to the local photocopying machine, a speedy means of avoiding the purchase of textual and related materials, the advent of inexpensive methods of transferring visual materials to computer memory creates an almost infinite variety of methods by which to violate copyright law. Another area of growing significance is the copying of computer programs, generally from a purchased master disk to a blank to avoid repurchase. An accompanying infringement is the photocopying of the instruction manual for the same software, since the manuals are rarely sold separately. Even though the publisher (owner) of copyrighted computer programs may not "copy protect" the software, the ownership of that material is still protected by copyright as long as the appropriate notice is affixed and the work incorporates restrictive verbiage. To provide an added level of protection, a pre-printed seal referring to these notices is commonly affixed to the wrapping of computer disks.

To avoid copyright infringement on protected software, administrators should obtain the "multiuser" releases now becoming widely available. These releases allow either unrestricted use on a network or, more generally the case, a specific number of uses before a new fee must be paid to the owner of the protected materials. It should be noted that the copyrighting of computer programs, both the source code and the object (machine-readable) code, has precipitated something just short of a raging debate regarding whether patents are a more suitable form of protection. Since the patent process is more expensive, and almost always an endurance contest, it is understandable that many prefer the generous protections of copyright.

Students and staff alike may find themselves in violation of copyright, though the occasions resulting in litigation or assessment of penalties are rare, primarily because the owner of the copyright is unaware of violations. Courts have indicated that the copying of protected materials may violate the law even though no resale or personal profit motive is involved (*Marcus* v. *Rowley*, 1983). The most frequent issue raised in copyright law as it concerns postsecondary educational institutions is the "fair-use" doctrine.

This doctrine allows the copying of protected materials, including sheet music and recordings, under a variety of conditions, the most salient being for scholarly and research purposes. There are specific restrictions on the number of copies that may be made and the extent to which they may be distributed. In the administrative setting, it is likely that copying of protected materials for any purpose will be considered at least a "technical" violation of the law, but the likelihood of legal action is small if no commercial use is made of the copies. It is sound practice to avoid any violations of copyright law, regardless of the probability of sanctions.

The copying of protected materials for private use, such as that by a student or a staff member, is an area yet to be fully explored; but in *Sony Corp. of America* v. *Universal City Studios, Inc.* (1984), the Supreme Court held that making videocassette copies of television programs for private use does not violate the copyright law. There are also exemptions to some of the provisions of the copyright law for duplicating materials for blind and deaf persons and for teaching and research at nonprofit schools for the deaf and the hearing impaired. "Library copying" is allowed under several circumstances, the most salient being a request for a copy of a portion of a published work in the library's collection. The law requires that no commercial use be made of the copy and that the library prominently display a copyright warning notice near where orders are placed and on any order forms. It goes without saying that the commercial copying of protected materials, even making individual copies for a fee, will generally be considered an infringement.

Penalties for violation of copyright law are invoked as the result of a lawsuit by the owner of the copyright or anyone with a royalty interest in the protected property, after the materials have been registered with the U.S. Copyright Office. Suit must be brought in a federal district court within three years of the infringement, although common law suits may be brought in state courts for pre-1978 violations. A successful suit may result in damages and injunctive relief. Damages may extend from reimbursement for the owner's lost profits to recovery of the profits of the violator. Statutory damages may be elected, ranging from $100 upward to $50,000, depending on the nature of the case. There are criminal penalties for willful violation of the law, including fines and imprisonment.

It is the conventional wisdom of those concerned about copyright that institutions should develop a written policy on copyright, generally modeled after the *Guidelines for Classroom Copying* (United States House of Representatives, 1976), a document now widely in use after it was presented as part of the legislative history of the new copyright law.

Tax Questions

Provisions of the Tax Code of the United States have been interpreted by the Internal Revenue Service to place severe restrictions on the tax-exempt status of a wide range of activities that many institutions routinely conduct. These interpretations apply to both private and public institutions. In general, to avoid complications, institutions should restrict their business constituency to faculty, staff, and enrolled students. Recent trends in revenue rulings indicate that the IRS is increasingly intolerant of activities previously thought to be marginal, particularly in the realm of fund raising and athletics. It is not yet clear what impact the Tax Reform Act of 1986 will have on rulings of interest to institutions, but significant changes are expected.

Given the complexity of these matters, administrators are advised to consult with counsel before undertaking income-generating activities that may ultimately be interpreted as unrelated business income, requiring the filing of a number of federal reports and the possible payment of taxes or, in severe instances, actually jeopardizing the institution's tax-exempt status.

Other questions regarding taxes may relate to whether local real estate or entertainment taxes should be paid by institutions. Since the fact situation and the specific statute will control, this question is difficult to discuss in broad terms. Administrators should, however, be aware of this potential problem and seek advice before developing additional programs and activities where these questions may arise.

Athletics

An area of growing legal significance for student affairs administrators is that of intercollegiate athletics and oversight by the National Collegiate Athletic Association (NCAA). The capacity of the NCAA to regulate certain activities of participating post-secondary institutions rises to the scope of national legislation, albeit nongovernmental. A discussion of the status of NCAA actions can be found in *Arlosoroff* v. *National Collegiate Athletic Association* (1984). The association's constitution, bylaws, regulations, and recommended policies are published in its manual (National Collegiate Athletic Association, 1986). These rules govern a wide range of athletic recruiting and administrative actions. The growth of drug-testing programs for athletes (and other persons) is to some extent fostered by the activities of this association and is bound to be a fertile source of litigation for the foreseeable future (see Chapter Four in this volume). Penalties for violation of the NCAA rules vary with the nature of the infraction but may include termination of the institution's membership in the association and the so-called "death penalty," resulting in the suspension of the right to conduct a sport for up to two years (Enforcement, sec. 7(d)(1)).

State Laws

Many states have enacted legislation dealing with other activities that are typically a part of the institutional work load. Especially important are the laws concerning open records, open meetings (Sunshine Acts), and computer crimes. Since the content of these laws and the extent of state jurisdiction over institutions vary by state, it is essential to refer to counsel or other local sources of information to avoid potential difficulties. As mentioned earlier in this chapter, it may be necessary to reconcile the provisions of state laws with those of overlapping or preemptive federal jurisdiction. The penalties for violating these statutes may be quite severe, including personal liability on the part of the administrator.

Summary

The legal aspects of administration are increasingly complex, requiring more than a passing knowledge of statutory and judicial requirements. The issue is further complicated by the need for an administrator to interpret statutory and judicial findings within the context of his or her own institution. Whether the institution is public or private, statutory or constitutional, residential or commuting can raise significant distinctions and questions regarding the applicability of certain cases and statutes. It is therefore critical that administrators minimize uncertainty, to the extent that anything can for very long be genuinely clear in our system of laws, by obtaining the assistance of a qualified legal adviser. This chapter presented an overview of relevant federal statutes not discussed elsewhere in this volume, but it is only a modest point of departure, suggesting directions for further serious inquiry.

References

American Association of Collegiate Registrars and Admissions Officers. *A Guide to Postsecondary Institutions for Implementation of the Family Educational Rights and Privacy Act of 1974, as Amended.* Washington, D.C.: American Association of Collegiate Registrars and Admissions Officers, 1976.

National Collegiate Athletic Association. *1986–87 Manual of the National Collegiate Athletic Association.* Mission, Kans.: National Collegiate Athletic Association, 1986.

United States House of Representatives. *Guidelines for Classroom Copying.* House Report No. 94-1476, 2d Session. Washington, D.C.: U.S. House of Representatives, 1976.

Shari R. Rhode
Melissa Gasser Math

8

Student Conduct, Discipline, and Control: Understanding Institutional Options and Limits

One of the prime areas of responsibility for student affairs administrators on most college campuses is student discipline. In addition, there is a widely held expectation that control will be exercised over the behavior of students and nonstudents on institutional property. The purpose of this chapter is to provide student affairs administrators with background information in order to develop policies and options for *decision choices*. It is not meant to substitute for specific legal advice. Legal implications vary within each state depending on state and local law. Within the same locale, legal requirements may change because of what may appear to the layman as a slight change of facts. If administrators have any doubts about a specific requirement, they should seek legal advice.

The standards of conduct with which a student must comply are established by university policies, as well as by federal, state, and local law. Laws establish the procedures to be followed to determine whether a particular law has been violated and, if it has, what sanctions may be imposed. University policies should also set forth the procedures to be followed to determine whether these policies have been violated and, if so, what sanctions may be imposed on the violator. As previously indicated, there are differences in what can be done in the area of discipline and control between public and private institutions (see Chapters Three and Four in this volume for a discussion of these questions). This chapter will review the expected parameters of due process that should be provided within the disciplinary system, including both academic and conduct judicial systems. A review of concurrent jurisdiction with civil authorities will be provided. Search and seizure questions, issues related to behavior problems, and policy issues regarding physical and mental illness will also be discussed.

Due Process

Due process claims can be either procedural or substantive. Procedural due process focuses on the fairness and validity of rules and policies. Substantive due process prohibits arbitrary and capricious conduct on the part of university officials by a showing that there was no rational basis for the university's decision or that the decision was motivated by bad faith or ill will unrelated to academic performance (*Schuler* v. *University of Minnesota*, 1986; *Board of Curators of the University of Missouri* v. *Horowitz*, 1978).

Constitutional guarantees of due process apply to public schools but not to purely private schools. However, the constitutional provisions will apply to private institutions' activities that constitute state action—that is, when there is such substantial government involvement in the activities as to make it impossible to distinguish between private and public action. If the activity at the private institution receives a substantial amount of federal funds, is heavily regulated by the government, and is subject to government involvement, the court may find state action to be present. For example, if a private college or university accepts significant financial assistance from the state, the school may be subject to the same constitutional restrictions and liabilities for violation of those restrictions as is a public institution. But state aid alone may not convert the actions of a private institution into state action (see *Rendell-Baker* v. *Kohn*, 1982). Government aid must be directly linked to the challenged action (*Adickes* v. *S. H. Kress & Co.*, 1970). Since there is no clear test to determine whether an activity constitutes state action, administrators at private colleges and universities should discuss with their legal counsel the circumstances that may create a state action finding and the legal obligations such a finding will impose. (See Chapter Four in this volume for a discussion of these issues.)

Protected Interests. The Constitution protects a variety of interests in the educational setting. The two most important for the purposes of this discussion are property and liberty interests. "Property interests . . . are created and their dimensions defined by existing rules and understandings that stem from an independent source such as state law—rules or understandings that secure certain benefits and that support claims of entitlement to those benefits" (*Board of Regents* v. *Roth,* 1972, at 2701). In addition, "agreements implied from the promisor's words and conduct in the light of the surrounding circumstances" may also be independent sources of property interests (*Perry* v. *Sindermann,* 1972, at 2699). To determine whether entitlement exists so as to create a property interest, one must look to state statutes or university policies, procedures, and practices. The expectation should be generally understood; and, in cases based on university policies or procedures, those policies and procedures should be official institutional statements. For example, a student has a protected interest in continuing his studies (*Regents of the University of Michigan* v. *Ewing,* 1985). The basis for constitutionally protected property interests may be found in admissions policies as well as policies concerning academic or disciplinary dismissal.

Liberty interests, though not subject to precise delineation, encompass the right to contract, to acquire useful knowledge, to marry and to raise children, and to pursue an occupation (*Roth*). To forestall the potential serious effects of government actions on identified liberty interests, the Supreme Court held that when a person's "good name, reputation, honor, or integrity is at stake" because of government action, that person is entitled to notice and an opportunity to be heard (*Wisconsin* v. *Constantineau,* 1971, at 510). In institutions of higher education, liberty interests may be involved when a university suspends a student because he has been *charged* with plagiarism but has not been given an opportunity to respond to the charges. Additionally, where the university's decision to refuse enrollment is based on an allegation or belief that the potential student is mentally ill, such decision may impose a stigma on or foreclose opportunities for the student, thereby infringing on protected liberty interests.

Liberty interests have been broadly construed by the courts. A reasonable expectation of continued enrollment free from arbitrary or capricious interruption by a college or university is such an interest. If a student has such an interest, how can one tell whether that student has been or is about to be deprived of it? Unless there is a deprivation of a protected interest, due process never comes into play.

A clear example of deprivation of a student's liberty interest occurred in *Greenhill* v. *Bailey* (1975). Greenhill was dismissed from medical school for unsatisfactory performance. The assistant dean of the medical school completed a Change of Status Form indicating that Greenhill was dismissed "due to Poor Academic Standing and that the apparent reason therefor was 'lack of intellectual ability or insufficient preparation'" (*Greenhill*, at 7). The Change of Status Form was sent to the Liaison Committee on Medical Education of the Association of American Medical Colleges in Washington, D.C. The court found that "the action by the school in denigrating Greenhill's intellectual ability, as distinguished from his performance, deprived him of a significant interest in liberty, for it admittedly 'imposed on him a stigma or other disability that foreclose[s] his freedom to take advantage of other . . . opportunities'" (*Greenhill*, at 8; quoting *Roth*, at 2707). The school transmitted more than the factual information that Greenhill had failed his junior year; it also provided an interpretation of the reason for his failure to other medical schools. Other opportunities for medical education could thus be denied to Greenhill without an opportunity for him to state his version of the record. The court found that "at the very least, Greenhill should have been notified in writing of the alleged deficiency in his intellectual ability, since this reason for his dismissal would potentially stigmatize his future as a medical student elsewhere, and should have been accorded an opportunity to appear personally to contest such allegations" (at 9). The court acknowledged that a graduate or professional school was in the best position to judge the academic performance and ability of its students. At the same time, the court recognized that giving the student opportunity, even on an informal basis, to meet with the administrative person or body dismissing him would not unduly burden the educational process.

Once it is determined that a liberty or property interest is at stake, the next question to be answered is: What process is due to that particular student in the particular setting before the student can lawfully be deprived of the protected interest? The United States Supreme Court has stated that three elements must be examined to determine what process is due: "first, the private interest that will be affected by the official action; second, the risk of an erroneous deprivation of such interest through the procedures used, and the probable value, if any, of additional or substitute procedural safeguards; and finally, the government's interest, including the function involved and the fiscal and administrative burdens that the additional or substitute procedures would entail" (*Mathews* v. *Eldridge,* 1976, at 334). (For a full discussion of this key case on due process, see Golden, 1981–82.)

There is no constitutional right to postsecondary education. Property interests must therefore be based on the legal relationship created between the institution and the student. A contract of enrollment may be the basis of such a legal relationship. The terms of the contract may be defined in several documents, such as an admissions form, the student handbook, established rules and regulations with which the student is expected to comply, or any other documents that specify the rights and obligations of the student and the institution in relation to each other. (See Chapter Five in this volume.)

For private institutions, the courts will look to the contract that exists between the student and the school to determine what process is due. The contract that exists between a public institution and a student may also provide some definition of the process due, but it will not be the sole source of that determination, as it would be with a purely private institution. Is the institution safe from actions if no constitutional deprivation can be established by the student? What about a breach of contract argument? What happens if a student alleges that the university has failed to observe its own grievance procedures? These questions will have particular interest to private institutions, which, in general, are not subject to constitutional due process claims.

Academic Due Process. Guidance can be found for both public and private schools in the recent Supreme Court decision in *Regents of the University of Michigan* v. *Ewing* (1985). Ewing was dismissed from a joint degree program when he failed a national examination with the lowest score recorded in the history of the program. Ewing sought and was denied both readmission to this program and the opportunity to retake the exam. He filed suit in federal court, alleging, in part, that the university's action constituted a breach of contract. The trial court found for the university; however, the decision was reversed by a federal appeals court, and the university then appealed that decision to the U.S. Supreme Court. The Court noted that "Ewing was the only student who, having failed the test, was not permitted to retake it . . . [and] . . . students were 'routinely' given a second chance" (at 510). Additionally, Ewing cited language in university publications, such as "everything possible is done to keep qualified medical students in Medical School. This even extends to taking and passing National Board Exams. Should a student fail either part of the National Boards, an opportunity is provided to make up the failure in a second exam" (at 510). The trial court, however, found no evidence to conclude "that the [university officials] bound themselves either expressly or by course of conduct to give Ewing a second chance" to retake the exam (at 509–510).

The trial court's decision was based, in large part, on a finding that Ewing had not been arbitrarily dismissed and, therefore, that any implied contractual right to continued enrollment free of arbitrary dismissal had not been violated. The appropriate committees made their decisions conscientiously and with careful deliberation, based on Ewing's entire academic record. That record constituted a situation significantly different from that of any other student who had been allowed to retake the exam. In affirming the judgment, the Supreme Court once again demonstrated its reluctance to substitute its judgment for the academic decisions made by faculty in institutions of higher education where such decisions require "an expert evaluation of cumulative information" (*Board of Curators of the University of Missouri* v. *Horowitz*, 1978, at 954–

955). Absent a substantial departure from accepted academic norms, judicial intervention is unlikely.

While no action by a university can eliminate every lawsuit that might be based on an alleged breach of contract, preventive measures can be taken to minimize the likelihood of successful claims. Donin (1986) describes the following preventive measures:

1. Review university publications to ensure accuracy and consistency.
2. If policies are subject to change during the student's course of study, make sure the policy states that fact. Avoid published statements that suggest the rules and regulations in effect at the time of enrollment control throughout the term of study.
3. If general policies may be supplemented by more detailed rules within a division or department of the institution, state that fact. In addition, state that it is the student's responsibility to be apprised of such rules.
4. Include a statement reserving the university's right to terminate any student's affiliation for appropriate reasons. If the reasons are to be stated, consider giving general reasons, such as failure to meet standards of academic progress, and include a caveat that the general reasons given are not all-inclusive.
5. Provide some procedure through which the student is given notice of proposed termination and an opportunity to present his position. Courts have traditionally been hesitant to become involved in oversight of an educational institution's academic decisions. Judicial involvement has been limited because academic dismissals are based on professional academic judgment. Students who allege that decisions were not fundamentally fair have the task of proving that university officials acted in bad faith or in an arbitrary, capricious manner, and that there was no rational basis for the decision (*Board of Curators of the University of Missouri* v. *Horowitz*, 1978; *Schuler* v. *University of Minnesota*, 1986).

Students dismissed for academic reasons are entitled to due process, but the requirements of academic due process generally are satisfied by notice of academic deficiencies, an opportunity for students to correct the deficiencies, and notice of the possibility of sanctions if they fail to do so. A hearing prior to academic dismissal is not required, but some opportunity for students to present their points of view is highly recommended.

One of the earliest cases discussing the tradition of judicial nonintervention in academic decisions is *Connelly* v. *University of Vermont and State Agricultural College* (1965). The plaintiff was a third-year medical student who was dismissed after he failed 25 percent or more of his third-year courses. The student alleged that his dismissal was arbitrary and unjust. The federal district court first noted that the university officials were uniquely qualified to judge whether the student deserved a passing grade, and that decision was left wholly to them. The court then indicated that, if the student could prove that his dismissal was motivated by arbitrariness, capriciousness, or bad faith, the court would order the university to provide the student with an impartial hearing on his dismissal. The court found that, in the absence of a showing of bad faith or arbitrary action, a predismissal hearing was not required.

In the cases decided after *Connelly*, the courts generally adopted the "arbitrary, capricious, or bad-faith" test set out in *Connelly* and did not require a hearing prior to an academic dismissal. For example, the Alabama court in *Mustell* v. *Rose* (1968) refused to order a predismissal hearing for a medical student, noting that even the federal courts did not require a student to be given notice and an opportunity to be present when the dismissal decision is made. In later cases, courts determined that students should receive at least minimal notice, prior to suspension or expulsion, that they are not meeting the required academic standards. In *Gaspar* v. *Bruton* (1975), the court determined that a student who was informed that her performance was deficient and would lead to dismissal if not corrected received all the due process to which she was entitled.

The U.S. Supreme Court did not review an academic due process case until it heard *Board of Curators of the University of Missouri* v. *Horowitz* (1978). Horowitz was a medical student who performed well in her courses but was dismissed from medical school for deficiencies in clinical skills and personal hygiene. The faculty's dissatisfaction was conveyed to the student, along with the

possible sanctions if her deficiences were not corrected. Responding
to the student's allegation that she was entitled to a hearing to rebut
the evidence relied upon for her dismissal, the Court determined
that there was no right to a hearing and that the student had
received at least as much due process as the Constitution required.
The Court reasoned that, because the dismissal was based on the
evaluative academic judgment of university officials, it (the Court)
would not ignore the academic judgment or formalize it by
requiring a hearing. Noting that "courts are particularly ill-
equipped to evaluate academic performance," the Court made it
clear that due process requirements for academic dismissal are
minimal and that courts should not readily interfere with the
academic decision-making process.

   While *Horowitz* established that a student is not entitled to
a hearing prior to an academic dismissal, the Court did not directly
discuss whether notice of deficiencies was required. Since Horowitz
had repeatedly been notified of her deficiencies, the Court concluded that the notice received was adequate. The Court's statement
is not helpful to university officials who want to determine whether
notice is necessary. As a practical matter, nearly every university
provides its students with a description of the school's academic
requirements and a notice of a student's academic deficiencies.
Many provide the opportunity for at least an informal discussion
before ordering an academic dismissal. These practices are highly
recommended. Despite the fact that most of the case law discussed
involves medical students, due process is an issue of concern with
regard to all students, irrespective of their discipline.

   Case law indicates that any existing notice requirements can
be met fairly easily. Prior published notice of a university's
academic requirements and sanctions for failing to meet the
criteria—usually contained in catalogues, bulletins, or admissions
documents—should satisfy nearly every court that establishes a
notice requirement in academic dismissal cases (*Bleicker* v. *Board
of Trustees of the Ohio State University College of Veterinary
Medicine*, 1980). Similarly, if a student receives notice of unsatisfactory academic performance before dismissal, due process requirements will usually be deemed to be satisfied, although—in addition
to notice of deficiencies—an opportunity for students to explain

poor academic performance has been looked upon favorably by some courts (*Stoller* v. *College of Medicine,* 1984).

While the Supreme Court stated in *Horowitz* that academic dismissals need not be accompanied by all of the due process requirements associated with a trial, many of the subsequent state and federal cases indicate that some prior notice of a student's unsatisfactory performance should be given, and some cases have required students to be given an opportunity to be heard, at least informally.

Disciplinary Due Process. The Fifth Circuit Court in *Dixon* v. *Alabama State Board of Education* (1961) determined that, prior to expelling students at a public institution for misconduct, an institution must give the students notice and some opportunity for a hearing. Though not requiring a complete judicial hearing, the Court stated that the students must receive notice of the specific charges; participate in an adversarial type of hearing, with the opportunity to present a defense; and have access to the results and findings of the hearing. In 1975, the Supreme Court extended the applicability of requirements of notice and opportunity for a hearing to public school students who face suspension for less than ten days (*Goss* v. *Lopez,* 1975). Notice should generally consist of a clear statement of the alleged conduct and the rule that the conduct violates. The Court in *Goss* noted that the hearings could be informal and need not provide the students with an opportunity to obtain private counsel, cross-examine witnesses, or present witnesses on their behalf. However, the Court also stated that expulsions and suspensions of ten days or more may require more formal procedures to further protect against unfair deprivations of liberty and property interests.

Notice of charges and a hearing may quickly follow the misconduct, but, in most cases, the hearing must precede the suspension or expulsion. The exceptional case exists when a student presents a continuing danger to persons or to the property of others. In the exceptional case, the student may be removed from school immediately and then provided with a hearing (*Goss*).

Most courts have agreed that students in disciplinary proceedings are not entitled to have their defenses presented by private legal counsel (*Henson* v. *Honor Committee of the Univer-*

sity of Virginia, 1983). However, some courts have required that
private attorneys be allowed to be present at the proceeding to advise
their clients. In *Esteban* v. *Central Missouri State College* (1969), a
federal appeals court held that a student was entitled to have outside
counsel brought in at his expense but that the attorney could only
advise the student, not conduct the defense. Such a procedure—that
is, allowing a student to retain private legal counsel at his own
expense, while restricting the attorney to an advisory role—
minimizes the adversarial nature of the hearing and, at the same
time, gives the student access to counsel. If the university is to be
represented by legal counsel, the student should be allowed the same
privilege. Where the student is charged with a serious disciplinary
violation and is also facing criminal charges for the same offense,
the student is entitled to have a lawyer present at the student's
expense *Gabrilowitz* v. *Newman,* (1978). Again, however, the
attorney may be restricted to the role of adviser, not advocate.

Under disciplinary due process, the student has the right to
have the matter resolved by an impartial fact-finder, either an
administrator or a committee. The committee may be advisory or
may make the actual decision, depending on university policy. The
fact that an administrator may be asked to rule on the disciplinary
recommendation of another administrator in the same institution
does not constitute impartiality in and of itself. The decision maker
should not be the individual bringing the charge, nor should it be
anyone who the student can show has an actual bias in the
situation. Other matters, such as the right to open or closed
hearings and the right to a transcript, are left to institutional choice
but should be addressed in the appropriate policy documents.

Courts have evaluated the adequacy of the due process
provided on a case-by-case basis, in order to preserve the needed
flexibility of the educational institutions while still protecting the
individual student's rights. It is difficult, therefore, to delineate
exact procedures that colleges and universities must follow to satisfy
the notice and hearing requirements of *Dixon* and *Goss.* The more
specific and detailed the notice of dismissal criteria, the less formal
the hearing requirements need to be. In the recent past, universities
have been granted substantial deference in their disposition of
student discipline cases. Courts will examine the procedural aspects

to ensure that the basic due process elements of notice of charges and a hearing are provided, but they will not restructure the disciplinary process used by an educational institution.

University-Created Procedures. When an educational institution has established its own procedures to be applied in academic and disciplinary cases, the law generally requires that the procedures be substantially followed. However, courts have repeatedly held that a university's noncompliance with its own procedures, in and of itself, does not violate an individual's rights if the procedural safeguards afforded the individual met or exceeded the requirements of the Fourteenth Amendment (*Schuler* v. *University of Minnesota,* 1986).

Academic or Disciplinary Sanctions. The categorization of sanctions as disciplinary or academic is a crucial factor in determining the procedural safeguards that must be provided to the student. The distinctions between the two classifications are not always clear cut, however. While cheating is usually considered a disciplinary matter, courts deciding cases involving cheating have not always required the standard of substantial evidence of the violation required in disciplinary cases, because the violation is unique to the academic community (*McDonald* v. *Board of Trustees of the University of Illinois,* 1974). A dismissal for reasons other than poor grades is not necessarily a disciplinary dismissal. A medical student who failed to meet qualifications deemed necessary by the school to become a competent professional was dismissed, and the court noted that grades are not the only measure of student proficiency (*Wong* v. *Regents of the University of California,* 1971). In *Horowitz,* the U.S. Supreme Court suggested that issues requiring evaluative judgment of professionals, rather than resolution of disputed questions of fact, should be considered academic issues. If a student is being dismissed for reasons based on the expert's evaluative determination, that student is not entitled to the greater procedural rights due in disciplinary cases.

Qualified Immunity. Qualified immunity is a legal doctrine that provides state and federal officials, acting reasonably, with the authority to make difficult decisions and to exercise discretion without fear of exposing themselves to monetary liability (see *Wood* v. *Strickland,* 1975). Unless a plaintiff can demonstrate that the administrator's conduct was "unreasonable under the applicable standard," the plaintiff is not entitled to compensation (*Davis* v. *Scherer*, 1984). It is reasonable for an administrator to rely on factual information supplied by others when a prompt decision is required in order to respond to a student's threatened or actual disruption. Qualified immunity will apply even when the decision maker makes no independent investigation of the facts on which he or she relies, where such reliance is reasonable under the circumstances.

Student affairs administrators are often concerned that they will not be upheld by the courts if their decisions involve a procedural error. In general, the courts have upheld administrators when their conduct "does not violate clearly established statutory or constitutional rights of which a reasonable person would have known" (*Harlow* v. *Fitzgerald*, 1982, at 2738). If the quoted language applies, an administrator is probably shielded from damage liability under the doctrine of qualified immunity.

Nonstudents. University administrators are sometimes forced to deal with nonstudents who enter university property and are disruptive or cause damage. The university's inherent power to protect itself from disruptive students by instituting disciplinary action is unfortunately inapplicable to nonstudents. Campus police can escort nonstudents off campus if they are disruptive or are trespassers. To file any civil or criminal charges, university officials must go outside their own disciplinary system and must consult local law enforcement officials.

Criminal and Institutional Charges

Courts have uniformly held that when a student is facing charges both on campus and in criminal court for the same conduct, the university need not stay its disciplinary proceedings until the criminal trial is complete. Double jeopardy protects an individual from being tried twice for the same crime by the same governmental authority, but when a student is disciplined by the university and also prosecuted by the city or state for the same offense, this does not constitute double jeopardy (*Nzuve* v. *Castleton State College*, 1975). Similarly, a university may institute civil charges to recover for damages caused by a student who was disciplined, and this will not constitute double jeopardy. Neither can a student properly claim entitlement to the Fifth Amendment protection against self-incrimination, because that amendment applies only to criminal matters, not to university disciplinary proceedings.

Where a student is charged both criminally and under the student conduct code, a criminal defense attorney often will attempt to have the university's student conduct proceedings delayed or abandoned. The criminal defense attorney will correctly argue that any evidence introduced or statements made during the disciplinary procedure could be used in a pending criminal proceeding. Furthermore, a university proceeding generally has no procedure for allowing the student charged to refuse to testify without penalty or presumption, as would be available under the Fifth Amendment in a criminal case. Additionally, university procedures rarely include methods that may be utilized to exclude evidence obtained in a manner the student believes is unfair or even unconstitutional. The institution therefore has to make a policy decision on whether it will, in serious matters, abandon its internal proceedings in favor of a criminal proceeding. While it is certainly more pleasant to do so, the institution is viewed by many as having an obligation to maintain discipline and decorum within its own institution.

The university could decide to stay its disciplinary proceeding until the criminal matter has been resolved. This decision requires a weighing of the competing interests of the institution's desire to deal with problems in an expeditious manner and its desire not to make the criminal defense any more difficult for the student than otherwise necessary. If the institution determines not to postpone its disciplinary proceeding, the student has to decide whether to participate actively or not. If the student chooses not to participate actively, there is significant potential that he or she will be subject to some disciplinary sanction but will be unable to respond in any significant detail to the accusations. On the other hand, if the institution decides to stay its internal proceedings until the criminal matter has been resolved, there should be a written agreement between the parties that the matter is being stayed at the request of the student to allow for disposition of the pending criminal matter. It is certainly reasonable to include in that agreement a provision that a finding of guilt under the criminal law will automatically constitute a finding of guilt under the student conduct code if the charges arise out of the same set of facts. In contrast, a finding of not guilty by the courts will not be conclusive and may not be relevant to the matter in the discipline procedure. The standard of proof is very different in each proceeding. An individual must be found guilty beyond a reasonable doubt to be convicted of a crime; but an individual need only be found guilty by a preponderance of the evidence in an institutional proceeding unless the institutional procedures require a higher standard of proof.

The university must be careful not to make any presumptions from the fact that a student has been charged with a criminal offense, even if that charge comes in the form of an indictment. The student/criminal defendant is entitled to a presumption of innocence until proven guilty. Unless the university has sufficient information to lead to a reasonable belief that the student is a danger to other students or to the institution itself, the fact that the student has been charged with violating a criminal law, in and of itself, is insufficient for a public institution to take action. In purely private institutions, however, a student may be temporarily or permanently suspended for almost any reason reserved by the school as a sufficient basis in its contractual arrangement with the student. The court in *Aronson* v. *North Park College* (1981) affirmed the required withdrawal of a student from a private institution where the catalogue read, "The institution reserves the right to dismiss at any time a student who in its judgment is undesirable and whose continuation in the school is detrimental to himself or his fellow students. Such dismissals may be made without specific charge."

Search and Seizure

Educational administrators occasionally find it necessary to conduct searches of students, their dormitory rooms, and their personal belongings, to protect campus order and discipline. Searches and seizures are regulated by the Fourth Amendment, which provides: "The right of the people to be secure in their persons, houses, papers, and effects, against unreasonable searches and seizures, shall not be violated, and no warrants shall issue, but upon probable cause, supported by oath or affirmation, and particularly describing the place to be searched, and the persons or things to be seized." Evidence seized during a search that violated the Fourth Amendment is generally inadmissible in criminal trials, and arrests made in contravention to the Fourth Amendment's dictates will not stand.

In *Burdeau* v. *McDowell* (1921), the United States Supreme Court held that these limits apply to governmental action only, so administrators at private institutions are generally not limited by Fourth Amendment restraints. However, if government agents (local, state, or federal law enforcement officers) specifically instigate or participate in a search or seizure, the actions will probably be deemed subject to Fourth Amendment restrictions.

Search Warrants. Searches and seizures conducted pursuant to search warrants that satisfy the requirements of the Fourth Amendment are deemed reasonable. Conversely, as a general rule, warrantless searches are deemed unreasonable unless they come within the parameters of certain judicially created exceptions, which will be discussed below. The courts are not in agreement about whether searches and seizures at educational institutions can be conducted only if there is a showing of full probable cause, as required by the Fourth Amendment, or whether administrators and campus police need only meet a lesser standard of proof and show that there is a reasonable suspicion of illicit activity. In *Moore* v. *Student Affairs Committee of Troy State University* (1968), a federal district court held that full compliance with the Fourth Amendment is not required in a college setting. After receiving word from informers that marijuana might be found in dormitory rooms, two narcotics agents and the dean of men searched Moore's room in his presence but without his consent. The search revealed a small amount of marijuana, and the student was arrested. The court rejected Moore's contention that the seach violated his Fourth Amendment rights. The court stated that an educational institution has a responsibility to protect campus order and discipline; and if its regulations and actions are necessary to fulfill its responsibility, they will be presumed reasonable, even if they infringe somewhat on a student's Fourth Amendment rights. The court determined that the college authorities had a right to search the room, even though the search was based on a suspicion of criminal activities, because they had a reasonable belief that the student was using the room for a purpose that would seriously obstruct campus discipline.

Other courts have determined that administrators are not free to ignore the requirements of the Fourth Amendment and conduct warrantless searches even on a reasonable suspicion. In *Piazzola* v. *Watkins* (1971), the court stated that a regulation about inspection of rooms "cannot be construed or applied so as to give consent to a search for evidence for the primary purpose of criminal prosecution. Otherwise, the regulation itself would constitute an unconstitutional attempt to require a student to waive his protection from unreasonable searches and seizures as a condition to his occupancy of a college dormitory room" (at 289). In determining whether warrantless searches violate students' constitutional rights, courts have examined the expectation of privacy associated with dormitory rooms. One federal court stated that a student's "dormitory room is his house and home for all practical purposes, and he has the same interest in the privacy of his room as any adult has in the privacy of his home, dwelling, or lodging" (*Smyth* v. *Lubbers,* 1975, at 779). However, a state court recently determined that a student who invited others to her room to participate in illegal drug transactions had no reasonable expectation of privacy (*State* v. *Dalton,* 1986). Thus, the expectation of privacy associated with dormitory rooms can be waived by the student, and this waiver may affect the necessity of satisfying all of the Fourth Amendment's requirements.

Since the case law is not entirely clear on the applicability of the Fourth Amendment's mandates to universities, administrators should be cautious about entering student rooms uninvited and without a warrant.

Warrantless Searches. While searches should be conducted pursuant to a warrant in many circumstances, the law does not provide that college authorities must always make a full showing of probable cause before entering a student's room. Certain exceptions to the Fourth Amendment have developed, and many, if not all, of them apply in the college setting.

First, the university and the student are in a landlord-tenant relationship, and it has been established that a landlord may enter the premises for certain limited purposes, such as to make repairs. As a practical matter, the right to enter for such purposes is usually expressly reserved in housing contracts.

Second, university administrators may enter students' rooms in emergency situations to protect health and safety. Entry would be allowed if the building were on fire or if a resident were in distress and in need of emergency treatment. Note, however, that in the emergency situation and in the previously discussed landlord-tenant situation, administrators or their representatives are permitted access to a student's room without a warrant, but only for the limited purpose described. Entry is not allowed for the purpose of making a general search on the basis of suspicion of illegal activity.

A third exception to the Fourth Amendment mandates is known as the "plain view doctrine." Under this doctrine, if a police officer, while in a place where he has a legitimate right to be, inadvertently discovers incriminating evidence in "plain view," the officer may seize the property without first obtaining a warrant. The plain view doctrine was recently held to apply to universities in *Washington* v. *Chrisman* (1982). In *Chrisman,* a campus police officer who was questioning a student was waiting in the doorway of a dormitory room for the student to return with his identification. While waiting, the officer observed contraband belonging to the student's roommate on a desk in the room. The officer entered, seized the contraband, and arrested the roommate to whom it belonged. The Supreme Court upheld the roommate's conviction, stating that the officer had a legitimate, though unrelated, reason to be where he was and the evidence was in his plain view, so no constitutional violation occurred.

Finally, a student may consent to a dormitory room search and alleviate the need for a warrant. Courts carefully examine the circumstances, however, to ensure that the student's consent was voluntarily given—because, in these circumstances, the interaction between the student and the administrator may be confrontive and not lend itself to a truly voluntary giving of consent. Before searching a student's room on the basis of consent, the university official must inform the student of his legal rights and thereafter must not use force or coercion to obtain consent. *People* v. *Whalen* (1982) provides a classic example of coerced consent. At approximately 4 o'clock on a Sunday morning, a student in a dormitory who was suspected of perpetrating a theft was escorted to his room by campus police. After waking the suspect's roommate, the police told both students that, unless they consented to a room search, their room would be "sealed" until a search warrant could be obtained. Both students consented, but the court determined that their consent was not voluntarily given, considering the circumstances. The police had no authority to "seal" the room, and a warrant could not be obtained until Monday at the earliest; so the suspect and his roommate would be without accommodations unless consent was given for a search. Consent after being told "Consent or get out!" is not voluntary.

A suspect's roommate may give consent to a search of the premises in some circumstances, even if the suspect would not have done so. In *State* v. *Radcliffe* (1986), the court held that a roommate in a trailer could give consent to a search of jointly owned areas where the suspect had no reasonable expectation of privacy. Considering the space limitations of a dormitory room, at most a small portion of the room might be considered "jointly owned"; so campus officials should avoid searching an entire dormitory room without consent from all roommates.

Housing contracts and regulations may be drafted to authorize university officials to enter student rooms, and students may consent to these searches by signing the contract. These regulations may only provide for consent to searches reasonably necessary to further the university's responsibility to provide an educational atmosphere, and they must specify the purposes for which such a search is permitted. A university should not draft regulations so as to give consent for broad, general searches or searches for evidence of criminal violations, since it is likely that such searches would violate the Fourth Amendment.

Handicapped Students and Discipline

Just as it is important to consider whether a student problem is an academic or a nonacademic problem, it is important to determine whether behavioral problems are in fact the result of acting out or whether they result from a physical or mental condition that may be classified as a handicap under Section 504 of the Rehabilitation Act of 1973 and comparable state laws. (See Chapter Six in this volume for a full discussion of Section 504.)

One of the difficulties in determining whether a student is a qualified handicapped student is that "handicapped" is often a self-identified status. It is obvious that an individual in a wheelchair is handicapped under the law; but many other conditions that are not easily visible also qualify as handicaps and therefore are subject to special consideration under Section 504. A student with epilepsy or another disease may, without medication, behave in a manner that appears to be disruptive and violative of a student conduct code. When administrators are faced with behavioral acting out on the part of the student, they should be sensitive to the possibility that the student might be handicapped. If the student does not explain that he has a medical or psychiatric problem, the administrator might consider whether the situation warrants asking the student specifically whether he is acting under some physical or mental handicap. Substance abuse is a very real problem in postsecondary education, and at times drug addiction and alcoholism may constitute physical or mental impairment. However, the mere fact that a student is handicapped does not mean that the student cannot be removed or excluded from a program in which he or she receives federal financial assistance, because the handicapped student must be qualified in order to participate. As the Secretary of Health and Human Services has stated:

> [I]t cannot be emphasized too strongly that the statute and the regulation apply only to discrimination against qualified handicapped persons solely by reason of their handicap. The fact that drug addiction and alcoholism may be handicaps does not mean that these conditions must be ignored in determining whether an individual is qualified for services or employment opportunities. On the contrary, a recipient may hold a drug addict or alcoholic to the same standard of performance and behavior to which it

holds others, even if any unsatisfactory performance
or behavior is related to the person's drug addiction or
alcoholism. In other words, while an alcoholic or
drug addict may not be denied services or disqualified
from employment solely because of his or her condition, the behavioral manifestations of the condition
may be taken into account in determining whether he
or she is qualified [34 C.F.R. Part 104, Appendix, at
303].

Instead of utilizing the traditional disciplinary process for
students who demonstrate behavioral problems, administrators may
be tempted to mandate an involuntary withdrawal for medical
reasons. On the surface, this might seem a more expeditious and less
offensive way to remove an unruly student. However, a determination as a matter of public record that a student has been removed
for medical reasons—or, more important, for psychiatric reasons—
may impose a stigma on the student. The resulting stigma would
entitle the student in the public setting to constitutionally required
due process.

When a constitutionally protected interest is involved, due
process has as its operative principle that a student should not be
removed for failure to meet institutional standards that do not state
with precision what is or is not acceptable. The language of
applicable regulations should be sufficiently specific so as to
prevent multiple interpretations by various administrators and not
lead to arbitrary interpretation or discriminatory application.

In *Board of Curators of the University of Missouri* v.
Horowitz (1978), the U.S. Supreme Court gave significant discretion
to academic determinations and evaluations made by public
administrators. The courts generally will intervene only when there
is clear error of judgment, such as a decision made before the facts
have been gathered or a decision that bears no relationship to an
exercise of professional judgment and is fundamentally unfair.

If a public institution intends to utilize involuntary withdrawal, including medical/psychiatric withdrawal procedures, the
student should be provided with a hearing prior to the withdrawal;
or, if the student is considered a danger to the institution or to other

students, the hearing should take place very shortly after the recommended dismissal. Where a predeprivation hearing is to be provided to a student, administrators should consider allowing the student to obtain an independent medical or psychiatric assessment. There is certainly a significant chance that the student will have a protected liberty and/or property interest in continued enrollment and freedom from the stigma that may attach to the result of an involuntary medical or psychiatric withdrawal based on a finding of an emotional or mental illness (*Wisconsin* v. *Constantineau,* 1971; *Board of Regents* v. *Roth,* 1972).

In *Lombard* v. *Board of Education of the City of New York* (1974), John Lombard, a teacher in a public school system, was terminated on the basis of, among other things, an accusation that his conversations were illogical and disoriented, evidencing unfitness for duty. Because Lombard was a probationary employee, he had no property right in his position. He did, however, have a liberty interest in a reputation as a person who was presumably free from mental disorder. Because Lombard was not given a right to confront witnesses before the termination of his probationary employment on the basis of mental disorder and unfitness for duty, his constitutional rights of due process under the Fourteenth Amendment were violated. "A charge of mental illness, proportedly supported by a finding of an administrative body, is a heavy burden for a young person to carry through life. A serious constitutional question arises if he has had no opportunity to meet the challenge by confrontation" (*Lombard,* at 637–638).

Even a public institution subject to constitutional requirements of due process need not develop internal procedures that mimic the adversarial criminal justice system when dealing with such problems. Drafting complex procedures may simply exacerbate an already difficult situation. The institution should develop a simple set of procedures that meet the minimum elements required by the court, such as notice, opportunity to respond, and the right to a decision based on the facts. Administrators should make sure that the system provides for basic fairness and that the established procedures are followed. Additional unnecessary problems are created when an institution unwillingly or inadvertently fails to follow its own procedures.

When disciplinary problems appear to be based on behavioral problems, one alternative is to require counseling as a sanction. Many mental health professionals oppose counseling as a sanction because they believe that counseling must be voluntary if it is to be useful and helpful. Careful decisions must be made in the use of this alternative to traditional discipline, in order to preserve the effectiveness of the counseling function on campus. It also has limitations that must be respected. The student and the counselor will engage in a privileged relationship. The institution has no right to the information about what goes on in the counseling sessions. It is not unreasonable to require the student to give the counselor permission to acknowledge that the student attended the session, but it is an invasion of privacy for the institution to attempt to destroy the confidential nature of the relationship in order to gain information regarding the topics discussed at the session. The advantage of a counseling sanction, however, is that it may take care of the behavioral problem. Whether the counseling sessions address the cause of the difficulties suffered by the student or merely the acting-out symptoms, it is the behavioral problem with which the institution must be concerned in this setting.

If whatever sanctions are imposed fail to resolve the student's disciplinary problems, a more severe sanction of suspension or dismissal may be in order. If the university determines that it has no alternative but to dismiss the student, and the student sues the institution, the court will look favorably on the efforts made by the institution to deal with the problems in a way short of depriving the individual of the privilege of continuing in the educational institution.

If the acting out is not merely a behavioral problem but the symptom of a mental or physical handicap, the institution is not without a remedy. Section 504 does not necessarily mandate different procedures. It does require more carefully reasoned decisions. It is much more difficult to deal with the cause of a problem than it is to deal with the symptoms that manifest themselves because of the problems. Some of the determinations of how to handle what may appear to be disciplinary but are actually handicap problems will depend on the institution's philosophy.

Section 504 still provides for deference to professional decision makers in the academic arena, but the laws provide protection for qualified handicapped students. The term *qualified* means that, with reasonable accommodations, those students must still meet the established academic expectations in order to reap the benefits of attending the institution. It is imperative that individuals with handicaps be treated on an individual basis. Generic assumptions about handicapped individuals and their qualifications will expose institutions to liability for handicap discrimination.

Potential Liability Issues

AIDS. The most difficult handicap to accommodate today is acquired immune deficiency syndrome (AIDS). Research is relatively new, and information is being gathered every day. Medical science has no cures or ways to prevent the illness, and the best approach today is public awareness of the facts that are known and precautions that can be taken to reduce the likelihood of acquiring or transmitting the disease.

The best medical information is that AIDS is not spread through casual contact. AIDS is transmitted through an exchange of body fluids, such as through intimate sexual contact, sharing of intravenous needles, or transfusion of blood products. Because of the high mortality rate, the social stigma associated with the largest-known classes of AIDS victims (homosexual men and drug users), and the lack of public education about the disease, the risk of reaction rather than action increases potential legal risks for the college or university.

Institutions must balance their obligations to protect members of the university community and the public from reasonably foreseeable dangers while they protect the individual student's rights to privacy. In addition, the institution that is subject to Section 504 is obligated to make reasonable accommodations for students with AIDS or AIDS-related complex (ARC) if they are otherwise qualified. To best safeguard all concerned parties, an institution should have a well-publicized program of public education, constantly updated to reflect the most recent research developments. As with all other handicaps, AIDS cases must be evaluated and accommodated on an individual basis.

The institution in which an AIDS victim is enrolled may also be liable to third parties for negligence. The institution must balance the privacy rights of the individual with AIDS against the responsibility or duty, if any, that the institution has to other individuals who may come in contact with the individual with AIDS. Since current medical information indicates that AIDS is not spread through casual contact, it is unlikely that the institution owes any duty to third parties because of their casual contact with an individual with AIDS. The potential for liability may change, however, if the university fails to advise an individual in a special relationship to the AIDS victim of the existence of the disease (since the special relationship may create a duty where none previously existed). Special relationships may exist with respect to roommates or teammates or opponents in contact sports where there is a significant potential for bleeding injuries to occur. The special relationship problem with roommates may be avoided by giving the AIDS student a private room.

If the institution is aware that a student has AIDS, regular monitoring of the student's condition might well be advised, to ensure that necessary precautions are taken. Provisions for isolation must be available when medically needed for a student who, because of the immunity deficiency, contracts a disease that may be easily transmitted to a third party.

Whatever medical information the institution has about a specific student's condition should be held within the strictest confidence that is reasonable under the circumstances. The student has a right not to be labeled as an AIDS victim by the institution itself; but because others may need to be informed of the fact that a student has AIDS, though not of the specific medical details, confidentiality may be somewhat infringed upon. Medical personnel should be apprised of the situation, and possibly housing authorities if the student lives on campus. The stigma that may attach to the student's status as an AIDS victim if publicized must be weighed against the institution's potential liability if other students are adversely affected because they have not been warned. In *Tarasoff* v. *Regents of the University of California* (1976), liability was imposed for failure to warn the potential victim of threats made against her life. However, in *Bradshaw* v. *Rawlings* (1979), the court held that duties must be realistic in order to impose them. The court held in part that "[t]he college, on the other hand, has an interest in the nature of its relationship with its adult students as well as an interest in avoiding responsibility that it is incapable of performing" (at 140). Steinbach (1986) has prepared a helpful summary for college administrators on this subject, which includes statements from James O. Mas, Acting Secretary for Health, and a statement from the United States Public Health Service. Determination on a case-by-case basis is important when one is dealing with AIDS. If exclusion is even considered, the student affairs administrator should obtain both legal and medical advice prior to making such a decision.

Mental Disorders. Potential exposure to liability also exists when the institution provides help for psychologically disturbed students. In *Tarasoff,* a therapist employed by the university was found liable in a wrongful death action brought by the parents of a student who was brutally murdered by one of the therapist's clients. The basis of the therapist's liability was his failure to warn either the young woman or the authorities that a psychotic patient of his had expressed the intent to kill her. The court specifically found that there was a special relationship between the therapist and the patient and that the therapist had knowledge that the patient was dangerous and that the plaintiff was a foreseeable victim. The court, therefore, found that the therapist owed a duty of care to the woman who was murdered and that he failed to take any reasonable steps to discharge that duty of care.

The reasoning in *Tarasoff* puts the institutional psychologist or therapist in a very difficult situation. Without the confidential nature of the client-therapist relationship, many patients would never seek the assistance of a therapist. While *Tarasoff* is controlling in California, not all courts have been as willing to find that the therapist owes an independent duty to third parties, such a finding being prerequisite to the determination of liability if a patient harms a third party. No single piece of legal advice can be given. The ethical constraints of the therapist will ultimately control what he or she does in a professional relationship. If the college or university has a counseling center or a therapist available for the students, administrators should ask the university's legal counsel what legal constraints exist in their state and how to best deal with them given the objectives of the institution.

Summary

The law in its many forms influences what may be done on college campuses in the areas of conduct, discipline, and control. Both federal constitutional issues and statutes may influence policy formation and implementation. Student affairs administrators do, however, have policy and decision choices within the parameters of the law. Due process issues must be considered when either academic or disciplinary sanctions are to be invoked. Special and careful consideration should be given to policy formation involving any category of handicapped students. Mental and psychiatric disorders affecting behavior can be confronted in ways that protect the rights of both the student and the institution. The current concern about AIDS raises special legal questions, which must be resolved in the context of the law and the campus. Finally, search and seizure procedures must be developed to balance the competing rights of individual privacy and institutional responsibilities.

References

Donin, R. B. *"Regents of University of Michigan* v. *Ewing:* The Private University Perspective."* Paper presented at the Twenty-Sixth Annual Conference of the National Association of College and University Attorneys, San Francisco, June 23, 1986.

Golden, E. J. "College Student Dismissals and the *Eldridge* Factors: What Process Is Due?" *Journal of College and University Law,* 1981-82, *8*, 496-504.

Steinbach, S. E. "AIDS on Campus: Emerging Issues for College and University Administrators." *College Law Digest,* 1986, *16,* 113-128.

9

Margaret J. Barr

🌿   🌿   🌿

Institutional Liability: What Are the Risks and Obligations of Student Services?

Many factors have contributed to the growing concern by student affairs administrators regarding liability. Among these are the increasingly litigious nature of our society, the growing national concern for consumer protection, the increased cost of insurance, and the increasing number of contractual disputes. Prevention of and defense against liability claims within institutions of higher education are complex and difficult. In the typical business setting, reduction of liability hazards has been rather straightforward. Counsel is sought, policies and practices are reviewed, potentially harmful policies and practices are modified, assignment of responsibility is made, and insurance is purchased to cover unforeseen circumstances. Today, however, even business organizations are having difficulty in obtaining appropriate insurance coverage at a reasonable cost. In higher education, the issues are even more complex.

First, many policies and procedures have evolved through tradition, and there is great variability within the institution regarding application and enforcement. Second, decision-making and enforcement power is often diffuse, and change comes slowly. Third, in many institutions, authority is not clearly defined;

therefore, responsibility is difficult to pinpoint. Fourth, many institutions operate under the incorrect assumption that they are protected from strict legalistic interpretations of their actions. Finally, administrators have not been aware or informed of the legal implications of their actions or inactions. Given the ambiguity in the environment, it is understandable that a student affairs professional can be confused about liability questions.

Aiken (1976) identifies several major sources of liability claims: bodily injury and property damage, civil rights claims, the changing status of sovereign immunity, the status of a good-faith defense for actions by administrators, and contractual disputes with students and employees. The most common form of liability action falls under the doctrine of torts. "A tort is broadly defined as a civil wrong, other than a breach of contract, for which the courts will allow a damage remedy" (Kaplin, 1985, p. 55). Tort actions may be either a direct invasion of some legal right of the individual or the infraction of a public duty or obligation to the individual. The most common form of tort liability faced by administrators is that of negligence.

Negligence

Legally, there are three elements in a negligence claim: (1) that the defendant owed a duty of care to the claimant; (2) that the defendant breached that duty; and (3) that the breach of duty was the proximate cause of the injury. The key to determining negligence rests on the legal relationship existing between the individual claiming negligence and the institution. Is there a duty of care, and was that duty breached in some way? The answer may depend on the status of the claimant. There are three legal definitions of the status of the claimant in negligence suits: invitee, licensee, or trespasser.

When an individual is invited to the campus, either directly or indirectly, the courts have held that the institution owes that individual the duty of ordinary and reasonable care with respect to the conditions of the premises (*Brown* v. *Oakland*, 1942; *Leahey* v. *State*, 1944; *Sandoval* v. *Board of Regents of New Mexico State University*, 1965). The Second Circuit found that, in order to impose liability for injury caused to an invitee to the premises, the dangerous condition that caused the injury must have been known by the institution (*Mortiboys* v. *St. Michael's College*, 1973). Ordinary hazards, such as ice and snow, are not, in and of themselves, a cause for liability to attach.

A licensee is on the property for his or her own convenience but at the sufferance of the owner of the property (Flora, 1970). The institution owes a licensee the duty of maintaining the property in a reasonably safe condition; however, if ordinary hazards, such as ice and snow, exist and the licensee has been injured, the university has not been held liable.

A trespasser enters on the property at his or her own risk and without permission of the owners. Under these conditions, a college or university may have diminished legal responsibility to an individual seeking damages under a claim of negligence. Students and invited guests to the campus, thus, have a stronger legal claim in negligence cases.

Sexual Assault. A number of cases involving sexual assault and rape have been litigated where students or their agents have claimed negligence on the part of a college or university. In North Carolina, a cheerleader was abducted from the campus and was raped and murdered. Her family brought suit, claiming that the institution had a special duty of care which was violated. The court held that the injury was not foreseeable, that there was no evidence of repeated criminal activity, and that adequate security was in place. The institution was not held liable (*Brown* v. *North Carolina Wesleyan College, Inc.*, 1983). Negligence was found in *Peterson* v. *San Francisco Community College District* (1984). The court held that a special relationship or duty existed when a female student was assaulted by a man hiding in the foliage near a parking lot, that a college has a duty to warn students of known dangers posed by criminals on campus, and that the college's failure to warn students and cut down the bushes was part of the cause of the attack. In New York, when a student was raped in her campus residence hall, the court held that there was a special duty arising from the landlord-tenant relationship. Further, the failure of the university to lock the outer doors of the residence hall was a contributing factor in the rape (*Miller* v. *State of New York*, 1984), and negligence was found.

The highest court in Massachusetts upheld a jury verdict against Pine Manor College and its vice-president for operations, awarding damages to a female student raped on campus by an unidentified assailant (*Mullins* v. *Pine Manor College,* 1983). The student was not required to show evidence of prior criminal acts on campus in order to hold the college liable.

Other Injuries. The University of California, Santa Barbara, was not held liable for attacks on two men using the college beach at night (*Hayes* v. *State,* 1974). The court held, in part, that a warning was not necessary, since "the public is aware of the incidence of violent crime in unlit and little used places" (at 857). In Tennessee, when a student was injured in the fall of an elevator, the court held that an executive committee consisting of institutional officers of the university was personally liable for the injuries because they knew of the dangerous condition and failed to correct it (*Gambet* v. *Vanderbilt University,* 1918). In a New York case, *Scully* v. *State* (1953), a woman was injured in a fall on a stairway at a movie on campus, and the university was not held liable. No defect in the stairway was either claimed or proven in *Scully.* At a private university in Texas, the Court of Civil Appeals held that "the mere fact that plaintiff fell on the steps did not establish negligence on the part of the defendants" (*Yost* v. *Texas Christian University,* 1962, at 363). If, however, the institution knew of a dangerous condition and yet still allowed persons to use the property and injury resulted, then liability could ensue.

If a person assumed the risk of the injury that occurred, then liability claims against institutions or their agents have not been upheld in most courts (*Rubtchinsky* v. *State University of New York at Albany,* 1965; *Dudley* v. *William Penn College,* 1974). The legal status of an injured party can also make a significant difference in tort liability claims. In *Lumbard* v. *Fireman's Fund Insurance Co.* (1974), a student at Southern University was injured when she slipped on a floor while on her way to class. Using the standard of reasonable care to determine the responsibility of the institution for the injury, the court held that as a student or invitee she could expect such care. In *Mintz* v. *State* (1975), the State University of New York at New Paltz was not found to be liable when two students drowned on a canoe trip sponsored by a student organization. Weather conditions rather than any action or inaction on the part of the institution were cited as the cause of the death, and liability did not attach.

Failure to correct a known hazard or failure to make a correct decision about a potential hazard also has potential for liability findings for administrators and institutions. Hazards that are unknown to administrators today may, in the future, result in liability. Such potential liability may be reduced if institutional authorities attempt to deal with issues such as safety, security, drugs, and alcohol before any problems develop in the area. Good, sound educational efforts in areas of great risk can be the strongest defense an institution has in avoiding liability claims.

Summary. In cases of negligence, the courts have required three elements to be present: duty to the plaintiff, breach of that duty, and breach of duty shown as the proximate cause of the injury. The institution does not have an obligation to warn of possible dangers unless a special relationship exists with the injured party. Students and other invitees to the premises have been seen by the courts as having that special relationship causing duty on the part of the institution. If the courts determine that duty is involved, the second question revolves on whether that duty was breached. If an institution has attempted to provide security and good maintenance and has procedures to warn of possible dangers, the courts are less likely to find that the duty of the institution was breached. Of course, there must be a finding that the plaintiff was damaged for liability to attach. Finally, the breach of duty must be shown as the proximate cause of the damage; that is, there must be a relationship between the action or inaction on the part of the institution and the damages.

Alcohol Liability: A Special Case

Steinbach (1985) lists four roles of institutions regarding alcohol: as a supervisor of student conduct, as a property owner, as a seller of alcohol, and as a social host. Each role brings special questions of liability. Buchanan and Oliaro (1986) indicate that the greatest risks arise from several sources. First, if a custodial relationship is established between a student and an institution and the student is injured in an alcohol-related incident, liability may attach. Second, if institutional personnel serve a minor, the institution may be held liable. Third, if a student is involved in a drunk-driving incident after consuming alcohol on institutional premises or at an institutional function, liability may attach. Further, they indicate that either criminal or civil liability may attach under any of the three circumstances. They outline other criminal law applications as follows (p. 50):

1. Group liability: A student group votes to perform a criminal act, such as selling liquor without a license.
2. "Constructive" liability: A student group takes no vote but has a past pattern of illegal conduct that is continued, such as getting eighteen-year-old pledges drunk.
3. Accessory liability: A student group or an institution provides a facility or resources for unlawful behavior.

Clearly, the area of liability associated with alcohol is complex and reflects changing law and societal attitudes in this area.

Student Conduct. Bradshaw v. *Rawlings* (1979) is often cited as a leading case regarding potential alcohol liability. In *Bradshaw,* a student was severely injured returning from a class picnic while in a car with an intoxicated driver. Class funds supported the picnic, the adviser aided in planning the event, and publicity was allowed on campus. Over one million dollars in damages were awarded by a jury in trial court against the institution. On appeal, the appellate court reversed, holding that the college had no legal duty that could keep an individual from getting into a car with an intoxicated person and placing himself at risk. A California court also ruled in favor of the college in *Baldwin* v. *Zoradi* (1981) when, after illegal drinking occurred in a college residence hall, a student was injured by another student in an off-campus drag race. In part, the court found no cause to believe that the college was responsible for the drag race after the illegal drinking occurred.

Property Owner. Steinbach (1985, p. 34) states that "the university is not an insurer of the safety of those who come onto the campus; it cannot be held responsible simply because a student injures himself or another on school property. But a college or university may be held liable if it fails to remedy a foreseeable state of affairs of which it is aware or should be aware." An Oregon court found a fraternity liable for injuries caused by an intoxicated driver returning from a fraternity-sponsored party (*Wiener* v. *Gamma Phi Chapter of Alpha Tau Omega*, 1971). State law varies widely and is extremely important in this area. In Nevada, for example, the fraternity was not held to be liable under similar circumstances (*Bell* v. *Alpha Tau Omega Fraternity*, 1982). In *Zavala* v. *Regents of the University of California* (1981), residence hall staff served alcohol to an intoxicated person, and he subsequently fell and was injured. Although he played a part in his own injury, the institution was held to be partially liable under California law.

In *Whitlock* v. *University of Denver* (1987), a student was injured jumping on a trampoline while suffering from a hangover. The trampoline was located in the front yard of a recognized fraternity renting premises from the university. As part of the lease, the fraternity agreed to nominal supervision from the university. Trampolines owned by the university were closely supervised, but fraternity trampolines were not. "Liability was imposed against the university because of its negligent failure to ban the use of unsupervised trampolines" (Roth, 1986, p. 53), although the liability award was reduced by the court because of the student's own negligence. The Colorado Supreme Court reversed the judgment, declaring, in part, that the university held no duty of care to Whitlock.

Selling Alcohol. Many colleges and universities have established pubs or other areas where alcohol is sold. These facilities pose special liability concerns. "Liability in connection with the commercial sales of alcoholic beverages has been imposed by statute and/or case law in thirty-nine states and the District of Columbia" (Roth, 1986, p. 50). The scope of individual state laws varies considerably, and the criminal and civil liabilities that may attach under the law also vary. Nonetheless, the sale of alcohol is clearly a high-risk situation for colleges and universities. Negligence liability often is based "on the failure to conduct an activity as a reasonably prudent person would under similar circumstances" (Roth, 1986, p. 49). Issues of determining what a prudent person would do, how to determine whether a person is intoxicated, and what results may come from failure to act are difficult to resolve but are a part of standard legal procedure.

Potential liability connected with the sale of alcoholic beverages also extends to student organizations. Off-campus parties and events where alcohol sales are a part of the event raise special liability questions. Again, state law will exhibit great variability. Some states will require a temporary seller's license and insurance for such events. Others will not. Even when dram shop laws and insurance requirements are in place, caution should be exercised. Many insurance policies held by student organizations exclude coverage for events where alcohol is involved or severely limit the amount of coverage provided. Insurance is no guarantee that risk will be reduced. In any case, liability for injury associated with alcohol sold at the event may result.

Social Host. Attachment of liability to a social host is a relatively new development in alcohol law. "A university is likely to be a social host where it, its agents, or employees actually serve alcoholic beverages such as at an official reception or ceremony" (Steinbach, 1985, p. 36). Roth (1986, p. 50) indicates that social host liability is being imposed by courts in Colorado, Georgia, Indiana, Iowa, Louisiana, Michigan, New Jersey, Pennsylvania, Washington, and Wisconsin. Specific statutes in Alabama, Oregon, and New Mexico also authorize social host liability under some conditions. In other states, legislation has been introduced to bring social host liability into law. Social host liability is a rapidly changing area of the law. It would be prudent for institutions to monitor this area and develop policies to respond to it.

Summary. Alcohol-related liability is clearly an appropriate area of concern for student affairs administrators. It is becoming an increasing concern in society and thus will be felt on the campus. Policies should recognize all applicable laws, be consistent and fair, and clearly state that inappropriate behavior related to alcohol will result in disciplinary measures. Further, the institution must respond quickly to disturbances related to alcohol and take preventive measures to stop recurrence. Obviously, the special case of alcohol deserves careful attention and action.

Defamation and Libel

Tort liability claims for defamation and libelous activities raise complex legal questions. Liability claims regarding defamation and the publishing of libelous material are of particular concern to student affairs administrators in two areas: staff supervision and student publications.

Defamation claims arise when "oral or written publication of material tends to injure a person's reputation" (Kaplin, 1985, p. 61). For defamation to occur, the material must have been published or made public by a third person and must have been capable of injuring the claimant's reputation. Several key cases have been brought by faculty members alleging defamation by their supervisors in evaluating their performance. In *Greenya* v. *George Washington University* (1975), the court held that "educational officers and faculty members enjoy a qualified privilege to discuss the qualifications and character of fellow officers and faculty members if the matter communicated is pertinent to the functioning of the educational institution" (*Greenya*, at 563). In order to prove defamation, the court held, a plaintiff must prove that the material was handled outside of normal channels or that the normal manner of publication resulted in an unreasonable degree of publication or that malicious intent was involved.

The strongest defense against a claim of defamation is that the published information was true. For public institutions, a further defense against defamation claims has also been upheld by the courts. Under circumstances when a defendant publishes defamatory material in the performance of official duties, the court held that such material may be published (*Shearer* v. *Lambert*, 1976). A third defense against defamation also arises if the complaining individual is a "public figure." Under the First Amendment, "public figures" cannot claim defamation because such alleged defamation may be considered protected speech. When such a defense is made, a court must determine whether the individual is indeed a public figure (*Avins* v. *White*, 1980). If a person is a public figure, then the institution or another person will not be held liable unless the comment was knowingly false or made "in reckless disregard of whether it was true or false" (*Garrison* v. *Louisiana,* 1964, at 74).

For student publications, the issue is even more complex because of First Amendment protections governing a free press. (Chapter Sixteen in this volume provides a full discussion of this matter.) Common law and constitutional law doctrines indicate that it is not enough for the statement to be false or misleading. In addition, nominal injury must be caused, and the libelous material must be attributable to some fault by the organization or individual who published it. When a public figure is involved, a higher standard is required to attach liability. Policy issues in this area are complex, and decisions must be made regarding the relationship of the institution to the student publication to limit institutional liability (*Mazart* v. *State,* 1981).

Civil Rights Liability

Potential liability for civil rights claims exists with both institutional employees and students. Section 1983 of the Civil Rights Act provides:

> Every person who, under color of any statute, ordi-
> nance, regulation, custom, or usage of any State or
> Territory or the District of Columbia subjects, or
> causes to be subjected, any citizen of the United States
> or other person within the jurisdiction thereof to the
> deprivation of any rights, privileges, or immunities
> secured by the Constitution and laws, shall be liable
> to the party injured in an action at law, suit in equity,
> or other proper proceeding for redress [42 U.S.C. sec.
> 1983].

This liability area is not limited to public institutions; private institutions may fall under the law if they receive federal financial assistance. The definition of federal financial assistance is still not clear, but case law is providing new insights. *Grove City College* v. *Bell* (1984) is a leading case in describing what constitutes federal financial assistance to private institutions and thus makes them accountable under federal law. In *Grove City,* the college received no direct federal or state financial assistance, but students did in the form of grants under the Basic Educational Opportunity Grant program. The United States Supreme Court ruled that student aid constitutes aid to the college and that aid can be withdrawn if the college does not comply with applicable federal regulations. However, in *Grove City,* the court limited the definition of a program or activity to the school's financial aid program and did not extend the definition to include the entire institution. (See Chapters Six and Seven in this volume for a full discussion of these issues.) Conceivably, under the definition, parts of an institution would not be subject to antidiscrimination law. Clearly, this area of case law will need to be monitored in the future. As of this writing, legislation has been introduced to amend the statute to broaden the interpretation of what constitutes a program or activity. Prudent institutions, public and private, should therefore attempt to be in full compliance with all applicable statutes.

The *Wood* v. *Strickland* (1975) decision has been viewed by many as a landmark case in the area of personal liability under the Civil Rights Act for school administrators. Although it is a secondary school case, it has broad implications for higher education administrators. In *Wood,* suit was brought under Section 1983 when students were expelled on the grounds of violating a school regulation prohibiting the use of intoxicating beverages at school activities. The students claimed that their federal rights of due process were violated. A federal district court had directed verdicts in favor of the school board members on the grounds that "the petitioners were immune from damage suits absent proof of malice in the sense of ill will toward the respondents" (*Wood,* at 995). On appeal, the United States Court of Appeals for the Eighth Circuit reversed the decision, finding a violation of the students' rights to substantive due process. A petition for rehearing *en banc* was denied, and certiorari was granted to consider whether this application of due process was warranted and whether the district court's expression of a standard governing immunity for public school board members from liability for compensatory damages under Section 1983 was correct. The findings of the Supreme Court on the question of immunity in this case are the basis of much of the concern about liability for school officials.

In a previous case, *Scheuer* v. *Rhodes* (1974), the Supreme Court had found that government officials, including a university president, had qualified immunity under Section 1983 when all the circumstances were considered as they reasonably appeared at the time. Thus, reasonable discretionary judgment, coupled with good-faith nonmalicious action, had been held to provide qualified immunity for government and the other school officials under Section 1983. In *Wood*, however, the court set two standards for immunity: a subjective and an objective test. Two questions must be answered: Did the school officials act without malice? Did they know or should they reasonably have known that their actions would violate a constitutionally protected right of a student? "Therefore, in the specific context of school discipline, we hold that a school board member is not immune from liability for damages under Section 1983 if he knew or reasonably should have known that the action he took within his sphere of official responsibility would violate the constitutional rights of the student affected or if he took the action with the malicious intention to cause a deprivation of constitutional rights or other injury to the student" (*Wood,* at 1001). This decision has caused many administrators to examine the extent of their personal liability. Forgotten, however, in the furor raised by the decision was the holding of the court regarding compensatory damage awards: "A compensatory award will be appropriate only if the school board member has acted with such impermissible motivation or with such disregard of the student's clearly established constitutional rights that his action cannot reasonably be characterized as being in good faith" (*Wood,* at 1001).

Subsequent analysis of the case has supported this doctrine when applied to higher education. Claque (1976, p. 341) states: "It is doubtful that the individual administrator will be made liable for restitutionary remedies for university policies that are found to be violative of constitutional norms." The *Harvard Law Review* analysis ("Developments in the Law," 1977) notes that, although *Wood* broadens the potential for damages under Section 1983, "*Wood* and *Scheuer* taken together make it clear that the immunity extended to state officials is in fact a defense—a defense on the merits involving both state of mind and reasonableness of conduct" (p. 1213).

In *Carey* v. *Piphus* (1978), the United States Supreme Court reduced some of the concern regarding compensatory damages under the Civil Rights Act. The court ruled that the plaintiff must prove that he actually was injured by the deprivation of his rights before he could recover damages.

Harlow v. *Fitzgerald* (1982) deleted the subjective question of deciding immunity in *Wood*. The Supreme Court held in part that "allegations of malice should not suffice to subject government officials either to the cost of trial or the burdens of broad reaching discovery. We, therefore, hold that government officials performing discretionary functions generally are shielded from liability for civil damages insofar as their conduct does not violate clearly established statutory or constitutional rights of which a reasonable person should have known" (*Harlow*, at 2738). Although decided prior to *Harlow*, *Perez* v. *Rodriguez Bou* (1978) also illustrates the objective test set in *Wood*. Students brought a civil rights suit against the university and the chancellor after they were summarily suspended. The court held that the chancellor should have known that such a suspension would violate constitutionally protected rights of students.

Immunity from Suit

Many public college administrators have claimed that the Eleventh Amendment protects both them and their institution from suit. The Eleventh Amendment provides that the state may not be sued. In general, the courts have not upheld this claim or have granted only limited immunity. First, the Eleventh Amendment bars suit only in federal court and does not provide state court protection. Second, since *Scheuer* v. *Rhodes* (1974), the doctrine of sovereign immunity of the state has been struck down in many courts. Finally, the Eleventh Amendment only affords protection from liabilities that must be paid from state treasuries. In *Hander* v. *San Jacinto Junior College* (1975), the Fifth Circuit held that the college was not immune from damages under the Eleventh

Amendment but that individual members of the board of regents were immune. In *Slaughter* v. *Brigham Young University* (1975), no damages were awarded against individual administrators. The Seventh Circuit held in *Hostrop* v. *Board of Junior College District No. 515* (1975) that individual board members were protected by the doctrine of official immunity. New ground was broken in *Pence* v. *Rosenquist* (1978), where the court broadened the effect of *Wood* to part-time employees. In *Taliaferro* v. *State Council of Higher Education* (1977), the court held that officials were not liable individually but were liable in their official capacities. Aiken (1976, p. 191) also supports this reasoning, stating that "institutional personnel sued in their official capacities are not thereby subject to personal liability but are sued as an alter ego of the institution."

Administrators have also been protected from personal liability for inherited decisions. *Pinkney* v. *District of Columbia* (1977) held that the refusal of a newly appointed president to reopen a dismissal case did not render him individually liable if he did not play a part in the termination decision.

State law is the primary influence on whether an institution and its employees have immunity from civil suit. Pennsylvania law, for example, provides that colleges are subject to the claim of sovereign immunity. A Kentucky statute giving the University of Louisville power to sue and to be sued in its corporate name was not found to constitute a waiver of Eleventh Amendment rights. In Tennessee, the court found that the University of Tennessee charter, which contained a provision that the university may sue and be sued, meant that "consent to be sued inescapably subjects the University to the hazard of having a money judgment rendered against it" (*Soni* v. *Board of Trustees of the University of Tennessee*, 1975, at 353). In the same state, Memphis State University, because it did not have comparable language in the charter, was found to be protected by the Eleventh Amendment.

The question of college and university immunity from suit rests on several factors: whether the university was engaged in state action, whether state law or an institution's charter uphold or waive such immunity, and whether damages will be paid from the state treasury. It is clear, however, that the doctrine of sovereign immunity for public institutions does not provide blanket protection from liability claims. Further, private institutions must not assume that they are immune from such claims.

In summary: Prudent administrators will keep informed about developments in the law to ensure that they will meet the standard of reasonable knowledge that their actions might involve deprivation of a right. "The state of law under Section 1983 and the Eleventh Amendment, taken together, gives administrators of public postsecondary institutions no cause to feel confident that either they or other institutional officers or employees are insulated from personal civil rights liability" (Kaplin, 1985, p. 84).

Contract Liability

There are six elements that must be present for a contract to be legally binding. First, the parties to the contract must have the legal capacity to contract, the contract must cover subject matter that is within the legal mission of the institution, and the parties contracting must have authority to do so. Second, the contract must be based on an offer, either direct or implied. Third, the contract must be accepted by either promise or performance. Fourth, there must be mutual agreement to the terms and conditions of the contract. Fifth, there must be performance under the terms and conditions of the contract in order for one or both parties to be bound by the contract. Sixth, in order to be binding, a contract must be entered into for a legal purpose (Hammond, 1977). Thus, the issue of contracts is very complex, and involvement of legal counsel in the formation of contracts is essential if legal problems are to be avoided. Not only must administrators be concerned with contractual issues involving staff, faculty, and outside persons but a new body of law is redefining the relationship of students and the institution as contractual. (Chapter Five in this volume discusses this emerging area of law in detail.)

"The postsecondary institution's main concern in managing liability should be the delineation of the contracting authority of each of its agents. By carefully defining such authority, and by repudiating unauthorized contracts of which they become aware, postsecondary administrators can protect the institution from unwanted liability" (Kaplin, 1985, pp. 65-66). *Brown* v. *Wichita*

State University (1975) illustrates the complexity of determining authorization. Wichita State University had a separate corporation for athletics; however, both the university and the corporation were sued following a plane crash in which members of the football team and others were killed. Representatives and relatives of the deceased passengers sued the university and the Physical Education Corporation for breaking an agreement to provide passenger liability insurance. The court ruled that the Physical Education Corporation was an agent of the university and that the athletic director had implied power to enter into a contract and bind the institution. However, not all courts have found institutional authority for unauthorized acts. Utah State University was not held liable when the institution refused to pay for stocks ordered by an employee who did not have authority to do so (*First Equity Corp. of Florida* v. *Utah State University*, 1975).

Other defenses that can be used against contract liability claims are fraud by the other party and breach of the contract. Such claims rely on the contract and the agreement of the parties involved; therefore, each contract should be carefully construed.

Insurance

Many feel that insurance coverage mitigates concern with liability questions. Such feelings are inaccurate. The cost of insurance, the ability to get insurance, and the exclusions in insurance policies have all reduced the sense of comfort in this area. Administrators should understand the terms, conditions, and limitations of any insurance coverage provided by the institution. Several professional associations, including the American Association of Counseling and Development and the National Association of Student Personnel Administrators, also offer individual liability insurance. Coverage under such policies should be carefully explored by the practicing administrator.

Mandatory student health and accident insurance coverage is being adopted by many institutions. Although most institutions offer optional insurance, student participation is not high. Many times, subunits of the institution also require medical insurance for participation in field trips, sports, or study abroad. But unless such policies are enforced, such requirements are useless and may even put the institution in a situation where liability will be found on the basis of nonenforcement of its own rules. Competent, qualified advice is needed in the area of insurance, and all practitioners are urged to seek it out and use it.

Summary

In this litigious society, liability claims continue to grow. The prudent administrator attempts to reduce such claims through sound practice, staff education, prevention techniques, and consistent legal advice. Early detection of potentially harmful situations and immediate action to correct hazards are the best defenses against liability claims. Further, policies should be carefully written, enforceable, and consistently applied. Finally, constant review of both policies and physical facilities is necessary in order to reduce successful liability claims.

A number of areas related to liability still have not been resolved. Although state law varies widely, some states have recognized third-party and vicarious liability. Under such doctrines, the institution can be held responsible and thus face liability claims for the actions of third parties, such as student organizations. (See Chapter Fifteen in this volume for a discussion of these issues.) It is clear that the legal relationship between the institution and the third party lies at the heart of the liability question. In this case, sound student affairs practice and defense against liability may be in conflict.

References

Aiken, R. J. "Legal Liabilities in Higher Education: Their Scope and Management." *Journal of College and University Law,* 1976, *3* (2), 127-298.

Buchanan, E. T., Jr., and Oliaro, P. M. "Law, Alcohol and Higher Education." In T. G. Goodale (ed.), *Alcohol and the College Student.* New Directions for Student Services, no. 35. San Francisco: Jossey-Bass, 1986.

Claque, M. "Suing the University 'Black Box' Under the Civil Rights Act of 1871." *Iowa Law Review,* 1976, *62,* 337–379.

"Developments in the Law, Section 1983 and Federalism." *Harvard Law Review,* 1977, *90* (6), 1135–1360.

Flora, C. A. "Tort Liability and Insurance." In A. S. Knowles (ed.), *Handbook of College and University Administration.* New York: McGraw-Hill, 1970.

Hammond, E. H. "Risk Management In Student Affairs." Paper presented at the annual law conference of the Texas Association of College Student Personnel Administrators, Austin, Texas, June 1977.

Kaplin, W. A. *The Law of Higher Education: A Comprehensive Guide to Legal Implications of Administrative Decision Making.* (2nd ed.) San Francisco: Jossey-Bass, 1985.

Roth, R. A. "The Impact of Liquor Liability on Colleges and Universities." *Journal of College and University Law,* 1986, *13* (1), 45–64.

Steinbach, S. "Student Alcohol Abuse: Who Will Pay the Price?" *Educational Record,* 1985, *66* (4), 32–38.

Part Three

Strengthening the Legal Basis of Student Affairs Policy and Practice

Part One of this volume focused on the legal foundations for student affairs practice. In Part Two, major legal issues influencing policies, procedures, and practice in student affairs were discussed in detail. Obviously, not all legal issues that could potentially involve student affairs were covered. However, the major constitutional, statutory, judicial, and administrative rulings having a daily influence in student affairs were highlighted. Part Three attempts to apply the legal principles discussed in the preceding chapters to specific areas of practice in student affairs. Each chapter is written by an experienced student affairs administrator. All the authors give specific guidance for the application of diverse sources of the law in both private and public colleges and universities.

In Chapter Ten, Edward Boehm focuses on the constitutional, statutory, and agency rulings influencing admissions policies and practice. The complex area of the legal ramifications of residence life programs and residence hall supervision is carefully covered by Donald Buckner in Chapter Eleven. Management of facilities—including student unions, recreation centers, athletic

197

facilities, and residence halls—is part of the daily responsibility for student affairs administrators. Chapter Twelve provides specific guidance for policy development and implementation in facility management. Counseling and health centers have specific legal constraints relating to confidentiality, ethics, and practice. David Emmerling provides guidance in developing policies for agency management in Chapter Thirteen.

Discipline seems to take a great deal of time and effort on any college campus. In Chapter Fourteen, William Bracewell provides practical advice on the development of discipline policies and procedures. Glenn Maloney discusses the equally complex area of student organizations in Chapter Fifteen. His analysis of the issues involved in this area as well as his recommendations for practice will be most valuable for practitioners.

Working with the student press can be both frustrating and rewarding, as any administrator knows. John Schuh outlines the legal implications inherent in relationships with the press in Chapter Sixteen.

Maintenance of a sound, legally correct record-keeping system is vital to the administration of student affairs. In Chapter Seventeen, Larry Ebbers provides specific guidance for establishing policies and procedures in this area. Employment and supervision can provide the greatest number of legal challenges for the student affairs administrator. Jon Dalton, in Chapter Eighteen, provides specific guidelines for practice regarding employment issues based on identified legal constraints. Chapter Nineteen focuses on conclusions and future implications for practice.

Part Three of this volume should provide specific, practical guidance for student affairs practitioners by translating legal constraints on actions into specific policies and procedures that work within an educational context. The law is only one parameter in policy development and program implementation. By understanding the law, student affairs practitioners can increase their ability to meet their educational goals within the institution.

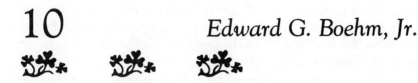

10   *Edward G. Boehm, Jr.*

Admissions Policies
and Procedures

The admission of new students is the lifeblood of any institution of higher education. However, the current climate for admissions officers is not without problems. Legal constraints as well as educational standards influence the admissions process. Issues are now more complex than ever before in the history of American higher education. Some of these issues emerge from societal pressures; others are the result of the increased influence of the law on college and university campuses.

The history of American higher education reflects changing admissions policies and standards as well as changes in the larger society. In the early years of American higher education, there were no uniform standards for admission to higher education. An applicant found many and varied criteria used in the admissions process at different institutions. In a partial response to this lack of standardization, the College Board and the Carnegie Unit were established at the turn of the twentieth century. These efforts resulted in potential students' increased understanding of the expectations of the academy.

After World War II, a series of societal changes also influenced the admissions process. The return of veterans with government financing for their education radically changed the student and applicant populations in colleges and universities. Shortly thereafter, the civil rights movement required institutions to confront both the legal and ethical issues involved in college admission. Legal challenges to admissions decisions became more frequent. A landmark case (*Regents of the University of California v. Bakke,* 1978), discussed later in this chapter, was decided by the Supreme Court. New federal legislation governing the use of student records was introduced and influenced the information available to admissions officers in the decision process. The Family Educational Rights and Privacy Act of 1974 caused many to avoid providing nonstandardized information to colleges and universities during the admissions process, although that was not the intent of the legislation. (See Chapter Seven in this volume for a full discussion of these issues.) State legislatures have recently also become involved in the admissions process by establishing standardized tests to determine the competency of high school and college students. Admissions officers clearly must now adhere to a number of statutory and administrative rulings in the admissions process.

It is possible, however, even with the massive changes in legislation and court decisions, for the admissions process to be fair as well as legally sound. Recruitment activities to generate students for colleges (from the local community college to the state university) can be designed to produce results without litigation. Attention to detail and honesty ahead of time can prevent student or parent dissatisfaction and future legal action.

In this chapter, the basic legal constraints influencing admissions will be discussed, with a focus on application of these constraints to admissions policies and practices. Suggestions will be offered to aid the practitioner in designing admission procedures, admissions publications, and recruitment procedures. Unresolved issues in the area of admissions will be identified, and a philosophical approach to admissions—which balances the potential student's rights, institutional needs, and the applicable legal constraints on the admissions process—will be presented.

Basic Legal Requirements

Certain federal statutes prohibit discrimination on the basis of race, sex, handicap, and age if an institution or enrolled students receive funds from the federal government. (See Chapter Six in this volume for a discussion of applicable statutes.)

Title VI: Race Discrimination. Title VI of the Civil Rights Act of 1964 prohibits discrimination on the basis of race, color, or national origin in any program or activity receiving federal financial assistance. A majority of the Supreme Court in the *Bakke* case confirmed this statute as identical to the equal protection clause of the Fourteenth Amendment. In another case, however, the Supreme Court upheld the application of protected class status under civil rights legislation (*Guardians Association* v. *Civil Service Commission of the City of New York,* 1983). An independent educational institution may have to show that recruitment and admissions practices resulting in a disproportionate underrepresentation of minorities have not been motivated by impermissible racial considerations (American Association of Collegiate Registrars and Admissions Officers, 1985). Although the *Bakke* decision relates to state institutions, it should offer a word of warning to independent institutions as well. While race can be one of the factors used in a preferential admissions program, no mathematical formulas, quotas, or separate admissions procedures may be used in the process. Title VI permits affirmative action programs consistent with *Bakke.* If a history of discrimination is determined, the courts may require affirmative action.

Title IX: Sex Discrimination. "While the Education Amendments of 1972 (Title IX) prohibit using a student's sex as a criterion for admission to any program or activity receiving federal financial assistance, certain exceptions exist for independent institutions. For instance, traditionally all-female and all-male independent institutions of undergraduate higher education and institutions governed by a religious organization are exempted when the requirements are in conflict with the religious beliefs of the institution. Affirmative action programs are required if past discrimination can be proved. Additionally, they are permissible in the absence of past discrimination" (American Association of Collegiate Registrars and Admissions Officers, 1985, p. 28).

Following the adoption of Title IX, all institutions receiving federal financial assistance for their programs were required to follow a series of procedures in evaluating their programs and then to take the necessary steps to modify and eliminate those not in compliance. They were prohibited from engaging in practices that would violate the Title IX regulations.

Under the equal opportunity clause of the Fourteenth Amendment, a state institution can be sex-segregated only if state systems provide other educational opportunities equal to the excluding institution. Thus, sex segregation is permitted if it is reasonable, not arbitrary, and rests on fair or justifiable grounds of difference (*Reed* v. *Reed,* 1971). Title IX prohibits sex discrimination in admissions in graduate schools, vocational schools, or professional schools unless they are part of an undergraduate institution permitted to be single sex. Additionally, institutions are restricted from giving preference to or ranking applicants separately by sex, applying numerical limitations on the basis of sex, or treating one group differently from another on the basis of sex. In fact, institutions cannot treat sexes differently on the basis of "actual or potential parental, family, or marital status"; discriminate because of pregnancy or conditions relating to childbirth; or make preadmission inquiries regarding marital status (34 C.F.R. sec. 106.23).

The landmark case involving *Grove City College* v. *Bell* (1984) affects not only Title IX but Title VI and Section 504 of the Rehabilitation Act of 1973 as well. Mandates become program specific only to those parts of the institution receiving federal funds, and it is not always clear what constitutes a "program" that must comply with Title IX mandates or Title VI or Section 504.

Women who believe that they have been discriminated against in admission, on factors of both age and sex, sometimes fail to realize that the burden of proof of institutional discrimination rests with the applicant. A thirty-nine-year-old woman who was denied admission to the University of Chicago sued the university on the grounds of sex discrimination (*Cannon* v. *University of Chicago,* 1979). Her thesis was that her denial of admission was discriminatory because women traditionally interrupt their education and even a neutral age policy in admissions works against them. The Supreme Court ruled in the case that under Title IX there was a private right of action but that the plaintiff had to prove institutional discrimination.

Section 504: Discrimination on the Basis of Handicap. The

provisions of Section 504 of the Rehabilitation Act of 1973 prohibit both public and independent institutions that receive federal financial assistance from discriminating against an "otherwise qualified handicapped individual." A "qualified" handicapped person would be defined as one who meets the academic standards required for admission or for participation in the institution's educational programs or activities. For example, in *Southeastern Community College* v. *Davis* (1979), a student was denied admission to a registered nurse (RN) program because she was deaf. She sued the college under Section 504. The college declared that a deaf person could not function as an RN, whereas the student contended that the college should have focused on her academic qualifications, not on her handicap. The Supreme Court ruled that colleges and universities do not have to modify their programs or lower their requirements to allow handicapped persons to participate. It is important to note that Section 504 does not ban the requirement of "reasonable physical qualifications" for programs where these qualifications are important.

Age Discrimination. A graduate program may require specific preparation as admissions criteria. However, the time elapsed since date of completion of the undergraduate degree is not a reasonable eligibility factor, since more recent activities could have a more substantial impact on readiness for graduate work. There are two basic concepts to remember in connection with age discrimination. The law does not hold as high a standard of justification against discrimination on the basis of age as it does for race. The federal Age Discrimination Act was amended in 1978 to make the standards stronger. For example, a fifty-one-year-old woman who was denied admission to a graduate program in educational psychology sued the University of Utah, claiming that she met or exceeded all admissions criteria and was rejected solely on the basis of her age (*Purdie* v. *University of Utah*, 1978). The Supreme Court of Utah agreed, stating that the denial of admission violated the equal protection provisions of the United States Constitution and the state's constitution.

Race Discrimination. As *Purdie* illustrates, courts have held that the equal protection clause of the Fourteenth Amendment of the United States Constitution has been found applicable to higher education (see also *Brown* v. *Board of Education,* 1954; *Geier* v. *University of Tennessee,* 1979; *Plessy* v. *Ferguson,* 1896). This stance has also been supported by administrative and legislative action governing tax laws. For example, the Department of Education and the Internal Revenue Service require private schools that desire tax-exempt status not to discriminate on the basis of race. In fact, the Internal Revenue Service requires that all institutions receiving federal assistance must include a statement of a racially nondiscriminatory policy in all its brochures dealing with student admissions, programs, and scholarships as well as in other written advertising that it uses as a means of informing prospective students of its programs. The statement must be used in both the print and broadcast media to all segments of the general community served by the institution. The requirements include factors such as frequency, circulation, location, print size and typeface, as well as records showing frequency, time of day, duration, and market. If the institution draws from a large geographical area, the use of newspaper or radio spots is encouraged but optional (American Association of Collegiate Registrars and Admissions Officers, 1985).

Institutions receiving federal financial assistance must conduct their recruitment activities in a manner that enables them to reach all groups of potential students without regard to race, color, or national origin.

Affirmative Action Programs. Affirmative action programs that are designed to increase the number of minority persons enrolled in institutional programs have been affirmed in a number of court cases, including *DeFunis* v. *Odegaard* (1973) and *Regents of the University of California* v. *Bakke* (1978). The courts have held that, *if* no past discrimination exists, an institution may permit but is not required to have affirmative action programs for admissions. If an affirmative action program is implemented, an institution may take a uniform differential or preferential approach to admissions. In any case, the goal of the program must be to ensure open and fair opportunities for students regardless of race, color, or national origin. An institution that has never employed discriminatory policies may develop recruitment procedures to become more visible to groups of students not previously served. Methods include neighborhood visits, school visits, and media campaigns that will reach students not previously recruited by the institution. *Geier* v. *Dunn* (1972) and *Lee* v. *Macon County Board of Education* (1972) provide support for these approaches.

Contracts. Chapter Five in this volume discusses contract theory in great detail. Usually, state law governs the interpretation of the contract between the institution and the students. The courts have recognized authorized and unauthorized statements by institutional representatives as a part of the contract, as well as any written statements in publications, advertising, or brochures.

Application of Legal Constraints

College and university administrators must adhere to four constraints in determining and carrying out policies:

1. They cannot be arbitrary or capricious.
2. They must honor published admissions standards and honor admissions decisions.
3. They must not have procedures that unjustly discriminate on the basis of race, sex, age, handicap, or citizenship.
4. They must ensure that their records are in compliance with the provisions of the Family Educational Rights and Privacy Act of 1974 (the "Buckley Amendment") as soon as a student is enrolled in their institution.

Constitutional Constraints. Courts have traditionally kept "hands off" the area of academic qualifications as long as an institution was acting in good faith and the policies in question were reasonable. However, they are ready to interfere if they observe that "good faith," fairness, and reasonableness are lacking. Two specific cases illustrate the courts' concern for fairness and reasonable standards. In the first case, *State ex rel. Bartlett* v. *Pantzer* (1971), the University of Montana's law school informed a candidate that he would be accepted if he completed a course in financial accounting. After receiving a *D*, he was told that the grade was "acceptable" but not "satisfactory" for admission. The court found this action "unreasonable" and ruled against the law school. The student was admitted. In the second case, *Evans* v. *West Virginia*

Board of Regents (1980), a student was denied readmission to a state School of Osteopathic Medicine. He had completed two years with a *B+* average before taking a medical leave of absence. He sought readmission and was supported by his physician, but the school rejected his application. The court held that the student had a property right in continuing his education unless the school could show intervening circumstances. In other words, his entitlement to due process was no different from that of any other continuing student.

Institutions will basically be left alone by the courts if standards for admission, matriculation, retention, and graduation are reasonable, fair, and not arbitrary or capricious. An institution should make sure that entering students are aware of its policies prior to their arrival on campus. For example, students should be informed of specific terms and conditions of admission, degree requirements and proposed changes, the confidential nature of their admission and permanent records, and the "satisfactory" progress requirements necessary for scholarship and financial aid consideration.

Contractual Constraints. A representative of the institution can be seen as entering into a contract through implied or direct promises to applicants. In New York, plans were announced and applications accepted for a new School of Podiatry. The admitted students were notified by the dean of the school that their admissions were final. The students then declined other offers only to find out a month later that, because of budgetary problems, the opening would be deferred. The court ruled against the state university because the representations made by officials disadvantaged the students and the budget savings were minor compared to the injury suffered by the students (*Eden* v. *Board of Trustees of the State University of New York,* 1975).

It is also generally accepted that private institutions enter into a contractual relationship with matriculants and that recruitment promises become part of that contract. A student applied for admission to the Chicago Medical School, a private institution, and paid his $15 application fee. After being rejected, he sued the school for failing to evaluate his application and those of other applicants according to the academic entrance criteria printed in the school's bulletin. He charged that the school's decision regarding his application was based on nonacademic matters and that the acceptance of the application fee created a contractual obligation to evaluate applicants in accordance with the criteria published in the bulletin. The court agreed, noting that the school's brochure was an invitation to make an offer, that the student responded to the offer, and that the school's retention of the application fee of $15 constituted an acceptance of that offer. The court concluded that the applicant and the school entered into an enforceable contract and that the applicant was entitled to have his application judged according to the school's published criteria (*Steinberg* v. *Chicago Medical School,* 1976).

State institutions fall under the same requirement when they make changes in the original contractual agreement and fail to give students proper notice of such changes. For example, a student was admitted to a graduate program, registered for fall courses, and received a receipt for the courses at the rates listed in the school catalogue. The college then raised the fees, and the student paid the new fees under protest. The court ruled against the college and ordered a refund to the student. Again, the catalogue statement constituted an offer that was accepted by the student (*Silver* v. *Queens College of City University,* 1970).

Institutional Representatives. Statements made on behalf of the institution by representatives or recruitment officers when they do not hold the power and authority to make such promises can also be damaging (*Blank* v. *Board of Higher Education of the City of New York,* 1966; *Healy* v. *Larsson,* 1973). If the students *believe* that the representative has the power to make exceptions or alter policy within the institution, the courts have generally held that institutions were bound to honor these statements even though they were contrary to institutional policy and beyond the authority of the representative to change.

Admissions Requirements. The courts have continued to support fair and reasonable admissions requirements. Public and private institutions do have the right to require diplomas and degrees. In *McCall* v. *Penegar* (1975), a member of the Knoxville police force who did not have a high school diploma or a bachelor's degree applied to the University of Tennessee law school. The university denied his admission on the grounds that he failed to meet the minimum standards of the university as well as requirements of the state, the American Bar Association, and the Association of American Law Schools. He then brought suit, stating that his constitutional rights were violated by the university's action. The trial court ruled in favor of the law school, and the state appeals court supported that judgment.

The requirement that students must be graduates of accredited high schools and colleges also has been supported by the courts. In *Pappanastos* v. *Board of Trustees of the University of Alabama* (1977), a student was denied admission to a Master of Laws program at the University of Alabama because he had not graduated from a law school accredited by the American Bar Association. His suit stated that the university's action constituted discrimination in violation of the equal protection clause of the Fourteenth Amendment. The university responded that such a requirement was essential to the accreditation of the entire program. The court ruled against the student, noting that the alleged discrimination did not involve a suspect classification and did not impinge upon a fundamental right. The court also agreed that the State of Alabama had a legitimate interest in having its law program accredited by the ABA.

In the area of Section 504, the institution should be aware that "good faith" is not enough of a defense for noncompliance. Unlike racial discrimination cases, the courts have stated that Section 504 sets its own criteria. Students must demonstrate that they were otherwise qualified and denied solely because of a handicap. If a student is successful in this regard, the institution must prove that the denial was based on reasons other than the handicap. The student must then prove that the reasons presented by the institution are faulty (*Pushkin* v. *Regents of the University of Colorado*, 1981).

Institutions should be aware of the implications of Section 504 of the Rehabilitation Act of 1973 (Subpart E, dealing with admissions and recruitment), which indicates that institutions must not exclude *qualified* handicapped persons from programs through prescreening, information dissemination, or recruitment practices. Institutions, therefore, may *not:*

1. Limit the number or proportion of handicapped individuals offered admission.
2. Use any test or criterion for admission that has a disproportionate adverse effect on handicapped persons *unless* the test or criterion has been validated as a predictor of success in the program and alternate tests are not available.
3. Use admissions tests that reflect the applicant's impaired sensory, manual, or speaking skills (except where those skills are factors that the test purports to measure).
4. Make *preadmission inquiry* about whether the applicant for admission is handicapped, unless answers to such an inquiry are optional, will remain confidential, and will not cause adverse treatment.

After admission, institutions can make confidential inquiries regarding handicapping conditions if the purpose is to ascertain the need for accommodation to the handicapped. In addition, colleges and universities may develop predictive measures for grades and use them in admission but should conduct periodic validity studies to ensure that the prediction equation is not discriminatory against handicapped or other applicants (Biehl, 1978).

Readmission or Conditional Admission. An offer of readmission or conditional admission must be made in good faith and must provide the student a genuine opportunity for success. In *Paulsen v. Golden State University* (1979), a law student who had failed to meet requirements for graduation was permitted to reenroll for a fourth year but was told that, regardless of his grade point average, he would not be awarded a degree. While he informed the school that the conditions were unacceptable, he proceeded to enroll, indicating on his registration form that he was a degree student and paying his tuition at that rate. The school, in fact, had no nondegree program except for attorneys or graduates of accredited law schools. After completing the requirements for graduation, the student was denied a degree. He therefore brought suit against the university. The court ruled that, although it was within the university's absolute discretion to deny the student readmission, the readmission condition imposed was arbitrary and capricious. Therefore, the law school was ordered to award the student a degree.

Institutions must be precise when using provisional or conditional admission policies, and they are better off denying admission outright if the policy is fair and reasonable rather than creating impossible standards for success. In *Koutsis* v. *Polytechnic Institute of New York* (1981), a student was permitted to register and complete two-thirds of his master's degree requirements on a provisional basis. In fact, it took seven months for the institution to act on his provisional status and to deny him admission. The court ruled against the college, stating that it had abused its discretion and acted in bad faith. This was a case of procedural flaws, which allowed the student to begin his work without exact knowledge of expectations and thus placed him in an unfair position. In contrast, the plaintiff in *Ramos* v. *Texas Tech University* (1977) was denied admission to the master's degree program at Texas Tech University but was given permission to take courses in the graduate school. She sued the university, claiming that it had discriminated against her and deprived her of her "liberty" and "property" interests without due process of law. The court upheld the university's actions, noting that an applicant has only a unilateral expectation of admittance. Since Ramos had never been admitted, her unilateral expectation of admission did not rise to the level of a legitimate claim of entitlement; therefore, no due process rights of the student were violated.

Suggestions for Practice

These legal constraints require an institution to review, consolidate, and—if necessary—revise processes, procedures, and publications related to admission to the college or university.

Preadmission. The chief admissions officer should be sure that institutional admissions policies are based on proper criteria; distributed through adequate channels, so that the potential students are aware of the selection process; procedurally correct in recruiting, admitting, and retaining students within the institution; and reviewed on a regular basis, so that the institution is protected from legal action (Federal Interagency Committee on Education, 1978).

The application form should not require information that students believe might work against them in the admissions process. Usually, an application may ask for age, sex, race, marital status, and health as long as such information is *not required* for admission consideration. The publications that accompany the application should be clear and concise; the requirements specified in these publications should be fair and reasonable and must not violate anyone's rights. In distributing the publications, the admissions officer must make sure that *all* prospective students have access to institutional requirements, mailings, and school visits.

Institutional Representatives. Anyone representing the institution in the admissions process must clearly understand the legal as well as the moral implications of his or her actions. Training is required for the admissions staff and others who will represent the institution in the admissions process, including alumni, students, faculty, parents, other staff, and athletic department personnel. Such training should focus on the permissible admissions criteria, interview procedures, and the legal implications of statements and commitments made on behalf of the institution. All representatives should be aware of the contractual obligations binding the institution and should understand how proposed changes in admissions procedures might affect these obligations or the institution.

The courts seem a little more tolerant of oral commitments made by representatives of the institution. An Illinois appellate court held that an alleged statement made by college representatives to a student who was dismissed because of academic problems did not constitute a binding and enforceable oral contract (*Abrams* v. *Illinois College of Podiatric Medicine*, 1979). Nonetheless, although the court ruled in favor of the institution in this case, institutional representatives should not promise more than can be delivered or lure students to the institution under false pretenses. This caution will help prevent charges of fraud and misrepresentation.

Public Versus Private Institutions. Regardless of the public or private status of the institution, each is bound by a set of requirements of operation. These requirements may be contained in a "statement of purpose" or a charter or in federal or state statutes. Whether public or private, an institution has the right to establish reasonable standards and procedures for admission, matriculation, termination, and expectations for student accomplishment. It has the right to authorize administrators, faculty, and staff to enforce these standards. As long as the enforcement is fair, reasonable, and without bias, the institution is usually on safe ground. The key here is that the student is aware of the conditions and expectations prior to and during matriculation (especially if changes occur).

A certain amount of discretion on the part of private institutions has been upheld by the courts (*People ex rel. Tinkoff* v. *Northwestern University*, 1947). Private institutions, however, are also accountable for equal access and may not discriminate on the basis of race in the admissions process. Colleges and universities, especially in the private sector, have been supported by the courts in their efforts to establish fair and reasonable entrance, retention, and graduation requirements (*Mewshaw* v. *Brooklyn Law School*, 1976).

The courts have upheld the rights of state institutions to have differential criteria for out-of-state applicants and also even to give preference to children of alumni living out of state. For example, in *Rosenstock* v. *Board of Governors of the University of North Carolina* (1976), the court ruled that an admissions policy allowing for preferential treatment of in-state applicants as well as out-of-state applicants who are children of alumni does not constitute a denial of equal protection guarantees of the federal Constitution. In addition, preferential treatment of applicants who, because of low socioeconomic backgrounds, may not meet regular admissions standards but who demonstrate that they could complete the university's academic program is also permissable.

Required Information. Even though the federal government ordinarily does not interfere in the area of college and university publications, it does insist that certain consumer information be available to students and parents. These regulations are a part of the *Code of Federal Regulations* (34 C.F.R. Part 178) and have been in effect since 1977. Although the regulations require only that this information (admissions and scholarship criteria, total costs, refund policies, retention and placement information) be made available on request, institutions should consider including it in their catalogues or other materials sent to all prospects.

These requirements were further supported in 1979, when final regulations for the Guaranteed Student Loan program were adopted (34 C.F.R. Part 682). Additionally, every institution offering instruction in the health professions and receiving federal funds under Title VII or VIII of the Public Health Service Act must develop and publicize a written policy statement of nondiscrimination on the basis of sex. The statement should be included in each bulletin, catalogue, and application form. The institution *should not* imply in thought, word, or deed that it treats applicants, students, or employees differently on the basis of sex (American Association of Collegiate Registrars and Admissions Officers, 1985).

Information must also be provided on the range and scope of federal financial aid programs administered by the institution. Other types of information for students should include programs authorized under Title IV, programs administered by the "home" state of the institution, the institution's own student financial aid program, and the institution's refund policy. Each participating institution is required to make a "good-faith" effort to provide prospective students with a complete and accurate statement, including written materials about the institution, before they obligate themselves to accept the offer and pay tuition or fees.

Refund Policy. An institution's publications for prospective students should provide a written statement containing an explanation of its refund policy. This information must be available prior to acceptance or initial enrollment of the student. The school must also make its refund policy known to currently enrolled students. If the school changes the refund policy, the institution must ensure that all students are made aware of the new policy.

In determining whether a refund policy is fair and equitable, administrators should ask the following questions:

1. Does the policy take into consideration the period for which tuition, fees, and room and board charges were paid?
2. Does the policy take into consideration the length of time the student was enrolled at the school?
3. Does the policy take into consideration the kind and amount of instruction, equipment, and other services received by the student?

4. Does the policy provide for refunds in reasonable and equitable amounts in consideration of the length of time the student was enrolled?

A school may retain reasonable fees, for the period for which tuition and other fees were required, to cover application, enrollment, registration, and other similar costs. The policy should provide that all monies paid the school by the student, except for "reasonable fees," will be refunded if the student notifies the school of his or her decision not to enroll prior to the sixtieth day before the scheduled date of enrollment (Hornby, 1980).

Publications. All written materials sent to prospective students should be carefully reviewed and read from the point of view of a prospective student rather than an admissions officer. Furthermore, staff members should be sensitive to the truth-in-advertising concept and should make sure that they adhere to their own published criteria. In *Donnelly* v. *Suffolk University* (1976), the court held that the use of letters of recommendation did not breach the published admissions criteria because the catalogue explicitly gave the institution flexibility in implementing criteria for admission. Another case illustrating the need for correct wording is *Mahavongsanan* v. *Hall* (1976), where a student sued Georgia State University because it allegedly had neglected to provide information regarding changes in academic requirements. The court found that the university had made reasonable attempts to notify students of changes in requirements for graduation. The institution clearly is entitled to modify requirements so as to properly exercise its educational responsibility. In two other cases, *Craft* v. *Board of Trustees of the University of Illinois* (1981) and *Anderson* v. *Banks* (1981), the courts supported the rights of colleges to change requirements after admission and matriculation as long as the changes were made without malice or discrimination.

Catalogue editors need to be informed about legislation and regulations affecting college promotional and informational publications. Publications should fairly and accurately represent the institution's size, location, accreditation, admissions requirements, degrees offered, expenses (real costs), financial aid available (renewal criteria and amount of award over a one- to four-year period), housing (real opportunities for renewal and requirements to maintain "on-campus" housing for all four years), and food plans (optional or required five- to seven-day plans—real costs, not estimated "starvation" rates). For example, editors should be wary of describing a campus setting as grassy and tree lined, suggesting a countryside, when the college is really located in the inner city; they should not announce a "major" in music when the school offers only three courses taught by a part-time faculty member; they should not advertise a scholarship program without also explaining that the scholarships cover only a student's first year; and they should not proclaim that the school provides on-campus housing without also explaining that students are not guaranteed a place on campus after the freshman year. If students (and their parents) do receive incorrect impressions from the school's publications, they must be informed of the truth before admission and matriculation. The courts are beginning to take to task those institutions that surprise students.

Provision of the requisite information would place the institution within the spirit of the Commission on Self-Regulation of the American Council on Education. The need to provide adequate information was highlighted by the president of the Carnegie Foundation for the Advancement of Teaching, who asks colleges to demystify the selection process and to help students rather than merely filling an entering class (Boyer, 1987).

With a diminishing applicant pool, we must also be careful as admissions officers not to promise more than we can deliver. A student in Connecticut claimed that the University of Bridgeport was in breach of contract because the actual content and rigor of a course did not live up to the level that the students expected as a result of reading the catalogue (*Ianiello* v. *University of Bridgeport*, 1977). The court did not allow the case to go to jury and the institution was spared only because the student did not present "expert testimony" to refute the university's claim.

Unresolved Issues

A number of issues related to admission of students either have not been tested or have not been fully resolved by legislation, administrative regulation, or court decisions.

Accreditation. A panel of educators has recommended several modifications in the procedures used by the federal government in recognizing accrediting agencies. The group has urged the Department of Education to set higher standards in judging accrediting agencies. In particular, accrediting agencies should be judged by their willingness to enforce truth in advertising by institutions. All institutions, according to the National Advisory Committee on Accreditation and Institutional Eligibility, should promise only what they can deliver. Furthermore, accrediting agencies should enforce stricter standards in this area (Palmer, 1986).

As a result of a growing dissatisfaction with the public system of secondary education, many parents are taking direct responsibility for their children's education by withdrawing them from the traditional public and private schools. Parents in Texas who teach their children at home are waiting to see whether they can continue without violating the law. The agreement being considered by the courts calls for parents teaching their children at home to develop a written curriculum and to provide a building that meets state fire and safety codes. If the conditions are met, then the home school becomes a private school and does not violate the law. However, while the courts can rule on compliance, only the state legislature can change the compulsory attendance law.

If home schools become legal, college registrars will have to determine how to treat students who graduate from these "private schools" (Chandler, 1986) and other nontraditional private schools. The key words to consider here are "small," "unaccredited," and "private." Can the school really provide the subject-matter instruction by qualified teachers necessary for success in college? Why has the school sought to bypass the state accrediting process? Some unaccredited schools are excellent, with strong faculties and curriculum, but college registrars and admissions officers should have written policy statements to protect themselves from any schools that are suspect (not in intent but in substance). They should use these statements early in the process with the student and not after verbal communication has colored the process.

Students do have the right to attend a high school of their choice, but public and private colleges and universities have retained the right to exclude on the basis of accreditation. With the rise in home-bound education and other educational alternatives, however, this issue is far from resolved.

AIDS. A legal opinion released in June 1986 by the U.S. Department of Justice directly affects people who have AIDS or who are known to have been exposed to the AIDS virus and are seeking protection from discrimination in admission or continuing enrollment in the college of their choice (Biemiller, 1986). According to the opinion, programs that receive federal funds are prohibited from "discrimination based on the disabling effects that AIDS and related conditions have on victims." However, the ability to transmit a disease such as AIDS cannot itself be considered a handicap. Section 504 of the Rehabilitation Act of 1973 does not prohibit discrimination rooted in fear of transmission of the disease. Proof of discrimination as a result of disease's "disabling effects" rather than the potential (real or perceived) ability to transmit the disease is the issue facing both students and institutions in the near future.

Learning Disabilities. It is presently estimated that individuals with learning disabilities comprise 10–12 percent of the United States population. Institutions have been slow in developing admissions standards for these potential students (Bowen, 1986). What are the ethical obligations and the legal responsibilities of undergraduate institutions to those with learning disabilities? These questions are answered specifically by the Rehabilitation Act of 1973, Section 504. Some colleges and universities have tried a variety of approaches for attracting, admitting, and graduating these students, but many have ignored the fact that these learning disabilities exist.

Some institutions deal with the students on a case-by-case basis by allowing alternative courses for admission as well as untimed entrance examinations. The course exceptions most commonly occur in the areas of foreign language, computer science, and certain natural sciences (Faigel, 1985). While these students and their parents may have been passive in the past, colleges that avoid the problem by being oblivious to learning disabilities can expect future legal action. For example, a college senior sued the University of Massachusetts at Amherst for failure to expedite the university's procedure for waiving the foreign language requirements for dyslexic students, thereby placing an unfair burden on them. The university responded that the hearing board established to handle these requests did not meet regularly and that it could take up to nine months to process the waiver request ("Dyslexic Student Sues University . . . ," 1986). The suit was not successful, but institutions should be more aware of their responsibilities in both admissions and policies and make certain that they are in compliance with Section 504.

Financial Aid. New regulations limiting access to Guaranteed Student Loan funds may influence admissions procedures at institutions with open-admissions programs. For example, a university with an open-admissions policy permitting adults to register for a certain number of credit hours without providing transcripts or other personal information may face conflicts with the newest financial aid regulations. All loan applicants will now have to certify that they are not in default on any Department of Education loan and do not owe a refund on a Department of Education grant at any institution. Under the new laws governing student aid administration, the federal government places more responsibility on institutions to coordinate admissions and financial aid procedures (National Association of College Admissions Counselors, 1985).

Athletic Eligibility. In many instances, what the National Collegiate Athletic Association, high school counselors, and the school system accept as courses fulfilling academic units and what the college or university expects are not exactly the same. How involved should the admissions officer be with prospective student athletes to ensure compliance with eligiblity requirements? There are two aspects of this dilemma to consider: (1) the athlete as a student who is or is not eligible for admission to the institution; (2) the student as an athlete who is or is not eligible to compete for the institution. Admissions officers should direct their efforts toward the first concern and leave the second to others within and outside the institution who have been charged with that responsibility.

Admissions Exceptions. Many institutions have provisions for admitting students who do not meet published entrance requirements. Potential problems, however, are looming ahead for our institutions in the area of athletic exceptions. If exceptions are made for athletes, should exceptions also be available for others? Otherwise, a *Bakke* type of suit might arise, in which a nonathlete who is denied admission but knows that he has better academic credentials than athletes who have been accepted alleges academic discrimination.

Confidentiality of Records. All staff, especially student workers, should be reminded of the need for confidentiality on a regular basis. It may be useful for staff to sign statements acknowledging their understanding of the procedures protecting confidentiality. Awareness or training sessions should be offered, with emphasis on the consequences of breaching confidentiality of records. Students, parents, and high school counselors frequently are put in awkward situations because of wrongful or unauthorized release of information. Review of the process to determine who oversees the release and content of lists and letters during and after the admissions process is sound management.

Standardized Testing. Suits have been brought by minority groups on the use of standardized tests in the admissions process. Standardized testing also relates to institutional results in the area of retention and outcome assessment. In other words, are certain groups admitted "on condition" and then expected to compete in a curve type of classroom atmosphere that eliminates the bottom portion?

In 1980, the Educational Testing Service was challenged by test consumers as well as state and federal legislators. Leading the charge in New York were parents, teachers, students, minorities, and labor groups. The New York state legislature has passed three bills to extend the nation's first "truth-in-testing" law, effective January 1, 1986 ("New York Legislature Approves Three 'Truth in Testing' Bills," 1986). The original laws required test companies to disclose to students, on request, a copy of their exam and responses as well as the correct answers and internal studies on test validity, what the test scores meant, and how well they might predict future achievement. At one time, as many as twenty states considered similar legislation, and a national "truth-in-testing" bill was introduced in the House of Representatives. Regardless of any further state or federal action, an institution has a better chance of avoiding a lawsuit if it does not overemphasize standardized testing in making admissions decisions.

Institutions also might consider providing alternative ways for students to demonstrate ability to succeed in college (Skinner, 1980). These alternatives range from essays and personal questionnaires to various types of problem-solving tests. The former president of the National Organization for Women charges that standardized tests are used as "gate keepers" to prevent women and minorities from attending college and achieving powerful positions in society. She predicts future lawsuits against testing companies and colleges that use standardized tests (Jaschik, 1986). The legislature and the courts seem to stay away from both truth in advertising and truth in testing as long as they perceive that an institution is attempting to clarify and publish policies.

Conclusions

Institutions should follow the recent recommendation in Section I of the recent Carnegie report, which deals with the transition from high school to college. The study found that the path from high school to college is poorly marked and that admissions officers have to do more to advise students about their alternatives (Boyer, 1987). Furthermore, the study urges college to serve the interests of students, not to just fill the spaces in the entering classes. Students who will not benefit from a particular college should not be accepted and should be referred to institutions that will better serve their needs and abilities. An annual review of policies and procedures will provide a healthy outlook for the legal requirements of each institution.

The *Statement of Principles of Good Practice* for members of the National Association of College Admissions Counselors (1985) provides a useful summary of current admissions issues. The statement sets forth the following general principles:

> High schools, colleges, universities, and other institutions and organizations dedicated to the promotion of formal education believe in the dignity, the worth, and the potentialities of every human being. They

cooperate in the development of programs and services in postsecondary counseling, admissions, and financial assistance to eliminate bias related to race, creed, sex, political affiliation, or national origin. Believing that institutions of learning are only as strong ultimately as their human resources, they look upon counseling individual students about their postsecondary plans as an important aspect of their responsibilities [p. 27].

It then lists the following specific tenets:

1. Admissions officers should be professional staff members of the institution and receive a fixed salary rather than a commission or bonuses.
2. Admissions officers should not initiate contact with students who have paid deposits or enrolled at another institution. To do so would be infringing on the rights and contractual relationship established between the student and the other institution.
3. The admissions officer should assume full responsibility for the admissions procedures initiated and followed by the institution.
4. Admissions officers should ensure that the procedures are known to all concerned students, parents, and high school counselors; that procedures or requirements are not changed without public notice or in the middle of the process; the records are handled in confidence; and that deadlines and notification dates are public knowledge.
5. The admissions officer should work with the appropriate parties in the university to ensure that the student is treated fairly, reasonably, and without prejudice during the admissions process.
6. The public should be informed of all types of financial aid available, the process for accessing those institutional funds, and the required deadlines.
7. Another issue is the need to address admission without regard to the financial need of the applicant. This is particularly

important for private institutions, which often attempt to achieve diversity in their student bodies through provision of financial aid to needy students or those with culturally different backgrounds. If, however, such aid is directly tied to ethnicity or race, other applicants denied such financial aid might bring suit.

8. Care must be taken to inform all applicants of any advanced-standing programs available at the institution. Such programs, in fact, offer an opportunity for students to shorten their collegiate experience by giving credit for courses required for graduation. Such opportunities must be made equally available to all applicants.

9. Preadmission information must be carefully reviewed and evaluated. The goal of a good admissions program is to assist both the institution and the student. Adherence to applicable legal constraints assists in meeting this goal.

References

American Association of Collegiate Registrars and Admissions Officers. *Legal Guide for Admissions Officers and Registrars.* Washington, D.C.: American Association of Collegiate Registrars and Admissions Officers, 1985.

Biehl, G. R. *Guide to the Section 504 Self-Evaluation for Colleges and Universities.* Washington, D.C.: National Association of College and University Business Officers, 1978.

Biemiller, L. "Justice Department Curbs Right of People with AIDS to Fight Discrimination." *Chronicle of Higher Education,* July 2, 1986, p. 9.

Bowen, E. "Good Timers Need Not Apply." *Time,* April 21, 1986, p. 70.

Boyer, E. *College: The Undergraduate Experience in America.* New York: Carnegie Foundation for the Advancement of Teaching, 1987.

Chandler, L. "Decision on Schools Delayed . . . Home Instruction Agreement Revised." *Fort Worth Star-Telegram,* Aug. 8, 1986, p. 20a.

"Dyslexic Student Sues University of Massachusetts." *Chronicle of Higher Education,* July 2, 1986, p. 2.

Faigel, H. C. "The Learning Disabled Go to College." *Journal of American College Health,* Aug. 1985, pp. 18–22.

Federal Interagency Committee on Education. *Keeping Your School or College Catalog in Compliance with Federal Laws and Regulations.* Washington, D.C.: Federal Interagency Committee on Education, 1978.

Hornby, D. B. *Higher Education Admission Law Service.* Princeton, N.J.: Educational Testing Service, 1980.

Jaschik, S. "Feminist Leader Urges Critics of Tests to File Law Suits and Stage Protests." *Chronicle of Higher Education,* Dec. 17, 1986, pp. 1, 8.

National Association of College Admissions Counselors. *Statement of Principles of Good Practice.* Skokie, Ill.: National Association of College Admissions Counselors, 1985.

"New Law Changes Student Aid Program Administration." *NACAC Bulletin,* June 1986, p. 2.

"New York Legislature Approves Three 'Truth in Testing' Bills." *Chronicle of Higher Education,* July 9, 1986, p. 80.

Palmer, S. E. "Change Sought on U.S. Policy on Accrediting," *Chronicle of Higher Education,* Dec. 17, 1986, p. 24.

Skinner, F. "Nader and ETS Clash on Standardized Testing." *Higher Education and National Affairs,* Jan. 1980, *29,* 2.

11

Donald R. Buckner

Residence Life Programs

The administration of residence life programs is described by Schuh (1984, p. 57) as "high-risk territory." These programs can indeed be fraught with possibilities for exposure to legal challenges and litigation, which could become highly stressful and financially draining. In this chapter, the current status of residence halls will be discussed, with specific attention given to the areas of contracts, constitutional constraints, liability, and risk reduction. The chapter closes with a summary of policy implications for the residence hall administrator. Although the focus in this chapter is on traditional residence hall environments for undergraduates, the material discussed can be applied to housing for married students, graduate students, and other facilities such as apartments. Of particular note for readers interested in these types of facilities are the sections on contractual and liability issues.

The Environment

Residence life administrators simultaneously operate multimillion-dollar businesses and complex educational endeavors. As part of their job, they must manage "cities" comprised almost entirely of adolescents living in high-density enclaves. The primary life stage of their clientele, late adolescence, is typically a volatile one, often involving risky experimentation, defiance of authority, serious emotional problems, active sexual behavior, and a sense of immortality. Alcohol and drug abuse, the pressures of growing up in modern society, and the anxieties generated by functioning in a competitive academic milieu may further lead to instances of rebellious, disturbed, and dangerous conduct in the residence halls. Many students, of course, do not exhibit such problems and are responsible and responsive members of both the residential community and the institution. They seek and expect living arrangements that are well maintained, safe, and supportive, and that provide ways to help them become involved in the life of the campus. The key to a successful residence hall program is to provide a comprehensive service meeting the needs of a diverse group of students.

Well-designed residence life programs can help residents adapt themselves to the demands of the contemporary college experience and, in the process, may reduce the institution's susceptibility to legal action. For example, effective programs can provide learning assistance and developmental programming opportunities; offer social, cultural, and recreational outlets; and supply counseling, crisis intervention, and referral services. Residence halls can make a positive difference in the health and well-being of college students.

One challenging aspect of residence life administration is ensuring the safety and security of the living environment. Many residence halls are aging and may be overdue for preventive maintenance or rehabilitation. Damage levels can run high. The high concentration of young people make residence halls a logical target for thieves, fly-by-night vendors, and those seeking to prey on women. Security is frequently inadequate, since residence halls were often built with more attention given to convenience of entry and exit than to security. These architectural deficiencies can be exacerbated by the inclination of youth to be more concerned about freedom of access and movement than personal safety. On the more clearly educational side, the residence hall living environment is an ideal setting to focus the delivery of a college's full array of student personnel services. Along with the benefits these services provide to residents, there are associated legal risks, as described in other chapters of this book. Although most residence life administrators do not have personal exposure to financial losses, their actions are always under legal scrutiny because of the nature of the territory. A sensitivity to evolving legal issues, principles, and risks can help administrators develop effective and prudent managerial and student development strategies.

The Changed Legal Climate

Prior to the 1960s, as Kaplin (1985, pp. 4–5) has noted, the courts afforded to higher education a privileged and essentially autonomous status in its relationship with students. This status was based on the doctrine of *in loco parentis,* which had filtered down from early English common law and was strongly reaffirmed in *Gott* v. *Berea College* (1913). Wide discretion was afforded to college officers to act in place of parents in regulating the physical, mental, and moral conduct of students. Termination of a student's affiliation with the college was considered to be the prerogative of the institution (*Hamilton* v. *Regents of the University of California,* 1934). Relatively few legal actions were initiated by students, and many of those that were initiated tended to be disallowed on grounds of governmental or charitable immunity of the institution.

During that era, the residence halls became the logical focal point for the exercise of *in loco parentis.* The resulting restrictive regulations appeared to be oriented primarily toward keeping the sexes separated from each other. By today's standards, this practice resulted in women's being treated in a clearly discriminatory fashion. In many institutions, they alone were subjected to curfews, weekend travel restrictions, and such regulations as having the window shades in their rooms drawn by dusk. In addition, college administrators could—and frequently did—dismiss both male and female students for residence hall infractions without due process, enter rooms without reasonable cause, and prohibit students from personalizing their living environment.

In the past two decades, many important changes in our society have had a profound effect on the administration of residence life programs and related legal issues. (See Chapter Four in this volume for a review of these issues.) The federal government became not only a major partner in the funding of higher education but also a significant force in regulating its relationship with students. Federal legislation now protects the privacy of student records and mandates the equal and equitable treatment of women, minorities, veterans, and the handicapped. The sanction of removal of federal funding for infractions extends these protections to both public and private institutions.

Court decisions reflecting these societal changes, such as *Dixon* v. *Alabama State Board of Education* (1961) and *Healy* v. *James* (1972), essentially dismantled the doctrine of *in loco parentis.* This major change in legal philosophy had a profound influence on the administration of residence life programs. Students came to be treated by the courts as full-fledged citizens who no longer surrendered their constitutional rights when they moved into a residence hall. The legal relationship of student to institution became a contractual one, not unlike that between a normal consumer and a supplier of services. These changes, along with the erosion of the doctrines of governmental and charitable immunity in negligence cases, opened up many more possibilities for students to pursue litigation. Today's residence life professional clearly faces a more complex and tenuous legal environment. However, the movement away from the previously imposed role of "surrogate authoritarian parent" has opened up new and broader opportunities for influencing the quality of life and education in residence halls. An essential element in defining this new relationship is the residence hall contract.

The Contractual Relationship

During the era of *in loco parentis,* the residence hall contract tended to be pro forma. It frequently was incorporated into a document that served as both a residence hall application and a contract. Most undergraduates had no choice regarding where they lived. Residence hall living arrangements were often uniform, without lifestyle or meal options offered. Contract terms were usually limited to a terse statement of financial conditions, with perhaps an oblique reference to a publication, to be supplied later, containing residence hall rules and regulations. Eviction did not need to be addresssed as an issue, since students were removed from both the residence halls and class enrollment if their conduct in housing was deemed unacceptable.

In today's legal climate, such a generalized and one-sided contract would be viewed as one of adhesion and therefore quite possibly unenforceable. Miller (1983, p. 51) correctly identifies the contemporary residence hall contract as "at the core of the relationship between residential students and the institution." An appropriate contract details what students can expect from the college in their housing arrangements and, in turn, what the institution will expect from the residents. The full range of topics covered in the document and the emphasis and detail provided will depend on the type of institution involved and its past experience with specific issues. Generally, residence hall contracts will encompass such items as financial matters; assignment policy; terms of occupancy, including holiday closings; conditions of use; alcoholic beverages and drugs; visitation and noise restrictions; damage assessments; cooking and appliances; security and safety; commercial solicitation; room entry and search; guests; food service; telephones; pets; miscellaneous housing regulations; a statement of the applicability of federal, state, and local criminal statutes; disclaimers; reservation of rights; and enforcement provisions. Residence life administrators may not realize that, in addition, statements made about housing facilities in any college publication may be interpreted by the courts as a binding promise and read into the housing contract. Although some judicial leeway is allowed for "gilding the lily" in institutional public relations, it would be judicious to review publications prior to their issuance. (See Chapter Five in this volume.)

Attention must also be given to the contractual relationship between the institution and those residing in institutional facilities other than residence halls. Again, the institution must clearly identify the terms and conditions of such arrangements and the responsibilities of both the institution and the tenant.

Housing contracts may be structured either as leases or licenses (Shur, 1983, p. 36). A lease establishes a formal landlord-tenant relationship and ties the agreement to the state's housing laws, which typically include a protracted eviction process. In those states allowing it, a license arrangement seems clearly preferable from the institution's point of view. In a decision in Illinois (*Cook v. University Plaza*, 1981), a license was defined as "an agreement which merely entitles one party to use the property subject to the management and control of the other party." In this case, it was noted that the student licensee had no property right to a specific room and therefore could be moved by the institution from one room to another.

Many areas of potential friction between the institution and the student "renter" may be rectified through remedies written into the residence hall contract, so that the institution is not required to utilize the due process requirements of campus disciplinary proceedings (*Miller* v. *Long Island University,* 1976). Contract enforcement provisions may include specified administrative fines for violations of designated housing standards; temporary removal of meal privileges as a possible prelude to eviction for overdue rent; damage assessments, including a notice that all floor residents will be held responsible for anonymous damage to communal areas on residence hall floors; transfers to another room or residence hall; denial of contract renewal; and eviction. A written warning, where feasible, prior to the imposition of the more stringent contractual remedies, is always a desirable practice. Prior to the final implementation of a contractual remedy, students desiring such should be afforded the opportunity to relate their side of the situation to an appropriate housing or other institutional official.

The preparation of the housing contract by residence life staff, in consultation with legal counsel, should become an important element of the planning process of identifying how the residence halls and other housing facilities will be programmed, managed, and administered. For students, the contract can serve as an essential reference to review prior to making a housing commitment and as a source of information, rights, obligations, and recourse during the term of residency. A well-thought-out, comprehensive, just, and enforceable housing contract becomes a valuable compact for facilitating the type of harmonious, growth-producing, and satisfying living and learning environments that institutions strive to deliver and residents are entitled to experience. If this desired relationship breaks down, the contract serves as a point of departure for redress within institutional channels or, in extreme cases, in the courts.

The Constitutional Imperative

An important goal of the residence life program is to facilitate the development of a living/learning environment that is conducive to the personal growth and development of residents. According to Grant (1974, p. 71), the four needs basic to human development are freedom, stimulation, security, and order. Needless to say, during the era of *in loco parentis,* residence hall living environments were heavily oriented toward maintaining order and frequently did not allow for sufficient freedom, stimulation, or privacy.

As previously noted, the legal ground rules changed dramatically in the 1960s, beginning with *Dixon* v. *Alabama State Board of Education* (1961). In that case, a federal appeals court held that students must be extended due process prior to expulsion from a public institution of higher education, and the U.S. Supreme Court let that decision stand. This landmark decision was the prelude to a series of federal court decisions that extended full constitutional rights to students at public colleges. According to Kaplin (1985, pp. 16–31), such rights under certain circumstances were also applicable to students attending private colleges. Selected constitutional rights and their implications for residence life administration are discussed below as they apply to freedom of expression, due process, and privacy.

Freedom of Expression. The First Amendment to the United States Constitution protects freedom of speech, religion, assembly, and association. These rights are the basis for life in a free society. Clearly, these freedoms must be nurtured in the residence life area, not merely to meet the letter of the law but also to establish living/ learning environments that support the institution's educational mission.

The exercise of freedom of expression by individuals in a residence hall living environment may, under certain circumstances, impinge unreasonably on the rights of others to privacy, peace, and tranquility. Fortunately, the courts, as detailed by Kaplin (1985, p. 431), do permit the regulation of the time, place, and manner in which First Amendment rights are exercised. Such regulation, in order to be upheld, must serve a significant governmental interest (such as the protection of rights to privacy and security) and may in no way serve to censor the content of the material being expressed. The manner in which freedom of expression is exercised can become an issue in a residence life setting in such areas as demonstrations, political canvassing, commercial solicitation, and the use of facilities for religious worship.

Ideas and protest may be legally expressed in public institutions of higher education through demonstrations and mass gatherings (*Healy* v. *James*, 1972). Such demonstrations must be structured so that they do not materially affect normal operations, interfere with the rights of others, or involve violence or the destruction of property (*Tinker* v. *Des Moines Independent School District*, 1969). Demonstrations may not compromise the freedom of movement of nondemonstrators, disrupt meetings, or disturb the study and sleep of others (*Buttney* v. *Smiley*, 1968). So as not to create the impression in the midst of a demonstration that restrictions are being issued arbitrarily, residence living administrators may want to publish, distribute, and enforce institutional guidelines governing the time, place, and manner of demonstrations in the residence halls.

Residence hall populations have also become an important target for solicitation by commercial vendors and political canvassers. Before the 1960s, many residence hall systems were totally closed to commercial activities. Political canvassing did not become a significant issue until 1970, when the minimum age for voting was lowered from twenty-one to eighteen. Clearly, the exercise of freedom of speech for the purpose of contacting voters as part of the electoral process is essential to the democratic process. However, even such a fundamental exercise of First Amendment guarantees is subject to time, place, and manner restrictions (*James* v. *Nelson*, 1972). The courts have been ambivalent concerning whether residence hall living areas, which are not normally regarded as a public forum, need to be opened up to door-to-door political canvassing. In the *James* case, the court held that some provision for door-to-door political canvassing must be enacted but that such canvassing could be reasonably delimited. In addition to time and manner restrictions, students were permitted to post signs on their individual doors declaring their room off-limits to canvassers. Such residents were prohibited, however, from declaring the entire residence hall building off-limits by referendum. In direct contrast, the Pennsylvania Supreme Court upheld the right of the university to ban door-to-door noncommercial canvassing in residence halls where a majority of the students had voted to preclude access (*Brush* v. *Pennsylvania State University*, 1980). The court noted that canvassers had many alternative avenues of communicating—for instance, by mail and telephone or in dining halls, lobbies, and conference rooms. At another public university, a federal court ruled that, for the purpose of registering voters, the central areas of the residence hall provided a sufficient channel for communication and denied the complainant the right to go door to door (*Harrell* v. *Southern Illinois University*, 1983). The subject of commercial solicitation in residence halls has also been extensively explored in litigation initiated by American Future Systems, a purveyor of china and crystal typically sold in group presentations. In a series of cases (*American Future Systems, Inc.* v. *Pennsylvania State University*, 1980, 1982, 1983, 1984), a number of principles have evolved.

It is clear that commercial solicitors do not have freedom to roam about, hawking their wares on residence hall living floors. Such excursions would constitute trespass. Vendors may be prohibited from taking orders and receiving funds anywhere in the residence hall except in a student's own room and only then if previously and specifically invited to be there by that resident. Institutions may oversee any commercial activity authorized in the residence hall, to ensure that it is not misleading or illegal.

Although public institutions of higher education have been given considerable leeway to place restrictions on the access of commercial vendors to the residence halls, regulations that censor or unreasonably curtail the mere dissemination of commercial information may infringe on the First Amendment. Aside from the legalities involved, it would seem unwise for residence life administrators to mount an aggressive campaign motivated by a desire to shield students entirely from the "real world" of commercial activity. A better approach would be to conduct ongoing programming in the area of consumer education, with some emphasis on the need for prospective buyers to beware.

The appropriateness of allowing formal religious activities to take place in the residence halls of public institutions has also been the source of some confusion. The First Amendment to the Constitution requires the neutrality of the government toward religion. Such neutrality, however, may not extend to discriminating against campus religious organizations or interfering with the individual's right to the free exercise of religion. In *Keegan* v. *University of Delaware* (1975), the court held that public institutions may not deny students the opportunity to hold religious services in the common areas of residence halls. Six years later, in *Widmar* v. *Vincent* (1981), the United States Supreme Court similarly concluded that the Constitution requires public institutions of higher education to allow religious activities to take place in campus areas normally open to other student activities uses.

The constitutional rights of students to associate freely with others in organizations and the prerogatives of a free press can also become issues within the residence life program. The legal ramifications of these rights are covered in detail in Chapters Fifteen and Sixteen, respectively.

Due Process, Privacy, and Order. The extension of constitutional rights to students has included a basic form of due process in disciplinary matters under the Fifth and Fourteenth Amendments and the right to be secure from unreasonable searches and seizures as provided by the Fourth Amendment. It is important for residence life professionals to be aware of the legal principles involving these rights as they influence housing management. A proper understanding provides a firm foundation for respecting important civil liberties and builds an awareness of avenues available for maintaining a level of order necessary for preserving the quality of life in the residence halls for all.

The previously cited case of *Dixon* v. *Alabama State Board of Education* (1961) altered the reigning legal theory that attending a public institution is a privilege that may be revoked by the college without affording due process. The amount of due process that came to be required by the courts is related to the maximum penalty that could be anticipated for the violation under consideration. Therefore, adjudication of relatively minor residence hall offenses (such as noise or a water fight), in which sanctions as a letter of warning or a work sanction might be involved, should require only a simple form of due process: an oral or written presentation of charges, an explanation of the evidence against the alleged offender, and an opportunity for the student to present his or her side of the case to a school official (*Goss* v. *Lopez,* 1975). Students at public institutions facing more serious penalties, such as lengthy suspensions or dismissals from housing, would be entitled to more elaborate due process. However, even in these instances, a true adversarial type of hearing, as in a courtroom, is neither required nor recommended (*Whiteside* v. *Kay,* 1978).

The courts have acknowledged the educative function of discipline in higher education and do not require that institutions utilize a criminal justice model of adjudication (*Zanders* v. *Louisiana State Board of Education,* 1968). However, as the pendulum began to swing sharply away from *in loco parentis,* many institutions complicated, elongated, and diluted the responsiveness of the judicial process by establishing legalistically oriented student judicial boards and providing seemingly endless levels of appeal. Pavela (1983, p. 29) notes that, although there may be some institutional reasons for providing each, there are no legal precedents mandating either.

The Fourth Amendment states that "The right of the people to be secure in their persons, houses, papers, and effects, against unreasonable searches and seizures shall not be violated." A public institution may not require that students relinquish their constitutional rights to privacy when they move into a residence hall (*Morale* v. *Grigel,* 1976). Private institutions, although not similarly bound (*Walter* v. *United States,* 1980), may not legally conduct a search that is in any way in collusion with the police (*People* v. *Cohen,* 1968). Both Pavela (1983, pp. 22-23) and Hood (1981, p. 14) list a number of circumstances under which school officials can legitimately enter, inspect, and in some cases seize evidence without a search warrant. These circumstances include room entry in response to emergencies (such as a fire or a blaring clock radio), for health and safety inspections announced in advance, and for maintenance functions. Staff may also enter a residence hall room for rule enforcement if they have "reasonable cause" to believe that a violation of college regulations is occurring.

"Reasonable cause"—based on judgment of what a "reasonable person of ordinary prudence" would deduce—is a lower level of test than the constitutionally required "probable cause" in criminal cases. Therefore, this basis for entry should be used only if the situation is to be handled as an internal disciplinary matter. When staff enter a student's room for any of the authorized reasons listed above, evidence in plain view may be seized and used in campus disciplinary proceedings (*Washington* v. *Chrisman,* 1982).

Sometimes the perceived rights of individual students and requirements necessary for preserving the common good come into conflict in a residence life setting. Familiarity with both the constitutional rights of residents and institutional prerogatives in the areas of freedom of expression, due process, and privacy are enormously helpful in equitably resolving such dilemmas.

Liability and Reduction of Risk

A survey conducted by Gehring (1983b) revealed that the preponderance of litigation emanating from the college housing area since 1975 has involved tort actions alleging negligence. The law governing negligence is complex and evolving. According to Moore and Murray (1983), for negligence to be proven and damages awarded against staff and/or the institution, the following elements must be present: (1) the institution must have a duty recognized by legal precedent to conform to a certain standard of care to protect others against unreasonable risks; (2) there must be a failure to deliver the appropriate standard of care; (3) such a failure must be the proximate cause of the resulting injury; and (4) actual damage must be suffered by the injured party. The following discussion of liability and risk reduction in residence halls focuses on the issues of security, safety, alcoholic beverage misuse, and staff training and supervision.

Security. The courts have held that colleges have an obligation to take reasonable steps to protect residents from criminal assault under circumstances where an attack is foreseeable (*Duarte* v. *California,* 1979) and must exercise reasonable care in the design and implementation of residence hall security systems (*Mullins* v. *Pine Manor College,* 1983). There are many barriers to providing tight security in a residence hall setting. A recurring problem is the lackadaisical attitude that students exhibit toward security, especially at institutions located away from large urban areas. Freedom of movement and convenience are often afforded a much higher priority than adherence to security measures. As a result, individual room doors are left unlocked, corridor entrance doors are propped open, and strangers are allowed to roam unescorted and unchallenged. These factors, combined with the large number of entrances and exits found in a typical residence hall, make it both difficult and very costly to implement an effective security system. In order to provide a satisfactory system, a combination of measures should be employed. Such a comprehensive building security plan would include well-trained and supervised security guards; the registration of guests; the enforcement of policies requiring hosts to escort their guests; stringent master key security; and the employment of modern technology, such as video cameras, alarm systems, key-operated elevators, walkie-talkies, and direct telephone lines to the police. To maximize the effective utilization of this system, an ongoing and creative publicity campaign needs to focus the attention of residents on foreseeable dangers and personal security measures.

Safety. Fire safety is the number-one priority in residence life administration. This awareness has been heightened in recent years in the aftermath of tragic fires in high-rise hotels. Too often, students contribute to the potential for losses by creating fire hazards, "playing" with fire, setting off false alarms, and using fire extinguishers inappropriately. To reduce risk, ongoing fire safety education programs should be supplemented with preannounced room safety inspections; prohibitions against cooking, use of candles, and the storage of combustibles; and the assessment of stringent penalties for acts that endanger the safety of others. False fire alarms should be responded to with immediate and thorough police and fire department investigations, large institutional rewards for the apprehension of offenders, and the placement of glass enclosures over pull stations to decrease the ease and temptation of triggering false alarms. A well-designed fire evacuation plan supported by periodic fire drills, carefully trained staff, and floor fire marshals is a must. Consideration should also be given to installing state-of-the-art computer-monitored smoke detection systems, which supply greater reliability, permit earlier and more specific fire detection, and have features that can reduce the incidence of false and phantom alarms.

Lack of ongoing responsive maintenance, along with the presence of hazardous conditions and attractive nuisances, can create significant exposure to liability in residence halls. Illustrative cases show institutions being held liable for such diverse hazards as an icy sidewalk (*Shannon* v. *Washington University*, 1978) and glass doors at the end of an exercise area (*Eddy* v. *Syracuse University*, 1980). Staff at all levels need to be constantly alert for conditions that may constitute a hazard to the safety of residents. Once a hazard is detected, a system for rapid reporting should be in place along with a channel for immediate corrective action.

Alcoholic Beverage Misuse. Institutional liability for the dangerous conduct of students following drinking in the residence halls has been the subject of much discussion. In *Baldwin* v. *Zoradi* (1981), the California courts held that practicality of enforcement prevented the imposition of a legal duty on the college to control student drinking in the residence halls. This litigation involved a student who had become intoxicated in the residence halls and subsequently injured another individual during a drag race. In an earlier case in Pennsylvania (*Bradshaw* v. *Rawlings*, 1979), Delaware Valley College was not held liable on appeal for a crippling traffic injury following an official off-campus sophomore class party, even though the faculty adviser had cosigned the check for the purpose of the beer. The court noted in finding for the college that the state of Pennsylvania does not hold hosts civilly liable for the actions of persons who become intoxicated at a "private party." It is important to note, however, that this decision might have gone against the institution in states with more stringent laws governing host responsibility. Kaplin (1985, p. 60) warns that colleges with alcoholic beverage regulations more stringent than state laws may assume third-party liability for injuries caused by residents following excessive drinking in the residence halls.

Staff Training and Supervision. A high level of effectiveness on the part of residence hall staff is essential to the delivery of an appropriate standard of care and the avoidance of claims of negligence. Central to this enterprise are the undergraduate resident assistants (RAs) or floor advisers who live with, counsel, advise, supervise activities, and discipline students under supervision of residence hall directors. These student staff members are typically young and inexperienced. Training sessions for such staff should begin after selection, resume in a preschool workshop format, and continue at periodic intervals throughout the year. Potentially, the most effective ongoing training can be focused in weekly one-to-one conferences between the resident assistant and his or her professional staff supervisor. At these conferences, the week's activities should be reported, reveiwed, and analyzed, with particular emphasis on any events that could impose legal liability.

Normally, a large portion of residence hall staff training and supervision serves to develop and assist individuals to perform as prudent and reasonable persons. Although this training in itself should reduce the risk of negligence, more focused training is warranted. The first and perhaps most important related training objective is to raise the awareness of RAs to their passage from the status of "carefree student" to that of a staff member. RAs must come to understand that they are agents of the institution and that their job-related actions (which in live-in positions are all-encompassing) can create legal liability for the institution. An effective vehicle for accomplishing this objective is to build a strong and supportive sense of working community between the RAs and the professional staff. This sense of community will do much to reinforce the RAs' identification with staff status and develop their sensitivity to the importance of performing as responsible institutional representatives. The value of maintaining floor security must be emphasized. Perhaps paramount to this goal is the need for RAs to guard their floor master key from loss, theft, or use by any other person. Too often, resident assistants may jeopardize the security of an entire floor or floors through the loss of a master key. Institutions should give serious consideration to developing viable alternatives that greatly reduce the number of staff to whom master keys are issued and the frequency with which they are carried.

Rule enforcement is also frequently difficult for new staff members. Training emphasis needs to be placed on their legal duty to enforce published rules consistently and equitably, to refrain from extending liability to areas not included in the institution's purview (for instance, by supervising off-campus social functions), and to follow meticulously all institutional policies governing room entry and search.

Professional staff must guard against the tendency of some resident assistants to overestimate their skills and sense of autonomy. Policies on reporting exceptional circumstances to professionals must be established, communicated, and reinforced. Reportable conditions should include such areas as hazardous situations, breaches of security, accidents, floor emergencies, and serious disciplinary and emotional problems of residents. Especially important to the ongoing supervision of RAs is the monitoring of interactions with emotionally disturbed students. RAs must recognize their limits as peer counselors, be sensitive to the need for receiving case management assistance from their supervisors, and be able to utilize referral sources appropriately. Most important, resident assistants must realize the critical importance of notifying the professional staff immediately if a student threatens suicide and the legal obligation of all staff members to break confidentiality if there is a warning sign of a confidant's intent to inflict serious harm on another (*Tarasoff* v. *Regents of the University of California,* 1976).

Although such extensive training and supervision may be very time consuming, it will prove to be time very well spent. The personal development of student staff and the quality of their service to residents can be enhanced immeasurably. In the process, the level of institutional risk in the residence life area should be significantly reduced.

Summary and Policy Implications

Today's housing professionals clearly face a complex and tenuous legal environment. However, the changes in the legal climate have provided new opportunities for positively influencing the quality of life and education in residence halls apart from the previously imposed repressive role of "surrogate authoritarian parent." A sensitivity to evolving legal issues, principles, and risks in the residence life area can help professionals develop effective and prudent managerial and student development strategies. From these legal principles, a number of policy implications are apparent.

Utilization of the Contract.

1. The residence hall contract becomes the core of the legal relationship between the student living in the residence halls or other facilities and the institution.

2. Contracts must be carefully constructed and updated annually with the aid of legal counsel; they must include in specific detail what is being offered and must spell out current policies, conditions of use, and college regulations.

3. In addition to the standard contract, supplemental contracts should be utilized for residential programs that have unique conditions and regulations (such as quiet lifestyle floors and academic residential programs).

4. If possible, the residence hall contract needs to be structured as a simple license rather than a lease, in order to avoid creating a landlord-tenant relationship. This relationship could tie an institution to that state's entire body of landlord-tenant law, which may include cumbersome civil eviction proceedings.

5. All institutional publications that include information on the residence halls need to be reviewed for accuracy by housing officials. These statements may be viewed by prospective students and ultimately the courts as binding promises.

6. Specific remedies and procedures for redressing breaches of contract should be written into the document. Contractual remedies may be used to resolve a wide range of matters covered in the contract, so that housing officials need not become involved unnecessarily in the lengthy due process requirements of campus disciplinary systems.

Constitutionally Related Matters.

1. Students who live in residence halls in public institutions do not forfeit their constitutional rights to freedom of speech, assembly, association, or religion. Residence life administrators

may, however, regulate the time, place, and manner in which these rights are exercised, provided that such regulation serves a significant governmental function (such as protection of rights to privacy and security) and is not directed at censoring the content of the material being expressed. The subject of when, where, and what constitutional rights the courts will hold applicable to students at private institutions is a complex one, requiring legal advice for specific situations. On both educational and public relations grounds, private institutions may also wish to consider following many of the principles detailed below.

2. Institutions should develop, publish, and distribute explicit policies addressing the time, place, and manner for political canvassing, commercial solicitation, and demonstrations in the residence halls.

3. Provisions must be made for allowing orderly demonstrations, no matter how bizarre the cause. Regulations may specify the means, lead time, and conditions required for reserving and utilizing residence hall space for this purpose. Such mass gatherings must not be allowed to interfere with the freedom of movement, safety, or privacy of nondemonstrators.

4. Court decisions have been contradictory regarding whether political canvassers have the right to go door to door in the residence halls at specified times or may merely reserve spaces in the central areas of buildings to register and inform resident voters. Residence life educators should consider, however, providing means beyond the legal minimums to facilitate the electoral process.

5. Commercial solicitation may and should be more strongly regulated than political canvassing. The order-taking and money-exchange part of sales presentations may be disallowed. A total prohibition in public institutions on the mere dissemination of commercial information in central areas may infringe on the First Amendment.

6. Rather than engaging in an aggressive and possibly illegal campaign to provide a totally "commerce-free" residence hall environment, staff may wish to focus some of their energies on providing programs designed to enhance consumer awareness and skills.

7. Religious activities may facilitate such educational

objectives as the development of ethical values and a philosophy of life. Contrary to earlier misunderstandings by some, students do have the legal right to utilize residence hall space in public institutions for religious purposes on the same basis as other student activity users.

8.   Students are entitled to a form of procedural due process in disciplinary matters. The severity of the potential sanction determines the formality and extent of the process due (in no case is an adversarial trial style of hearing required or recommended).

9.   The extensive use of student judicial boards and elaborate appeal processes are not legally required. Institutions should consider streamlining their residence hall disciplinary process in order to reduce the time gap between the occurrence of the disciplinary incident and the levying of the sanction (especially for relatively minor infractions).

10.   Because of the complexity and sensitivity of matters involving the privacy of students in residence halls, each instition should include in its residence hall contract a detailed institutional policy concerning entry into and search of residence hall rooms. Provisions may be included for staff to enter areas—but not search without warrants—for announced safety inspections, maintenance, emergencies, and "reasonable cause" to believe that housing violations are occurring.

Reducing Liability.

1.   In our litigious society and in the complex operating environment of modern-day residence halls, the preponderance of court cases coming out of the college housing area involve claims of negligence. A major effort needs to be devoted to providing the legally required standard of care, both to reduce the possibility of litigation and to serve residents more satisfactorily.

2.   Fire safety is the number-one priority in the administration of residence life programs. A comprehensive and coherent plan of fire prevention, detection, and emergency evacuation must be skillfully formulated and diligently carried out.

3.   The institution has a duty to take reasonable measures to protect residents against criminal assault. Such measures would

typically include both well-executed residence hall security systems and ongoing campaigns to educate and motivate residents to utilize security plans rather than finding ways to undermine them.

4.   The presence of hazardous situations in residence halls is a frequent source of litigation. A strong and coordinated team effort needs to be developed among residence hall staff, maintenance personnel, outside contractors, and students for the prevention, detection, reporting, and expeditious correction of situations potentially hazardous to the safety of residents.

5.   The abuse of alcoholic beverages by students is a universal concern. Institutions should be careful, however, not to assume third-party liability for the intoxicated behavior of students through the promulgation of unrealistic and unenforceable regulations that go beyond the tracking of state law.

6.   Critical to the delivery of an appropriate standard of care to students and the avoidance of claims of negligence is the effectiveness of the residence hall staff, especially that of undergraduate floor advisers. Therefore, ongoing staff training and supervision must be oriented toward ensuring quality performance, especially in areas that impose the greatest risk of legal liability.

References

Barr, M. J. (ed.). *Student Affairs and the Law.* New Directions for Student Services, no. 22. San Francisco: Jossey-Bass, 1983.

Gehring, D. D. (ed.). *Administering College and University Housing: A Legal Perspective.* Asheville, N.C.: College Administrative Publications, 1983a.

Gehring, D. D. "Consumerism in College Housing: An Empirical Analysis of Litigation." *Journal of College Student Personnel,* 1983b, *24* (11), 502–506.

Grant, W. H. "Humanizing the Residence Hall Environment." In D. A. DeCoster and P. Mable (eds.), *Student Development and Education in College Residence Halls.* Washington, D.C.: American College Personnel Association, 1974.

Hood, A. B. "Fourth Amendment Rights in the College Residence Hall." *Journal of College and University Housing,* 1981, *11* (2), 13–15.

Kaplin, W. A. *The Law of Higher Education: A Comprehensive Guide to Legal Implications of Administrative Decision Making.* (2nd ed.) San Francisco: Jossey-Bass, 1985.

Miller, S. T. "Contracts and Their Use in Housing." In D. D. Gehring (ed.), *Administering College and University Housing: A Legal Perspective.* Asheville, N.C.: College Administrative Publications, 1983.

Moore, D. R., and Murray, L. "Torts: Your Legal Duties and Responsibilities." In D. D. Gehring (ed.), *Administering College and University Housing: A Legal Perspective.* Asheville, N.C.: College Administrative Publications, 1983.

Owens, H. F. (ed.). *Risk Management and the Student Affairs Professional.* Monograph Series, Vol. 2. Columbus, Ohio: National Association of Student Personnel Administrators, 1984.

Pavela, G. "Constitutional Issues in Residence Halls." In D. D. Gehring (ed.), *Administering College and University Housing: A Legal Perspective.* Asheville, N.C.: College Administrative Publications, 1983.

Roe, B. "Staff Liability in Residence Halls." *Journal of College and University Residence Halls,* 1979, *9* (2), 6-10.

Schuh, J. H. "The Residential Campus: High Risk Territory!" In H. F. Owens (ed.), *Risk Management and the Student Affairs Professional.* Monograph Series, Vol. 2. Columbus, Ohio: National Association of Student Personnel Administrators, 1984.

Shur, G. M. "Contractual Relationships." In M. J. Barr (ed.), *Student Affairs and the Law.* New Directions for Student Services, no. 22. San Francisco: Jossey-Bass, 1983.

12

Margaret J. Barr

🍀❄   🍀❄   🍀❄

Facility Management

A state political party wants to hold a fund raiser in the student center. A national church group wants to hold a week-long conference using food service, residence halls, and academic buildings. Members of a new congregation ask if they can meet regularly in the ballroom until their church is finished. A local teenage swimming team wants to use the swimming pool for practice. Members of a Bible society want to distribute free Bibles to students at a desk in the registration line. A local vendor asks for space in the student center to sell products at a substantial discount. The local Little League wants to use the intramural fields for games. A black student group wants a prominent lounge assigned to it for its exclusive use.

None of these requests are unusual. In fact, most student affairs administrators deal with them on a daily basis. Colleges and universities attract such interest because often they have unique facilities or provide a combination of facilities that are attractive to both on- and off-campus groups. Often, the facilities requested for use fall under the domain of student affairs administration. Although the types of facilities requested may range from a residence hall to a swimming pool, the legal concerns remain the same.

Thus, the response of the student affairs administrator to each request is critical, for precedents can be set. An unlawful refusal can cause expensive and time-consuming litigation. Policies must be developed and be consistently followed in order to protect both the institution and the individual administrator. Development of policies depends on several factors, including the public or private nature of the institution, the type of group (whether it is a campus organization or an off campus group), legal questions, institutional philosophy, and facility availability. In this chapter, these factors will be discussed and guidelines provided to aid administrators in both policy development and implementation.

Public Versus Private Institutions

As indicated in Chapters Three and Four in this volume, public institutions have greater statutory and constitutional constraints on the conduct of their business than private institutions do. Private institutions are not immune from such constraints under certain conditions, such as state constitutional provisions (*State* v. *Schmid,* 1980). However, "Whether public or private, postsecondary institutions have considerable authority to determine how and when their property will be used" (Kaplin, 1985, p. 418). Property law of the state provides a protected interest by the institution in the use of its buildings and grounds.

Use of facilities by members of the campus community (students, faculty, and staff), in both public and private institutions, is governed by the contractual relationship the institution has with the party involved. Public institutions must further comply with provisions of the federal Constitution, their state's constitution (see Chapter Four), and the state's statutes governing the use of state property (Kaplin, 1985, p. 419). Private institutions, however, are not immune from constitutional constraints if they are engaging in state action (see Chapters Three and Four); and, under certain other conditions, they may be subject to certain federal laws (see Chapters Six and Seven). Private institutions, therefore, should have clear regulations governing the use of their facilities and should consistently follow their own rules. Although the focus in this chapter is on public colleges and universities, the suggestions presented can provide valuable guidance for administrators in private institutions.

Students and Student Organizations

The courts have held that students do have First Amendment protections on the college campus (see Chapters Three, Four,

Eleven, and Fifteen in this volume). A distinction has been made in the courts between freedom of speech and assembly, on the one hand, and, on the other hand, speech or action that constitutes a clear or immediate danger to the university community or has the potential to interfere substantially with institutional activities. The burden of proof is on the institution to show that prohibited behavior or expression would be disruptive (*Tinker* v. *Des Moines Independent School District,* 1969; *Bayless* v. *Martine,* 1970).

An institution may regulate the time, place, and manner of expression, not the content of the ideas expressed (*Smith* v. *Ellington,* 1971). In *Cox* v. *Louisiana* (1965), for example, the Supreme Court held: "The rights of free speech and assembly while fundamental in our democratic society still do not mean that everyone with opinions may address a group at any public place or time" (at 454). Regulations governing speech of students and their right to hear outside speakers must not be vague or overbroad (*Smith* v. *University of Tennessee,* 1969; *Stacy* v. *Williams,* 1969), and institutional officials may not exercise unrestrained discretion in enforcing regulations (*Hammond* v. *South Carolina State College,* 1967).

The freedom of students to demonstrate or hold peaceful assembly has also been upheld by the courts when it has not materially and substantially interfered with the normal educational process or invaded the rights of others (Wright, 1969, p. 1043). However, the university may restrict demonstrations to certain areas of the campus and to facilities appropriate to the activity. Care must be taken in developing regulations and policies, so that such regulations do not "go farther than [their] intended application" (Wright, 1969, p. 1045). Broad and vague regulations could open the door to selective enforcement and to charges of interference with constitutionally protected rights.

Freedom of association of students and student groups has also been firmly upheld by the Supreme Court in *Healy* v. *James* (1972). (See Chapter Fifteen in this volume for a complete discussion of the issues involved.)

In negligence liability cases, students and student organizations have been seen as invitees to the campus. When policies and procedures are developed, attention must be given to making the

environment as safe as possible to avoid litigation. (See Chapter
Nine in this volume.) Finally, the institution must comply with
applicable state and federal statutes when managing facilities for
the use of students.

Many of these same issues also are of concern when institutional facilities are to be used by nonaffiliated persons or groups.
These issues include constitutional and statutory constraints at the
federal, state, and local levels.

Constitutional Rights of Nonaffiliated Persons or Groups

Nonaffiliated individuals and groups have five federal
constitutionally protected rights, which must be taken into account
in the development of facility use policies: freedom of religion,
freedom of the press, freedom of speech, equal protection under the
law, and due process. Additionally, in some states, provisions of the
state constitution may influence policy development (see Chapter
Four in this volume).

Freedom of Religion. The principle of separation of church
and state has long been used as a basis for denying permission to
religious groups to use public educational facilities. Complete
exclusion of religious groups, however, may neither be prudent nor
legally defensible, as court cases illustrate.

In *Lemon* v. *Kurtzman* (1971), the Supreme Court held that
acts of the state must have a secular legislative purpose and that
there may not be excessive governmental entanglement with
religion (at 2112). In *Hunt* v. *McNair* (1973), the Court held that the
primary effect of any act by the state may be neither to aid nor to
inhibit religion. The right to free expression of religious beliefs in
a public park was upheld by the Supreme Court in *Fowler* v. *Rhode
Island* (1953).

State courts faced with cases involving use of facilities by
religious groups at public colleges and universities have followed
the same logic. In *Keegan* v. *University of Delaware* (1975), the
Delaware Supreme Court held that neutral accommodation is
permitted in the facilities of a state university. The institution could
not show a compelling state interest to deny the free exercise of
religion. Moreover, religious groups must conform with the facility

use policies applicable to other organizations. When the board of regents rented a public university stadium to Billy Graham, a taxpayer brought suit, charging that the principle of separation of church and state had been violated (*Pratt* v. *Arizona Board of Regents*, 1974). The court held that rental of the facility on an occasional basis did not violate the constitutional principle of separation of church and state as long as a fair rental value was charged.

Finally, in *International Society for Krishna Consciousness of Atlanta* v. *Eaves* (1979), the Fifth Circuit affirmed two principles bearing on the separation of church and state. First, vague measures regarding religious activities permit low-level administrators to act as censors, and such measures cannot be permitted. Second, to treat exchanges of money for religious purposes differently from exchanges of money for commercial purposes amounts to discrimination on the basis of content; therefore, such discrimination is invalid.

Freedom of the Press. Marsh v. *Alabama* (1946) is often cited as precedent in determining the right of colleges and universities to regulate the sale or distribution of newspapers on campus (see Chapters Four and Sixteen in this volume). Several cases confirm the need for specific regulations in this area (*New Left Education Project* v. *Board of Regents of the University of Texas System*, 1970; *New Times, Inc.* v. *Arizona Board of Regents*, 1974). The court in *New Times* summarized the issue when it declared, "The state has already opened the campus to the public generally and may not arbitrarily restrict the freedoms of individuals lawfully on the campus to exercise their First Amendment rights" (at 173). (For a detailed analysis of public freedom of press issues, see the discussion of *Spartacus Youth League* v. *Board of Trustees of Illinois Industrial University* (1980) in Chapter Sixteen of this volume.)

Freedom of Speech. Early cases dealt only with outside speakers, but they have had a great influence on public access questions. Neutral priorities and coordination have been upheld, but once a university "opens its lecture halls, it must do so nondiscriminately" (*Stacy* v. *Williams*, 1969, at 971). If any outside speakers are permitted, then speakers cannot be barred solely on the basis of the content of their speech.

Restrictions on the use of campus facilities have been upheld in the courts as long as the restrictions are enforced in a fair and equitable manner (*Cholmakjian* v. *Board of Trustees of Michigan State University,* 1970; *American Civil Liberties Union of Virginia, Inc.* v. *Radford College,* 1970). The prime educational purpose of the institution may be protected through facility use policies (*State* v. *Jordan,* 1972). The question of commercial sales and solicitation on university property has also been challenged in the courts (*American Future Systems, Inc.* v. *Pennsylvania State University,* 1980, 1982, 1983, 1984). (See Chapter Eleven in this volume for a full discussion of these issues.)

Equal Protection. The federal Constitution provides that all citizens have equal protection under the law and that citizens may not be treated differently merely because of their particular status. (See Chapter Six in this volume for a full discussion of these issues.) Rental of an auditorium on a regular basis for a nominal fee during nonschool hours was judged by a court to be effective dedication of the auditorium for the exercise of First Amendment rights (*National Socialist White People's Party* v. *Ringers,* 1973). Elimination of certain groups from consideration for facility use because of their beliefs has not been upheld by the courts. "The state is not under a duty to make school buildings available for public gatherings, but if it elects to do so, it must be done with reasonable nondiscrimination equally applicable to all and equally administered to all" (*East Meadows Community Concerts Association* v. *Board of Education,* 1966, at 173).

Due Process. Chapter Eight discusses due process requirements for student discipline in detail. These same due process requirements must also be met in facility use policies (*Watson* v. *Board of Regents of the University of Colorado,* 1973; *Dunkel* v. *Elkins,* 1971). Also, "state and local governments have trespass or unlawful entry laws that limit the use of a postsecondary institution's facilities by outsiders" (Kaplin, 1985, p. 422). These laws have been upheld, in general, by the courts (*Braxton* v. *Municipal Court,* 1973; *Kristel* v. *State,* 1971). However, in *Grody* v. *State* (1972), a trespass statute was struck down on grounds of vagueness and overbreadth.

State Constitutional Protections. In some states, the state constitution provides even greater rights than the federal Constitution for nonaffiliated persons. New Jersey and Pennsylvania have litigated cases in this area (*State* v. *Schmid,* 1980; *Commonwealth of Pennsylvania* v. *Tate,* 1981). Both of these cases found a state constitutional right of access for nonaffiliated persons at private instititutions. Although each of these cases has findings limited to the state in question, they do indicate the need for legal counsel in the formation of policies in order to avoid litigation.

Statutory Constraints on Policy Formation

Statutes at the federal, state, and local levels must also be respected when facility use policies are developed and implemented. Since each state has a unique set of civil and criminal laws, the prudent administrator should test the statutory concerns outlined against the applicable set of state statutes.

Authority over Facilities. In Chapter Two, the legal organization and control of colleges and universities was discussed. Legal authority to govern facilities and their use can make a critical difference in the development of policies. The clear power and authority of the governing board to regulate facilities is the basis for administrative intervention. Finally, the authority to act in the name of the institution should, for the protection of both the institution and the administrator, be clearly defined.

Liability Concerns. Facility use policies for institutions of higher education should be developed and implemented in a manner that reduces the potential for liability claims against the institution. As discussed in Chapter Nine, that goal is often difficult to achieve. Governmental immunity has not, in recent years, provided a strong defense against a suit. If the institution is engaged in activity "which is commercial in character or is usually carried out by private individuals or is for profit, benefit or advantage of the governmental unit conducting the activity" (*Carroll* v. *Kittle,* 1969, at 23), then it is viewed as a proprietary function. Under such conditions, even limited immunity might not attach.

Determination of whether an institution is liable in negligence suits rests on the legal relationship between the institution and the claimant. The institution owes the duty of ordinary and reasonable care with respect to premise conditions for invitees. For licensees, if ordinary hazards exist and injury results, the institution has not been held to be liable. Under conditions where a person assumes a risk of injury and injury occurs, courts have not upheld liability claims against either institutions or their agents (*Rubtchinsky* v. *State University of New York at Albany*, 1965; *Dudley* v. *William Penn College*, 1974). These decisions are critical to institutions that lease facilities to nonaffiliated groups for events or that allow nonaffiliated persons to attend events on institutional property. In general, the courts have held that, when school property is leased to nonschool organizations, the lessee accepts the conditions of the facility by accepting the lease agreement. Such agreements should be negotiated carefully in order to reduce the potential liability claims for negligence.

Civil Rights Liability and Discrimination. Other chapters in this volume discuss issues of civil rights and discrimination in great detail. Case law clearly indicates that neither on their face nor by implication can institutional policies discriminate against any protected class of beneficiaries under federal law. In some locations, state statutes also affect this area. Priorities on the use of facilities can be set to meet legitimate educational needs, but they cannot be based on discriminatory criteria.

Antitrust Laws. The courts have held in the past that the Sherman Act and the Clayton Act do not apply to public postsecondary institutions when such institutions are engaged in governmental activities (*Parker* v. *Brown*, 1943; *Saenz* v. *University Interscholastic League*, 1976). However, in 1975, the Supreme Court declared that absolute exemption from antitrust coverage does not exist (*Goldfarb* v. *Virginia State Bar*, 1975). As institutions attempt to generate additional income by leasing facilities for commercial and proprietary enterprises, their officers must be aware of the potential for litigation under the claim of restraint of trade. Care should be taken to ensure that rental fees or charges are fair and equitable and that institutions do not combine with other educational institutions in the community to engage in price fixing on the cost of admission to events.

Unfair Competition. There has been a long history of litigation between public colleges and universities and the local business community on the claim of unfair competition. The rationale on which such cases are based is the legitimacy of using state tax-supported property to conduct business activities that compete directly with private enterprise. Court decisions have been based on several factors, including the legal authority of the institution to engage in such enterprise, the nature of the goods and services rendered, and the rationale for the institution to engage in such enterprise. Enterprises that are reasonably related to the prime educational mission of the institution haave been upheld (*Villyard et al.* v. *Regents of the University System of Georgia*, 1948) and do not constitute unfair competition. Additionally, if the institution has statutory authority to provide services to those not directly affiliated with it, it may do so (*University of North Carolina* v. *Town of Carrboro*, 1972).

Relationships with Local Governments. A distinction is made between governmental functions and proprietary functions in determining the superiority of the state institution over local ordinances regarding general health and safety. In California, a university was not permitted to lease facilities to a circus under conditions that were not allowed by local ordinance (*Board of Trustees* v. *City of Los Angeles*, 1975). Sales tax questions have also been litigated, and decisions have been based on the facts and the language of the exemption for the institution as found in the statutes. When the city of Boulder, Colorado, asked the court to compel the university to pay taxes on public events such as concerts, lectures, and plays, the court declined to do so, holding in part that "[a] person's acquisition of knowledge should not be taxed" (*City of Boulder* v. *Regents of the University of Colorado*, 1972, at 123). (Admission to athletic events was not exempt in *City of Boulder.*) In *New York University* v. *Taylor* (1937), the courts held that the language of the exemption made NYU free from a sales tax burden.

Even under conditions of municipal home rule, it usually is only those activities at public institutions clearly not related to education that can be governed by local ordinance. The various units of local government are creatures of state policy, and they are subservient to the state in governmental functions unless the state grants them authority to act (Fordham, 1975). Facility use policies, therefore, should conform to local ordinances when such policies govern activities that can be legally viewed as incidental enterprises.

Other Statutes. The civil code of each state has other statutes that can also influence facility use policies. Such statutes include those related to general public safety, public order and decency, abuse of public office, weapon control, and police authority. Public institutions are also subject to the general provisions of the state education code and the specific statutory entitlement of the institution. All these state laws must be considered in policy development for institutional facilities.

Policy Implications

Both public and private institutions need to have clear and unambiguous policies governing facility use. Generally, private or public institutions are not legally obligated to make institutional facilities available for use by nonaffiliated persons. As a practical matter, however, total exclusion of all nonaffiliated persons is difficult to achieve. Requests for use of facilities by students, faculty, and staff also require guidance for response. Reliance on the judgment of an individual staff member to accept or deny such requests without clear policy direction invites error. Thus, for each institution, the issue becomes one of determining the conditions under which facilities can be used.

Determination of facility use policies is difficult, but it is necessary in order to protect the institution and to ensure fair and equitable treatment of all who request the use of such facilities. The following list of guidelines for development of facility use policies is based on the known legal constraints on such policies. As already indicated, however, the law is always evolving. The prudent administrator should not only assess the institution's current policies against these guidelines but also develop a process that allows regular policy review on the basis of informed legal advice. Finally, although private institutions have greater latitude in such matters than do public institutions, sound administrative practice and educational philosophy require that some of these guidelines be adopted within the private sector.

- *Facility use policies must conform to the general criminal and civil statutes of the state.* An institution, whether public or private, is not an enclave of immunity from the law. Any policy should reflect adherence to such standards.

- *Facility use policies can regulate the time, place, and manner of use of institutional property.* This standard holds true for both affiliated and nonaffiliated persons or groups. Such regulations, however, should be reasonably precise and not vague or overbroad.

- *Facility use policies cannot discriminate on the basis of the beliefs or philosophy of the requesting organization.* The question of precedent is critical to this standard. Once the public institution opens its doors, it cannot discriminate on the basis of the philosophy of the group or individual. Private institutions do have greater latitude in this area, but care should be exercised in refusal and it should be linked to the institution's educational mission or purpose.

- *Facility use policies should set very specific standards for use of facilities by nonaffiliated religious, political, or commercial groups.* Again the question of legal precedent is important. If an institution allows one such group to use its facilities because it likes or accepts that group, it may be establishing a precedent that would not be easy to set aside for other groups deemed unacceptable. Public institutions must be particularly cautious in this area.

- *Policies governing the sale and distribution of off-campus publications should be specific and precise.* This standard is critical for public institutions and will make implementation decisions more fair and equitable in private institutions.

- *Facility use policies should stipulate the individuals who can make exceptions to the policy and should outline the procedures for appeal and review of decisions on facility use.* Such precision helps both the institution and the potential user. In addition to the legal requirements for public institutions, appeal procedures are sound public relations.

- *Facility use policies should specify criteria to be used by institutional agents in policy implementation.* If an institution's policy does not provide implementation guidance, uninformed decisions may be made by staff lacking an adequate base of knowledge or experience to make such decisions.

• *Facility use policies should stipulate the authority of the institution to refuse access under conditions where there is strong evidence that such use of property will disrupt the educational enterprise.* When such conditions occur, the burden of proof is on the public institution to show that the planned activity will materially and substantially disrupt educational efforts. Such proof is not easy, and careful use of this policy guideline must be made in the public sector.

• *Facility use policies must address tort liability issues.* This standard is critical for both public and private institutions. Litigation appears to be the first answer in most disputes involving injury. Careful construction of policies can protect the institution from unwarranted claims.

• *Facility use policies should comply with antidiscrimination statutes.* From both a legal and an ethical view, this standard is important for public and private institutions.

• *Facility use policies should be reasonably specific and precise regarding access to and use of campus facilities and property by nonaffiliated persons and groups.* Such a policy statement should reflect the priority of affiliated persons in the use of facilities and provide guidance to university agents in dealing with nonaffiliated and noninvited individuals and groups.

• *Facility use policies should define which areas of the campus, if any, are public areas, where free access and egress of nonaffiliated persons are permitted.* Again the policy should provide guidance for institutional agents in the performance of their duties. Further, such policies should give clear notice and warning of consequences for violation of the policy by nonaffiliated persons.

Policy Development and Implementation

In order to meet the minimum legal criteria set out in the preceding section, administrators must consider a number of procedural issues during the stages of policy development and implementation. Awareness of these procedural issues can assist them in developing facility use policies that are not only consistent with identified legal constraints but also reflect the unique needs of their institution.

Institutional Mission. Understanding the institution's educational and public service philosophy is the first step in development of a sound facility use policy. Indeed, this philosophical base is perhaps the most important factor in policy formation. To illustrate, a community-based institution and a highly selective university should both have parameters for facility use. The institution's philosophy and mission define the parameters within which the legal constraints on facility use policies must be met.

Legal Advice. While appropriate legal advice during the process of policy development does not guarantee that the resulting policy will withstand judicial scrutiny if it is challenged, it can ensure that all identified legal standards have been included in the policy. Legal review has great potential for increasing the possibility that the final policy will be fundamentally fair and reasonable.

Awareness of the Law. College and university administrators can no longer function in ignorance of the law. Every person who has policy formation responsibilities needs to acquire at least a minimal understanding of the legal constraints on facility use policies. Methods should also be developed to ensure that administrators are aware of new developments in the law.

Consolidation of Policies. A consolidated policy for all institutional facilities provides the best defense against internal inconsistency. At most institutions, regulations on facility use can be found in handbooks, procedure manuals, and internal memoranda. If it is not feasible to develop a consolidated document, then, at the very minimum, a cross-reference index to all applicable policies is necessary in order to reduce confusion, both for potential users of institutional facilities and for the institution's administrators.

Broad Policy Base. Policies need to be not only legally correct but also reasonable and useful to those charged with implementation. A policy document provides guidance for everyday decisions. When administrators who have responsibility for policy implementation are included in the policy development process, ambiguities can be resolved, potential problems can be identified, and clarity can be sought. An additional benefit is that a broad-based development process increases the knowledge base of all participants.

Ongoing Training. The least experienced staff often are required to implement policies. Training is essential to help these individuals do their job. Policy review and discussions of potential problems by involved staff can go a long way in reducing institutional risks.

Policy Review. As indicated before, the law is an ever-evolving standard. A consistent process for periodic review of all policies should be implemented in every institution. Review and amendment of policies can often reduce potential problems based on new case and statutory law. Failure to provide for such periodic review invites problems.

Summary

The development of legally sound, practical, and useful facility use policies for both public and private institutions is not an easy task. Although public institutions have many more legal constraints on their activities than do their private counterparts, each institutional type should have clear, concise, and enforceable policies for the use of facilities.

Institutions must define the conditions under which facilities and property can be used by both affiliated and nonaffiliated persons and organizations. Policies for the use of facilities should be fundamentally fair, clear, and concise, and they must provide adequate guidance for those charged with policy implementation. College and university administrators should anticipate problems with current policies, develop a sound procedure for revising them, and ensure that new policies meet identified legal standards. If they do so, then the institution's own definition of the proper use of its facilities has a greater chance of surviving a test in the courts.

References

Fordham, J. B. *Local Government Law: Legal and Related Materials.* Mineola, N.Y.: Foundation Press, 1975.

Kaplin, W. A. *The Law of Higher Education: A Comprehensive Guide to Legal Implications of Administrative Decision Making.* (2nd ed.) San Francisco: Jossey-Bass, 1985.

Wright, C. A. "The Constitution on Campus." *Vanderbilt Law Review,* 1969, *22* (5), 1027–1088.

13

David A. Emmerling

Counseling and Health Centers

In a society concerned with litigation, even the most well-intentioned professional incurs the risk of litigation. Thus, any modern professional in any setting needs to know the inherent risk of professional practice. The purpose of this chapter is not to review case law as it relates to counseling and health centers but to address the practical issues of effective management of these offices, with the goal of reducing risk and liability to their lowest possible incidence. Careful attention will be paid to the similarities and differences between counseling centers and health centers. Although they are intricate, counseling centers tend to be more specialized than the typical health center operation. Yet principles of ethics, integrity, and professionalism in professional practices are similar in both settings.

This chapter will identify areas of legal concern for practitioners, review policy questions, and provide examples for the application of professional and legal standards for the operation of mental health and health care facilities.

Values

The law itself is a value-laden system. Similarly, there are values held by individual professionals and endorsed by professional organizations; and these values have influenced and contributed heavily to the point of view expressed in this chapter. Specifically:

- An individual is responsible for his or her behavior.
- An individual is entitled to all reasonable information from any health care provider.

- Ethical guidelines established by the mental health and health care professions should serve as the standard of reasonable care to be provided to clients.

These values have strong implications for practice. They influence not only individual patient treatment but also record and management systems of providers. Individual patients need complete, accurate, and understandable information and are entitled to the best judgment of the professional staff member regarding consequences of potential decisions. Patients must make their decisions for action when they have and are able to understand all the available information. Further, patients must live with the consequences of their decisions.

Ethical guidelines must be followed, and the practitioner must also comply with applicable statutory requirements. The definition of a standard of reasonable care must be clearly understood by both practitioners and patients. Review of applicable standards and incorporation of those standards into the policies and procedures of the mental health or health care agency are essential. Staff members should participate in educational sessions regarding such ethical statements and standards and the way they are applied within specific agencies.

The ethical statements of the American Association of Counseling and Development, the American College Personnel Association, the American Psychological Association, and the American Medical Association should be reviewed and used where appropriate. Statements of particular value include *Standards for Providers of Psychological Services* (American Psychological Association, 1974); *Recommended Standards and Practices for a College Health Program* (American College Health Association, 1983); and the *CAS Standards and Guidelines for Student Services/ Development Programs* (Council for the Advancement of Standards, 1986).

General Issues

The law grants a variety of privileges and assigns numerous responsibilities to the professionals in both counseling and health centers. While there may be differences between professionals in each setting, the following issues are of general concern.

State laws will vary regarding what types of information and relationships are privileged and therefore protected from disclosure in legal proceedings. In most states, the relationship between the physician and his or her patient is considered a privileged relationship. Some states recently have extended their privileged communications laws to include mental health professionals. Others do not extend privileged communication to mental health professionals, although the relationship between these professionals and their clients usually is regarded as confidential. Confidentiality defines the nature of a relationship in all areas of mental health and health care.

In other areas, the law dictates a standard of care that directly affects the practice of a counseling and health center professional. State law will, in most instances, dictate appropriate procedures in the areas of child abuse and the provision of services to a minor child. In addition, state law can dictate professional practice with respect to a suicidal or homicidal individual who is known to the practitioner. Licensure for the professional involved in both counseling and health centers will also be available through the state or dictated by the state. During litigation, licensure and/or accreditation offers the means by which the practitioner or the agency can establish demonstrated adherence to a reasonable standard of care.

Other issues that more directly influence the operation of the health center but are not limited to a health center operation include (1) knowledge of sexual offenses and the procedures for gathering information and evidence regarding an alleged sexual offense; (2) gunshot wounds and their management; and (3) venereal disease. States often specify methods of reporting these occurrences.

Another relevant area is the area of institutional tort liability—for example, liability for injuries resulting from negligence or from defamation (libel and slander). While the number of libel and slander cases is relatively small, the professional is at risk in higher education when there is communication between parents and the professional regarding a given case. The specific institutional policy regarding release of information can also influence what can be shared with parents. (For a complete review of these issues, see Chapter Seven in this volume.) Similarly, libel and slander might be claimed in instances where a perceived abuse act toward children had been reported by a practitioner. In the area of negligence, a professional may be held liable for an injury sustained by an individual under the professional's care. Practitioners may be held accountable under the tort of negligence if the injury to the person should have been anticipated by someone offering a reasonable standard of care (Hummel, Talbutt, and Alexander, 1985, p. 69). For example, if a psychologist knew of a patient's suicidal intent and did not take steps to prevent it and the suicide occurred, then negligence might be found. (See Chapter Nine in this volume for further discussion of these issues.) Policies and procedures of the agency must establish the acceptable standard of care for a specific agency. Applicable state law and "reasonable care" standards established by the guidelines for practice within the individual's professional group should be part of the policy development process.

Confidentiality

Although confidentiality exists as an ethical concept in the practice of medical and mental health service, the law offers no specific protection for that information; in fact, it is the practitioner who decides to hold information in confidence. In contrast, the law does protect "privileged communications." In many states, the law dictates that communications between a medical or a mental health practitioner and a patient or client may not be made public except in extreme situations. It is important for each practitioner to know his or her rights under the law on a state-to-state basis. Practitioners also should remember that the concept of privileged communication is an extension of Fifth Amendment rights and is a privilege of the patient or client, not the practitioner (Hummel, Talbutt, and Alexander, 1985, pp. 55-57). Since the courts can modify this privilege, practitioners should not assume that it is absolute.

Exceptions. Where there is imminent danger either to the client or to others, the practitioner is bound to disclose this information, in order to protect the client or other individuals involved. As a standard of practice, and a legal requirement in many states, the practitioner must protect the patient if the patient's self-destructive or self-abusive behavior could result in injury or death, or if that individual is not competent to manage himself in a normal course of activity. The same responsibility under the law occurs in situations where the practitioner is aware of or suspects child abuse on the part of his or her client or patient. The practitioner must also intervene to warn or protect an individual who might be the victim of a homicidal act or an injury. Failure to protect a third party from a criminal act creates a situation for a legal action against the practitioner.

Group Counseling. Confidentiality becomes an even greater challenge to maintain in a group counseling situation or in programs offered by a health service prior to the prescription of birth control medication. Participants in family-planning or contraceptive seminars might consider their attendance a confidential matter, and public disclosure of their attendance could create a situation of risk for the health service. Similary, in counseling or mental health services, confidentiality must be examined and explained to the group as a whole. The group members should be informed that their interactions are confidential and that they must exercise sound judgment regarding the use of information that becomes available to them within the group.

Policies and Procedures. A mental health agency should develop a policy and procedure for informed consent and conscientiously follow it. Such a procedure should include information on confidentiality and privileged communication, the client's rights, and the process by which the client might review his or her records. An important component of this procedure is that the client be asked to sign a consent form, which verifies that the information has been provided and was read or presented by some means. Since there is a risk of liability with respect to management of information within agencies, the conditions governing the release of information and the manner in which records are to be maintained must be carefully covered in the policy; and the policy must be routinely followed by all practitioners. Procedures for release of information should include a standardized form for release of specific information, which clearly defines whom the information will be sent to, what information will be sent, the length of time that the release is valid, and the process by which the client can remove his or her approval for the release of information. Such a form is mandatory in providing information to other practitioners outside the agency; it can also be used, when appropriate, to provide information to the client.

When information is requested by other agencies or offices within the university, clearly established policies and procedures for those requests are required. Similarly, the patient should give prior approval to release that information. The Family Educational Rights and Privacy Act, as well as applicable state law, will dictate what information can be shared and under what conditions. It is also the responsibility of the health practitioner to assist the client in establishing the limits of the information that will be released. For example, judicial offices that refer individuals to mental health services on campus usually require some type of response by that service about a given individual's participation or success in the counseling situation. The individual client has the right to approve or disapprove the release of this information. It would be in both the client's and the counselor's best interest if judicial or disciplinary offices could be educated to the necessity for the counselor merely to verify the individual's attendance without disclosing the substance of the case material itself.

More difficult requests often come from areas such as residence life to both counseling and health services. Except in situations of imminent danger, there is not a legally defensible "need to know." Effective management of individuals and situations can be enhanced by consultation regarding specific incidents. Policies and procedures should clearly indicate the kinds of information that will be transferred to individuals outside the agency and the circumstances that would permit such a transfer of information. The mental health and medical practitioner can often assuage this need to know by providing information regarding the incidence of a physical illness or the dynamics of the situation in a consultation mode without discussing a specific content of a given case.

Finally, clearly established policies and procedures need to exist for responding to courts and agents of the court with respect to information on clients. These policies and procedures should be carefully reviewed by the university legal counsel, who will often be the conduit for such requests through the university. Information requested within a subpoena should be clearly defined by the subpoena itself. If a situation arises where there are no clear limits to the information requested, the professional is well advised to gain the assistance of the university legal counsel in establishing those limits. When the client is represented by legal counsel, that counsel with the written approval and consent of the client may have complete access to all information regarding the client.

When the maintenance of client records is considered, a variety of issues are present. First, client records, when well maintained, provide the practitioner with the clearest picture of the situation. The most defensible evidence of quality service delivery plus effective treatment and interventions is provided by careful case notes and records. Complete and accurate records are a standard of reasonable care. Yet the professional should be reminded that these records are available to the patient on request. This potential for patient review requires that language be concise, behaviorally oriented, and nonjudgmental, especially in the mental health area; in addition, reports on the patient should contain as few stigma-producing labels as is possible.

Records provide unusual challenges to both the mental health agency and the health care agency. In the case of the mental health agency, strict behavioral records that might be read by the client may not provide the therapist with notes on ideas that contribute to effective speculation in treatment. The idiosyncratic note-taking and description that can facilitate effective treatment are often needed in the mental health regime. Therefore, the therapist may decide to keep a separate set of files for his or her own use in managing cases. The health care agency, on the other hand, requires a file that will contain information provided by many health care professionals. The resulting record contains a diverse amount of information, ranging from medications to physical and psychological evaluations of a given patient. The confidentiality of these files may be compromised, since so many individuals have access to the information. This broad sharing of information does increase the risk of breach of confidence to the health service provider.

Finally, in both agencies, patients' records must be maintained in a secure and protected situation. As a minimally accepted standard, records should be kept in a locked cabinet or desk with access keys carefully controlled in a locked room within a locked agency. It should be recognized by all practitioners that a number of nonprofessionals have access to offices for a variety of reasons. As a result, record maintenance and security must be a priority in order that risk be minimized.

Liability

At present, there is little debate that a professional is most liable when assessing imminent danger. Since the practitioner's "duty to protect" has been clearly established, the definition of protection needs to extend to both the individual and others who may be at risk. Perhaps the most difficult task for any health care professional is to assess imminent danger to the person of the patient, as a result of suicidal intent or incompetence. The criteria for judging risk for both instances is soft at best and extremely subjective. In cases where others may be at risk—for instance, in cases of child abuse—the criteria are somewhat less subjective and will, especially in the area of child abuse, be clearly established by law. Even here, however, interpretations of a given set of statutes may vary. The individual practitioner should respond in a consistent and predetermined pattern, considering ethical practices, state statutes, and policies shared across a given agency.

Since a negligent act creates liability for the professional and the agency, and since that negligence is the result of a departure from acceptable professional standards, an agency must establish standards of care for all its professionals. These standards must be clearly documented in the protocols, policies, and procedures of that agency. Practitioners must understand that their actions or their omission of an action, or their failure to act in a given situation, may incur liability if these actions or inactions contribute to or cause injury to a patient, client, or related individual.

Since liability exists whether action is taken or not, each

agency needs to establish procedures to deal with individuals who are disturbing to the campus community. A mental health or health professional usually becomes involved when an individual appears to be out of control and in violation of the norms of the campus community. Others on the campus feel the need for skilled professional help in confronting the situation. In these instances, the professional must remember that the individual or situation has come to professional attention because of a request for assistance. Prior to intervening, the practitioner must understand what authority he or she is acting under and what legal limits are placed on such authority.

To illustrate: A mental health professional receives a call from a residence hall director reporting that during the past several weeks John Doe has become increasingly agitated and has been disturbing more and more individuals with a variety of bizarre verbalizations and inappropriate actions. He is now in the main lobby of the residence hall telling a resident assistant that he is being controlled by the Central Intelligence Agency through a brain implantation that occurred following a recent automobile accident. He also reports receiving instructions that he should harm certain individuals.

Diagnosis aside, it should be clear that this individual is asking for assistance in controlling uncontrollable thoughts and that the responsibility is upon the system—that is, the university— to respond appropriately. If we assume that this individual, because of his disruptive thinking, is unable to maintain or competently discharge care for himself, then steps must be taken to protect him. The obvious alternative is hospitalization. When that step is considered, the practitioner must know the legal procedure for both voluntary and involuntary commitment. Similarly, institutional policies would dictate the variety of consequences that may be created for the individual who refuses to comply with the directions of the practitioner as institutional representative.

Another case that has implications for both mental health and health care providers is that of the anorexic student who is experiencing significant physical and emotional difficulties associated with the illness. This type of case also has a profound impact on the university community, which is exposed to an individual who has become observably malnourished and whose behaviors may in fact become more and more bizarre, depending on the extent of the illness. Again, legal and ethical limits must be clearly defined in the minds of both medical and mental health practitioners, responsibility to the community taken into account, and the options for intervention within a given institution premeditated and consistently applied.

There are relatively few, if any, actions that do not create some degree of risk for the practitioner. However, a careful definition of standards of care, a thorough knowledge of legal and ethical practice, and professional behaviors that exceed acceptable standards of care can reduce the likelihood and incidence of negligence and related liability.

Specific Areas of Concern

One of the largest issues within medical and psychological practice today is avoiding liability. Each professional must understand the legal constraints in his or her practice and take steps to reduce liability claims. How is a healthy degree of "professional paranoia" established? Reaching a level of effective sensitivity that facilitates the relationship between the professional and the patient is the challenge. The current sensitivity to legal issues is not without a positive side. With the responsibility on the professional to share decision making with the patient and completely inform him or her of treatment procedures, and the consequences of a given course of action, patients are educated. Additionally, the lay public is better informed and participates more effectively, and the practitioner is demystified.

Within the area of confidentiality, a variety of issues exist, not the least of which is the professional's response to a known felony. Here the professional must give careful consideration to the legal consequences and liability created as a result of reporting or not reporting knowledge of a felony, which may include a risk of prosecution. After considering the consequences, the professional should decide how he or she will respond to information regarding felonies and should inform the client prior to the initiation of treatment about the limits of confidentiality and/or privileged communication.

Given the interest in the use of third-party coverage by both mental health and health care providers on university campuses, the issue of diagnostic labeling, which facilitates third-party payment, must be confronted. While there continues to be a greater acceptance of mental health treatment in this country, a significant amount of stigma is still inherent in the treatment.

Requests to transfer confidential information between offices within the university also present problems. As mentioned previously, there is occasionally pressure from judicial offices and offices of residence life on both health care and mental health facilities to provide information based on a need-to-know rationale. In situations where there is imminent danger, there is a clear mandate to provide that information. Yet a variety of student personnel professionals ask for more information than the law or ethical/professional practice permits of counseling or health center personnel. In response, the best information can be a clear description of not only the institutional policies and procedures about information transfer but the presentation of state statute where applicable and appropriate sections of ethical statements. This information is most often heard if provided prior to an incident. Likewise, an agency needs to remind each employee that incidental information regarding a client or patient should not be disclosed and that continued vigilance with regard to discussing cases in public areas needs to be routine. The adage of World War II "Loose lips sink ships" might also be true if accidentally released information damaged a client.

Certainly, some of the most critical problems in higher education today are those of AIDS, athletes and drugs, and liability insurance for practicing professionals. As the liability insurance industry continues to react to increased litigation in our society, the cost of liability insurance will continue to grow. Maintaining private coverage by the practitioner will no longer be a viable approach to ensure adequate protection. It is likely that greater responsibility will be placed on the institution to provide more comprehensive liability coverage, self-insure, or provide a stipend to those professionals for the purchase of liability insurance that provides both the institution and the individual effective coverage. In a different arena, issues such as AIDS and drug testing for athletes can create profound potential for litigation. What if a physician or psychologist is treating an individual who has been diagnosed with AIDS and is aware that that individual has refused to adopt any safe sex practices, or has refused to refrain from sexual contact with others? Would the imminent danger to the community prompt the professional to protect the known partners of this individual? Is a larger community at risk, and the professional with the knowledge liable for the indiscretion of a client? With the current questions of drug testing and an athlete's use of drugs, what should the health care or mental health professional do if he or she knows that an athlete is using a substance that would disqualify the athlete and the university from participation in a major competitive event? If the professional chooses not to disclose that information and, through a spot check or other means, it is determined that the athlete was using an unqualified substance, and as a result the institution forfeits not only the game but a substantial amount of present and future revenue, would that professional be liable?

Conclusion

If this chapter has raised issues of policy, procedure, and protocol for an individual or an agency, it has been successful. The answers are not supplied here. They are available in the current policies and procedures of a given agency or in state statutes or in the ethical guidelines of various professional groups. Clearly, the best protection from litigation is provided by adequate policies and procedures that reflect the best available knowledge of legal and ethical practice in either counseling centers or health services. Yet the policies and procedures, no matter how clearly written and how comprehensive, are only as good as the education that occurs within the staff regarding those policies, procedures, and protocols. If that knowledge is to be used and the institution adequately protected, each professional needs readily accessible information. Similarly, ongoing evaluation of policies and procedures must occur, and revisions should be made in accordance with revised ethical guidelines or changes in state statutes. Professional continuing education, which addresses practice and the law, needs to be a regular endeavor of each staff person. Staff also need to be trained and informed about the resources available in the office of the legal counsel for a given institution. Not only should the practitioner be well informed about the potential for using this resource; he or she must also understand its limits. Even if the most adequate policies and procedures and the best-educated practitioners exist, staff need to be rewarded and acknowledged by every conceivable means when they comply with those policies and procedures that protect themselves and, in effect, the institution.

References

American Association for Counseling and Development. *Ethical Standards.* Alexandria, Va.: American Association for Counseling and Development, 1981. (Originally published by American Personnel and Guidance Association.)

American College Health Association. *Recommended Standards and Practices for a College Health Program.* (4th ed.) Washington, D.C.: American College Health Association, 1983.

American Psychological Association. *Standards for Providers of Psychological Services.* Washington, D.C.: American Psychological Association, 1974.

American Psychological Association. *Ethical Principles of Psychologists.* Washington, D.C.: American Psychological Association, 1981.

Council for the Advancement of Standards. *CAS Standards and Guidelines for Student Services/Development Programs.* Washington, D.C.: Council for the Advancement of Standards, 1986.

Hummel, D. L., Talbutt, L. C., and Alexander, M. D. *Law and Ethics in Counseling.* New York: Van Nostrand Reinhold, 1985.

14

William R. Bracewell

Student Discipline

The administration of discipline programs is part of the responsibility of most divisions of student affairs. Sound management of the discipline process is essential, and the state of the law certainly influences that process. Although differences may and do exist between colleges and universities in this area of discipline, there are procedural guidelines that should be followed to protect both the rights of the individual and the legitimate interests of the institution. This chapter will cover a brief history of the relationship between the law and student discipline, define the essential procedural elements that need to be maintained in discipline proceedings, and provide practical guidance for the administration of student discipline systems.

Background

In 1961, the United States Court of Appeals for the Fifth Circuit upset more than two hundred years of legal and educational theory. By its decision in *Dixon* v. *Alabama State Board of Education,* it reversed a long line of case law. Some saw in this decision the death of the concept of *in loco parentis.* Others, more positively, saw the arrival of the American constitution on campus. The court in *Dixon* announced that the right to a state-supported education cannot be taken away from an individual without due process of law. Specifically, the court required public schools to demonstrate fundamental fairness in disciplinary proceedings by providing notice and an opportunity to be heard. Subsequent judicial decisions in this area of education law are but a footnote to the *Dixon* case. (See Chapter Four in this volume for additional information.)

During the remainder of the 1960s, numerous cases were brought to the courts as students tested their new standing in court, and administrators sought to assimilate due process into the academic community. All parties sought more definition for this imprecise legal doctrine.

In 1968, the judges in the Western District of Missouri, faced with three major cases from state-supported schools, sat *en banc* to draft a "General Order on Judicial Standards of Procedure and Substance in Review of Student Discipline in Tax-Supported Institutions of Higher Education" (45 F.R.D. 133). The judges asserted that colleges and universities may establish behavioral standards higher than those imposed on all citizens by civil and criminal law and may discipline students to secure compliance with these standards. But when severe sanctions, such as expulsion and suspension, are imposed, the institution must (1) give the student written notice of the specific grounds and the evidence on which the disciplinary proceedings are based; (2) provide an opportunity for a hearing in which the student can present his position, explanations, and evidence; and (3) initiate disciplinary action only when the charges against the student are supported by substantial evidence. The General Order, written after consideration of briefs and oral arguments, is only a further explication of the *Dixon* decision. The courts had said all they could in defining due process. It is not an inflexible procedure for all cases, but it is a concept sensitive to the circumstances of the individual case. The essential elements are notice, hearing, and decision.

While the courts defined due process, faculty and staff on campus sought ways to assimilate this concept into educational theories and policies. On the campus, the question of balance was the issue. How could they build a system that acknowledges and protects the rights of students while preserving the integrity and resources of the institution? A new vocabulary had to be learned, regulations written or rewritten, and hearing procedures drafted. Proceduralism was resisted in favor of the more traditional student-institution relationship. A strange amalgam of legalism and counseling was created.

In 1967, the year before the district court judges in Missouri published their General Order, the American Association of University Professors (AAUP) published its "Joint Statement on Rights and Freedoms of Students" in the *AAUP Bulletin* (vol. 52). In 1973, the American College Personnel Association (ACPA) created Commission XV to study campus judicial affairs and legal issues. Papers on due process appeared in all educational journals, and regional and national conferences were organized on the topic. From the combined experience and knowledge of educational administrators everywhere, systems serving the unique needs of each campus evolved. The state-supported institutions were required to develop their disciplinary system in compliance with judicial mandates. Private schools watched, learned, and saw the value of the structure that evolved. These institutions voluntarily began to develop procedures that suited their needs. Their procedures often go beyond what is required of the public schools.

Schools that had been comfortable with their authority to establish behavioral standards began to respect the constitutional rights of students and appreciate the benefits of a consistent, systematic response to student misconduct. In less than one decade, the courts went from the doctrine of *in loco parentis* to a constitutional definition of the student-institution relationship. In less than two decades, colleges and universities have accommodated this legal concept in their regulations and disciplinary procedures.

Essential Procedural Elements

It is strongly recommended that a single procedural framework be adopted by the institution. Such a procedural framework for both behavioral and academic discipline provides clarity and ensures that members of the community are treated equally regardless of their alleged offense. The first step in this process is developing an institutional commitment to fairness and respect for student rights. This attitude will facilitate the drafting of a document establishing procedures to be followed in all disciplinary proceedings. The stage is then set to allow the complete spectrum of institutional responses to individuals and groups who are accused of major or minor violations of regulations.

Notice. Notice begins with the publication of regulations governing student behavior. Regulations should contain precise descriptions of prohibited acts. This code of conduct is an important institutional statement, which sets the standards and creates an environment conducive to teaching and learning. University regulations should not duplicate the state criminal code but, instead, should specifically protect the unique interests of the academic community. Most important, the regulations should be consistently enforced. Unenforced regulations may lead to disrespect by all members of the community toward the code.

The regulations should be included in handbooks, catalogues, and other publications and should be widely distributed. Although ignorance of the regulations is no excuse for a violation, it is a part of fairness to do everything reasonable to make the rules readily available. Rules of particular importance (for instance, rules concerning academic honesty) may be addressed in pamphlets specially designed to prevent violations and to encourage student support for their enforcement.

When a student is suspected of violating a regulation, he or she should be contacted immediately and made aware of these suspicions. The regulation that may have been violated and the evidence supporting the complaint should be thoroughly discussed with the student. The purpose of the discussion is to determine whether or not a formal hearing should be scheduled, and more than one meeting may be necessary because witnesses may need to be interviewed. This preparation should not be hurried. The institution can afford to be patient during this period.

When the decision to conduct a formal hearing has been made, the student should be provided with a written statement of the specific allegations, which, if proven, will result in a finding of guilt and the assessment of sanctions. This statement should also include the location of the hearing and an evidence and witness list. A copy of the procedures to be followed at the hearing should also be provided. All this material must be given to the student as early as possible to allow the student time to prepare. Patience and attention to detail should characterize this period of preparation. This is also a time to help the student understand his or her responsibility and the institution's interest in the matter.

The Hearing. The hearing is the shortest part of the entire process and should be presented as a forum where both parties have a fair opportunity to present whatever they feel is important. Every effort should be made to avoid an adversarial confrontation. The institution is the complaining party, not an individual professor, staff member, or student. These individuals may participate as witnesses, but they should not be cast in the role of prosecutor.

Some institutions have trained staff or students who serve as university advocates and who organize and present the institution's case. Similarly trained individuals may also serve to assist the student in presenting his or her side in the hearing.

The hearing should be formal but not intimidating. Formal hearing procedures are designed to protect the student's rights. There are only four rules to observe. First, the institution should present its side first and has the burden of illustrating that a rule or rules have been violated. The standard of proof should be clear and convincing evidence. The other extremes, proof beyond a reasonable doubt or proof by a mere preponderance of evidence, should be avoided. One is not possible, and the other may not be fair. Second, the accused student has a right to hear all the evidence and testimony that is to be considered by the hearing body. Formal rules of evidence do not apply in disciplinary hearings, but the institution should have written policies defining any special rules of evidence (for example, the admission of hearsay evidence) used in its hearings. Third, the accused student has a right to present evidence and testimony or to remain silent, with no inference of guilt being drawn from the silence. Fourth, the student has a right to assistance in the preparation and presentation of evidence and witnesses.

Fairness requires that the student be able to participate fully in the hearing, and assistance may be necessary to guarantee that participation. The question is, who can provide this assistance? As mentioned, students and staff who are specifically trained are an ideal source. These individuals know the institution, the regulations, and the procedures, and they can truly facilitate the conduct of a hearing.

The participation of attorneys is often debated by college and university administrators. If the institution is represented by an attorney or some other legally trained person, the student should also be given this option (*French* v. *Bashful*, 1969). Also, if the disciplinary action stems from an incident resulting in criminal charges and the criminal case has not yet been heard, the student may have an attorney present to observe the hearing and to assist the student, but not to participate (*Gabrilowitz* v. *Newman*, 1978). In any case, the institution needs to decide whether the participation of an attorney will detract from or facilitate the hearing. If attorneys are made aware that they are bound by the procedures of the institution and clearly understand the nature of the hearing, they will not detract from the hearing and may make the student, and sometimes the student's family, more comfortable with the proceedings.

A record of the hearing must be maintained. Such a record becomes very important in the event of an appeal. The physical evidence should be received by the hearing body and kept with copies of all documents relating to the hearing. The simplest way to preserve the testimony is with a tape recorder. The tape and evidence can then be passed along during the appeal process and should be adequate to prevent the need for another hearing before an appellate body.

In summary, the hearing should exemplify a commitment to fairness. Everyone is assembled to hear all testimony and view all evidence, to participate fully and honestly, to assist the hearing body in understanding what happened, to determine whether a rule or rules were violated, and, if appropriate, to assess a penalty.

An Impartial Tribunal. Hearing bodies may be composed of people from all parts of the campus: students, faculty, and staff. They may be composed entirely of students or a combination of all three groups. The composition of the board may vary according to the nature of the case. In fact, one person may serve as a hearing officer. There is only one requirement for the individual or group conducting the original hearing or an appeal: impartiality. When the hearing begins, the hearing body must know nothing of the details of the case and must have no interest in the final outcome; it must have no direct connection with the complaining party or the accused student. The charge to the hearing body is simply to discover what happened and, if appropriate, assign a fair sanction.

Its decision must encompass the interests of both the institution and the accused.

Three elements are essential for an effective hearing body. First, its authority and jurisdiction must be carefully defined. An administrator usually has been assigned responsibility for student behavior. This delegation of authority must be understood and the limits on that authority defined. Preferably, the line of authority should be traced from the governing board, through the president, to deans or directors, and hence to the hearing body. This element is important in very serious cases and in an appeals process.

Second, the members of hearing boards or individual hearing officers, including faculty and staff participants, must be trained. The hearings must be conducted in an orderly fashion, and the institution's procedures must be scrupulously followed. Procedural errors at the hearing may lead to unnecessary appeals. Equally important, the accused student will lose confidence in the entire process if the hearing body is in disarray. Through training, the members of the hearing body will be comfortable with the procedures and able to concentrate on the presentation. Evidence and testimony must be carefully analyzed so that the decision can be well written and presented in the proper format.

Third, some office or individual must supervise the selection, training, and work of hearing panels. Ideally, this responsibility will reside in an individual or office that is involved in developing and revising regulations and procedures and is aware of the needs of various administrative units in the institution to respond to student behavior. The disciplinary system is static but should respond to the needs of the academic community. With this view of the campus, this administrator can develop a variety of responses to student behavior consistent with institutional policy.

A Variety of Tribunals. With a procedural framework in place and individuals recruited to conduct hearings, the institution can begin to design a system of tribunals to respond to specific incidents. This is not a due process concern or a legal issue. It is, rather, a matter of need and creativity. The following are illustrative examples.

Lesser offenses that will result only in warnings, oral reprimands, and other minor sanctions should be dealt with quickly and by staff closest to the situation. Residence hall staff are most familiar with this level of discipline. Individual staff members may conduct these hearings, or local judicial boards may be established. In either case, the institutional procedures can be modified to allow a hearing that is less formal but still sufficient to create a record of the incident and the disposition of the case. This record may become important if subsequent offenses by the same student require referral to a higher judicial board or authority.

Honor courts, the oldest judicial bodies on American campuses, were convened to rule on matters of academic dishonesty. Today it is not necessary, and may not be advisable, to distinguish academic misconduct from other forms of rule violations. The normal procedures designed to find fact are ideally suited to determining whether or not cheating occurred. Since, generally, the sanctions for academic dishonesty are more harsh and may involve both suspension or expulsion and loss of academic credit, the complete set of procedural safeguards should be employed. Since the courts have ruled that academic evaluations do not require due process (*Board of Curators of the University of Missouri* v. *Horowitz*, 1978), it is important to separate the penalty and the grade assignment. The hearing board assigns the penalty for a violation of a regulation based on the evidence presented at a hearing. The findings of fact are then referred to a faculty member, who assigns the grade. The grade is not a penalty but is an academic evaluation. It is important to preserve this dichotomy. The institution may develop an academic policy that defines the treatment of grades after cheating has been proven in a hearing; but, still, this is an academic decision, not the conversion of grades to penalties.

Related to academic dishonesty is the violation of ethical or professional standards in a graduate program. Schools of pharmacy, law, and veterinary medicine, for example, have codes that go beyond the institutional conduct regulations. Even violations of these codes may be adjudicated by means of the university-wide procedures. Since a professional career is potentially at stake, all the procedural safeguards need to be in place. The hearing board may be composed of faculty and students from the particular school or college, and special training with regard to the tenets of the professional code may be necessary.

The most critical hearing that can be conducted is one that might result in the revocation of a previously conferred degree. The standard procedures should be expanded to give notice through registered mail, and more time should be allowed for preparation prior to the hearing. Great care should be taken to guarantee a faultless hearing, with evidence carefully preserved. The initial hearing should determine whether or not a conduct regulation was violated, and these findings of fact should then be referred to the appropriate academic affairs unit, where the effect on the degree requirements will be assessed. The role of department heads, academic deans, the chief academic affairs officer, the president, and the governing board in awarding degrees must be understood. Each person who has a part to play in awarding the degree must be involved in revoking the degree, and the holder of the degree must be informed at each stage. Several cases that have been litigated in this very complex area uphold these suggestions (*Crook* v. *Baker,* 1984; *Waliga* v. *Board of Trustees of Kent State University,* 1986).

Student Groups. Regulations should also define the responsibility that student organizations have for the programs and activities they sponsor. While these groups do not have constitutional rights exactly like those of individuals, their members do have association rights protected by the First Amendment (*Healy* v. *James,* 1972). Irresponsible leadership that allows the group to disrupt the normal programs of the institution may lead to restrictions on the group's activities and access to institutional facilities and services. Again, a disciplinary hearing should be convened. As a result of this hearing, responsibility can be properly assigned, the prescribed behavior defined, and appropriate sanctions imposed.

Decisions and Appeals. Following the hearing, the student should receive a written decision, preferably delivered in person by the individual or individuals who made the decision. This document should contain the findings of fact in the case. Questions include: What acts were committed by the student as shown by the evidence presented? Do these acts violate conduct regulations? If a regulation was violated, what is an appropriate sanction? A well-written, logical decision with a sanction that is fair to both the student and the academic community goes a long way in helping the student understand his or her responsibility and the institutional interest in this matter.

Appeals are necessary to correct faults in the original hearing, but they do not need to go on forever. An appeal should be filed by a specified time, must be in writing, and must state specific grounds for the appeal. Usual grounds for an appeal are (1) that the hearing board did not have jurisdiction (authority) over the case; (2) that the board made a clearly erroneous finding of fact contrary to the substantial weight of the evidence, and the error materially affected the decision; (3) that the board did not correctly interpret a conduct rule or regulation, and the error materially affected the decision; (4) that the board deprived the student of a right given to the student by the rules and regulations governing disciplinary hearings, and this action materially affected the decision; or (5) that the penalty imposed by the board was clearly erroneous in light of the facts of the case. Mere dissatisfaction with the sanction is not grounds for appeal. Institutional or state system policies may define appellate procedures beyond the original hearing body, but generally the appeal should follow the line of authority and responsibility for student conduct.

The appeals body may be an individual or a small committee. It may review the entire record or such portions as it deems pertinent. In considering the appeal, the appeals body should keep in mind that (1) at the original hearing, the institution was required to prove by clear and convincing evidence that a rule or rules were violated; and (2) the original hearing body had an opportunity to observe all witnesses during their testimony. The appeals body may deny an appeal, may change a finding of guilt to a finding of innocence, may modify the penalty, or may order a new hearing to be held by the same or a new hearing body. In any case, the appeals process should be clearly defined, and students and student organizations should be informed about the appeals process and institutional regulations governing appeals.

Summary and Conclusion

Due process has arrived on campus and is here to stay. Although legal issues originally confounded institutional responses to student misconduct, it is now possible to review hearing procedures and develop a system that truly serves educational needs.

Several principles are important to remember when an institution is developing a disciplinary system. Due process is flexible and can be molded to fit the needs of each institution. Reduced to its simplest terms, it requires notice, a fair hearing, and a decision. Procedures should not unnecessarily encumber the resources of the institution but should demonstrate a commitment to fairness and respect for students. Regulations governing student conduct should be well publicized, and care should be taken to inform students of their rights and responsibilities within the discipline system. An effective disciplinary system can teach students that rules and laws protect the essential interests of the academic community and that individuals are responsible for their own conduct.

15

Glenn W. Maloney

🍀 🍀 🍀

Student Organizations
and Student Activities

Trends in educational legislation, social values, and political issues over the past twenty years have influenced colleges and student organizations. The civil rights movement and the Vietnam War motivated students to use campuses as backdrops for political protests, causing controversy and court involvement in student activities. These court decisions, combined with federal legislation, state statutes, and increased consumer awareness of the right to sue, have brought about profound changes in student activities.

This chapter will examine how legal developments affect the rights, responsibilities, and liabilities of student groups and the institutions with which they are affiliated. The right to associate, use of university facilities, student activity fees, fraternal organizations, alcohol liability, and other liability issues will all be addressed. Analysis of pertinent laws and court decisions will focus on implications for schools and organizations. Recommendations and guidelines are also offered, but these must be adapted to each institution's own mission, environment, location, and circumstances.

The Right to Associate

In 1972, the Supreme Court in *Healy* v. *James* determined that Central Connecticut State College showed no valid grounds for denying recognition to a local chapter of Students for a Democratic Society (SDS). The Court ruled that denial of official recognition without justification violated individuals' First Amendment rights to associate to further their personal beliefs. Central Connecticut State College based its denial of SDS on four points. First, the college did not like the local chapter's relationship with the national SDS. Second, the president determined that the group's philosophy of violence and disruption was inimical to the college's mission. Third, because of the philosophy and reputation of SDS, the president assumed that the group's activities would create campus disruption. Finally, the president also had reason to believe that the group would not agree to abide by campus regulations.

The Supreme Court found only "one potentially acceptable ground for denial of recognition" (*Healy*, 1972, at 2348). In response to the college's first point, the Court noted its disapproval of "denying rights and privileges solely because of . . . [an] association with an unpopular organization" (at 2348). In response to the second point, the Court said that "mere disagreement with the group's philosophy affords no reason to deny it recognition" and that Central Connecticut State "may not restrict speech or association simply because it finds the views expressed by any group to be abhorrent" (at 2349). Regarding the third point, the Court noted that "activities need not be tolerated where they infringe reasonable campus rules, interrupt classes, or substantially interfere with the opportunity of other students to obtain an education" (at 2350); but there was no evidence of such activity in this case. However, on the fourth reason for denial of recognition, the Court agreed that the SDS members had been evasive when asked what actions they might take to achieve their goals. If they planned to advocate for the change or elimination of campus regulations, the Court noted, such actions were permissible; but recognition "may be denied to any group that reserves the right to violate any valid campus rules with which it disagrees" (at 2352).

The *Healy* decision has made it virtually impossible for campuses to deny recognition to any group that complies with reasonable application procedures, unless the group openly admits to breaking university regulations. The decision has been tested several times since 1972, and each time that an organization denied recognition has brought the issue to court, the organization has won. Seven schools—the universities of Georgia (*Wood* v. *Davison*, 1972), New Hampshire (*Gay Students Organization of the Univer-*

sity of New Hampshire v. *Bonner,* 1974), Virginia Commonwealth
(*Student Coalition for Gay Alliance of Students* v. *Matthews,* 1976),
Missouri (*Gay Lib* v. *University of Missouri,* 1977), Austin Peay
State (*Student Coalition for Gay Rights* v. *Austin Peay State
University,* 1979), Oklahoma (*Gay Activitists Alliance* v. *Board of
Regents,* 1981), and Texas A&M (*Gay Student Services* v. *Texas
A&M University,* 1984), as well as the city of Anchorage, Alaska
(*Alaska Gay Coalition* v. *Sullivan,* 1978), and the state of Florida
(*Department of Education* v. *Lewis,* 1982)—have attempted to deny
gay students the right to associate, and all have lost. The arguments
used by each of the schools were basically the same: homosexuality
is illegal and abhorrent; the activities of such a group would harm
students; and sanctioning such conduct was not within the mission
of the institution (Stanley, 1983–84).

   None of the arguments used held up in court. To the
argument that homosexuality is illegal, the courts have responded
that advocacy is different from action and that a group could not
be denied recognition until it was actually found breaking the law.
To the argument that homosexuality is abhorrent, courts have
applied the *Healy* opinion that that is not a valid reason to restrict
association. As for the argument that these groups' activities would
harm students, the Supreme Court has responded that "undifferen-
tiated fear or apprehension . . . is not enough to overcome the right
to freedom of expression" (*Tinker* v. *Des Moines Independent
School District,* 1969, at 508). Finally, courts have consistently stated
that the granting of recognition by an institution does not imply
support, agreement, or approval of the organization's purpose.

   Although it is clear that colleges and universities cannot
deny recognition once student groups have complied with all
requirements and have agreed to follow university regulations,
there are few guidelines on what system or process to use in
recognizing groups. A survey done by Milani (1983) at the University of Pittsburgh shows that schools use one of four basic
recognition systems. Some schools require groups to file an
application through the student government. Others allow the
student government to make recommendations to a supervising
department. A third process involves the use of a board, allowing
students, faculty, and staff to participate. A final method used by

some schools gives responsibility for recognizing groups to an administrative unit. The advantage of this last method is that it speeds up the process by avoiding the need for committee meetings. It also allows for consistent and uniform application of the regulations. There is a danger that student governments or boards may make political judgments and attempt to evaluate a group's purpose, thereby violating constitutional rights. It is better not to put students or committees in the position of recognizing groups of a controversial nature, such as SDS or gay student groups, unless they are trained and advised by university officials regarding legal issues.

The process used to form new student groups is generally referred to as either a registration process or a recognition process. The terms *registration* and *recognition* are often used interchangeably (Milani, 1983). This usage does not cause a problem as long as the relationship between the institution and the student group is defined. On many campuses, clubs sponsored by departments receive special privileges and often represent the university. These groups—for instance, sports clubs, student government groups, and program and media boards—generally are required to register with the university. They may receive more benefits than other groups, but they also are subject to more control by the university. To acknowledge the difference between groups that are university supported and those that are not, schools should implement a two-tiered process. The first tier would be required of all groups and would be the standard registration process. The second tier would be completed only by those groups "officially sponsored" and should require the signature of a dean or department head. The requirement for a dean's signature is to ensure that the university is willing to assume the additional risk of being responsible for the organization's activities.

Once a group complies with all university application procedures, the group should be considered registered and eligible for privileges associated with use of campus facilities and services. But what application requirements can be imposed? Registration requirements often include the submission of a constitution, a list of officers, the name of a faculty or staff adviser, and a statement by the organization agreeing to abide by all institutional, local, state, and national laws, including antidiscrimination statutes. It is also wise to require groups to update their information at the beginning of every school year and during the year whenever there is a change of officers. They might also be asked to state whether they have any external affiliations, "to preclude the potential misappropriation of university resources, or the utilization of university students for what may amount to an external 'business' enterprise" (Milani, 1983, p. 8).

The courts have given only slight indications about which requirements are considered reasonable. A Supreme Court decision in 1958 stated that the National Association for the Advancement of Colored People could not be compelled to disclose its membership list (*NAACP* v. *Alabama*, 1958). In *Brown* v. *Socialist Workers '74 Campaign Committee* (1982), the Supreme Court held that the "First Amendment prohibits a State from compelling disclosures by a minor political party that will subject those persons identified to the reasonable probability of threats, harassments, or reprisals" (at 425). These rulings appear applicable to colleges and universities, since they are often called on to approve the applications of minority, political, social, and religious groups. Although such organizations probably can be required to list officers or a minimum number of members, it may be unconstitutional to require them to list all members as a condition of registration. In *Eisen* v. *Regents of the University of California* (1969), an organization officer sued the university for disclosing registration information to the public. The information included a statement of purpose and the names of the organization's officers. In its decision, the California appeals court noted that, although cases such as *NAACP* v. *Alabama* "clearly delineated the rights of rank and file members to remain anonymous, they did not deal with the question of whether the same right also applied to an officer of the organization" (*Eisen*, at 51). In this specific case, the court concluded that "the compelling interest of the public in being able to ascertain the information contained in the registration statement outweighs any minimal infringement of plaintiff's First Amendment rights" (at 52).

The courts also have upheld the right of a university to impose minimum academic standards on those who hold office in student government (*Sellman* v. *Baruch College of the City University of New York,* 1979) and have permitted the imposition of sanctions on groups that deny membership on the basis of race, color, or religion (*Sigma Chi Fraternity* v. *Regents of the University of Colorado,* 1966).

Use of University Facilities

Once student organizations are registered, they are generally entitled to use campus buildings and grounds for holding meetings, posting signs, distributing literature, raising funds, and sponsoring speakers and demonstrations. In some institutions, they also may have access to fees and use of the school name. They need not, however, be given access to resources such as typewriters, copiers, computers, or other equipment (Gehring, 1984). University regulations controlling the use of its facilities by student groups have been tested regularly in the courts. But opinions rendered by the Supreme Court and the federal appeals courts are consistent in their message: schools may enforce reasonable regulations of time, place, and manner that apply equally to all groups, regardless of the group's message.

In *Bayless* v. *Martine* (1970), a group of students challenged a university regulation that restricted demonstrations to specific locations between certain hours. The regulation also required forty-eight hours' notice for off-campus speakers. The Fifth Circuit determined that the rule was "a valid exercise of the University's right to adopt and enforce reasonable, nondiscriminatory regulations as to the time, place, and manner of student expression and demonstrations" (at 878). It also noted that the requirement of reserving the Student Expression Area forty-eight hours in advance was a reasonable method by which the problem of simultaneous and competing demonstrations could be avoided and was necessary in order to arrange "police protection for both the demonstrators and University property" (at 878).

In a similar case, a group of students challenged the following Grambling College regulation: "It is strictly forbidden for any group of students to gather in such a manner as to disturb the public peace [or to] do violence to any person or property. . . .

Any student who encourages, or in any way participates in, the formation or prolonging of such a gathering, who loiters in the vicinity of such a gathering, is subject to an immediate dismissal from the college" (*Jenkins* v. *Louisiana State Board of Education*, 1975, at 998). The court upheld the regulations as a code of general conduct, which "need not be drawn with the same precision as are criminal codes" (at 1004).

But the Fifth Circuit later struck down a Jackson State University regulation that stated: "All events sponsored by student organizations, groups, or individual students must be registered with the Director of Student Activities, who, in cooperation with the Vice President for Student Affairs, approves activities of a wholesome nature" (*Shamloo* v. *Mississippi State Board of Trustees, etc.*, 1980, at 625). In reviewing this regulation, the court pointed out that "there is one critical distinction between the regulation examined in *Bayless* and the Jackson State regulation. . . . Jackson State regulations provide that only 'activities of a *wholesome* nature' will be approved. . . . The presence of this language converts what might have otherwise been a reasonable regulation of time, place, and manner into a restriction on the content of speech" (at 629).

The following year, the Supreme Court confirmed the Fifth Circuit's opinion in holding that "a state regulation of speech should be content neutral" (*Widmar* v. *Vincent*, 1981, at 278). In this case, a religious group, Cornerstone, at the University of Missouri at Kansas City, was denied permission to use university buildings because of a regulation that "[n]o university buildings or grounds may be used for purposes of religious worship or religious teaching by either student or nonstudent groups" (footnote at 272). In overturning this regulation, the Supreme Court indicated that "having created a forum generally open to student groups, the University seeks to enforce a content-based exclusion of religious speech" (at 278). However, the Court also recognized that "First Amendment rights must be analyzed 'in light of the special characteristics of the school environment'. . . . A university differs in significant respects from public forums such as streets or parks. . . . A university's mission is education, and decisions of this Court have never denied its authority to impose reasonable regulations compatible with the mission upon the use of its campus and facilities" (footnote at 273).

"[T]he most important aspect of guidelines and policies is the principle of equal treatment for all student groups" (Cuyjet, Gilbert, and Conboy, 1983, p. 60). Policies that affect a particular group or attempt to solve a problem caused by a specific organization violate the Constitution. Courts will usually regard such policies as attempts to censor a single group because of the content of its activities. Privileges granted one group must be granted to all groups, and rules applying to one group must apply to all groups. A university might deny access to all off-campus speakers, but once a speaker has been allowed, all speakers must be accepted (Wright, 1969).

As for demonstrations, the *Widmar* opinion cautions that a university is not a public forum as are public parks, but "the Constitution forbids a State to enforce certain exclusions from a forum generally open to the public, even if it was not required to create the forum in the first place" (at 273). Thus, if a college permits an athletic pep rally in a certain location, it must also allow a rally protesting CIA recruitment. But colleges are not required to create forums. In *United States Postal Service* v. *Council of Greenburgh Civic Associations* (1981), the Supreme Court recognized that the "First Amendment does not guarantee access to property simply because it is owned or controlled by the government" (at 2684). Thus, decisions on where and when demonstrations can take place on a particular campus will depend on the nature of the location, as well as the past and normal activities of any particular place at any particular time. The critical point is that the Supreme Court has upheld the right of public institutions to establish reasonable regulations of time, place, and manner that are narrowly drawn, to protect a legitimate state interest.

Student Activity Fees

In order to conduct programs, many student groups rely on the use of student activity fees. In a 1976 survey of 217 public and private institutions, over 90 percent stated that they gave money to student organizations via a fee (Bauer, 1983). Student service fees or student activity fees are generally levied on all students and then allocated to various student service agencies or student organizations. Most campuses have a fee board or committee that determines who gets how much of the funds. The legal issues regarding fees fall into three categories: collection, control, and utilization (Meabon, Alexander, and Hunter, 1979).

Collection. As early as 1882, courts have held that governing boards of colleges and universities can impose mandatory fees on students for items other than teaching (Meabon, Alexander, and Hunter, 1979). In a 1934 case, the Montana Supreme Court stated that the responsibility "to manage and control the business and finances of the institutions carries with it the implied power to do all things necessary and proper . . . which would include the exaction of fees not prohibited, if fees are necessary to the conduct of the business of the institutions" (*State* v. *State Board of Education,* 1934, at 517). More recently, the Supreme Court of Washington upheld the right of the University of Washington to collect mandatory service and activity fees (*Good* v. *Associated Students of the University of Washington,* 1975). While recognizing the controversial nature of some programs funded by the fee, the court determined: "If we allow dissenters to withhold the minimal financial contributions required, we would permit a possible minority view to destroy or cripple a valuable learning adjunct of university life" (at 768).

Control. The question of who controls the mandatory fee usually depends on applicable state statute and institutional guidelines. The process for allocating the collected fees also varies among institutions. It may be handled by student government, or by a student/faculty committee, or by the vice-president for student affairs. In *Stringer* v. *Gould* (1970), the trustees of the State University of New York gave students the responsibility for assessing and allocating the mandatory activity fee. However, the court determined that "since the responsibility of administration and supervision in this area rests with the trustees, appropriation or expenditure of the fund in question may not be made without the approval of the trustees as to the purposes for such appropriation and expenditure" (at 312).

Utilization. The major legal controversies involving fees

have centered around the programs and activities funded by mandatory fees. "The courts have been willing to allow colleges and universities general discretion to determine programs to further the education of students, even if some of those programs are unpopular" (Meabon, Alexander, and Hunter, 1979, p. 11). Courts have upheld the right of schools to finance publications, speakers, student governments (*Veed* v. *Schwartzkopf*, 1973), and abortions (*Erzinger* v. *Regents of the University of California*, 1982) through mandatory student service fees. In general, it is permissible to use fees for purposes related to the educational mission of the institution; and—because states grant institutional boards the authority to set institutional policy—regents, not students, should determine the use of fees (Meabon, Alexander, and Hunter, 1979; *Erzinger*, 1982).

The most recent fee cases have involved the use of student fees to fund Public Interest Research Groups (PIRGs). PIRGs were started in September of 1970 by Ralph Nader. By 1974, more than 130 campuses in twenty-one states had PIRGs ("Activity Fees Support 'PIRG' Groups," 1974). Fishbein (1973–74, p. 192) described a PIRG as "a non-profit, politically unaligned corporation directed by students, employing non-student professionals such as lawyers and scientists on a full-time basis, and devoting its efforts to constructive social change by studying and working for change in such areas as consumer protection, environmental protection, occupational safety, and housing."

In 1972, Rutgers developed a policy whereby a mandatory fee would be collected from all students to support "student-sponsored programs and organizations, such as PIRG, that otherwise would not qualify for university financial support" (*Galda* v. *Bloustein*, 1982, at 161). The policy provided in part that, if there was an affirmative student referendum to support the fee, then the university would collect a mandatory fee to fund PIRG; however, a refund would be available on request. Students brought suit challenging this funding system because they were required to pay the fee as a condition of registration. Rutgers argued that a mandatory fee was justified because PIRG served legitimate educational purposes. The Third Circuit reversed the district court decision in favor of Rutgers and remanded the case back to the district court. After a two-week bench hearing, the district court again upheld Rutgers.

A second suit (*Galda* v. *Rutgers,* 1985) was later filed, seeking injunctive relief from the appellate court on the question of the collection of the mandatory, though refundable, fee. In this case, the Third Circuit held that "[t]he University has presented no evidence, nor do we believe it could, that the educational experience which it cites as justification could not be gained by other means which do not trench on the plaintiff's constitutional rights" (*Galda* v. *Rutgers,* at 1067). The Third Circuit clearly distinguished this impermissible mandatory fee from permissible mandatory fees: "PIRG's ineligibility for student activity funds—precisely because of its independent status—distinguishes PIRG from the other groups on campus which are funded by a standard 'student activity fee.' This fee, a lump sum used to subsidize a variety of student groups, can be perceived broadly as providing a 'forum' for a diverse range of opinion. The PIRG fee, in contrast, was segregated from the other charges listed on the students' term bills, and provides support for only one organization" (*Galda* v. *Bloustein,* 1982, at 166).

The opinions of the Third Circuit in the Rutgers cases provide some guidelines for universities to follow in administering fees. In upholding mandatory fees, the courts have held that such fees provide a forum of varying ideas, not one political or ideological stance. Thus, as long as one lump sum is collected to provide for many different purposes that have been deemed appropriate by the regents, the fee would be permissible even if it partially went to fund an issue or idea with which some students may disagree. On the other hand, if an organization or a program does not qualify to receive support from the lump-sum student service fee, but a large portion of students would support the activity, the institution can collect the fee on its bill, but it cannot mandate that all students be required to pay. An optional check-off system has been upheld by the courts in some instances (*Galda,* 1982, at 168). Although either a positive or a negative check-off system apparently is permissible, unless there is good reason not to, the university should require students who choose to pay the extra fee to so designate, instead of those who choose not to pay.

At institutions where part of the lump sum is allocated to student governments for further distribution to qualified groups, the institution should not attempt to influence the students' decisions. If student governments allocate fees to activities of a controversial nature, the students themselves can express opposing opinions and influence leaders to finance other points of view (Lauren, 1984).

Fraternities and Sororities

The Association of Fraternity Advisors (1981, p. 1) recommends that "the relationship between the host institution and the undergraduate Greek system be one of mutual cooperation, understanding, and conducive to meeting the goals of higher education." This objective can be accomplished in several ways. Many institutions own and operate individual fraternity and sorority houses. Others do not own the individual houses but control the Greek governing systems (the Interfraternity and Panhellenic Councils) that regulate the fraternities and sororities. Still other campuses have independent Greek houses and systems, which are not under university jurisdiction. Regardless of the type of relationship, it must be understood by all parties. Relationship statements should indicate the responsibilities and the limitations of the university and the individual chapters. Greek organizations that own their own houses and do not rely on university administration for support or advice are obviously less accountable to university officials than those that make greater use of university resources. Universities that control and operate the Greek systems are more accountable for the activities of those organizations.

The issue of accountability becomes very important as litigation involving hazing and alcohol increases. Even though it may be legal for Colby College to ban fraternities from university-owned housing—"trustees always retain the authority to change Colby's educational policies, including those related to housing" (Black, 1986a)—any attempt to ban Greeks from campus altogether is probably as unconstitutional as an attempt to ban all gay organizations. A university can limit the amount of support it wants to give fraternities and sororities, as long as it does not deny them the rights and privileges granted to other student organizations. But the reverse is also true. Fraternity and sorority acceptance of special university resources, such as housing, can be contingent on compliance with other university standards.

One regulation that fraternities and sororities have been exempted from is Title IX of the Education Amendments of 1972: "This part does not apply to the membership practices of social fraternities and sororities which are exempt from taxation under section 501(a) of the Internal Revenue Code of 1954, the active membership of which consists primarily of students in attendance at institutions of higher education" (34 C.F.R. sec. 106.14).

This exemption, however, may be threatened by the involvement of Little Sisters with fraternity activities and by the Supreme Court's decision in *Roberts* v. *United States Jaycees* (1984). The Court noted several reasons for its ruling prohibiting the Jaycees from excluding women from membership: "The undisputed facts reveal that the local chapters of the Jaycees are large and basically unselective groups. . . . Apart from age and sex, neither the national organization nor the local chapters employ any criteria for judging applicants for membership, and new members are routinely recruited and admitted with no inquiry into their backgrounds. . . . Indeed, numerous non-members of both genders regularly participate in a substantial portion of activities central to the decision of many members to associate with one another, including many programs, award ceremonies, and recruitment meetings" (at 3251).

The Association of Fraternity Advisors (1983, p. 1) supports Little Sister programs when "rights and privileges are granted that allow for significant partnership in the decision-making process of the fraternity." The association also recognizes that Little Sisters often participate in socials and rush. In some cases, they also have active roles in fraternity ritual. Harmon (1986b) points out that the more intertwined the fraternal organization is with the Little Sister organization, the better the challenge is to single-sex status. To avoid running afoul of the Supreme Court decision against the Jaycees, it is best to keep the Little Sister organizations and the fraternity separate and independent (Harmon, 1986b).

Another issue of great concern to those managing fraternities is hazing. At least sixty-one people have died as a result of hazing incidents in the past fifteen years. Hazing is against the law in nineteen states, and seven others are considering laws regarding hazing. And yet, despite these laws, antihazing statements by national fraternities, the AFA, and the Committee to Halt Useless College Killings (CHUCK), hazing continues to exist. Why? Because in the fraternity world, "reason is clouded by tradition, loyalty is equated with subservience, and . . . the ideal of brotherhood and sisterhood must be proven through the degrading of the individual" (Association of Fraternity Advisors, 1980, p. 1).

What can be done to stop hazing? "The relative absence of reported civil cases—and the fact that so few criminal prosecutions have been brought—suggest that the time is ripe for institutions to define their own level of liability and their own processes for dealing with hazing" (Buchanan and others, 1982). "It is the responsibility of the fraternity/sorority chapter and primarily its leaders in conjunction with their national organizations" (Association of Fraternity Advisors, 1980, p. 1) to protect pledges from hazing practices. Individual chapters, as well as campus administrators, must begin to take strong disciplinary action against those who are found to support, encourage, or initiate hazing activities. At the University of Texas at Austin, antihazing affidavits, for example, must be signed by all groups during the registration and reregistration processes. Officers from organizations that conduct any type of pledge or initiation activity also meet with university administrators on a regular basis. In addition to taking strong stands against hazing, university and national officials, along with the local chapters and students, must all work together to provide examples of positive pledge education programs (Association of Fraternity Advisors, 1980).

Alcohol Liability

"The alcohol issue is one of the hottest issues in our courts today. Volatile special interest groups, public frustrations, and political maneuvering can have enormous local influence on court decisions regarding alcohol incidents at any given moment" (BACCHUS, 1986, p. 12). "Individual students, student organizations, institutional faculty and staff, and institutions all may find themselves involved in both criminal and civil actions arising out of alcohol-related injury or death" (Buchanan, 1983, p. 4). The alcohol issue is complicated by the fact that laws vary from state to state and locality to locality. What is legal and risk free on one campus may cause a major liability suit for another. The best protection from criminal, civil, or university penalties is to know the laws. Sources of alcohol regulations include university rules, state law, alcoholic beverage control regulations, and case law (Janosik, 1983).

Forty states have laws setting the minimum drinking age at twenty-one, twenty-three states impose statutory liability on servers, and four more have laws placing limited liability on those who serve minors or intoxicated guests (Black, 1986c). Thirteen have case law establishing liability for vendors and social hosts. In the years 1980–1985, "the number of lawsuits is up over 400 percent" (Ingalls, 1985; quoting E. T. Buchanan III). Average damage awards granted by a jury total $100,000, and out-of-court settlements average $450,000 (Ingalls, 1985). "Recent cases have made it clear that a judgment or settlement involving the payment of several million dollars . . . is not an unusual occurrence" (Harmon, 1986a, p. 1).

In a recent Kappa Alpha lawsuit, where a fraternity member was permanently disabled during a fraternity function, a $21 million out-of-court settlement was divided by the fraternity and an individual member ("$21 Million Settles Fraternity Accident," 1985). The *ATO Letter* ("Parents Bring Suit Against Fraternity," 1985) reports the filing of a $1.5 million suit by parents following the death of their son after a fraternity party. And recent court decisions are beginning to erode the common law position that the intoxicated individual is responsible for his or her own behavior.

In *Wiener v. Gamma Phi Chapter of Alpha Tau Omega* (1971), the fraternity was found liable for an injury to a passenger in the car with a driver who had become intoxicated at a fraternity function. The party did not take place at the fraternity house but at a ranch off campus. The Oregon court stated that "the fraternity, not the owners of the land, should bear the responsibility for activities of guests who were negligently allowed to become intoxicated" (at 20). The New Jersey Supreme Court has held that a social host is liable if the host serves alcohol to a guest "knowing that the guest is intoxicated and will thereafter be operating a motor vehicle" (*Kelly* v. *Gwinnell*, 1984, at 1224). The court, recognizing that its ruling would "intrude on and somewhat diminish the enjoyment, relaxation, and camaraderie that accompany social gatherings at which alcohol is served," said that such a loss was "well worth the gain" (at 1224). When California created a similar precedent in *Coulter* v. *Superior Court of San Mateo County* (1978), the California legislature voided the opinion with a state statute granting immunity from third-party civil suits to all alcohol providers except for licensed establishments that furnish alcohol to an "obviously intoxicated minor" (*Cory* v. *Shierloh*, 1981, at 11). Meanwhile, the Pennsylvania Supreme Court ruled that "there can be no liability on the part of a social host who serves alcoholic beverages to his or her adult guests" (*Klein* v. *Raysinger*, 1983, at 511) but, on the same day, stated in a separate opinion that there can be liability "where an adult host has knowingly served intoxicants to a minor" (*Congini* v. *Portersville Valve Co.*, 1983, at 517).

"The most important common law tort case involving colleges in the last decade" is *Bradshaw* v. *Rawlings* (1979) (BACCHUS, 1986, p. 110). In *Bradshaw*, an automobile accident occurred following the annual college sophomore class picnic, at which the driver had become intoxicated. The picnic was held off campus, but the "advisor participated with the class officers in planning the picnic and co-signed a check for class funds that was later used to purchase beer" (*Bradshaw*, at 137). Bradshaw sued, arguing "that the college had knowledge that its students would drink beer at the picnic, that this conduct violated a school regulation and state law, [and] that it created a known probability of harm to third persons" (at 141). In finding for the school, the U.S. Court of Appeals for the Third Circuit noted that it is not uncommon for college students to drink, that today's society considers college students adults, and that "the modern American college is not an insurer of the safety of its students" (at 138). A California court reached a similar conclusion: "[A]lthough the consumption of alcoholic beverages by persons under 21 years of age is proscribed by law the use of alcohol by college students is not so unusual or heinous by contemporary standards as to require special efforts by college administrators to stamp it out" (*Baldwin v. Zoradi,* 1981, at 817).

Colleges tend to rely heavily on the Third Circuit's opinion in *Bradshaw,* but it is unclear whether that case would still be decided in the same way. In its 1979 ruling, the Third Circuit reasoned that "because the Pennsylvania Supreme Court has been unwilling to find a special relationship on which to predicate a duty between a private host and his visibly intoxicated guest, we predict it would be even less willing to find such a relationship between a college and its students" (*Bradshaw,* at 141). Would the 1983 decision in *Congini,* where the Pennsylvania Supreme Court did find that the host had a duty to his guest, change the decision of the Third Circuit today? The answer to this question seems to be a moving target. These examples point out the speed with which regulations regarding alcohol can change. We have gone from a society where a drunk was responsible for his or her own behavior, and where a minor was someone who was eighteen or under, to a society where the majority age for drinking alcoholic beverages in most states is twenty-one. Additionally, the public has become increasingly intolerant of intoxicated drivers, injured third parties are not hesitant to look for the deepest pocket from which to collect damages, and social hosts are just as likely to be sued as are those who provide alcohol for profit.

An organization, such as a fraternity, that does serve or provide alcohol at social functions can take precautionary measures to protect itself from costly liability suits. Of course, the safest step is not to have alcohol at organizational activities. If that is not possible or is unrealistic, valuable advice on ways to reduce an organization's legal exposure can be found in Harmon (1986a), Tracey (1986), and Alpha Tau Omega (1985). With insurance premiums tripling and some fraternities being dropped totally by insurance agencies, it may be virtually impossible to obtain insurance without adopting some or all of these recommendations. For example, organizations might check IDs to be certain that alcohol will not be served to minors; refuse to furnish alcohol to intoxicated guests; use trained bartenders; prohibit drinking games or contests; provide alternative nonalcoholic beverages in the same locations that alcohol is served; furnish food; arrange transportation, such as shuttle service, taxi chips, or a designated sober driver; refuse to cosponsor events with local distributors, or to sponsor events with a drinking theme, or to advertise the availability of alcohol; and limit the hours of social events. They should require all their officers and all those in charge of social functions to know all applicable state, local, and university regulations; and they should instruct all members and pledges on drinking laws, liability issues, intervention strategies, and emergency medical procedures. Finally, they should write an alcohol policy into their bylaws and then enforce it.

Following these guidelines not only helps protect officers' and members' personal liability but also provides an atmosphere that reduces the emphasis placed on alcohol. Such an atmosphere minimizes the risk of irresponsible drinking, which can lead to accidents involving guests or other persons.

The responsibility of the institution if one of its groups is alleged to be negligent is not always clear. Northern Kentucky successfully defended itself against a lawsuit involving an injury to a sorority woman who injured herself at a sorority party off campus. In his brief for the university, Gerald F. Dusing stated that registration of student groups does "not in any way evidence an agency relationship between the University and the Sorority. The University, through these rules, does not grant its consent nor exert control on policy of off-campus events nor does it authorize the sorority to represent it or act on its behalf" ("University Denies Ability to Control Greeks," 1984, p. 1). Other leading cases also indicate "that colleges and universities have no inherent duty—or any realistic ability—to control students who are acting in their personal capacities" (Gulland and Flournoy, 1986, p. 4).

However, in a very controversial decision, a jury found the University of Denver liable for an injury occurring in a fraternity's front yard, and set the award at $5.2 million (*Whitlock* v. *University of Denver*, 1985). Although Gulland and Flournoy (1986, p. 9) write that this "decision is a strong candidate for reversal in the Colorado Supreme Court," and although the decision has been called "unrealistic and unhealthy" (BACCHUS, 1986, p. 14), it has many university administrators concerned. These concerns are not unfounded. Manley (1984, p. 2) has noted: "It can be a difficult and

often expensive lesson, but increasing numbers of college administrators are realizing the dangers they embrace when they try to
exercise detailed control of the internal affairs of fraternities. The
more control that the college administration attempts to assert over
fraternities, the more liabilities the college administration imposes
upon itself." The Colorado Supreme Court agreed. On appeal, the
judgment against the university was reversed, and the court declared
that no duty of care was owed to Whitlock (1987). To limit an
institution's exposure to liability, the American Council on
Education recommends policies that are realistic and enforced
consistently and that emphasize students' personal responsibility
(Gulland and Flournoy, 1986). Schools should also foster alcohol
awareness programs (Buchanan, 1983) and teach students about
responsible drinking, the physical effects of consuming alcohol,
and the potential massive legal liabilities (Harmon, 1986a).

Other Liability Issues for Groups and Advisers

Student leaders and university advisers also should be aware
of liability that might arise in the areas of minimum standards of
care, contractual obligations, and fiduciary responsibilities.

Standards of Care. A "'minimum standard of care' is
normally defined as the minimum safety steps necessary to protect
an individual or group of individuals who are either using a
product or participating in an activity or program. Where standards
exist or are established, they should be adhered to. To recognize
reasonable standards of care in programs and services and then fail
to abide by them can be seen as a lack of care" (Black, 1986b, p. 7).
Often, organizations such as the Association of Fraternity Advisors
and the American Camping Association will publish standards.
University rules and regulations can also set or imply certain
standards of conduct. "Failure to follow rules or to enforce
regulations can create serious liability problems" (Black, 1986d,
p. 2). Standards of conduct or "duties" can also find their source in
"existing social values and customs" (BACCHUS, 1986, p. 14). But,
as was shown in the case of alcohol responsibility, the expectations
of society are subject to change. If an organization, or its adviser,

knowingly allows known standards to be broken, that organization or adviser "may be found guilty of breaching a standard of care and thus held personally liable for negligence" (Gehring, 1984, p. 138). Advisers at public institutions, who act in their official capacities, can often claim "official immunity," which may limit potential personal liability. To use such a defense, however, they must produce a written statement of the terms and conditions of the advising role (Gehring, 1984). In order to avoid legal entanglements with student organizations, universities should analyze their requirements of student groups to maintain university advisers. Universities that do require faculty or staff advisers should provide information and training to both the student group and the adviser regarding required responsibilities, university policies, and liability issues.

Contracts. Negotiating contracts is another area where student organizations need to exercise care. Titles given to student members do not always indicate who has the responsibility to bind the organization to future commitments. Organizations can create legal agents in different ways: by actually delegating the authority to act on behalf of the organization; by indicating to a third party that a member has the authority to conduct business; or by accepting the agreements of members who acted on their own (Black, 1986e). Even if a member exceeds his or her authority, the organization can be considered liable; and once an agreement is signed, all prior arrangements, oral or written, are void (Black, 1986f). The following guidelines are offered by *Perspective* (Black, 1986f) to assist organizations in contract agreements: read the contract completely; check to see that blanks are filled in appropriately; ask questions; understand the answers; make sure that all the points agreed upon are in the contract; verify that all terms are described so that a third party could clearly understand the intentions; know the length of the contract and any provisions for renewal; review appendixes and attachments; and use legal counsel when appropriate.

Fiduciary Responsibility. Contractual obligations often lead to another area of organization liability—fiduciary responsibility. The first step of proper money management is the development of a budget. Unfortunately, "the preparation of a budget and management of funds are among the most important and most frequently neglected functions of student organizations" (Hennessy and Lorenz, 1984, p. 89). The writing of a budget does not have to be a frightening or stressful experience. Nor does it require an MBA degree. It is simply a matter of stating how much money will be raised and from what sources and on what it will be spent. Budgets can be drawn up for individual programs or for an entire year. The budget represents "the goals of an organization expressed in terms of money. . . . It is a contract between the executive officers of an organization and the funding body to expend funds in a prescribed manner consistent with mutually accepted goals" (Hennessy and Lorenz, 1984, p. 90). Budgets often set the parameters for realistically deciding what an organization can accomplish.

A second aspect of fiduciary responsibility is the handling of funds. How is money collected? Is money kept in a checking account or savings account? Who is authorized to expend funds? Are there checks and balances? According to Hennessy and Lorenz (p. 109), "All organizations have an incumbent responsibility to manage their money in a business-like manner." Specifically, they should require more than one person to be responsible for financial transactions; maintain complete and accurate records of all income and expenses; and make regular financial reports to the membership. Besides developing a budget, an organization must follow federal, state, local, and university guidelines. Groups often think that tax-exempt status granted by the Internal Revenue Service (IRS) exempts them from paying and/or collecting state and local sales tax. However, the IRS can only grant an exemption from paying federal income tax. An organization's obligation to collect sales tax is dependent on state tax codes and on the organization's standing with the university. To prevent organizations from running afoul of applicable regulations, the university should provide regular training opportunities for officers.

Conclusion

This chapter has discussed both the rights and responsibilities of student organizations at institutions of higher education.

The courts have affirmed the rights of students to associate and express themselves. However, these rights are not absolute. The courts have also acknowledged the duty of educational institutions to preserve the educational environments for which they are formed. Schools can and should establish reasonable, content-neutral regulations of time, place, and manner. But once these rules are written, they must be followed by both the university and student groups. For if either students or university officials neglect their responsibilities, they may lose their respective rights.

References

"Activity Fees Support 'PIRG' Groups." *School Law Newsletter,* 1974, *4* (6), 147.

Alpha Tau Omega. *Resolution on Risk Avoidance.* Champaign, Ill.: Alpha Tau Omega, 1985.

Association of Fraternity Advisors. *Statement on Hazing.* Villanova, Pa.: Association of Fraternity Advisors, 1980.

Association of Fraternity Advisors. *Statement on the Relationship Between the University and the Greek System.* Villanova, Pa.: Association of Fraternity Advisors, 1981.

Association of Fraternity Advisors. *Statement on Little Sister Program.* Villanova, Pa.: Association of Fraternity Advisors, 1983.

BACCHUS of the United States and Inter-Association Task Force on Campus Alcohol Issues. *First National Conference on Campus Alcohol Policy Initiatives: A Timely Guide to Contemporary Campus Alcohol Policy Review and Development.* Washington, D.C.: BACCHUS of the United States and Inter-Association Task Force on Campus Alcohol Issues, 1986.

Bauer, J. B. "The Constitutionality of Student Fees for Political Student Groups in the Campus Public Forum: *Galda* v. *Bloustein* and the Right to Associate." *Rutgers Law Journal,* 1983, *15* (1), 135–184.

Black, D. R. (ed.). "Banned Fraternities." *Perspective,* no. 7. Madison: Magna Publications, 1986a.

Black, D. R. (ed.). "Cases Noted." *Perspective,* no. 2. Madison: Magna Publications, 1986b.

Black, D. R. (ed.). "Escaping Liquor Liability Off-Campus."
  Perspective, no. 4. Madison: Magna Publications, 1986c.

Black, D. R. (ed.). "Liabilities for Fraternities." *Perspective,* no. 8.
  Madison: Magna Publications, 1986d.

Black, D. R. (ed.). "Student Titles and Authority." *Perspective,* no. 7.
  Madison: Magna Publications, 1986e.

Black, D. R. (ed.). "What's in a Contract?" *Perspective,* no. 5.
  Madison: Magna Publications, 1986f.

Buchanan, E. T., III. "Alcohol on Campus and Possible Liability."
  NASPA Journal, 1983, *21* (2), 2-19.

Buchanan, E. T., III, and others. "Hazing: Collective Stupidity,
  Insensitivity and Irresponsibility." *NASPA Journal,* 1982, *20* (1),
  56-68.

Cuyjet, M. J., Gilbert, N. S., and Conboy, P. M. "Student Organi-
  zations: Some Legal Implications." In M. J. Barr (ed.), *Student
  Affairs and the Law.* New Directions for Student Services, no. 22.
  San Francisco: Jossey-Bass, 1983.

Fishbein, E. A. "Legal Aspects of Student Activities Fees." *Journal
  of College and University Law,* 1973-74, *1* (2), 190-198.

Gehring, D. D. "Legal Rights and Responsibilities of Campus
  Student Groups and Advisers." In J. H. Schuh (ed.), *A Handbook
  for Student Group Advisers.* Washington, D.C.: American
  College Personnel Association, 1984.

Gulland, E. D., and Flournoy, A. C. "Universities, Colleges and
  Alcohol: An Overview of Tort Liability Issues." In BACCHUS
  of the United States and Inter-Association Task Force on
  Campus Alcohol Issues, *First National Conference on Campus
  Alcohol Policy Initiatives: A Timely Guide to Contemporary
  Campus Alcohol Policy Review and Development.* Washington,
  D.C.: BACCHUS of the United States and Inter-Association Task
  Force on Campus Alcohol Issues, 1986.

Harmon, J. J. "Before Your Next Party . . ." *Fraternal Law,* 1986a,
  15, 1-4.

Harmon, J. J. "Little Sister or Fraternity Member?" *Fraternal Law,*
  1986b, *15.*

Hennessy, T. J., and Lorenz, N. "Budget and Fiscal Management."
  In J. H. Schuh (ed.), *A Handbook for Student Group Advisers.*

Washington, D.C.: American College Personnel Association, 1984.

Ingalls, Z. "Colleges in Growing Danger from Drinking-Related Lawsuits, Experts Say." *Chronicle of Higher Education,* March 27, 1985, p. 11.

Janosik, S. M. "Liquor Law Liability on the College Campus: When Are We Responsible?" *NASPA Journal,* 1983, *21* (2), 21-25.

Lauren, J. F. "'Fee Speech': First Amendment Limitations on Student Fee Expenditures." *California Western Law Review,* 1984, *20* (2), 279-311.

Manley, R. E. "College Administrators Should Avoid Control." *Fraternal Law,* 1984, *10,* 1-4.

Manley, R. E. "Campus Gang Rape." *Fraternal Law,* 1986, *16,* 1-4.

Meabon, D., Alexander, R., and Hunter, K. *Student Activity Fees: A Legal and National Perspective.* Columbia, S.C.: National Entertainment and Campus Activities Association, 1979.

Milani, T. E. "A Report Regarding the Recognition of Student Organizations and the Relationship Between Institutions of Higher Learning and Social Fraternities and Sororities." Unpublished report, University of Pittsburgh, 1983.

"Parents Bring Suit Against Fraternity." *ATO Letter,* Nov. 27, 1985, p. 4.

Stanley, W. "The Rights of Gay Student Organizations." *Journal of College and University Law,* 1983-84, *10,* 397-418.

Tracey, K. "Memorandum to Chapter Presidents." Letter from Executive Director, Sigma Alpha Epsilon, Evanston, Ill., March 19, 1986.

"$21 Million Settles Fraternity Accident." *Fraternal Law,* Nov. 1985, p. 1.

"University Denies Ability to Control Greeks." *Fraternal Law,* Nov. 1984, p. 1.

Wright, C. A. "The Constitution on Campus." *Vanderbilt Law Review,* 1969, *22* (5), 1027-1088.

16

John H. Schuh

The Student Press

"The student press. Those words are virtually guaranteed to give college administrators a case of the sputtering fits," writes Patrick Siddons (1986, p. 57). Administrators at times are so frustrated and chagrined by the student press that they have attempted to fire editors, limit the distribution of campus publications, or put the press out of business altogether. These actions often have resulted in complicated legal battles that generally have been decided in favor of the students.

In this chapter, a dozen fundamental issues pertaining to the relationship of administrators and the institution to the student press are identified, and suggestions are given for response. The legal environment is fluid; that is, what makes for good practice today could change tomorrow. If an administrator is not sure how to proceed on a legal issue, he or she should seek competent, professional counsel.

In this discussion, the terms *student press, periodical,* and *publications* are used interchangeably. They all refer to publications that are produced by students and typically include student newspapers, yearbooks, and literary magazines. While this chapter is not specifically designed to address student-operated radio and television stations, many of the principles discussed here apply to broadcast media in addition to print media. This chapter will provide information on issues of censorship and prior restraint, offensive and obscene material, statutory requirements, libel, and advertising. A discussion of the similarities and differences regarding legal issues and the student press in public and private institutions is given. Throughout the chapter, guidelines for practice are provided.

Censorship and Prior Restraint

Four questions arise in the area of censorship. May the institution reserve the right to approve the content of a student publication prior to printing and distribution? May an institution discipline or dismiss student editors or reporters if they print an objectionable story? Is it possible to change the funding formula of a student publication if it is objectionable? Finally, can the institution simply eliminate the student newspaper because it disapproves of its editorial policies?

Approval of Content. The content of a student publication is often a cause for concern by student affairs administrators. The student press may embarrass the institution or enrage or hurt an individual who plays a key role in the vitality of the institution. When such instances occur, questions arise about the ability of the administration to control the content of the student press. This issue has been reviewed a number of times by the courts, and the consistent conclusion has been that, in most instances, the institution does not have the right to approve content prior to publication.

Trager and Dickerson (1976, p. 18) point out that "once a public college or university makes an activity available to students, it must operate that activity in accordance with First Amendment principles (*Trujillo* v. *Love,* 1971). It cannot, for example, fund a student publication and then arbitrarily restrict the material it may publish (*American Civil Liberties Union of Virginia, Inc.* v. *Radford College,* 1970)." Gibbs and Stoner (1985, p. 200) caution even further, writing that "officials must abandon any prior official review of the content of those publications." Gehring (1986, p. 34) also cautions against exercising prior restraint. He refers to the case of *Antonelli* v. *Hammond* (1970), in which the president of Fitchburg State College in Massachusetts attempted to exercise prior restraint with respect to the student press. The court struck down this practice, indicating that "the state may not impose arbitrary restrictions on the matter to be communicated."

Even though judicial precedent clearly seems to be on the side of the student press, attempts still have been made to exercise prior restraint. For example, Behrens (1983) cites over twenty-five cases that were filed in 1982 dealing with censorship and prior restraint. "And the cases submitted dealt with censorship cases on well-known campuses where such controversies were thought to have been resolved years ago" (p. 14). Hollander (1978) also supports the conclusion that is extremely unwise to exercise prior restraint with respect to the editorial content of student publications. For no matter how laudable or well meaning the intention may be or how subtle the effort, there is substantial risk of losing litigation when such actions occur.

Discipline. "Colleges and universities retain little control over the content of those student publications they create and sustain" (Gibbs and Stoner, 1985, p. 200). In *Trujillo* v. *Love,* 1971, an adviser to the student newspaper attempted to suspend student Trujillo from the editor's position at Southern Colorado State College for printing potentially libelous material, violating the ethical canons of journalism, and other actions (Hotchkiss and Madson, 1978, p. 28). The court found on behalf of Trujillo, indicating that she was free to write as she pleased.

Gehring (1986) concludes that some administrators have reasoned that if the newspaper is supported by the campus through the collection of fees or the application of general fund money, then the editors are institutional employees and as a result could be suspended or fired for being insubordinate. However, Gehring notes, the courts have seen this type of reasoning as a subterfuge for violating the First Amendment (*Dickey* v. *Alabama State Board of Education,* 1967; *Schiff* v. *Williams,* 1975) and have found in favor of the student editors or reporters. It is clear that student editors or reporters cannot be dismissed from a position, even if they are employees, simply because they publish objectionable material. Dismissals on these grounds have been seen by the courts as a violation of First Amendment rights.

Funding. The question of changing the funding support for the student press as a means to control objectionable content has also been reviewed by the courts. Such methods can potentially involve another circuitous method of limiting the First and Fourteenth Amendment rights of the student press. Trager and Dickerson (1976) address this issue specifically in their discussion of *Antonelli* v. *Hammond* (1970) and *Joyner* v. *Whiting* (1973): "The courts said that colleges are under no affirmative obligation to establish student publications, but once such publications are established, administrative actions must be guided by the First and Fourteenth Amendments. Specifically, funds cannot be removed from student publications for reasons having to do with students' freedom of expression, nor can funds be stopped because the administration does not like the content of the publication" (p. 34).

Hotchkiss and Madson (1978) provide further analysis of the *Antonelli* case. In this situation, the newspaper printed four-letter words that the administration considered to be obscene. As a result, the president decided to withhold funds for the paper. The students sought relief from the courts and were successful.

Details of the *Joyner* case have also been analyzed by Gehring (1986), who indicates that in this situation the president of the university withdrew financial support from the campus paper and refunded that part of the activity fee which supported the newspaper to the student body. The dispute in this case was the editorial view espoused by the newspaper, where the campus administration disagreed with the position of the paper on several desegregation issues. Again, the students were successful in seeking relief from the courts. As a concluding comment, Gehring (1986) suggests that "terminating funding because of the content of those editorials was thus a violation of a protected First Amendment activity" (p. 35).

Gehring (1986) also cites a case at the University of Minnesota, Twin Cities Campus, where the administration attempted to allow students to seek a refund for the portion of their fees that was used to support the student newspaper. A group of students sued. The proposed change was prompted by a humor issue that met with administrative, but not student, complaints. The court found for the students (*Stanley* v. *Magrath*, 1983) on the basis that the university's actions violated the First Amendment.

Publication Elimination. Elimination of a newspaper by an institution because of disapproval of editorial policies is simply a variation of disciplining the editorial staff or changing the funding formula to limit the viability of the publication. Gibbs and Stoner (1985) point out that "once a university recognizes a student activity which has elements of free expression, it can act to censor that expression only if it acts consistent with First Amendment guarantees" (p. 198; citing *Bazaar* v. *Fortune*, 1973, at 228).

Given that guideline, it seems clear that eliminating the newspaper or forcing it off campus is not permissible. And, while a number of institutions have tried a number of ways to get rid of various student publications, the courts have found for the students' position very consistently. In the *Joyner* case cited earlier, the president attempted to remove the newspaper from the campus by restricting funding. He was enjoined from doing so. In the case of *Arrington* v. *Taylor* (1974), students objected to part of their activity fee being used to subsidize the campus paper. In a sense, the students were claiming that their First Amendment rights were being violated because the paper expressed views at variance with theirs. Consistent with other decisions, the court found on behalf of the student newspaper, indicating that the paper did not purport to speak for the entire student body and that its existence did not inhibit students from expressing their views (Kaplin, 1985, p. 333).

Summary. In the final analysis, then, administrators should realize that the courts view actions to restrict or censor publications very negatively. It is not permissible to restrict the content of the paper prior to its publication. Editors or writers may not be dismissed, the funding formula may not be changed, and the paper may not be eliminated because of disagreement with the editorial content of the paper. Perhaps a good way to view these questions would be to change the context and ask, rhetorically: What power do administrators have over the commercial press? The answer, quite obviously, is that they—like other private citizens—can attempt to persuade or influence. But they certainly cannot put the commercial press out of business, nor do they have any right of prior approval of content.

Offensive and Obscene Material

When a student publication prints material that is highly offensive, vulgar, or obscene, can the distribution of such material be limited on campus? If such material is found in an off-campus publication, may the institution limit distribution of the material on university property?

Student Publications. Healy v. *James* (1972) is often cited by institutions of higher education as giving them the right to regulate time, place, and manner of certain kinds of activities, such as protest demonstrations or picketing. Attempts to extend that right, however, to include the right to regulate the distribution of student newspaper and other publications have not been viewed favorably by the courts. The leading case in this area is *Papish* v. *Board of Curators of the University of Missouri* (1973), where a graduate student was expelled for violating an institutional regulation that prohibited the distribution of newspapers containing forms of indecent speech. The U.S. Supreme Court found for the student and against the university. Hotchkiss and Madson (1978, p. 29) make the following observation about this case: "It is clear that obscenity in a campus newspaper, even though offensive to much of the University population, is not apt to be considered significantly disruptive of the educational process to justify disciplinary action against the responsible newspaper personnel." Kaplin (1985, pp. 336–337) adds the following advice: "Administrators devising campus rules for public institutions are thus bound by the same obscenity guidelines that bind the legislators promulgating obscenity laws. . . . The permissible scope of regulation is very narrow."

Two other cases also speak to this general question. Alexander and Solomon (1972) write of a material and substantial interference as the test to determine whether the institution may deny distribution of printed materials. In one case (*Channing Club* v. *Board of Regents of Texas Tech University,* 1970), the court decided that the test had not been met. "There was no showing by the university of disruption, hostility, or infringement on the rights of other students" (Alexander and Solomon, 1972, p. 424). On the other hand, when students at East Tennessee State University through printed materials called on their colleagues to fight the institution, the university suspended them and had its position sustained through the courts (*Norton* v. *Discipline Committee of East Tennessee State University,* 1969). The court indicated that the university did not have to wait until a riot had begun to take action (Alexander and Solomon, 1972, p. 425). While material included in the student paper may be objectionable, vulgar, or even obscene, regulation of distribution of the paper is not permissible on those grounds. When a clear and present danger exists to the life of the university, because of the content of the publication, the university may act.

Off-Campus Publications. The reasoning of various courts has been consistent regarding off-campus publications, and the simple conclusion is that it is very difficult to be more restrictive in limiting distribution of off-campus publications than on-campus publications.

In their analysis of *Spartacus Youth League* v. *Board of Trustees of Illinois Industrial University* (1980), Gibbs and Stoner (1985) report that the university tried to prohibit nonaffiliated individuals from distributing materials in the student union. The court, however, decided that the student union was a public forum, and, as a result, the university could not deny access to it because of lack of institutional affiliation.

In a second case, *Solid Rock Foundation* v. *Ohio State University* (1979), the university provided over 140 locations for the distribution of the student newspaper but allowed only eight locations for the distribution of a publication by a student organization. The court decided that all publications had to be treated equally with respect to time, place, and manner of distribution (Gehring, 1986).

The third case involves the distribution of an off-campus commercial newspaper. In this case (*New Times, Inc.* v. *Arizona Board of Regents,* 1974), the university attempted to limit the distribution of the newspaper on the basis of the amount of litter it created. The court held that the newspaper was not responsible for the litter and that the university could not limit the distribution of the newspaper to just six locations on campus (Gehring, 1986).

Summary. These two questions regarding the distribution of the student newspaper and other publications, be they student or not, lead to several conclusions. The institution may not limit the distribution of the campus newspaper because it has an editorial position or stance with which the institution disagrees. Most likely, courts will find that attempts to limit distribution on the basis of editorial policy disagreement violate the First Amendment. Second, the distribution of other materials, be they student or nonstudent, commercial or not for profit, should approximate the procedures followed for the distribution of the campus newspaper. That the materials are produced by a nonstudent group, or by a commercial entity, does not influence this conclusion. Institutions of higher education create a number of public forums, and if such a forum has been created for some publications, then it must be declared such for all.

State and Federal Laws

While the student press enjoys many freedoms under the First Amendment, it is not immune from federal and state laws (Gehring, 1986). In a number of cases involving the application of state and federal laws to the student press, the courts have held that the press does not have special privileges.

Copyright and Privacy Laws. In *Mitcham* v. *Board of Regents, University of Texas System* (1984), the question before the court was to what extent the press could have access to copyrighted materials. The court indicated that the student press had no special privileges in that area. In *Marston* v. *Gainesville Sun Publishing Co., Inc.* (1976), the issue was whether or not material was protected under the Family Educational Rights and Privacy Act. The answer to this question was the same: The press cannot violate an individual's privacy rights under the law.

Obscenity Laws. In *Tinker* v. *Des Moines Independent School District* (1969), Justice Black indicated that "it is a myth to say that any person has a constitutional right to say what he pleases, where he pleases, and when he pleases" (cited by Hotchkiss and Madson, 1978, p. 30). Nonetheless, restricting the publishing of materials that may be, in the opinion of some administrators, obscene in advance of the publication is exceedingly difficult. Public institutions may discipline students for having published obscene materials, and they may even halt the publication if they carefully and conscientiously follow procedural safeguards (Kaplin, 1985).

The present standard for obscenity was defined in *Miller* v. *California* (1973, at 24). The basic definition is as follows: "A state offense must . . . be limited to works which, taken as a whole, appeal to the prurient interest in sex, which portray sexual conduct in a patently offensive way, and which, taken as a whole, do not have serious literary, artistic, political, or scientific value" (cited by Kaplin, 1985, p. 336).

In *Antonelli* v. *Hammond* (1970), a faculty advisory board had decided not to permit the publication of material on the grounds that it was obscene. The court found on behalf of students in this case because the system of prior review and approval used by the advisory board failed to place the burden of proof on the board, failed to provide for a prompt review and internal appeal of the board's decision, and failed to provide for a prompt final judicial determination (Kaplin, 1985, p. 335). As this case illustrates, establishing acceptable systems for review of material in advance of publication is very difficult and delicate.

Libel Issues. Libel laws apply to the student press as they apply to any other form of publishing media. The First Amendment does not protect the press from libel, obscenity, or slander suits (Trager and Dickerson, 1976). The general requirements for libel include the following conditions: that the statement be false, that the publication of the material causes at least nominal injury to the person libeled, and that the falsehood be attributable to some fault on the part of the person or organization publishing it (Kaplin, 1985, p. 337). (See Chapter Nine in this volume for a more complete discussion of these issues.)

The best defense against libel is that the statement published is true (Gehring, 1986, p. 39; citing *Mitcham* v. *Board of Regents, University of Texas System,* 1984). If the material that the student press has published is true, the chances of losing a libel case appear to be slim. On the other hand, it is entirely possible for student editors to lose libel suits. Gehring (p. 40) cites the case of *Madison* v. *Yunker* (1978), where the student editor accused the director of the university print shop of being a congenital liar and an incompetent. Even though a retraction to the statement was printed, the case was found in favor of the plaintiff and against the student editor.

Public figures have a more difficult time proving that they have been libeled. Actual malice needs to be shown in these cases, and it is useful to note that college athletes and institutions of higher education are considered to be public figures (Gehring, 1986).

When a libel suit is won against student editors, can the institution be implicated? Gibbs and Stoner (1985) cite the case of *Mazart* v. *State* (1981), where a libelous letter had been printed in the student newspaper. The court indicated that, even though the university did not provide the editors with guidelines or procedures to help them avoid libelous materials, it was not responsible for the paper's actions.

These cases seem to indicate that the student press, acting under First Amendment freedoms, must also be responsible for the material that is published. And it seems clear that, just as institutions are not permitted to interfere with the publication of student materials, they are not held responsible for any possible illegal results.

One other aspect of libel lawsuits deserves comment. From time to time, the student press will engage in a heated exchange with student government officers and others who are part of the campus political scene. In a noteworthy case, a student politician sued the student newspaper for libel after he was characterized in terms he did not like. The court found on behalf of the newspaper, indicating that since the systems of the press and government on campus were patterned after those off campus, there seemed to be no reason to develop different tests for libel (Trager and Dickerson, 1976).

Summary. Laws that apply to all citizens and organizations also apply to the student press. Members of the press have no more access to information that is protected under the several privacy acts than anyone else does. Members of the press may not violate copyright laws, and there are special stipulations that prescribe exactly what is covered under the copyright law and what is not. Finally, the questions of obscenity and libel are complex; however, the student press must take responsibility for its actions. The First Amendment does not protect the student press from obscenity laws. However, obscenity is difficult to prove in court, and generally it must be proved after the material has been published. It is extraordinarily difficult for an institution to exercise prior restraint in situations where it believes that the material about to be published is obscene. The student press is not immune from libel lawsuits. Specific criteria are involved in determining whether an individual has been libeled by the press, and it is very difficult for a public figure to prove libel. Nonetheless, several judgments have been won against the student press in libel cases. The best defense in a libel case is that the material published is true.

Advertising

From time to time, disputes arise over advertising that appears in the student press. Individuals or student organizations may feel that certain advertisements are degrading, racially discriminatory, or not in keeping with the values and regulations of the institution (for example, advertisements about term paper services or alcohol). Does the student paper have the right to refuse advertising? This issue has been studied by the courts on numerous occasions, and the answer seems clear. "American courts have ruled consistently that privately owned publications may accept or reject advertising" (Stevens and Webster, 1973, p. 63). However, Stevens and Webster believe that student publications should not reject editorial advertising, such as information that a candidate running for a student government position may wish to place, even though they apparently are free to do so. Instead, mechanisms for due process might be developed in these matters and an appeal to a committee provided for a student whose advertising has been rejected.

This question becomes more difficult, however, if the institution has promulgated guidelines concerning the kind of advertising that the paper may accept. Gehring (1986) has cited two cases (*Johnson* v. *Board of Junior College District 508,* 1975; and *Mississippi Gay Alliance* v. *Goudelock,* 1976) involving the rejection of advertising materials that resulted in different decisions by the courts. In each case, advertising material was rejected by the paper. In *Johnson,* the Illinois appeals court ruled against the paper, whereas a federal appeals court found in favor of the paper in *Mississippi Gay Alliance.* The primary difference between the two cases, as Gehring points out, is that in *Johnson* the university had promulgated guidelines concerning advertising, whereas in *Mississippi Gay Alliance* the editor made the decision to reject the advertising. When the university, as a state institution, develops such guidelines, rejection of the material becomes state action, and therefore a violation of the First Amendment (Gehring, 1986, p. 37).

Several other cases, which involved private, commercial newspapers, have resulted in the same decision by the courts. In both *Miami Herald Publishing Co. v. Tornillo* (1974) and *Pittsburgh Press Co. v. Pittsburgh Commission on Human Relations* (1973), the Supreme Court found on behalf of the newspaper. The editor was determined to have the right to reject advertising that the paper did not wish to publish.

Racial Discrimination. May a student newspaper practice racial discrimination in the advertising it rejects? This issue becomes a very difficult one, because competing interests are at work. On the one hand, the student press is guaranteed the right to publish under the First Amendment; on the other hand, it may not violate federal and state laws. This very issue was part of the *Joyner v. Whiting* (1973) decision, involving printed articles advocating segregation and an all-black university. The paper decided to employ only blacks and did not want to accept advertising from businesses owned by whites. The president terminated funding for the paper, and his decision was overturned by the courts. Several analyses of the opinion written in the case (Kaplin, 1985; Gehring, 1986) indicate that the president was heavy-handed in shutting down the press by terminating funding and that remedies are available to stop a paper from practicing racial discrimination. Although a permanent cut off of funds to support the paper was found to be unconstitutional by the court in *Joyner,* the court did hold that "freedom of the press furnishes no shield for discrimination" (at 456). The president must prohibit discrimination, although the specific action he took to do so was not constitutional.

Summary. Several conclusions can be drawn from this section on advertising. The editors of a publication have the right to determine the advertising that they wish to publish. If the institution has determined the guidelines that prescribe what the paper may include, then problems may arise because of the First Amendment and state action. The safest course is to let the editors decide. They need to be careful, however, not to violate federal or state laws in determining what advertising to reject, because there may be judicial remedies for advertisers who have suffered discrimination.

Private Versus Public Institutions

Most people believe that freedom of the press is inherently guaranteed by the First Amendment. The amendment reads, in part, "Congress shall make no law . . . abridging the freedom of speech, or of the press." Since very few institutions of higher education in the country are operated by the federal government, it would appear that this amendment does not apply to state-assisted institutions. Actually, the combination of the First Amendment with the Fourteenth Amendment is what applies to the student press. The Fourteenth Amendment indicates that "No State shall make or enforce any law which shall abridge the privileges or immunities of citizens of the United States." This amendment makes the rest of the Constitution apply to the states; in short, the states cannot abridge rights guaranteed to citizens by the federal Constitution; therefore, states cannot deny their citizens the right of a free press.

Neither amendment applies to private institutions of higher education as long as the private institution is not engaged in state action, so the thrust of the discussion moves from the legal arena to what makes for good educational practice. While it is true that a number of cases have been heard about just how much public involvement there is in private institutions, most often the courts have indicated that private institutions are just that and are not involved in state action (see *Grossner* v. *Trustees of Columbia University*, 1968). But a private institution still needs to resolve what it believes to be good educational practice with respect to providing freedom for the editors of student publications. (See Chapter Three in this volume for a detailed discussion of the inherent differences between public and private institutions.)

Conclusions

While the student press can be a perplexing and exasperating part of campus life, the legal environment for student publications seems relatively clear. With respect to public institutions of higher education, university officials generally should not attempt to restrain the content of student publications prior to their publication. Trying to fire editors, change the funding structure, or take other steps to restrict the operation of the student press has not been viewed favorably by the courts. Perhaps a better way to work with the student press is to use the experience as a solid educational experience for student journalists, select a professional adviser, and develop a publication board along the lines outlined by DeCoster and Krager (1986).

The distribution of student and nonstudent publications must be handled in an even-handed way. While the institution has some rights to regulate time, place, and manner, any restrictions on the distribution of materials must be well grounded. The distribution of off-campus publications must be treated much the same as the distribution of on-campus publications. And, whatever regulations are promulgated concerning the distribution of materials, the institution should not appear to be limiting access to the material.

Laws that apply to individuals and institutions generally apply to the student press. The press may not violate federal or state law. The press may not print obscenities (as defined by law), and the press does not have access to information that is restricted by statute. If individuals feel that they have been libeled by the press, they have recourse through the courts. Institutions that have a student press generally have not had to worry about being held responsible for the actions of the student press.

The press has a right to determine what advertising it will accept. However, a preferred practice is that student publications ought to make it possible for all points of view to be represented, if not through editorial content, then through paid advertising.

Public and private institutions are treated very differently with respect to the student press by the law and the courts. On constitutional grounds, private institutions generally have not been found to be engaged in state action, and so the First Amendment does not apply to them. Nonetheless, this may be an area of educational practice where the institution might want to create an independent student press so as to approximate the environment enjoyed by the private, commercial press off campus.

The best advice ever received from a journalist about the student press is this: While you may find the student press to be difficult and frustrating, few people tomorrow will remember today's headlines.

References

Alexander, K., and Solomon, E. S. *College and University Law.* Charlottesville, Va.: Michie, 1972.

Behrens, J. "Censorship: A 1982 Student Press Issue." *College Press Review,* 1983, *22* (3), 14.

DeCoster, D. A., and Krager, L. "Student Affairs Professionals and the Student Press." In J. H. Schuh (ed.), *Enhancing Relationships with the Student Press.* New Directions for Student Services, no. 33. San Francisco: Jossey-Bass, 1986.

Gehring, D. D. "The Student Press: A Legal Perspective." In J. H. Schuh (ed.), *Enhancing Relationships with the Student Press.* New Directions for Student Services, no. 33. San Francisco: Jossey-Bass, 1986.

Gibbs, A., and Stoner, T. D. "Student Publications as a Public Forum: Institutional Restraints and Individual Rights." *Journal of College Student Personnel,* 1985, *26* (3), 197–200.

Hollander, P. A. *Legal Handbook for Educators.* Boulder, Colo.: Westview Press, 1978.

Hotchkiss, C. W., and Madson, D. L. "A New Look at the Campus Press and the Law." *NASPA Journal,* 1978, *15* (4), 27–31.

Kaplin, W. A. *The Law of Higher Education: A Comprehensive Guide to Legal Implications of Administrative Decision Making.* (2nd ed.) San Francisco: Jossey-Bass, 1985.

Siddons, P. "The Frustrations and Rewards of College Journalism." In J. H. Schuh (ed.), *Enhancing Relationships with the Student Press.* New Directions for Student Services, no. 33. San Francisco: Jossey-Bass, 1986.

Stevens, G. E., and Webster, J. B. *Law and the Student Press.* Ames: Iowa State University Press, 1973.

Trager, R., and Dickerson, D. L. *College Student Press Law.* Terre Haute, Ind.: National Council of College Publications Advisers, 1976.

17

Larry H. Ebbers

Management and Use of Student Records

Questions surrounding maintenance, access to, and use of student records are part of the daily life of a student affairs administrator. Although record keeping should be a straightforward and easy task, it is not. Federal and state statutes, judicial decisions, and institutional policies have all complicated the task. Further, it is important that student affairs administrators understand the issues involved in record keeping and work actively to protect the rights of individuals about whom records are kept.

This chapter presents an overview of the issues involved in the management of educational records. Specific attention is given to the definition, classification, and retention of student records and to the unique problems involved in career planning and placement records, including recommendations. Suggestions are given on methods to approach policy development and implementation on a campus.

General Issues

Records management is not an issue exclusively for student affairs units. The entire institution is involved and is affected by records management policies and systems. Attention to legal and ethical questions on an institutional level can reduce complexity and ambiguity for practitioners. Prior to the establishment of any record management system, each institution should specifically identify how records are to be managed in the institution.

Approaches to records management and policy will vary between and among institutions. Whatever the system, each person involved in the use or maintenance of student records must be aware of policy and practice within the institution. In most cases, a records management committee serves as an excellent vehicle for the development of an appropriate retention schedule, maintenance access to a records system, and the needed security associated with the system. A joint student affairs, faculty, and administrative committee should be appointed to develop a master plan for the institution. This plan should specify record series and titles, the office responsible for retention of the placement record, the policy for release, and the length of time that a holder of permanent and nonpermanent records must retain the material.

For the purpose of this chapter, a record is defined as any information or data recorded in any medium designated as a record by the university or its representative. Notes or other supporting documents in any form used in generating a record are not considered part of the record unless specifically designated by the university or its representatives as such. This definition has been adopted by the Iowa State University Records Management Committee and is used as the basis for the entire university records management system.

The Family Educational Rights and Privacy Act of 1974 as Amended (FERPA) governs the right of access to educational records. Often referred to as the Buckley Amendment, the Act applies to most educational agencies and institutions in the United States. It is designed to protect the privacy of parents and students regarding school records. Parents are entitled to those rights until a student is eighteen years old or attends a postsecondary institution. At that time, the student obtains the rights, and the parents may no longer exercise them (Schatken, 1977) unless the student is a dependent for federal income tax purposes. Under those conditions, parents cannot be denied the right to see the student's records. (Chapter Seven in this volume provides a full description of the provisions of the Act.) The definition of students excludes anyone who has not been in attendance (Schatken, 1977). Thus, applicants for admission have no rights under FERPA.

Administrators should have a copy of this Act, as well as the implementing regulations (34 C.F.R. Part 99), in order to respond to all issues that may not be written as part of standard institutional policy or those that are not readily apparent with respect to protection of individual records. In addition, Kaplin (1985, pp. 358–359) outlines areas of the Buckley Amendment that are important for practitioners to understand. In most cases, students have rights to all those records that directly affect them and are maintained by the agency, but there are some exceptions. The exceptions include (1) certain personal and private records of institution personnel, (2) identified campus law enforcement records, (3) certain employment records, (4) some records regarding health care, and (5) certain records that relate to alumni information and files.

The American Association of Collegiate Registrars and Admissions Officers (1984a, 1984b) has published *A Guide to Postsecondary Institutions for Implementation of the Family Educational Rights and Privacy Act of 1974 as Amended* and an *Academic Record and Transcript Guide,* which provides guidelines for dealing with academic records and transcripts, continuing education unit records, transcript services, the security of records, and the release of academic record information and transcripts. Both of these sources are useful and helpful to practitioners.

In addition to FERPA, many states also have laws governing the maintenance and release of records. Such statutes should be carefully reviewed to determine whether provisions of the law are applicable in an institution. If the state has no statutory regulations regarding records, court cases need to be reviewed. In most states, courts recognize "a common law tort of invasion of privacy" (Kaplin, 1985, p. 359), which protects individuals against the disclosure of affairs considered private. A first step in developing a records management policy that is legally correct and educationally sound is to develop a classification system of records within the institution.

Record Classification

Classification of records for purposes of release clarifies questions of authority, responsibility, and law for both institutional employees and students. The following classification system is a useful way to approach this task:

> *Confidential by State and Federal Statute.* This type of record contains information that the university is bound to keep confidential and cannot release except upon court order or with permission of the person identified in the record.
>
> *Restricted by University Policy Under State Law.* This type of record contains information that the university *may* keep confidential in the interests of personal privacy under state law.
>
> *Privileged Under Common Law.* This type of record contains information that could not ordinarily be used as evidence in a civil lawsuit, since it is derived from a confidential relationship protected by common law (such as physician-patient or lawyer-client) or is protected under the common law tort of invasion of privacy. The record may not be released except with specific written permission of the person who is identified in the record or the person having a legal right to waive the claim of privilege.
>
> *Unrestricted, Provided Confidential Material Is Deleted.* This type of record is generally subject to release to any requesting person; however, certain identifying personal or otherwise confidential information must be deleted on the released copy.
>
> *Unrestricted.* This type of record is subject to release without restriction upon compliance with university policies governing payment of costs of copying and proper supervision under the applicable state statute.

Taking time to identify and classify records is worth the effort. Ambiguity is reduced, and guidance is given to personnel and students.

Record Retention Schedule

The most helpful way of clarifying an institutional record policy is to publish a separate document, which is made available to faculty, staff, and students. The retention or record schedule should include the record series title and description, responsible parties, release policy, and the holders of both permanent and nonpermanent records.

1. *Title and Description.* This is an important step in the development of any records management and retention system. The titles should be developed to ensure that they are the best descriptions of the actual record being kept—for example, Advanced Standing (placement examinations); Admissions Records (student); Test Out Language Requirements Cards; List of Graduating Seniors.
2. *Responsible Parties.* The office or organization responsible for retention of the permanent record should be noted—for example, the registrar, the department, the admissions office, or the dean of students.
3. *Release Policy.* The policy for release should follow closely the classification of records for purposes of release.
4. *Holder of Permanent Record.* This facet of the schedule identifies who is responsible and how long a particular record should be retained: permanently; retain until updated, then discard; retain as long as needed, then transfer to the archives.
5. *Holder of Nonpermanent Record.* These guidelines may include comments regarding how long nonpermanent records should be kept by personnel in each area. Directions may be given, for example, to retain the record until updated, then discard; retain one term, then destroy; or retain lists three years, then destroy.

Policy Issues

There are several areas that should be taken into consideration in developing a policy and system for records management. An official custodian should be designated for each permanent record system. If the institution does not have a comprehensive records policy, the institution's attorney or legal adviser should ensure that someone is charged with this important caretaking responsibility. All requests for information should be referred to the official custodian of the record. The primary responsibility for the release of all records then becomes the responsibility of the official custodian. Normally, the official custodian is the head of the administrative unit responsible for the retention of the academic record.

Retention. Official determination needs to be made regarding the length of retention of any records. Beyond the permanent transcript records, specific retention schedules for academic records should be provided to departments. If the institutional committee does not wish to set a schedule, each department should establish a schedule and report this schedule to the chief institutional officer designated as the official custodian of the records.

Guidelines should be included regarding when and where records should be sent to the archives of the institution. For some documents, such as honorary records and award documentation, annual disposition may be deemed appropriate. Finally, the record schedule should clearly indicate that personal papers and notes of faculty and staff members are not included in the system.

Guidance for development of such a schedule can be found in *Retention of Records* (American Association of Collegiate Registrars and Admissions Officers, 1987). This booklet discusses the legal aspects of student records retention and disposal, the process of developing a records retention and disposal program, retention schedule recommendations, the methods of storage, and the security of student records. Specific recommended retention schedules by type of record are listed, as well as a retention schedule for those records regularly maintained or used in the admissions process. In addition, retention recommendations are provided for certification data/documents, publications, statistical data/documents, and institution reports. The certification data should include enrollment verification, financial assistance records, Veterans Administration certification, and Social Security certification. The publication schedule should include catalogues, commencement programs, degree and enrollment statistics, and schedule of classes. A separate retention schedule is suggested for FERPA data and related documents, including requests for formal hearings, students' written consent for records disclosure, waivers for right of access, and students' requests for nondisclosure of directory information. AACRAO also recommends guidelines for retention of records with respect to methods of storage. They include paper (hard copy), micrographics, computer machine-readable records, and electronic image systems. Examples of records inventory forms, an institutional records policy, and pertinent federal regulation references are provided by AACRAO and may be particularly useful to the practitioner.

State Law. When establishing a records management system, institutions must recognize the continuing press for "right to know" and "sunshine laws" on the part of states to provide access to certain types of records held by academic institutions. States have not advanced significantly or varied much from the intent of the Buckley Amendment in that, if a student's right to privacy of records is challenged, the courts have sided with the provisions of the Buckley Amendment. Academic and personal records should be kept separate and treated accordingly. Guidelines and retention schedules need to be developed for each type of record maintained. These procedures prevent any unnecessary disclosure or access to inappropriate information.

Terminology. The use of the terminology in academic records and transcripts has been confused with respect to record keeping. The American Association of Collegiate Registrars and Admissions Officers (1984a) describes the academic record as "that internal document or electronic image maintained by the Office of the Registrar that reflects the unabridged academic history of the student at the institution. It is a chronological listing of the student's total quantitative learning experiences and achievements and may include any information pertinent to the evaluation thereof" (p. 4). The transcript is defined as "that document which, at the request of the student or former student, is forwarded to persons or agencies for their use in reviewing the academic performance of the student" (p. 16).

Special problems related to transcripts and appropriate record keeping are presented by the continuing education unit (CEU). Records on the necessity for recertification, identification of course units completed, and other efforts to identify completion of noncredit experiences should be maintained in a separate file and monitored by a separate release policy. The National University

Extension Association (1974) has published a set of guidelines entitled *The Continuing Education Unit—Criteria and Guidelines.* These guidelines define the CEU and indicate the basis and requirements for keeping appropriate records. The American Association of Collegiate Registrars and Admissions Officers (1979) has also developed a *Self-Audit Manual for Registrars,* which is particularly valuable in evaluating and updating a records system.

Information Systems. The major issues associated with transcripts and academic records in an electronic age revolve around the security and privacy of the information systems. The popular press has been replete with stories about students gaining access to and making changes on electronic data-keeping systems. This concern is highlighted by Ware (1984, p. 7): "Between the outreach of remotely provided computing services and the interconnectivity of modern day networking, the educational community finds itself in an ever increasing posture of exposure and subject to an increasing scope of threats: fraud, hacking, pirating of information, stealing of computer resources, destruction of records, invasion of privacy, physical damage to facilities."

Educational institutions must make every effort to protect the data and records that they hold. Although it may be beneficial to share some of the policies that institutions have regarding the protection of data and records, the need for confidentiality and the nature of information have made policies institution specific. Each institution must be willing to commit the financial resources and have an ongoing procedure for continuous review of its protection policy to ensure that its privacy is maintained. A comprehensive set of safeguards is needed to ensure the privacy of all records. A records management committee with appropriate representation from the registrar's office, the computer center, and the administrative data-processing center is critical to the development and implementation of guidelines.

Career/Placement Records

Another area of interest to student affairs personnel relates to the registration and maintenance of personal credential files, applications for graduate and professional schools, and other forms of career information, such as a student development transcript. All these and similar types of records come under the provisions of FERPA. The Act brought forth two options in the credentialing process. One option retains the individual's right to access to all materials and references in the file, and a second option provides a waiver of right of access. Each student using the placement service should be aware of these options, and requests for references should state the option chosen by the student. The following are examples of waiver statements:

> *Option A: Right of Access.* The Family Educational Rights and Privacy Act of 1974 gives you the right to review the statements in your file that were written on or after January 1, 1975. If you choose to set up a file to which you have access, the placement office will send you the necessary forms, and your old file (statements written before January 1, 1975) will be destroyed. Under no circumstances will the statements in the old file, written before January 1, 1975, be shown to the registrant. You must obtain new recommendations under this option.

> *Option B: Waiver of Right of Access.* If you wish to begin a confidential file, or if you wish to maintain a file that was established with our office before January 1, 1975, you must sign a waiver of your right of access to anything in your file which might be written after January 1, 1975. In this instance, you will not have the opportunity to review your file; therefore, the file will be totally confidential. In essence, our past policy of confidentiality will be maintained.

Most placement offices, admissions offices, and other offices that recognize both confidential and open-access information do not allow students to mix options. Once students make a choice regarding their options, they are irrevocable unless the student wishes to create an entirely new file under either of the options.

As a result of FERPA, institutions are required to have a

release form signed by the student before a set of credentials, application, or grades can be mailed to a requesting agency or employer. In some cases, placement offices have initiated the use of general release forms, but caution should still be maintained in the distribution of confidential files and records.

Conclusion

The laws and regulations regarding student records have been clarified considerably during the last few years. However, additional mandates regarding repayment of student loans and other financial aid records and academic records are certain to continue. A most recent example has been the requirement that transcripts be withheld under the bankruptcy law (Tanaka, 1986).

A number of sources help define and clarify records management questions. These include the *Federal Register;* documents from government agencies, including the United States Department of Education, the Veterans Administration (VA), the United States Public Health Service (PHS), the Internal Revenue Service (IRS), and the State Department; court documents; professional associations, such as AACRAO and the National Association of College and University Attorneys (NACUA); professional journals, such as the *AACRAO Journal;* and the *Journal of College and University Law.* Above all, a system must be developed, and it must be well understood and consistently enforced on campus. The time spent in developing an appropriate record-keeping system is well spent. Confusion is reduced, personnel and students understand their rights and responsibilities, and educational purposes can be met with minimal legal problems.

References

American Association of Collegiate Registrars and Admissions Officers. *Self-Audit Manual for Registrars.* Washington, D.C.: American Association of Collegiate Registrars and Admissions Officers, 1979.

American Association of Collegiate Registrars and Admissions Officers. *Academic Record and Transcript Guide.* (Rev. ed.)

Washington, D.C.: American Association of Collegiate Registrars and Admissions Officers, 1984a.

American Association of Collegiate Registrars and Admissions Officers. *A Guide to Postsecondary Institutions for Implementation of the Family Educational Rights and Privacy Act of 1974 as Amended, 1976.* Washington, D.C.: American Association of Collegiate Registrars and Admissions Officers, 1984b.

American Association of Collegiate Registrars and Admissions Officers. *Retention of Records—A Guide for Registrars and Admissions Officers.* Washington, D.C.: American Association of Collegiate Registrars and Admissions Officers, 1987.

Kaplin, W. A. *The Law of Higher Education: A Comprehensive Guide to Legal Implications of Administrative Decision Making.* San Francisco: Jossey-Bass, 1985.

National University Extension Association. *The Continuing Education Unit—Criteria and Guidelines.* Washington, D.C.: National University Extension Association, 1974.

Schatken, S. N. "Student Records at Institutions of Postsecondary Education: Selected Issues Under the Family Educational Rights and Privacy Act." *Journal of College and University Law,* 1977, *4* (3), 147–176.

Tanaka, P. *The Permissibility of Withholding Transcripts Under the Bankruptcy Law.* Washington, D.C.: National Association of College and University Attorneys, 1986.

Ware, W. H. "Information Systems, Security and Privacy." *EDUCOM,* 1984, *19* (2), 6–11.

18

Jon C. Dalton

Employment and Supervision of Student Affairs Personnel

A retiring student affairs vice-president suggested some years ago that one of the most important lessons he had learned from more than three decades in the profession was never to underestimate a personnel problem. His conviction that personnel issues almost always have the potential to become complex and serious legal problems has been confirmed by professional experience and seems to be shared by many colleagues in student affairs administration. Few areas of student affairs management seem to generate so many legal problems as supervision and employment practices. Even the most innocuous personnel issue can mushroom into litigation if not recognized and managed appropriately.

Student affairs employees do not have a long history of initiating legal actions to resolve personnel disputes. When such actions do occur, however, they have the potential to generate intense adversarial relations and considerable stress in the supervisor-employee relationship, which can spill over into the entire organization. Consequently, it is important for the student affairs supervisor to be familiar with potential areas of legal risk and to know how to employ effective prevention strategies to avoid legal problems.

Issues in employment practices and staff supervision are certainly not unique to student affairs. The principles remain the same regardless of the area of employment in higher education. However, since student affairs employs numbers of persons, this update is provided. In this chapter, some important areas of

334

potential legal risk in student affairs employment practices and supervision will be reviewed. In addition, some practical supervision approaches and strategies will be identified that can help the student affairs professional avoid legal problems in these areas.

Job Assignment and Hiring

Job Descriptions. One of the most common areas of legal difficulty concerns poorly constructed job descriptions. Often, student affairs job assignments are vague and general, partly because many of them encompass a wide variety of assignments and duties. The job description, which is essentially a form of contract between the employer and employee, contains the basic duties of the position. It summarizes the elements of accountability that apply to the job (Belker, 1986). Consequently, the job assignments that are summarized in the job description must accurately define the employee's scope of duties. It is impossible, of course, to detail every responsibility in the job description, but it should specify primary duties and responsibilities, indicate the priority or time commitment for each major area of responsibility, and provide a summary of general duties that may be expected of every employee. Job descriptions often contain the phrase "other duties as assigned." Such a reference is often needed because of the generalist responsibilities of many student affairs jobs. But an open-ended job specification can invite personnel conflict and abuse. Clearly, a student affairs supervisor needs authority to change work assignments as circumstances require, but the job description should not provide carte blanche authority for the supervisor by keeping duties of employees vague and subject to constant reformulation. It is better to make the job description as specific as possible, so that there is clear understanding of basic work assignments and responsibilities. Whenever job duties must be changed, job descriptions should be revised to reflect new duties.

It is the supervisor's responsibility to ensure accurate job descriptions before filling positions and to review systematically all job descriptions so that they reflect changing job duties. Used effectively, the job description can be an important management tool. It helps employees understand what is to be done on the job and what their primary duties are. It identifies the most important relationships in the work setting and provides the basis for performance evaluation. Finally, it is an essential tool in the hiring and placement of new employees.

Hiring Procedures. At the beginning of the hiring process, the supervisor should review the job description for the position to be filled. Once the duties of the position are clear, the specific skills, abilities, and experiences required to perform the duties of the job should then be specified. Minimum skills and qualifications should be clearly tied to job duties and performance standards. Other desirable credentials can be preferred but should not be stated requirements unless they are integral to the performance of the job.

In addition to a clearly defined job description, it is important to have search procedures specified *before search activities begin.* The standards and criteria used to guide decisions in the search process should be communicated to the search committee in writing and in advance, so that they are familiar to all involved in search activities. It is important to keep in mind that, as a general principle, the courts are more concerned with the *procedures* of personnel searches than with their *substance* (Kaplin, 1985).

One of the most common problems in the search process is inadequate orientation of the search committee. Often, there is pressure to move quickly because of lengthy search procedures and the need to fill the vacant position. Consequently, supervisors often hurry the search process and take insufficient time to orient search committee members to the job description and the standards and criteria to be used in evaluating candidates. This situation can lead to disagreement and conflict later in the search process. Student affairs supervisors should ensure that all searches begin with a thorough review of the job description and all criteria that apply to the search process. Search committee members must be clear about their role in selecting finalists and making the job offer. As a rule, it is usually best for the supervisor to reserve final authority for the hiring decision and to make sure at the outset that the committee members know that the supervisor has this authority, so that there is no misunderstanding.

Of all the legal problems that may arise in a search process, the most common and most serious is employment discrimination.

In no other area of employment and supervisory practice are there so many statutory and regulatory requirements. Kaplin (1985) points out that, in addition to state statutes governing fair employment practices, the federal government has eight major employment discrimination statutes and an executive order. (See Chapter Six in this volume for further information.) Whenever possible, the composition of the search committee should include protected-class individuals in order to promote diversity of viewpoint and sensitivity to affirmative action concerns. The search committee should also include staff and faculty from outside the hiring department as well as students, in order to gain additional input and promote community involvement.

What is said and not said during candidate interviews can often lead to personnel difficulties later. Chapter Six in this volume reviews civil rights law and identifies inappropriate and illegal statements and questions related to a candidate's age, race, sexual preference, marital status, religion, and physical characteristics. Such questions or statements can prejudice the integrity of the search process and constitute grounds for employment discrimination.

Other problems can occur when inaccurate information is conveyed about job duties and conditions. If candidates are given a set of expectations about job responsibilities and employment benefits that differ from actual conditions encountered on the job, employees may later have grounds to file employment grievances.

When discussing job responsibilities during the search process, interviewers should closely follow the stated job description and provide the candidate with a copy of this document. If at any time during the search process necessary changes are made in job duties or working conditions, these should be immediately communicated to candidates.

As search activities reach the final stages, another kind of problem can arise. In the time-consuming process of checking credentials, reviewing interview evaluations, and moving toward a hiring decision, candidates may not be kept informed of the progress of the search. These communication lapses are very often viewed by the candidate as inconsiderate or unprofessional treatment or, at worst, grounds for a formal complaint about the fairness of the search process. Failure to keep candidates notified about the progress of the search will almost assuredly exacerbate any other problem they may have encountered during the search process.

Qualifications. One final issue should be mentioned in discussing the hiring process. Serious problems can arise regarding the qualifications of the candidate *after* he or she has begun employment. For example, a new employee may not have completed a degree that was a stated requirement of the position. It is always important to talk directly with references, especially supervisors, who have knowledge of the candidate's stated qualifications before a job offer is tendered. Once the employee is on the job, it is difficult to take corrective action unless one can prove deliberate misrepresentation.

One way to certify degree status or completion date is to include a degree certification form in the offer-of-employment letter. Such a form requires the candidate to certify that the required degree has been completed or to indicate the projected completion date. If the latter, the form should clearly indicate that the job offer is contingent on the successful completion of the degree by the projected date. Another approach is to hire the individual on a temporary basis until the degree has been officially granted.

Grievances and Disciplinary Action

Grievance Procedures. Fox (1966) argues that dispute is inherent in employer-employee relationships. Legal problems commonly arise from the *process* by which employee grievances are handled as well as by the *manner* in which disciplinary action is conducted by the supervisor. The supervisor's first and most important requirement in handling disputes is to adopt a properly constructed grievance policy and procedure. The grievance procedure must be formally documented and publicized and should include the following steps: receiving and defining the nature of the grievance, gathering the facts, analyzing the facts, making a decision, applying the decision, and following up on the decision (Flippo, 1971). During the entire procedure, records of meetings must be kept; and all findings, decisions, and actions must be communicated in writing to the employee.

Almost all colleges and universities have some system of personnel classification that defines certain employee benefits and obligations. Typically, these personnel policies are set by governing boards or by the central administration or through the collective bargaining process and are administered by a central personnel office or some other administrative unit outside the student affairs area. The student affairs supervisor should understand the terms and conditions set forth in the institution's personnel classification system. Such classification systems generally specify the procedures, special rules, chain of command, and lines of communication to be followed in formal employee grievance procedures (Rhode, 1983).

In addition to institutional rules that apply to employee classification groups, student affairs organizations also should have their own personnel handbook, containing not only the pertinent institutional personnel guidelines but all other rules and procedures that are unique to student affairs staff. Such a handbook provides a valuable orientation to new staff members and helps to minimize employee grievances, which sometimes grow out of misinformation or lack of information.

Understanding Employee Grievances. Fortunato and Waddell (1981) claim that the most important needs of employees are recognition, security, adequate pay, reasonable working conditions, fair treatment, and opportunity for advancement. Employees typically initiate grievances because they feel they are being denied one or more of these primary needs. Of all these primary needs, fair and adequate compensation is most often the employee's first concern. An employer's foremost obligation is to compensate employees fairly. Student affairs supervisors should be particularly careful about pay inequities with respect to women and minorities. The Equal Pay Act of 1963 requires equal pay for equal work (Kaplin, 1985).

Although some grievances are capricious or malicious in character, employee grievances usually arise because of ineffective personnel management. When job descriptions are poorly written or ignored, when personnel procedures are not clearly articulated and honored, or when there is lack of attention to the primary needs of employees, grievances are likely to occur. There is no more effective way to prevent employee grievances than to have in place effectively written and administered personnel procedures.

When grievances do arise, the issue immediately becomes one of quick assessment and resolution. As a general rule, the longer it takes to resolve a grievance, the more likely it is that complications will occur. If possible, the grievance should be resolved in an informal manner. If it cannot be resolved in this way, the formal grievance procedure must be implemented without delay. The supervisor should never view an employee grievance as a personal insult or offense. Failure to be objective or to hear grievances with an open mind and a nonjudgmental attitude will assuredly magnify any complaint. Most grievances can, in fact, usually be resolved simply by giving the employee an opportunity to express his or her feelings.

Disciplinary Action. Disciplinary action is usually taken because of repeated failures in performance or a malfeasance of duty. Legal problems most frequently occur when a disciplinary action is construed by the employee as capricious or unwarranted. If an effective program of performance evaluation is in place, disciplinary action will usually occur as the final action in a series of efforts to correct performance problems. When disciplinary action occurs in the context of systematic performance evaluation, employees are much less likely to formally contest the disciplinary action taken, even though they may strongly disagree with it. Unfortunately, many student affairs officers do not have an effective system of performance evaluation in place. Meabon and colleagues (1978) found in a survey of chief student affairs officers that fewer than 50 percent of them conducted regular performance reviews with individual staff members.

Disciplinary action taken as part of a system of performance evaluation provides not only the documentation that protects the supervisor from legal action but, more important, a framework for correcting performance problems and encouraging the professional development of the employee. Disciplinary action should always be taken in private. Supervisors should keep in mind that the performance—not the person—is the object of criticism. Therefore, they should avoid statements that an employee might interpret as personal attacks. Instead of delivering an angry monologue, they should involve the employee in discussing the disciplinary action (Belker, 1986).

Whenever possible, disciplinary action should be taken early and in incremental stages. Employees should be given a reasonable opportunity to correct a problem as well as an indication of the consequences if the problem is not corrected. Disciplinary action should not be conveyed as punishment but as corrective action for failure in performance. It constitutes a formal warning or notice that such performance failure is unacceptable. When disciplinary action is taken, the principles of what Ardaiolo (1983) calls "fundamental fairness" should be followed. These principles include written notice, a statement of specific charges, a fair hearing, an opportunity to confront witnesses and review their statements, and an opportunity to speak in one's own defense.

Termination of an employee is justifiable when the employee has not performed on the job as he or she agreed, when the employee fails to comply with instructions given by the supervisor, or when the employee is judged to be incompetent (Robinson and Catena, 1972). Termination of employment is the action taken by an employer when all disciplinary efforts fail. It is the last step in a process of personnel review designed to correct problems in performance and establish consequences for continued performance failure. If this process of review and disciplinary action is managed appropriately, termination of employment should never come as a surprise to the affected employee. If termination is necessary, the grounds for the action should be clearly documented and justified by the performance evaluation review process and formally communicated to the employee.

There is an important difference between the termination of an employee's contractual relationship and the decision not to *renew* a contractual arrangement with an employee (Rhode, 1983). In situations where employing institutions use specified term contracts, there is no legal obligation to renew the employee's appointment from one contractual period to another. In these instances, termination of employment is accomplished by nonrenewal of the term contract. Dismissal of an employee for cause, on the other hand, is the termination of a contract and places on the employer a burden of proof to demonstrate that good-faith efforts have been made to honor the terms of the contract and that dismissal is clearly justified under the due process requirements of the contractual relationship.

Rewards and Recognition

How employees are rewarded and recognized for their performance is a frequent problem area in supervisor-employee relations. Decisions about salary changes receive the most attention because an employee's compensation is commonly regarded as the leading barometer of the employee's worth. Because salary is viewed as a key indicator of performance, even the smallest discrepancy in salary increments among staff can take on significant symbolic importance. Staff members often discuss and compare salary information, particularly at the time that salary increments are given; and perceived discrepancies often lead to discontent and grievances. Decisions about salary increments should never be made without reference to clearly established performance criteria and documentation. If employees have an opportunity to review their performance with their supervisor and realize that salary decisions are closely tied to performance evaluation, grievances are far less likely to occur. It is always wise to handle matters related to salary in a formal manner. If salary decisions are conveyed in a casual, incomplete manner, the impression can easily be conveyed that the decision (and the employee) has not been given careful attention.

Promotions are one of the most powerful means of rewarding staff performance; they can also be one of the most common sources of legal problems. The problems that arise are usually related to the criteria for promotion. Promotion is generally based either on merit or on seniority. In cases of promotion based on merit, a conscientious and systematic effort should be made to measure merit and to show that promotion is based on employee competence. When there is little effort to assess merit and to measure it in an objective manner, concern is quickly generated about equal treatment, due process, and favoritism.

Promotion of employees sometimes appears to conflict with

affirmative action efforts. Outright promotion of an individual, especially a nonminority, without any search activity can be perceived as skirting the spirit, if not the letter, of affirmative action requirements. Policies relating to promotion should be clearly publicized and familiar to employees. It is especially important that these policies demonstrate support for the overall goal of affirmative action, which is to accelerate the achievement of equal opportunity for minority groups, women, the handicapped, and Vietnam-era veterans (Fortunato and Waddell, 1981).

Whenever possible, all qualified employees should be given an opportunity to indicate an interest in a position vacancy before an outright promotion is made. The right of all persons to work and advance on the basis of merit and potential is a powerful principle in the work environment. Even though an employee may realize that he or she is not likely to get the promotion, the opportunity to discuss it with a supervisor and to be considered for it is very important to employee morale and perceived fairness.

Working Conditions

In a narrow sense, the term *working conditions* refers to job provisions and employee benefits specified by the employment contract: work hours, work-space assignment, organizational communications, access to necessary equipment, and a safe work environment. In a broader sense, it refers to all aspects of the physical and psychological environment of the workplace. Working conditions can greatly influence the quality of life for employees on the job. The following are some important issues related to working conditions that often create legal problems for the supervisor.

Work Hours. Student affairs staff often feel that they work the longest hours of anyone in higher education. Because they staff the residence halls, advise student activities, and provide counseling and health services, they are frequently on duty during evenings and weekends and on call around the clock. Except under collective bargaining agreements, student affairs staff, like other campus professional staff, usually have no compensatory time arrangements. Long working hours are almost always a source of concern for student affairs staff.

Because of the diversity of roles within student affairs organizations, the work schedules of staff members vary greatly. In most situations, there is no practical way to have complete uniformity in work-hour arrangements for all staff. Consequently, arrangements must be made to accommodate the special work-hour requirements of some staff positions. Flex time or compensatory time arrangements can be a useful personnel benefit for the long and irregular work schedules of student affairs employees. However, problems with perceived fairness are quick to arise when flex time or compensatory time policies are not clearly communicated or administered. Exceptions to the formal work-hour policy should be clearly justified and communicated in order to avoid problems with perceived fairness.

Health and Safety. In the employee's hierarchy of personal needs, safety and security on the job occupy a place of importance second only to basic life-support needs. Among the health and safety concerns of importance to employees are such matters as asbestos in the workplace; chemical exposure; well-lit parking lots; adequate heating, cooling, and lighting; safety training for required equipment use; and appropriate space for work activities. The current "wellness" movement has done much to focus attention on health issues in the work setting.

Many health and safety standards for the workplace are established and monitored by the Occupational Safety and Health Administration (OSHA). Periodic audits are performed by OSHA to assess employee working conditions, and student affairs supervisors should be familiar with the standards required by this federal agency as well as state and local regulations for occupational safety. Additional health and safety requirements may be specified by collective bargaining agreements.

Communications. Student affairs staff often complain that they are given inadequate information about matters directly or indirectly affecting their job responsibilities and performance. Problems with organizational communications can be a source of employee grievance if the employee believes that the lack of information negatively affects his or her job status or performance evaluation.

Communications problems often occur because information

is shared in both formal and informal ways in most organizations. Because of informal personal networking, some individuals become privy to information that other staff do not have. This situation can create the perception of "selective" communication, which can damage staff morale and undermine supervisor-employee relations.

One of the best ways to prevent such problems is to have effective departmental and divisional communication systems. Such systems should include formal communications, such as newsletters and other forms of written information, as well as information dissemination through a structured network of staff meetings. Communication can also take place through face-to-face contact, group meetings, an open-door policy, a departmental complaint system, committee meetings, and "round-table" sessions where the supervisor meets with employees. Experience suggests that staff within an organization tend to emulate the behavior of organizational leaders. When leaders share information through established channels, maintain confidences, and avoid the rumor mill, staff are more likely to trust the communications they receive and to model good communications themselves.

Conclusion

Supervision and employment practices are areas with significant potential for serious legal problems. Careful attention to detail and clear communication are needed at all times. Specific attention must be paid to job descriptions, to ensure that such descriptions correctly reflect the expectations of the supervisor and the needs of the position. Hiring procedures must conform to both the law and institutional expectations. Care must be taken that any committee involved in the hiring process understands its role. Staff members and others involved in interviewing candidates should be made aware of the legal constraints on interview questions. Impermissible questions could lead to legal challenges later, with claims of employment discrimination. Clear and unambiguous grievance, evaluation, and discipline procedures should be established within the organization. Attention must be given to rewards and recognition of staff to sustain both morale and productivity. Working conditions must be monitored to ensure compliance with applicable state and federal laws. The ability to recognize these high-risk issues that are likely to expand into full-blown legal problems is a necessity for successfully negotiating the terrain of student affairs administrative practice.

References

Ardaiolo, F. P. "What Process Is Due?" In M. J. Barr (ed.), *Student Affairs and the Law*. New Directions for Student Services, no. 22. San Francisco: Jossey-Bass, 1983.

Belker, L. B. *The First Time Manager: A Procedural Guide to the Management of People*. New York: American Management Association, 1986.

Flippo, E. B. *Principles of Personnel Management*. New York: McGraw-Hill, 1971.

Fortunato, R. T., and Waddell, D. G. *Personnel Administration in Higher Education: Handbook of Faculty and Staff Practices*. San Francisco: Jossey-Bass, 1981.

Fox, S. *Management and the Law*. New York: Appleton-Century-Crofts, 1966.

Kaplin, W. A. *The Law of Higher Education: A Comprehensive Guide to Legal Implications of Administrative Decision Making*. (2nd ed.) San Francisco: Jossey-Bass, 1985.

Meabon, D. L., and others. "Management Techniques in Student Affairs." *Journal of College Student Personnel*, 1978, *19* (3), 221–224.

Rhode, S. "Use of Legal Counsel: Avoiding Problems." In M. J. Barr (ed.), *Student Affairs and the Law*. New Directions for Student Services, no. 22. San Francisco: Jossey-Bass, 1983.

Robinson, W. G., and Catena, A. P. *Business Law: Legal Aspects of Management Decisions*. Boston: Allyn & Bacon, 1972.

Sims, J. M. and Foxley, C. H. "Job Analysis, Job Descriptions, and Performance Appraisal Systems." In C. H. Foxley (ed.), *Applying Management Techniques*. New Directions for Student Services, no. 9. San Francisco: Jossey-Bass, 1980.

Margaret J. Barr

✿✿✿   ✿✿✿   ✿✿✿

Conclusion: The Evolving Legal Environment of Student Affairs Administration

This volume has presented the pertinent areas of the law that influence student affairs administration. Not every legal concern influencing higher education has been covered. Other sources, listed in the Annotated Bibliography at the end of this volume, are designed to provide a comprehensive legal perspective on the enterprise of higher education. Our purpose here was to identify legal concerns for student affairs practitioners and to translate what is known about the law into principles of practice and administration in student affairs.

Emerging Themes

Several themes emerge from this volume. First, the law is always in a process of change and modification. The increased volume and scope of statutes, judicial decisions, and administrative rules bear stark witness to this theme. Such a volatile environment requires student affairs professionals to stay informed of changes in the law and be able to translate those changes into effective policies and procedures for the campus. Further, a changing, evolving legal environment requires a high tolerance for ambiguity on the part of the administrators. Answers to legal questions are dependent on the specific facts involved and the current state of the law. Reliance on good judgment is not enough! Astute practitioners must carefully consider both the legal and educational implications of their actions.

Second, the legal implications for student affairs practice will increase rather than decrease in the years ahead. Although sound risk management principles mandate careful attention to legal questions, student affairs administrators are not likely to avoid litigation. Some lawsuits will be brought that are frivolous; others will be threatened on grounds that have already been litigated; and still others will raise new legal questions. Fear of legal proceedings should not, however, substitute for sound administrative judgment. The law and attorneys provide advice; administrators must make the best decision they can based on the facts at the time.

Third, the law is not something to be either feared or merely tolerated. Although the rising number of rules, regulations, statutes, and judicial decisions can seem overwhelming and at times create an onerous burden, the influence of the law is not all negative. Protection of individual rights, ethical and humane treatment, and responsible actions are principles on which student affairs is founded. The emerging trend toward legalism is in part a response to lack of adherence to these principles in the past. Administrators do not have the freedom that they experienced in the early years of American higher education. Arbitrary and capricious actions by administrators will be challenged within the legal system. But, more important, such practices are simply not good ways to conduct business. The result can and should be a more thoughtful and careful decision-making process on campus. On the other hand, the degree of legalism we are experiencing today is frustrating and can be confusing even to those acting in good faith.

Fourth, students, faculty, and staff in public institutions do have protected constitutional and statutory rights. Although private institutions are not legally required to recognize constitutional rights unless the institution is engaging in state action, many private institutions elect to do so. Thus, the lines of demarcation between public and private institutions from a legal perspective are becoming less clear. Both types of institutions must follow their own rules, and the courts have held that principles of fundamental fairness must prevail.

Fifth, the definition of the relationship between the student and the institution is changing to that of a contract. Both public and private institutions must examine publications, representations, and documents to ensure that they are not promising more than they can deliver. Litigation based on contract theory will continue to grow in the decades ahead.

Sixth, liability questions are becoming pervasive in all aspects of student affairs administration. Risk management plans, clear policies, staff training, and common sense can help reduce liability claims. The increase in liability judgments, coupled with rising insurance costs or the inability to obtain coverage, has created a crisis in higher education. Of particular concern are liability claims associated with negligence and alcohol. The astute administrator will audit current policies and procedures and attempt to reduce the potential for liability claims as much as possible.

Seventh, colleges and universities are no longer viewed as enclaves where legal issues are not of concern. Both public and private institutions must be responsible to a wide range of laws, including those associated with employment, health and welfare of students and employees, and record keeping. Each of these statutory provisions mandates a careful administrative response to avoid litigation or penalties.

Eighth, student affairs administrators should know when to seek qualified legal advice. The complex nature of the law requires that such advice be sought at the policy development stage, so that legal counsel can engage in preventive law. Such a goal cannot be accomplished unless there is clear and open communication between legal counsel and administrators. The burden for seeking such advice lies with the administrator, but it cannot be exercised unless the administrator is aware of the potential legal issues involved in his or her work.

Ninth, student affairs administrators must become more aware of the law. Graduate preparation programs should include courses and materials to help practitioners understand the law. Professional associations and staff development programs should intentionally focus on such issues. For the good administrator is the aware and prepared administrator.

Finally, the legal constraints identified in this volume provide the parameters for policy development and implementation. Within that framework, the student affairs administrator must exercise judgment based on the characteristics of the institution and the educational goals involved. There are, however, a number of legal questions that have not been answered and will be the subject of future legal challenges. Some of these have been specifically referred to in this volume; others are identified as emerging themes.

Future Directions

Among the challenges facing student affairs administrators in the future are the following:

Influence of State Constitutions. The cases in New Jersey referred to in Chapter Four may be the beginning of a trend. If the applicable state constitution has provisions similar to the Bill of Rights in the federal Constitution, private institutions may experience more litigation on state constitutional grounds. Each college or university should carefully research the provisions of the applicable state constitution and ensure that compliance exists on the campus.

Role of Legal Counsel. There is no current legal definition of the role of a college or university legal counsel. Colleges and universities differ markedly from governmental and corporate organizations, and thus the role of an attorney is different. Thompson (1987) defines sixteen roles for the university attorney and indicates that each institution must know what is wanted or needed from legal counsel. Although many models exist for legal representation—including outside counsel, in-house counsel, state representation through the attorney general's office, and the like—each college should clearly communicate and understand the expectations of those who provide legal advice.

Role of Standards. In recent years, the courts have increasingly relied on standards of practice to guide decisions. Many professional associations have responded and have promulgated standards for practice. Such a trend has both positive and negative implications. Adherence to standards by the institution can aid in limiting liability claims. Lack of knowledge of such standards and failure to follow them can increase potential liability for the institution. Buchanan (1987) has presented a comprehensive review of available standards in all areas of higher education. For student affairs, the Council for the Advancement of Standards (1986) document can provide helpful guidance in this arena.

Drug Testing. The current concern with illicit drugs in athletics, employment, and society has led to demands for mandatory drug testing. Such testing, however, raises serious constitutional questions that will be the basis for future legal challenges. Blood testing has already been recognized as constituting a search within the meaning of the Fourth Amendment (Brown, 1987; see also *Schmerber* v. *California*, 1966; and *Capau* v. *City of Plainfield*, 1986). In general, there must be a reason to suspect drug use prior to mandatory testing. The current NCAA policies on drug testing before championship games will inevitably be tested in court. Institutions should be extremely cautious in adopting any program of random or mandatory drug testing for students.

Institutional Regulations Regarding Drugs. This issue is related to drug testing but has a much more pervasive scope and impact. With increased societal pressure to curb the use of illicit drugs on campus, many colleges and universities are responding with more specific regulations regarding the use and sale of drugs. Such policies should be carefully fashioned and provide due process for students accused of drug use or sale. The ramifications of linking a student conduct code to off-campus behavior of students must also be carefully considered in policy development. Many institutions have developed systems that differentiate between first-time offenses of use or possession and sale, distribution, and manufacture. Such a course of action appears to be prudent and would assist the student affairs professional in creating policies that can be enforced and are educationally sound.

Communicable Diseases. AIDS or related diseases are currently in the forefront of health-related issues for colleges and universities. Because of the fatal nature of the disease, AIDS has created a whole set of moral, ethical, and legal questions for student affairs administrators. Protection of the rights of victims as well as other students must be considered in the development of any policy. Legal challenges under the Rehabilitation Act are already emerging to policies that exclude victims from higher education. Other legal challenges on other grounds are sure to follow. Although the most serious disease facing administrators is AIDS, other communicable diseases—such as measles, chickenpox, and hepatitis—also raise policy questions. A careful balance will need to be achieved in health-related policies between the rights of victims and those of the rest of the academic community.

Testing. As indicated in Chapter Ten of this volume, legal challenges to the use of standardized tests for admissions and placement are just beginning. Allegations of cultural bias, lack of due process, and breach of confidentiality have all been made. Many states have passed or are considering truth-in-testing legislation to protect the public from testing abuse. Concurrently, many of those same states are instituting competency tests for graduation. Finally, challenges are beginning to be heard regarding the validity and reasonableness of classroom tests. Hollander (1982) recommends that care be exercised in testing by ensuring that the tests employed are valid and reasonable.

Control of Monetary Awards. During the last few years, monetary judgments in liability cases have risen dramatically. The results have been difficulty in gaining insurance and costly appeals. Many states, such as Texas, have introduced tort reform legislation limiting damages and attorneys' fees when litigation is successful. This area should be carefully monitored and the potential impact of such legislation on university policies assessed.

Relationships with Student Organizations. Legal liability arising from the actions of student organizations has caused many institutions to reconsider their relationship with student organizations. This area will also need to be monitored, for the fear of potential legal consequences has caused unsound educational and student development policies to emerge. While new legal relationships may be appropriate in the future, severing all ties with student organizations for fear of liability is not the answer.

There are, of course, other potential areas for legal concern. If, however, sound administrative judgment is exercised within the appropriate legal framework, problems should be diminished. The law is one of the many tools available to educators to meet goals of honesty, justice, fairness, and responsibility. Our legal framework provides a strong foundation, as cumbersome as it may seem, for correct actions. For as Aristotle said, "We become just by the practice of just actions."

References

Brown, M. R. "Constitutional Objections to Drug Testing." Unpublished paper presented at the Eighth Annual Law and Higher Education Conference, Stetson University College of Law, Clearwater Beach, Fla., Jan. 1987.

Buchanan, E. T., III. "Standards and Guidelines in College Administration." Unpublished paper presented at the Eighth Annual Law and Higher Education Conference, Stetson University College of Law, Clearwater Beach, Fla., Jan. 1987.

Council for the Advancement of Standards. *CAS Standards and Guidelines for Student Services/Development Programs.* Washington, D.C.: Council for the Advancement of Standards, 1986.

Hollander, P. A. "Legal Context of Educational Testing." In A. Wigdor and W. Garner (eds.), *Ability Testing: Uses, Consequences, and Controversies.* Part II. Washington, D.C.: National Academy Press, 1982.

Thompson, L. R. "Defining the Roles of the University Attorney." Unpublished paper presented at the Eighth Annual Law and Higher Education Conference, Stetson University College of Law, Clearwater Beach, Fla., Jan. 1987.

Sources of
Additional Information

Alexander, K., and Solomon, E. *College and University Law.* Charlottesville, Va.: Michie, 1972. Provides an excellent review of the relationship and implications of the law for colleges and universities.

Biehl, G. R. *Guide to the Section 504 Self-Evaluation for Colleges and Universities.* Washington, D.C.: National Association of College and University Business Officers, 1978. Contains helpful information to assess both the spirit and the letter of compliance of institutions under Section 504.

Carnegie Council on Policy Studies in Higher Education. *Fair Practices in Higher Education: Rights and Responsibilities of Students and Their Colleges in a Period of Intensified Competition for Enrollments.* San Francisco: Jossey-Bass, 1979. Provides guidance for both students and institutions regarding admissions, recruitment, financial aid, and enrollment procedures.

Duscha, J., and Fisher, T. *The Campus Press: Freedom and Responsibility.* Washington, D.C.: American Association of State Colleges and Universities, 1973. A handbook that presents historical background, philosophical discussions, and legal issues concerning the college press.

Edwards, E. T., and Nordin, V. D. *Higher Education and the Law.* Cambridge, Mass.: Institute for Educational Management, Harvard University, 1979 (with periodic supplements). An excellent sourcebook containing edited texts of leading court opinions, source materials, and other information covering a wide range of issues in higher education.

Fox, S. *Management and the Law*. New York: Appleton-Century-Crofts, 1966. A good overview of the legal issues involved in employment and supervision. Readers should be cautioned, however, to research developments in the law since the publication date.

Gehring, D. D. (ed.). *Administering College and University Housing: A Legal Perspective*. Asheville, N.C.: College Administration Publications, 1983. An excellent handbook, written in lay language, on the legal issues relevant to the administration and supervision of college housing.

Hollander, P. A. *A Legal Handbook for Educators*. Boulder, Colo.: Westview Press, 1978. Valuable because of the scope of topics covered, the clear language, and the concise organization of the text.

Kaplin, W. A. *The Law of Higher Education: A Comprehensive Guide to Legal Implications of Administrative Decision Making*. (2nd ed.) San Francisco: Jossey-Bass, 1985. A comprehensive, clearly organized reference; an excellent source of information on a wide range of legal issues influencing higher education.

Laudicina, R., and Tramutola, J., Jr. *A Legal Overview of the New Student as Educational Consumer, Citizen and Bargainer*. Springfield, Ill.: Thomas, 1976. Although over ten years old, still a helpful study of the student consumer movement from a legal perspective.

Meabon, D. L., Alexander, R. E., and Hunter, K. E. *Student Activity Fees: A Legal and National Perspective*. Columbia, S.C.: National Entertainment and Campus Activities Association, 1979. Provides an excellent overview of the practical and legal issues surrounding the collection, allocation, and disbursement of student activity fees.

National Association for Foreign Student Affairs. *Faculty Member's Guide to U.S. Immigration Law*. Washington, D.C.: National Association for Foreign Student Affairs, 1986. An aid in understanding the complex issues surrounding the legal status of international students in college and universities.

Owens, H. F. (ed.). *Risk Management in Student Affairs.* Columbus, Ohio: National Association of Student Personnel Administrators, 1985. A good discussion of the issues associated with liability reduction for both institutions and student affairs personnel.

Schuh, J. H. (ed.). *A Handbook for Student Group Advisors.* Washington, D.C.: American College Personnel Association, 1984. Contains a wealth of information concerning both the educational and legal responsibilities of advisers to student organizations.

Young, D. P., and Gehring, D. D. (eds.). *The College Student and the Courts.* Asheville, N.C.: College Administration Publications, 1973 (with quarterly supplements). Provides excellent reviews and commentaries on recent case law directly affecting students and institutions.

Glossary of Legal Terms

AFFIRMED. A higher court agrees with the decision of a lower court.

APPEAL. Resort to a superior court for review by an inferior court.

BURDEN OF PROOF. In a criminal proceeding, the duty of the state to present evidence proving the defendant guilty "beyond a reasonable doubt." In noncriminal proceedings, the duty of the plaintiff (the party who filed the lawsuit claiming damages) to present a preponderance or greater weight of the evidence to support his or her claims.

CASE LAW. The body of law that emerges as the result of judicial decisions in specific lawsuits.

CERTIORARI, WRIT OF. The Latin term means "to be informed of." In the United States, the writ of certiorari is used by the United States Supreme Court as a discretionary device to choose the cases it wishes to hear. If a writ is denied, the Supreme Court declines to hear the case, and the decision of the lower court becomes final. Certiorari is sometimes abbreviated, as in the expression *cert. denied.*

CIVIL. In legal terminology, civil contrasts with criminal. A civil action is instituted by a private individual seeking redress, usually monetary, for a harm done another.

COMMON LAW. The body of law, brought to the United States from England, that is derived from court decisions based on custom and precedent. The term *common law* is often used in contrast with the term *statutory law,* which refers to laws enacted by legislative action.

359

CRIMINAL. In legal terminology, criminal contrasts with civil. In a criminal action, the state brings action against a wrongdoer on behalf of the person harmed. Since the law that was broken was made by the state legislature, it is actually the state that was wronged.

DAMAGES. The award or verdict, by a judge or jury, for financial loss suffered by an injured party in a lawsuit.

DECREE. A declaration of the court announcing the legal consequences of the facts found.

DEFAMATION. Oral or written publication of matter, published by some third person, that tends to injure a person's reputation. The material must be understood to be referring to the plaintiff.

DEMURRER. An admission by a defendant that the allegations set out against him or her are true but are not sufficient to form a cause of action against the person.

DEPOSITION. The testimony of a witness under oath, taken outside the court, usually in the office of a lawyer. A word-by-word account of the deposition is taken in writing, and this transcript is admissible in court.

DISCOVERY. Pretrial devices used by one party to obtain facts and information about the case from the other party. This information is used in preparing the case for trial.

DUE PROCESS. In general, a constitutional concept (Fourteenth Amendment) that no person shall be deprived of life, liberty, or property without legal protection in the form of being present at a hearing, having the opportunity to be heard, and having the opportunity to present evidence.

EN BANC. All judges in a district or circuit or on the Supreme Court convene and hear a case together.

ESTOPPEL, DOCTRINE OF. Legally treating an unauthorized act as if it had been authorized, in order to prevent injustice to persons who had justifiably relied on the unauthorized act.

IMMUNITY. Exemption from doing something that the law requires.

IMMUNITY, CHARITABLE. A claim that private institutions and other nonprofit ventures are not subject to suit because of the nonprofit legal status of the organization.

IMMUNITY, QUALIFIED. A claim that under certain specific

circumstances an individual acting in his or her official capacity may not be sued.

IMMUNITY, SOVEREIGN. A claim that the state may not be sued because it is protected by the Eleventh Amendment of the United States Constitution.

INFRA. A Latin word meaning "below," "after," or "later."

INJUNCTION. A form of relief granted by a court, which forbids the defendant from continuing a certain act or from beginning a certain act.

INTERROGATORIES. A pretrial discovery device consisting of a series of written questions submitted by one party to another party or witness. The person who answers the interrogatories signs a statement swearing that the information given is true.

INVITEE. An individual who is on or using the property of another at the express invitation of the owner.

LESSEE. An individual who is renting or leasing the property of another for a specified time under specified terms and conditions.

LIABILITY. In legal terminology, liability has a very broad definition. Generally, it means responsibility for possible or actual loss, penalty, evil, expense, or burden. Liability is often used to mean liability for damages, an amount determined by a trial on the facts of the case.

LIBEL. For a statement to involve libel, it (1) must be false; (2) must cause at least nominal injury to the person, including reputation; and (3) must be the fault of the person or organization publishing it. This is a highly complex legal concept with different standards for public persons.

LICENSEE. An individual who is on the property of another for his or her own convenience but at the sufferance of the owner.

MALICE. Intent, without just cause or reason, to commit an unlawful act that will result in injury to another.

MANDAMUS, WRIT OF. The Latin word means "we command." An order of a superior court to an inferior court commanding it to perform the act specified in the writ. Writs of mandamus can also be issued to corporations, public officials, and executive officers, commanding them to perform an act within the scope of their particular authority.

NEGLIGENCE, TORT OF. Negligence will be found if one party owed a duty to the injured party but failed to exercise due care to avoid the injury.

PLAIN VIEW DOCTRINE. The doctrine that a searcher may seize evidence of a crime that was in plain view during a legal search but was not the original reason for the search.

PRIVILEGED COMMUNICATION. Statements made by a person to someone with whom that person has a relationship involving trust and confidence, such as the relationship between lawyer and client, doctor and patient, or priest and penitent. Privileged communications may not be revealed at a trial without the permission of the person who made them.

REMAND. To send a case from a superior court back to the court from which it came, for the purpose of having some further action taken.

RESPONDANT SUPERIOR. A Latin term meaning "let the master answer." The legal doctrine that holds a master responsible for the legal acts of his servant if the acts are committed while the servant is engaged in the master's business. This doctrine holds for a principal-agent relationship.

STATUTORY LAW. The body of law created by legislative enactments.

SUPRA. A Latin word meaning "above" or "over." In a sentence, *supra* indicates that the proposition, or the source, referred to was stated in full earlier in the text.

TORT. A violation of a duty that results in a private or civil wrong or injury, for which a court can provide a remedy in the form of an action for damages.

List of Cases Cited

Abrams v. *Illinois College of Podiatric Medicine,* 395 N.E.2d 1061 (Ill. App. 1979).

Adickes v. *S. H. Kress & Co.,* 398 U.S. 144, 90 S. Ct. 1598 (1970).

Alabama Education Association v. *James,* 373 So. 2d 1076 (Sup. Ct. Ala. 1979).

Alaska Gay Coalition v. *Sullivan,* 46 U.S.L.W. 2624 (1978).

American Civil Liberties Union of Virginia, Inc. v. *Radford College,* 315 F. Supp. 893 (W.D. Va. 1970).

American Future Systems, Inc. v. *Pennsylvania State University,* 618 F.2d. 252 (3d Cir. 1980).

American Future Systems, Inc. v. *Pennsylvania State University,* 688 F.2d 907 (3d Cir. 1982).

American Future Systems, Inc. v. *Pennsylvania State University,* 568 F. Supp. 666 (M.D. Pa. 1983).

American Future Systems, Inc. v. *Pennsylvania State University,* 464 F. Supp. 1252 (1979), 752 F.2d 854 (3d Cir. 1984).

Americans United for Separation of Church and State v. *Blanton,* 433 F. Supp. 97 (M.D. Tenn. 1977).

Anderson v. *Banks,* 520 F. Supp. 472 (S.D. Ga. 1981).

Anthony v. *Syracuse University,* 224 A.D. 487, 231 N.Y.S. 435 (1928).

Antonelli v. *Hammond,* 308 F. Supp. 1329 (D. Mass. 1970).

Arizona Board of Regents v. *Harper,* 495 P.2d 453 (Ariz. 1972).

Arlosoroff v. *National Collegiate Athletic Association,* 746 F.2d 1019 (4th Cir. 1984).

Aronson v. *North Park College,* 418 N.E.2d 776 (Ill. 1981).

Arrington v. *Taylor,* 380 F. Supp. 1348 (M.D.N.C. 1974).

Aryan v. *Mackey,* 462 F. Supp. 90 (N.D. Tex. 1978).

Brown v. *Wichita State University*, 217 Kan. 279, 540 P.2d 66 (1975), *vacated in part* 219 Kan. 2, 547 P.2d 1015 (1976).

Browns v. *Mitchell*, 409 F.2d 593 (10th Cir. 1969).

Brush v. *Pennsylvania State University*, 375 A.2d 810 (Pa. Sup. Ct. 1977), 414 A.2d 48 (Pa. 1980).

Burdeau v. *McDowell*, 256 U.S. 465, 41 S. Ct. 574 (1921).

Burton v. *Wilmington Parking Authority*, 365 U.S. 715 (1961).

Buttney v. *Smiley*, 281 F. Supp. 280 (D. Colo. 1968).

Cannon v. *University of Chicago*, 441 U.S. 677 (1979).

Capau v. *City of Plainfield*, 643 F. Supp. 1507 (D.N.J. 1986).

Carey v. *Piphus*, 435 U.S. 247, 98 S. Ct. 1042 (1978).

Carr v. *St. John's University, New York*, 17 A.D.2d 632, 231 N.Y.S.2d 410, *affirmed* 12 N.Y.2d 802, 187 N.E.2d 18 (1962).

Carroll v. *Kittle*, 203 Kan. 841, 457 P.2d 21 (1969).

Cazenovia College v. *Patterson*, 45 A.D.2d 501, 360 N.Y.S.2d 94 (1974).

Channing Club v. *Board of Regents of Texas Tech University*, 317 F. Supp. 688 (N.D. Tex. 1970).

Cholmakjian v. *Board of Trustees of Michigan State University*, 315 F. Supp. 1335 (W.D. Mich. 1970).

City of Boulder v. *Regents of the University of Colorado*, 179 Colo. 420, 501 P.2d 123 (1972).

Clayton v. *Trustees of Princeton University*, 608 F. Supp. 413 (D.N.J. 1985).

Cloud v. *Trustees of Boston University*, 720 F.2d 721 (1st Cir. 1983).

Cohen v. *Temple University of Commonwealth System of Higher Education*, 578 F. Supp. 1371 (D.C. Pa. 1984).

Commonwealth of Pennsylvania v. *Tate*, 432 A.2d 1382 (Pa. 1981).

Congini v. *Portersville Valve Co.*, 470 A.2d 515 (Pa. 1983).

Connelly v. *University of Vermont and State Agricultural College*, 244 F. Supp. 156 (D. Vt. 1965).

Cook v. *University Plaza*, 100 Ill. App. 3d 752, 427 N.E.2d 405 (1981).

Cory v. *Shierloh*, 629 P.2d 8 (Cal. 1981).

Coulter v. *Superior Court of San Mateo County*, 577 P.2d 669 (Cal. 1978).

Cox v. *Louisiana*, 85 S. Ct. 453 (1965).

Craft v. *Board of Trustees of the University of Illinois,* 516 F. Supp. 1317 (N.D. Ill. 1981).

Crook v. *Baker,* 584 F. Supp. 1531 (E.D. Mich. 1984).

Cuesongle v. *Ramos,* 713 F.2d 855 (1st Cir. 1983).

Daniels v. *Williams,* 106 S. Ct. 662, 88 L. Ed. 2d 662 (1986).

Davidson v. *Cannon,* 106 S. Ct. 668, 88 L. Ed. 2d 677 (1986).

Davis v. *Scherer,* 104 S. Ct. 3012 (1984).

DeFunis v. *Odegaard,* 507 P.2d 1169 (1973), *dismissed as moot* 416 U.S. 312 (1973), *remanded* 529 P.2d 438 (Wash. 1974).

Delta School of Business, Baton Rouge, Inc. v. *Shropshire,* 399 So. 2d 1212 (Ct. of App. 1981).

Department of Education v. *Lewis,* 416 So. 2d 455 (Fla. 1982).

DePrima v. *Columbia-Greene Community College,* 392 N.Y.S.2d 348 (Sup. Ct. Albany County 1977).

d'Errico v. *Lesmeister,* 570 F. Supp. 158 (D.N.D. 1983).

Dickey v. *Alabama State Board of Education,* 273 F. Supp. 613 (M.D. Ala. 1967).

Dixon v. *Alabama State Board of Education,* 294 F.2d 150 (5th Cir. 1961), *cert. denied* 368 U.S. 930, 82 S. Ct. 368 (1961).

Donnelly v. *Suffolk University,* 3 Mass. App. Ct. 788, 337 N.E.2d 920 (1976).

Doyle v. *University of Alabama in Birmingham,* 680 F.2d 1323 (5th Cir. 1982).

Duarte v. *California,* 151 Cal. Rptr. 727 (1979).

Dudley v. *William Penn College,* 219 N.W.2d 484 (Iowa 1974).

Dunkel v. *Elkins,* 325 F. Supp. 1235 (D. Md. 1971).

East Meadows Community Concerts Association v. *Board of Education,* 18 N.Y.2d 129, 219 N.E.2d 172 (1966).

Eddy v. *Syracuse University,* 433 N.Y.S.2d 923 (S. Ct. App. Div. 1980).

Eden v. *Board of Trustees of the State University of New York,* 49 A.D.2d 277, 374 N.Y.S.2d 686 (1975).

Eisele v. *Ayers,* 63 Ill. App. 3d 1039, 381 N.E.2d 21 (1978).

Eisen v. *Regents of the University of California,* 269 Cal. App. 2d 696, 75 Cal Rptr. 45 (1969).

Erzinger v. *Regents of the University of California,* 137 Cal. App. 3d 389, 187 Cal. Rptr. 164 (1982).

Escobar v. *State University of New York, College at Old Westbury,* 427 F. Supp. 850 (E.D.N.Y. 1977).

Esteban v. *Central Missouri State College,* 277 F. Supp. 649 (W.D. Mo. 1967), *affirmed* 415 F.2d 1077 (8th Cir. 1969).

Evans v. *West Virginia Board of Regents,* 271 S.E.2d 778 (W. Va. 1980).

Fazekas v. *University of Houston,* 565 S.W.2d 299 (Tex. Civ. App. 1972).

First Equity Corp. of Florida v. *Utah State University,* 544 P.2d 887 (Utah 1975).

Fleming v. *Moore,* 229 Va. 1, 325 S.E.2d 713, *cert. denied* 472 U.S. 1032 (1985).

Fowler v. *Rhode Island,* 345 U.S. 67, 73 S. Ct. 526 (1953).

French v. *Bashful,* 303 F. Supp. 1333 (E.D. La. 1969).

Gabrilowitz v. *Newman,* 582 F.2d 100 (1st Cir. 1978).

Galda v. *Bloustein,* 686 F.2d 159 (3d Cir. 1982).

Galda v. *Rutgers,* 772 F.2d 1060 (3d Cir. 1985).

Gambet v. *Vanderbilt University,* 138 Tenn. 616, 200 S.W. 510 (1918).

Garcia v. *San Antonio Metropolitan Transit Authority,* 105 S. Ct. 1005 (1985).

Garrison v. *Louisiana,* 379 U.S. 64 (1964).

Gaspar v. *Bruton,* 513 F.2d 843 (10th Cir. 1975).

Gay Activists Alliance v. *Board of Regents,* 638 P.2d 1116 (Okla. 1981).

Gay Lib v. *University of Missouri,* 558 F.2d 848 (8th Cir. 1977).

Gay Student Services v. *Texas A&M University,* 737 F.2d 1317 (5th Cir. 1984).

Gay Students Organization of the University of New Hampshire v. *Bonner,* 509 F.2d 652 (1st Cir. 1974).

Geier v. *Dunn,* 377 F. Supp. 573 (M.D. Tenn. 1972).

Geier v. *University of Tennessee,* 597 F.2d 1056 (6th Cir. 1979).

Giles v. *Howard University,* 428 F. Supp. 603 (D.D.C. 1977).

Gilinsky v. *Columbia University,* 488 F. Supp. 1309 (S.D.N.Y. 1980).

Girardier v. *Webster College,* 563 F.2d 1267 (8th Cir. 1977).

Goldfarb v. *Virginia State Bar,* 421 U.S. 773 (1975).

Hostrop v. *Board of Junior College District No. 515,* 523 F.2d 569 (7th Cir. 1975).

Hunt v. *McNair,* 413 U.S. 734, 93 S. Ct. 2868 (1973).

Ianiello v. *University of Bridgeport,* Conn. Trial Ct. (1977).

In re Antioch University, 418 A.2d 105 (D.C. App. 1980).

In re Eichelberger, 6 Bankr. Rptr. 705 (S.D. Miss. 1980).

In re Nunn, 788 F.2d 617 (9th Cir. 1986).

Ingram v. *Madison Square Garden Center, Inc.,* 482 F. Supp. 414 (S.D.N.Y.), *affirmed* 709 F.2d 807 (1983).

International Society for Krishna Consciousness of Atlanta v. *Eaves,* 601 F.2d 809 (5th Cir. 1979).

Isaacs v. *Board of Trustees of Temple University,* 385 F. Supp. 473 (E.D. Pa. 1974).

Jackson v. *Metropolitan Edison Co.,* 419 U.S. 345 (1974).

James v. *Nelson,* 349 F. Supp. 1061 (N.D. Ill. 1972).

Jansen v. *Emory University,* 440 F. Supp. 1060 (N.D. Ga. 1977).

Jenkins v. *Louisiana State Board of Education,* 506 F.2d 992 (5th Cir. 1975).

Johnson v. *Board of Junior College District 508,* 334 N.E.2d 442 (Ill. App. 1975).

Johnson v. *Edinboro State College,* 728 F.2d 163 (3d Cir. 1984).

Jones v. *Vassar College,* 59 Misc. 2d 296, 299 N.Y.S.2d 283 (1969).

Joyner v. *Whiting,* 477 F.2d 456 (4th Cir. 1973).

Keegan v. *University of Delaware,* 349 A.2d 14 (Del. 1975).

Kelly v. *Gwinnell,* 96 N.J. 538, 476 A.2d 1219 (1984).

Keys v. *Sawyer,* 353 F. Supp. 936 (S.D. Tex. 1973).

King v. *American Academy of Dramatic Arts,* 425 N.Y.S.2d 505 (1980).

Klein v. *Raysinger,* 470 A.2d 507 (Pa. 1983).

Koutsis v. *Polytechnic Institute of New York,* 11 Col. Law. Dig. 19 (1981).

Kristel v. *State,* 13 Md. App. 482, 284 A.2d 12 (1971).

Krotkoff v. *Goucher College,* 585 F.2d 675 (4th Cir. 1978).

Krynicky v. *University of Pittsburgh,* 742 F.2d 94 (3d Cir. 1984).

Kwiatkowski v. *Ithaca College,* 368 N.Y.S.2d 973 (Sup. Ct. 1975).

Lai v. *Board of Trustees of East Carolina University,* 330 F. Supp. 904 (E.D.N.C. 1971).

Lamphear v. *State,* 458 N.Y.S.2d 71 (App. Div. 1982).

Landrum v. *Eastern Kentucky University,* 578 F. Supp. 241 (D. Ky. 1984).

Lau v. *Nichols,* 414 U.S. 563, 94 S. Ct. 786 (1974).

Lavash v. *Kountze,* 473 F. Supp. 868 (D. Mass. 1979).

Lavoie v. *State,* 458 N.Y.S.2d 277 (Sup. Ct. App. Div. 1982).

Leahey v. *State,* 46 N.Y.S.2d 310 (Ct. Cl. 1944).

Lee v. *Macon County Board of Education,* 317 F. Supp. 103 (M.D. Ala. 1970), *stayed in part* 453 F.2d 524 (5th Cir. 1971), *degree granted by stipulation* 468 F.2d 956 (5th Cir. 1972).

Lemon v. *Kurtzman,* 403 U.S. 602, 91 S. Ct. 2105 (1971).

Lendall v. *Cook,* 432 F. Supp. 971 (E.D. Ark. 1977).

Lieberman v. *Marshall,* 236 So. 2d 120 (Fla. 1970).

Lombard v. *Board of Education of the City of New York,* 502 F.2d 631 (2d Cir. 1974), *cert. denied* 420 U.S. 976 (1975).

Lowenthal v. *Vanderbilt University,* Davidson County, Tenn., Docket No. A-8325, Memorandum Opinion (1977).

Lumbard v. *Fireman's Fund Insurance Co.,* 302 So. 2d 394 (Ct. App. La. 1974).

Lyons v. *Salve Regina College,* 565 F.2d 200 (1st Cir. 1977).

McCall v. *Penegar,* 543 S.W.2d 69 (Tenn. 1975).

McCrary v. *Runyon,* 515 F.2d 1095 (4th Cir. 1975), *affirmed* 427 U.S. 160 (1976).

McDonald v. *Board of Trustees of the University of Illinois,* 375 F. Supp. 95 (N.D. Ill. 1974), *affirmed* 503 F.2d 105 (7th Cir. 1974).

McDonald v. *Hogness,* 598 P.2d 707 (Wash. 1979).

McDonnell Douglas Corp. v. *Green,* 411 U.S. 792 (1973).

Madison v. *Yunker,* 589 P.2d 126 (Mont. 1978).

Mahavongsanan v. *Hall,* 529 F.2d 448 (5th Cir. 1976).

Marcus v. *Rowley,* 695 F.2d 1171 (9th Cir. 1983).

Marsh v. *Alabama,* 326 U.S. 501, 66 S. Ct. 276 (1946).

Marshall v. *Regis Educational Corp.,* 666 F.2d 1324 (10th Cir. 1981).

Marston v. *Gainesville Sun Publishing Co., Inc.,* 341 So. 2nd 783 (Fla. App. 1976).

Martin v. *Helstad,* 578 F. Supp. 1473 (W.D. Wis. 1983).

Mathews v. *Eldridge,* 424 U.S. 319, 96 S. Ct. 893 (1976).

Mazart v. *State,* 441 N.Y.S.2d 600 (Ct. Cl. 1981).

Mewshaw v. *Brooklyn Law School,* 383 N.Y.S.2d 648 (1976).

Miami Herald Publishing Co. v. *Tornillo,* 94 S. Ct. 2831 (1974).

New Times, Inc. v. *Arizona Board of Regents,* 110 Ariz. 367, 519 P.2d 169 (1974).

New York University v. *Taylor,* 251 A.D. 444, 296 N.Y.S. 848 (1937).

Niedermeyer v. *Curators of the University of Missouri,* 61 Mo. App. 654 (1895).

Norton v. *Discipline Committee of East Tennessee State University,* 419 F.2d 195 (6th Cir. 1969).

Nuttleman v. *Case Western Reserve University,* 560 F. Supp. 1 (N.D. Ohio 1981).

Nzuve v. *Castleton State College,* 335 A.2d 321 (Vt. 1975).

Papish v. *Board of Curators of the University of Missouri,* 410 U.S. 667, 93 S. Ct. 1197 (1973).

Pappanastos v. *Board of Trustees of the University of Alabama,* No. 77-380-N (M.D. Ala. 1977).

Parker v. *Brown,* 317 U.S. 341, 63 S. Ct. 307 (1943).

Parrett v. *Taylor,* 451 U.S. 527 (1981).

Paulsen v. *Golden Gate University,* 93 Cal. App. 3d 825, 156 Cal. Rptr. 190 (1979).

Paynter v. *New York University,* 66 Misc. 2d 92, 319 N.Y.S.2d 893 (1971).

Pence v. *Rosenquist,* 573 F.2d 395 (4th Cir. 1978).

People ex rel. Cecil v. *Bellevue Hospital Medical College,* 14 N.Y.S. 490 (Sup. Ct. 1891), *affirmed* 28 N.E. 253 (1891).

People ex rel. Tinkoff v. *Northwestern University,* 77 N.E.2d 345 (Ill. 1947), *cert. denied* 335 U.S. 829 (1948).

People v. *Boettner,* 362 N.Y.S.2d 365 (Sup. Ct. 1974), *affirmed* 50 A.D.2d 1074, 376 N.Y.S.2d 59 (1975).

People v. *Cohen,* 292 N.Y.S.2d 706 (Dist. Ct. 1968).

People v. *Kelly,* 195 Cal. App. 2d 669, 16 Cal. Rptr. 177 (1961).

People v. *Ware,* 368 N.Y.S.2d 797 (App. Div. 1975).

People v. *Whalen,* 443 N.E.2d 728 (Ill. App. 1982).

Peretti v. *State of Montana,* 464 F. Supp. 784 (D. Mont. 1979), *reversed* 661 F.2d 756 (9th Cir. 1981).

Perez v. *Rodriguez Bou,* 575 F.2d 21 (1st Cir. 1978).

Perry v. *Sindermann,* 408 U.S. 593, 92 S. Ct. 2694 (1972).

Peterson v. *San Francisco Community College District,* 36 Cal. 3d 799, 205 Cal. Rptr. 842, 685 P.2d 1193 (1984).

Piazzola v. *Watkins,* 442 F.2d 284 (5th Cir. 1971).

Pickering v. *Board of Education,* 391 U.S. 563 (1968).

Pinkney v. *District of Columbia,* 439 F. Supp. 519 (D.D.C. 1977).

Pittsburgh Press Co. v. *Pittsburgh Commission on Human Relations,* 413 U.S. 376, 93 S. Ct. 2553 (1973).

Plessy v. *Ferguson,* 163 U.S. 537 (1896).

Plyler v. *Doe,* 457 U.S. 202 (1982).

Powe v. *Miles,* 407 F.2d 73 (2d Cir. 1968).

Pratt v. *Arizona Board of Regents,* 110 Ariz. 466, 520 P.2d 514 (1974).

Professional Association of College Educators v. *El Paso County Community College,* 703 F.2d 258 (5th Cir.), *cert. denied* 83 L. Ed. 2d 186 (1984).

Prusack v. *State,* 498 N.Y.S.2d 455 (App. Div. 1986).

Purdie v. *University of Utah,* 584 P.2d 831 (Utah 1978).

Pushkin v. *Regents of the University of Colorado,* 658 F.2d 1372 (10th Cir. 1981).

Rackin v. *University of Pennsylvania,* 386 F. Supp. 992 (E.D. Pa. 1974).

Ramos v. *Texas Tech University,* 441 F. Supp. 1050 (N.D. Tex. 1977).

Reed v. *Reed,* 404 U.S. 71, 92 S. Ct. 251 (1971).

Regents of the University of California v. *Bakke,* 438 U.S. 265 (1978).

Regents of the University of Michigan v. *Ewing,* 106 S. Ct. 507 (1985).

Rendell-Baker v. *Kohn,* 457 U.S. 830, 102 S. Ct. 2764 (1982).

Roberts v. *United States Jaycees,* 104 S. Ct. 3244 (1984).

Robertson v. *Haaland,* Penobscot County Super. Ct. Docket No. 77-170, slip opinion p. 3 (Maine 1977).

Robinson v. *Davis,* 447 F.2d 753 (4th Cir. 1971), *cert. denied* 405 U.S. 979 (1972).

Roemer v. *Board of Public Works of Maryland,* 426 U.S. 736 (1976).

Rosenstock v. *Board of Governors of the University of North Carolina,* 423 F. Supp. 1321 (M.D.N.C. 1976).

Rubtchinsky v. *State University of New York at Albany,* 46 Misc. 2d 679, 260 N.Y.S.2d 256 (Ct. Cl. 1965).

Saenz v. *University Interscholastic League,* 487 F.2d 1026 (5th Cir. 1976).

Spartacus Youth League v. *Board of Trustees of Illinois Industrial University,* 502 F. Supp 789 (N.D. Ill. 1980).

Splawn v. *Woodard,* 287 S.W. 677 (Tex. Civ. App. 1926).

Stacy v. *Williams,* 306 F. Supp. 963 (N.D. Miss. 1969).

Staheli v. *University of Mississippi,* 621 F. Supp. 449 (N.D. Miss. 1985).

Stanley v. *Magrath,* 719 F.2d 279 (8th Cir. 1983).

State ex rel. Bartlett v. *Pantzer,* 158 Mont. 126, 489 P.2d 375 (1971).

State ex rel. Curators of the University of Missouri v. *Neill,* 397 S.W.2d 666 (Mo. 1966).

State ex rel. Peterson v. *Quinlivan,* 268 N.W. 858 (Minn. 1936).

State v. *Dalton,* 716 P.2d 940 (Wash. App. 1986).

State v. *Jordan,* 53 Hawaii 634, 500 P.2d 560 (1972).

State v. *Mora,* 307 S.2d 317, 423 U.S. 809 (1975), 330 S.2d 900 (Supreme Court, Louisiana, 1976), *cert. denied* 429 U.S. 1004 (1976).

State v. *Radcliffe,* 483 So. 2d 95 (Fla. App. 1986).

State v. *Schmid,* 423 A.2d 615 (N.J. 1980).

State v. *State Board of Education,* 33 P.2d 516 (Mont. 1934).

Steinberg v. *Chicago Medical School,* 41 Ill. App. 3d 804, 354 N.E.2d 586 (1976).

Stern v. *Lucy Webb Hayes National Training School for Deaconesses and Missionaries,* 381 F. Supp. 1003 (D.D.C. 1974).

Stewart v. *New York University,* 430 F. Supp. 1305 (S.D.N.Y. 1976).

Stoller v. *College of Medicine,* 562 F. Supp. 403 (M.D. Pa. 1983), *affirmed* 727 F.2d 1101 (3d Cir. 1984).

Stringer v. *Gould,* 314 N.Y.S.2d 309 (1970).

Student Coalition for Gay Alliance of Students v. *Matthews,* 544 F.2d 162 (4th Cir. 1976).

Student Coalition for Gay Rights v. *Austin Peay State University,* 477 F. Supp. 1267 (M.D. Tenn. 1979).

Taliaferro v. *State Council of Higher Education,* 372 F. Supp. 1378 (E.D. Va. 1977).

Tarasoff v. *Regents of the University of California,* 551 P.2d 334 (Cal. 1976).

Tate v. *Dravo Corp.,* 623 F. Supp. 1090 (D.N.C. 1985).

Taylor v. *Wake Forest University,* 191 S.E.2d 379 (N.C. 1972).

Tedeschi v. *Wagner College,* 49 N.Y.2d 652, 404 N.E.2d 1302 (1980).

Tinker v. *Des Moines Independent School District,* 393 U.S. 503, 89 S. Ct. 733 (1969).

Tinkoff et al. v. *Northwestern University et al.,* 33 Ill. App. 224, 71 N.E.2d 156 (1947).

Toll v. *Moreno,* 102 S.Ct. 2977 (1982).

Trujillo v. *Love,* 322 F. Supp. 1266 (D. Colo. 1971).

Trustees of Columbia University v. *Jacobsen,* 53 N.J. Super. 574, 148 A.2d 63 (1959).

Trustees of Dartmouth College v. *Woodward,* 17 U.S. 518 (1819).

Turkovich v. *Board of Trustees of the University of Illinois,* 143 N.E.2d 229 (Ill. 1957).

United States Postal Service v. *Council of Greenburgh Civic Associations,* 101 S. Ct. 2676 (1981).

United States v. *Barbera,* 514 F.2d 294 (2d Cir. 1975).

United States v. *El Camino Community College District,* 600 F.2d 1258 (9th Cir. 1979).

United States v. *Garrahan,* 614 F. Supp. 152 (N.D. Fla. 1985).

United States v. *Institute of Computer Technology,* 403 F. Supp. 922 (E.D. Mich. 1975).

United States v. *Phoenix Union High School District,* 681 F.2d 1235 (9th Cir. 1982).

University of Colorado v. *Silverman,* 555 P.2d 1155 (Colo. 1976).

University of Missouri at Columbia–National Education Association v. *Dalton,* 456 F. Supp. 985 (W.D. Mo. 1978).

University of North Carolina v. *Town of Carrboro,* 15 N.C. App. 501, 190 S.E.2d 231 (1972).

University of Pittsburgh, 7 O.H.S.C. 2211 (1980).

University of Vermont and State Agricultural College, 223 N.L.R.B. 423 (1976).

Veed v. *Schwartzkopf,* 353 F. Supp. 149 (D. Neb. 1973), *affirmed* 478 F.2d 1407 (8th Cir. 1973), *cert. denied* 94 S. Ct. 878 (1974).

Villyard et al. v. *Regents of the University System of Georgia,* 204 Ga. 517, 50 S.E.2d 313 (1948).

Vincent v. *Taylor,* 106 U.S. 57 (1986).

Wagner v. *Cooper Union,* N.Y.L.J. Feb. 11, 1976 (p. 7, col. 1) (Sup. Ct. N.Y. Co. 1976).

Waliga v. *Board of Trustees of Kent State University,* 22 Ohio St. 3d 55, 488 N.E.2d 850 (1986).

Wall v. *Board of Regents of the University of California,* 102 P.2d 533 (Cal. 1940).

Walter v. *United States,* 447 U.S. 649 (1980).

Washington v. *Chrisman,* 455 U.S. 1, 102 S. Ct. 812 (1982).

Water v. *University of South Carolina,* 313 So. 2d 346 (S.C. 1984).

Watson v. *Board of Regents of the University of Colorado,* 182 Colo. 307, 512 P.2d 1162 (1973).

Weise v. *Syracuse University,* 522 F.2d 397 (2d Cir. 1975).

White v. *Davis,* 13 Cal. 3d 757, 553 P.2d 222 (1975).

Whiteside v. *Kay,* 446 F. Supp. 716 (W.D. La. 1978).

Whitlock v. *University of Denver,* 712 P.2d 1072 (Colo. App. 1985), *cert. granted* No. 85 S.C. 391 (Colo. 1986).

Wickstrom et al. v. *North Idaho College,* 725 P.2d 155 (Idaho 1986).

Widmar v. *Vincent,* 102 S. Ct. 269 (1981).

Wiener v. *Gamma Phi Chapter of Alpha Tau Omega,* 485 P.2d 18 (Or. 1971).

William v. *Stein,* 100 Misc. 667, 166 N.Y.S. 836 (1917).

Williams v. *DeKalb County,* 582 F.2d 2 (5th Cir. 1978).

Wilson v. *Illinois Benedictine College,* 112 Ill. App. 3d 932, 445 N.E.2d 901 (1983).

Wisconsin v. *Constantineau,* 400 U.S. 433, 91 S. Ct. 507 (1971).

Wong v. *Regents of the University of California,* 15 Cal. 3d 823, 93 Cal. Rptr. 502 (1971).

Wong Wing v. *United States,* 163 U.S. 28 (1896).

Wood v. *Davison,* 351 F. Supp. 543 (N.D. Ga. 1972).

Wood v. *Strickland,* 402 U.S. 308, 95 S. Ct. 992 (1975).

Woody v. *Burns,* 188 So. 2d 56 (Fla. 1966).

Yost v. *Texas Christian University,* 362 S.W.2d 338 (Tex. Civ. App. 1962).

Zanders v. *Louisiana State Board of Education,* 281 F. Supp. 747 (W.D. La. 1968).

Zavala v. *Regents of the University of California,* 125 Cal. App. 3d 648, 178 Cal. Rptr. 185 (1981).

Zumbrun v. *University of Southern California,* 25 Cal. App. 3d 1, 101 Cal. Rptr. 499 (1972).

Case Index

Subject Index

A

Abernathy, C., 111, 127

Academic dismissals, and contracts, 78–82

Academic services, and civil rights, 125

Academic tradition, as source of law, 14

Accessibility, and civil rights, 126

Accreditation, and admissions, 216–217

Acquired immune deficiency syndrome (AIDS): and admissions, 217; and counseling and health centers, 271; and future, 351–352; and liability issues, 175–177

Activity fees: collection and control of, 292; and student organizations, 291–295; and student press, 310, 311, 312; utilization of, 292–295

Administrative practices: analysis of, 129–151; and athletics, 150; background on, 129–130; and contracts, 95–97; and copyright, 146–149; and educational records, 130–135, 141, 142; and financial assistance, 135–139; and immigration issues, 140–142; and labor laws, 144–146; and labor standards, 142–144; and rules and regulations as source of law, 12–13; and state laws, 150; summary

on, 150–151; and tax issues, 149

Admissions: and accreditation, 216–217; and affirmative action, 204–205; and age discrimination, 203; and AIDS, 217; analysis of legal basis for, 199–223; and athletic eligibility, 218; background on, 199–200; and civil rights, 120, 124–125; conclusions on, 220–222; conditional, 209–210; and confidentiality of records, 219; and constitutional issues, 205–206; and contracts, 77–78, 205, 206–207; exceptions for, 218–219; and financial aid, 218; and handicaps, 202–203, 208–209, 217–218; information required for, 212–213; and institutional representatives, 207, 211; issues in, 215–220; and learning disabilities, 217–218; legal constraints on, 205–210; legal requirements for, 200–205; and preadmission, 210–211; in public or private institutions, 211–212; and publications, 214–215; and race discrimination, 201, 203–204; and refund policy, 213–214; requirements for, 207–209; and sex discrimination, 201–202; and standardized testing, 219–220; suggestions for, 210–215

Advertising: and racial discrimination, 319; in student press, 318–320